BEYOND Sexuality

BEYOND Sexuality

Tim Dean

the
UNIVERSITY
of CHICAGO
PRESS

CHICAGO
and LONDON

TIM DEAN teaches English at the University of Illinois, Urbana-Champaign, and is author of *Gary Snyder and the American Unconscious: Inhabiting the Ground* (1991).

The University of Chicago Press, Chicago 60637
The University of Chicago Press, Ltd., London
© 2000 by The University of Chicago
All rights reserved. Published 2000
Printed in the United States of America
09 08 07 06 05 04 03 02 01 00   1 2 3 4 5
ISBN: 0-226-13934-4 (cloth)
ISBN: 0-226-13935-2 (paper)

Library of Congress Cataloging-in-Publication Data

Dean, Tim, 1964–
    Beyond sexuality / Tim Dean
        p.   cm.
    Includes bibliographical references and index.
    ISBN 0-226-13934-4 (cloth : alk. paper)—ISBN 0-226-13935-2 (pbk. : alk. paper)
    1. Sex (Psychology) 2. Psychoanalysis. 3. Lacan, Jacques, 1901– I. Title.

  BF175.5.S48D49   2000
  155.3—dc21

                                                                    99-086743

for Alice A. Jones

Contents

Acknowledgments

This book has been a long time in the making, and I have incurred numerous debts along the way. Earlier incarnations of most of these chapters were presented to audiences at Berkeley, University of Chicago, George Washington University, Harvard, Johns Hopkins, University of Missouri-Columbia, Pomona College, and the Institute for Psychoanalytic Education and Training, New York City. I am grateful to my audiences and sponsors on these occasions for providing me the opportunity to discuss the ideas developed in this book.

For critical readings of various chapters and for inspiring dialogue, I wish to thank Parveen Adams, Leo Bersani, Mark Bracher, Daniel Buccino, Judith Butler, Susan Cahn, Joan Copjec, Paul Darrah, Cynthia Dyess, Mary Esteve, Jerry Aline Flieger, Jonathan Goldberg, Russell Grigg, Allen Grossman, Judith Feher Gurewich, Graham Hammill, Phillip Brian Harper, Heather Lukes, Jane Malmo, Karol Marshall, Rita Mercedes, Elizabeth Povinelli, Ellie Ragland, Frances Restuccia, Jacqueline Rose, Julia Saville, Charles Shepherdson, Kaja Silverman, Susan Tucker, Joseph Valente, and Suzanne Yang. Two readers for University of Chicago Press provided enormous encouragement and a number of very helpful suggestions. For useful comments at various points I'm grateful also to Henry Abelove, Dennis Altman, Daniel Boyarin, Robert Caserio, Drucilla Cornell, Christina Crosby, Jonathan Dollimore, Richard Feldstein, Maria Gough, Marcia Ian, Martin Jay, Claudia Klaver, David Metzger, Paola Mieli, Robert Miklitsch, Stephen Orgel, Tova Perlmutter, Ross Posnock, Gerardo Réquiz, Paul Robinson, Robert Samuels, and Carole-Anne Tyler.

At University of Washington my colleagues and friends Gregg Crane and Lauren Goodlad remain invaluable interlocutors; their discussions of sex and sexuality were always illuminating—and invariably entertaining—as I worked on this book. At Stanford University Anston Bosman's and Edmund Valentine Campos's friendship and advice on all matters sexual sustained me through the penultimate draft. At University of Illinois my new colleagues and friends Michael Bérubé, Matti Bunzl, Janet Lyon, and Bob Parker provided the stimulation and support necessary to finally complete *Beyond Sexuality*. My graduate students have asked searching questions, made useful objections, and reminded me of what is most helpful in my work. I have revised this book with them in mind and would like to acknowledge especially Nick Anderson, Merrill Cole, Gabrielle Dean, Colbey Emmerson, Raymond Harris, Scott Herring, Bret Keeling, Kimberly Lamm, Shannon McRae, Robert Mitchell, Anne Raine, and Lawrence White.

An enormous debt of gratitude goes to the two people who have read every chapter more than once and whose scrupulous, loving attention helped improve the manuscript immeasurably: Jason Friedman and Christopher Lane. The love and advice of my partner, Ramón Soto-Crespo, brought the book fresh eyes and me a new lease on life. My psychoanalyst, Alice Jones, helped me let go of the book. My parents, Margaret and Jim Dean, gave me their emotional and financial support. At University of Chicago Press my editor, Doug Mitchell, has been an endless source of encouragement, support, wit, and insight. Together with Robert Devens, he transformed a potentially stressful process into a pleasure.

The departments of English at Johns Hopkins and University of Washington provided material assistance at various stages of this project. I completed the penultimate draft of this book at the Stanford Humanities Center and am grateful to the Center and its director, Keith Baker, for their splendidly generous fellowship support.

An earlier version of chapter 3 was originally published in *October* 63 (1993); an earlier version of chapter 4 appeared in *JPCS: Journal for the Psychoanalysis of Culture and Society*, volume 2 (1997); and an earlier version of chapter 5 was published in *Pre / Text*, volume 15 (1994). Each chapter has been revised extensively for inclusion in this book.

I am grateful to Ed Ruscha for permission to reproduce his painting *Desire* (1969) on the book cover and jacket.

Abbreviations

SE   *Standard Edition of the Complete Psychological Works of Sigmund Freud*. 24 vols. Ed. and trans. James Strachey. London: Hogarth, 1953–74.

Works by Jacques Lacan

"Desire"   "Desire and the Interpretation of Desire in *Hamlet*" (portion of *Seminar VI*). In *Literature and Psychoanalysis, The Question of Reading: Otherwise*. Ed. Shoshana Felman, 11–52. Baltimore: Johns Hopkins University Press, 1982.

E   *Écrits: A Selection*. Trans. Alan Sheridan. New York: Norton, 1977.

Four   *The Four Fundamental Concepts of Psychoanalysis (Seminar XI)*. Ed. Jacques-Alain Miller, trans. Alan Sheridan. Harmondsworth: Penguin, 1977.

"Intervention"   "Intervention on Transference." In *Feminine Sexuality: Jacques Lacan and the École Freudienne*. Ed. Juliet Mitchell and Jacqueline Rose, trans. Jacqueline Rose, 61–73. New York: Norton, 1982.

"Kant"   "Kant with Sade." Trans. James B. Swenson Jr. *October* 51 (1989): 55–104.

"Names"   "Introduction to the Names-of-the-Father Seminar."
               In *Television*, 81–95.

"Of Structure" "Of Structure as an Inmixing of an Otherness Prereq-
               uisite to Any Subject Whatever." In *The Structuralist
               Controversy: The Languages of Criticism and the Sciences
               of Man*. Ed. Richard Macksey and Eugenio Donato,
               186–200. Baltimore: Johns Hopkins University
               Press, 1972.

"Position"   "Position of the Unconscious." In *Reading Seminar XI:
               Lacan's Four Fundamental Concepts of Psychoanalysis*. Ed.
               Richard Feldstein, Bruce Fink, and Maire Jaanus,
               259–82. Albany: SUNY Press, 1995.

SI   *The Seminar of Jacques Lacan*. Book 1: *Freud's Papers on
               Technique, 1953–1954*. Ed. Jacques-Alain Miller,
               trans. John Forrester. Cambridge: Cambridge Univer-
               sity Press, 1988.

SII   *The Seminar of Jacques Lacan*. Book 2: *The Ego in Freud's Theory
               and in the Technique of Psychoanalysis, 1954–1955*.
               Ed. Jacques-Alain Miller, trans. Sylvana Tomaselli.
               Cambridge: Cambridge University Press, 1988.

SIII   *The Seminar of Jacques Lacan*. Book 3: *The Psychoses,
               1955–1956*. Ed. Jacques-Alain Miller, trans. Russell
               Grigg. New York: Norton, 1993.

SVII   *The Seminar of Jacques Lacan*. Book 7: *The Ethics of Psy-
               choanalysis, 1959–1960*. Ed. Jacques-Alain Miller,
               trans. Dennis Porter. New York: Norton, 1992.

SVIII   *Le séminaire, livre VIII: Le transfert, 1960–1961*. Ed.
               Jacques-Alain Miller. Paris: Seuil, 1991.

SXVII   *Le séminaire, livre XVII: L'envers de la psychanalyse,
               1969–1970*. Ed. Jacques-Alain Miller. Paris: Seuil,
               1991.

SXX   *Le séminaire, livre XX: Encore, 1972–1973*. Paris:
               Seuil, 1975.

Television   *Television: A Challenge to the Psychoanalytic Establish-
               ment*. Ed. Joan Copjec, trans. Denis Hollier, Rosalind
               Krauss, Annette Michelson, and Jeffrey Mehlman.
               New York: Norton, 1990.

BEYOND THE COUCH

This book is about sexuality at the end of the twentieth century and about the discourse that has made sexuality central to our understanding of who and what we are—psychoanalysis. Although psychoanalytic practice and, indeed, most sexual practices take place largely on the couch, I am more interested in what happens beyond the couch. In the pages that follow, I devote my attention to how psychoanalysis and sexuality function in social and cultural domains, rather than in strictly individual or clinical settings. I find Jacques Lacan's theory of the symbolic order particularly useful for this enterprise, in part because it makes fully evident how the private, individual realm of subjectivity ultimately cannot be separated from the public realm of social life.[1] To condense an argument I develop in greater detail below, let me just say that Lacan theorizes the subject as coming into being only by way of *the Other,* a term he uses to designate not other persons or disenfranchised groups, but cultural systems of meaning.

By theorizing this inseparability of subject and Other, Lacan also indicates where and how psychoanalysis departs from psychology. "[P]sychology is itself an error of perspective on the human being," he

---

1. In a recent article, Lauren Berlant and Michael Warner treat as axiomatic for queer theory the notion that "there is nothing more public than privacy," though they decline to develop in a psychoanalytic direction what I take to be their fundamentally Lacanian insight. See Lauren Berlant and Michael Warner, "Sex in Public," *Critical Inquiry* 24 (1998): 547–66.

remarks (*SI* 278). In pushing psychoanalysis beyond psychology, Lacan also pushes it beyond the couch—that is, beyond a framework comprising specific interactions between persons. And hence Lacan's account of symbolic subjectivity contributes more to social theory than to psychological theories of the individual. Part of Lacan's challenge—but also his fascination—for an English-speaking audience lies in this impulse toward outmoding the individual as a tenable category of analysis.

I will have more to say about this later, but I want to make clear from the outset that when I refer to psychoanalysis I mean a specific tradition of speculative thought that begins with Freud and is developed by Lacan, Jean Laplanche, and others. This Continental psychoanalytic tradition remains quite distinct from—and is often antithetical to— the various American traditions of psychoanalytic empiricism, which historically have harnessed Freudianism to an ideological project of boosting individualism rather than questioning it. My claims on behalf of psychoanalysis should be read with this distinction in mind, especially since one of this book's aims is to generate a sharper perspective on psychoanalysis by rendering it less rather than more recognizable. In other words, I intend to clarify current debates—ranging from the "sex wars" to the "Freud wars"—by defamiliarizing psychoanalysis, making it new. Given that we inhabit a therapeutical culture whose effects are more often debilitating than beneficial, I want to show how psychoanalysis is less an inevitable part of the world we live in—with its television trash-talk shows and its relentless psychologizing of all relationships— than a genuine alternative to that world.[2]

In intellectual circles, the alternative perspective offered by my psychoanalytic tradition has largely been neglected in favor of a philosophically oriented political challenge to psychological theories of sexuality that is attributable to Michel Foucault. Foucault argues that sexuality must be understood not psychologically but historically—and, specifically, discursively—in terms of the overarching deployment of what he calls biopower, as distinct from juridical power. Foucault's concept of biopower separates our understanding of sex from law and repres-

2. Here I find myself in sympathy with John Forrester's caustic remark that "[n]ot only does everyone know what Freud wrote and what everything Freudian 'really means,' everyone also knows what all the fuss is really about. So the process of writing about Freud must always be one of uneducating one's readers" (*Dispatches from the Freud Wars: Psychoanalysis and Its Passions* [Cambridge: Harvard University Press, 1997], 12).

sion, emphasizing instead how the category of sexuality is used to create subjective effects by molding bodies and regulating erotic practices.[3] In the sense that Foucault too is concerned with sex primarily beyond the couch, my project could be described as Foucaultian. Indeed, Foucault concurs with Lacan in the effort to move beyond psychology, affirming, in *Madness and Civilization,* that "[i]t is not psychology that is involved in psychoanalysis: but precisely an experience of unreason that it has been psychology's meaning, in the modern world, to mask."[4] From this point of view, psychoanalysis represents not so much a subdivision of the larger discipline of psychology, but a demystification of that field's assumptions and procedures.

Yet in spite of the valuable perspective on sexuality that it furnishes—and in spite of this observation in *Madness and Civilization*—Foucault's critique ends up reobscuring distinctions between psychoanalysis and psychology, as well as between psychoanalysis and psychiatry. In order to conceptualize sexuality *beyond* psychology, it is crucial to elaborate rather than glossing over the fundamental incompatibilities between the Continental psychoanalytic tradition, on one hand, and psychological—even psychiatric—canons of thought, on the other. My effort throughout this book to understand sexuality outside the terms of the ego, the individual, or the self culminates in my final chapter's discussion of the impersonality of desire. Thus rather than abandoning categories of sexuality and desire in favor of those of bodies and pleasures, as Foucault advocated, I try to show the steps necessary for thinking about sexuality and desire in different, less psychological terms.

In so doing, I am preoccupied less by Foucault's own relation to psychoanalysis or its status in his work (issues that have received admirable treatment elsewhere)[5] than by his widespread influence on subse-

3

3. Michel Foucault, *The History of Sexuality,* vol. 1, *An Introduction,* trans. Robert Hurley (New York: Random House, 1978).

4. Michel Foucault, *Madness and Civilization: A History of Insanity in the Age of Reason,* trans. Richard Howard (New York: Random House, 1965), 198. According to his recent editors, Althusser attributed to Lacan the rigorous distinguishing of psychoanalysis from psychology. See Louis Althusser, *Writings on Psychoanalysis: Freud and Lacan,* ed. Olivier Corpet and François Matheron, trans. Jeffrey Mehlman (New York: Columbia University Press, 1996), 4.

5. See especially Jacques Derrida, " 'To Do Justice to Freud': The History of Madness in the Age of Psychoanalysis," trans. Pascale-Anne Brault and Michael Naas, *Critical Inquiry* 20 (1994): 227–66; Jacques-Alain Miller, "Michel Foucault and Psychoanalysis," in *Michel Foucault, Philosopher,* ed. and trans. Timothy J. Armstrong (London: Harvester Wheatsheaf, 1992), 58–64; and, most recently, Christopher Lane, *The Burdens of Intimacy: Psychoanalysis and Victorian Masculinity* (Chicago: University of Chicago Press, 1999), 12–26.

quent accounts of sexuality, particularly those generated from within feminism, gay studies, and, most recently, queer theory. These progressive theories of sexuality form part of that school of thought known as social constructionism; they tend to either assimilate psychoanalysis to an essentially Foucaultian epistemology or repudiate it as an avatar of the ahistorical, universalizing view of sexuality that social constructionism rightly sets out to dismantle. Thus by way of amiable hermeneutic domestication, on one hand, or misguided rejection, on the other, what is most valuable about psychoanalysis disappears completely.

This is not so much Foucault's fault as that of the Anglo-American reception of Foucault *and* of Lacan. What happened to Freud in the United States has also been happening to his French successors. Transatlantic enthusiasm for these Continental thinkers has gone hand in hand with caricaturing and ultimately defanging them. Indeed, the concept of sexuality remains as much the sticking point now as it was ninety years ago, when Freud first traveled to America, to speak at Clark University, in 1909. In order to rethink sexuality, I expend much of my energy on disentangling psychoanalysis from its proponents and detractors alike, hoping that the distinctness of psychoanalysis may fall into greater relief. If in pursuing this metacritical project I sometimes appear too harshly critical of scholars I debate, I can say only that I'm interested in maintaining neither Lacanian orthodoxy nor what increasingly appears to be a Foucault-inspired antipsychoanalytic orthodoxy, but in confounding both.

Toward this end, I articulate a psychoanalytic theory of sexuality with a gay critique of psychoanalysis, not only to show their respective limits, but, more fundamentally, to push both to a new place. I consider it necessary to stake out a new position by way of the series of critiques that follows because the terms currently available for discussing sexuality—generally comprehended under the rubric of essentialism versus constructionism—represent false alternatives, and therefore they continue to mislead us in both theory and practice. Attempting to formulate an account of sexuality that is neither essentialist nor constructionist—and mounting a critique of Foucaultian positions in queer theory, as well as of certain sacred cows in Lacanian theory—I am aware that I risk alienating all parties in these debates. This risk seems to me unavoidable given the current state of sexuality and sexual practices at this fin de siècle. My efforts in this book are based on the assumption that the dawning historical perspective afforded by AIDS requires a fundamental reconceptualization of sexuality and its place in our lives. In my view, psychoanalysis still holds an untapped potential for assisting with this reconceptualization.

Sexuality and the Unconscious

The longstanding gay critique of Freud is right to decry institutionalized psychoanalysis's blind spots vis-à-vis same-sex object-choice, yet wrong to conclude from this history of institutional oppression that Freudian thought offers nothing but trouble for lesbians and gay men. This skeptical attitude toward psychoanalysis is neatly encapsulated in a wonderful line from Mark Merlis's debut novel, *American Studies* (about closeted Harvard literary critic F. O. Matthiessen's undoing in the McCarthy era), in which the narrator declares, "Of course I have never actually read Freud and so am prepared to dismiss him as readily as any other right-thinking faggot."[6] From this point of view, hostility toward psychoanalysis remains a sign of allegiance, a necessary credential for one's political identity as lesbian or gay. And even though this political view is currently being challenged by lesbian and gay psychoanalysts, therapists, and the more progressive elements of our mental health establishment, the terms of this challenge invariably remain those of minority rights—and hence of personhood. In other words, when North American analysts argue—against their homophobic colleagues, led by Charles Socarides—that it's OK to be gay, they do so on nonpsychoanalytic grounds, insisting that, as the editors of *Disorienting Sexuality* put it, "both sexuality and gender are historical constructions which serve to create boundaries between what is forbidden and allowable, defining both deviance and normality."[7] While it is necessary to acknowledge

5

6. Mark Merlis, *American Studies* (New York: Houghton Mifflin, 1994), 40.

7. Thomas Domenici and Ronnie C. Lesser, introduction to *Disorienting Sexuality: Psychoanalytic Reappraisals of Sexual Identities,* ed. Domenici and Lesser (New York: Routledge, 1995), 9. The following characterization of their project by the editors of this important volume seems to me accurate:

> This book is an attempt by lesbian, gay, and heterosexual psychoanalysts to reshape the psychoanalytic discourse on sexuality in a new image. The shared vision of each author is one which respects diversity, does not privilege one form of sexuality over another, confronts the uses of categorization, hierarchization, and the use of the "abnormal" within psychoanalytic theory, is suspicious of the power plays which underlie essentialist assumptions, and views gay, lesbian, and heterosexual identities as historical and cultural productions. Rooted in the gay, lesbian, and feminist movements, Foucauldian

that any sustained attempt by North American clinicians to consolidate a nonpathologizing discourse about homosexuality represents a historically significant step in the right direction, regrettably these psychoanalysts seem unable to formulate this affirmative discourse in anything but standard Foucaultian terms.

As several commentators on *Disorienting Sexuality* have noted, approaching sexuality by way of Foucault tends to minimize consideration of the unconscious. British psychoanalyst Joanna Ryan observes:

> Notions of the fluidity of identities, of diversity, of erotic flexibility and mobility, are all important in helping us listen to and understand the experiences and conflicts of patients without imposing rigid presuppositions or pathologizing categories. But they are not themselves elaborated psychoanalytic concepts, and it is easy to feel that [in *Disorienting Sexuality*] they are being made to take more weight than they can bear. They do not alone speak to and of the unconscious (although they could). Furthermore, they can just as easily become normative requirements or reified concepts themselves, albeit of a different kind.[8]

Ryan raises a number of issues that I pursue in *Beyond Sexuality,* particularly the question of norms and normativity in psychoanalysis. Given Foucault's argument that modern power functions less through repressive force than through techniques of normalization, the problem of psychoanalysis's role in normalizing sexual expression remains vitally pressing. Since I consider this question at length in my final chapter, I want to focus here on the category of the unconscious.

Extrapolating from Ryan's comments, I suggest that any theory of nonnormative sexuality is extremely difficult to sustain without a psychoanalytic, depsychologized understanding of the unconscious. In other words, without an appreciation of the unconscious, queer sexualities themselves become normalizing (paradoxical though that sounds), insofar as sexuality becomes wedded to identity. Hence although *Beyond*

6

---

theory, as well as social constructivist and postmodern critiques of sexuality, the views presented in this book, however, are not monolithic. (6)

See also Adria E. Schwartz, *Sexual Subjects: Lesbians, Gender, and Psychoanalysis* (New York: Routledge, 1997).

8. Joanna Ryan, "Reflections on *Disorienting Sexuality*," *Gender and Psychoanalysis* 2 (1997): 182. This journal contains a cluster of responses and counterresponses to the essays collected in *Disorienting Sexuality;* see, in particular, Donald Moss's "*Disorienting Sexuality:* A Commentary," 185–90.

Sexuality criticizes identitarian claims within the arena of sexual politics, it does so differently than Foucaultian critiques of identity politics. My argument that any theory of nonnormative sexuality collapses without a psychoanalytic concept of the unconscious makes sense only once we distinguish what we mean by the unconscious from its conventional resonances of interiority, mental depth, and chthonic powers.

Lacan depsychologizes the unconscious by treating it as linguistic and thus as transindividual: "The unconscious is that part of the concrete discourse, in so far as it is transindividual, that is not at the disposal of the subject in re-establishing the continuity of his conscious discourse" (*E* 49). With respect to its transindividuality, Lacan's sense of the unconscious requires distinguishing from Jung's collective unconscious— the assemblage of archetypes that Jung considered transhistorical. In direct contrast to Jung, Lacan identifies the unconscious as thoroughly historical, both conceptually and for the subject: "What we teach the subject to recognize as his unconscious is his history" (*E* 52). Lacan specifies this further, adding that "[t]he unconscious is that chapter of my history that is marked by a blank or occupied by a falsehood: it is the censored chapter" (*E* 50). On the face of it, this alignment of the unconscious with a subjective history may seem utterly conventional. But Lacan's emphasis on language—specifically, his attention to the symbolic inscription of historical events significant for the subject— reorients this standard view of the unconscious as referring simply to the patient's history, childhood memories, and so on. By emphasizing that the censored chapter of my history "has already been written down elsewhere," Lacan reinterprets that "other scene"—the *andere Schauplatz* Freud speaks of when describing the unconscious—in terms not of more or less private mental space, but of public discourse, the symbolic domain of language and culture, which is necessarily transindividual yet also historical.[9] Hence his insistence that "[t]he subject is as such historicised from one end to the other" (*SII* 255).

9. Lacan anatomizes this "elsewhere," this other scene where the censored chapter of my history has already been inscribed:

  —in monuments: this is my body. That is to say, the hysterical nucleus of the neurosis in which the hysterical symptom reveals the structure of a language, and is deciphered like an inscription which, once recovered, can without serious loss be destroyed;
  —in archival documents: these are my childhood memories, just as impenetrable as are such documents when I do not know their provenance;
  —in semantic evolution: this corresponds to the stock of words and acceptations of my particular vocabulary, as it does to my style of life and to my character;

The question of what psychoanalysis means by "history"—and of what Lacan means by the imperative to historicize—is too complex to pursue here.[10] Suffice it to say that the psychoanalytic tradition I discuss in this book remains far from indifferent to history and historical explanations, despite what many critics charge. The common dismissal of psychoanalysis *tout court* on the basis of its ahistoricism seems to me unwarranted, even though it isn't hard to find flagrant examples of psychoanalytic insensitivity to cultural and historical difference. In chapter 1, I discuss some methodological issues concerning the relationship between psychoanalysis and historicism, since I want to lay out from the start the principal stakes of employing psychoanalytic categories for cultural study. In that chapter, I argue against the historicist reduction of psychoanalytic concepts to the circumstances of their historical emergence; but I also want to indicate at this point that Lacan views the unconscious as a historically determined concept:

> [O]ne should see in the unconscious the effects of speech on the subject—in so far as these effects are so radically primary that they are properly what determine the status of the subject as subject. This proposition was intended to restore the Freudian unconscious to its true place. Certainly, the unconscious has always been present, it existed and acted before Freud, but it is important to stress that all the acceptations given, before Freud, to this function of the unconscious have absolutely nothing to do with the Freudian unconscious.
>
> The primal unconscious, the unconscious as archaic function, the unconscious as veiled presence of a thought to be placed at the level of being before it is revealed, the metaphysical unconscious . . . above all the unconscious as instinct—all this has nothing to do with the Freudian unconscious, nothing at all. (*Four* 126)

—in traditions, too, and even in the legends which, in a heroicized form, bear my history;

—and, lastly, in the traces that are inevitably preserved by the distortions necessitated by the linking of the adulterated chapter to the chapters surrounding it, and whose meaning will be re-established by my exegesis. (*E* 50)

10. The best discussion of this question may be found in Joan Copjec, *Read My Desire: Lacan against the Historicists* (Cambridge: MIT Press, 1994). See also Charles Shepherdson, "History and the Real: Foucault with Lacan," in *Rhetoric in an Antifoundational World: Language, Culture, and Pedagogy*, ed. Richard R. Glejzer and Michael F. Bernard-Donals (New Haven: Yale University Press, 1998), 292–317.

Lacan's claim is that when we think about the concept of the unconscious historically, we find that Freud means something fundamentally
different by this term *unconscious* than those who preceded him. Furthermore, though it is commonplace to observe that in the twentieth century Freudian categories have so thoroughly permeated our culture that
it is almost impossible to think without them, I maintain that in certain
crucial respects we still use the idea of the unconscious in an essentially
pre-Freudian sense, coining it as a psychological category. Lacan is at
pains to demonstrate that the Freudian unconscious is neither psychological nor strictly cultural, but something else entirely. In taking a conceptual term with widespread currency—the *unconscious*—and making it
inextricable from sexuality, Freud fundamentally altered the meaning
of both sexuality and the unconscious. It is for this reason that in a
project devoted to thinking differently—I might even say thinking
queerly—about sexuality, I regard it as indispensable to meditate on
this concept of the unconscious.

9

Trying to specify a genuinely psychoanalytic concept of the unconscious, I have become increasingly aware how this basic Freudian idea
constantly threatens to dissolve into something more recognizably psychological—even in the works of psychoanalysts themselves. Both Lacan and Laplanche have argued, in different ways, that Freud represses
the most radical dimension of his own discovery—specifically, that his
tripartite model of the mind (ego, id, superego), which replaces the
earlier topographic and dynamical conceptions of the unconscious, effectively institutes a repression within psychoanalytic theory itself.[11] In
other words, the Continental psychoanalytic tradition tends to regard
Freud's substitution of one model of mind for another in psychical,
rather than purely epistemological, terms. Far from compromising psychoanalysis's legitimacy, however, Freud's repression or forgetting of
his own conceptual innovation paradoxically substantiates what is, after
all, an empirically unverifiable discovery.

Lacan takes this evanescent quality of the unconscious as essential
rather than accidental in his understanding of it, describing the unconscious in terms of temporal pulsation (*Four* 123–48). His idea that the
unconscious may be registered only as it disappears, in the moment of

---

11. For this view of Freudian theory, see in particular Jean Laplanche, *Life and Death in Psychoanalysis,* trans. Jeffrey Mehlman (Baltimore: Johns Hopkins University Press, 1976).

its closing up, suggests just how difficult this fundamental psychoanalytic concept is to grasp. Indeed, if the Continental reading of Freud is on target in this respect, it follows that any discourse *on* the unconscious—including mine—necessarily engages an uphill task, given the elusiveness of its object. As I explain in my first chapter, Lacan's infuriating verbal style functions in part to remind his audience of this elusiveness, since unlike other concepts describing mental life, that of the unconscious resists objectification and, hence, systematization.

Why Does Freud Contradict Himself?

Another way of framing this problem involves emphasizing the contradictions in psychoanalytic theory. It isn't only the case that Freudian theory has been misapplied by homophobic and heterosexist therapists whom we might contextualize as inevitably "products of their time"; beyond the myriad injustices perpetrated throughout the institutional history of psychoanalysis there remain fundamental problems within Freudian theory itself. Following various French readings of him, it now seems less plausible to regard Freud's inconsistencies as evidence of sloppy thinking than as signs of difficulties inherent in mental life as such. Indeed, as Derrida puts it, "[t]he contradiction is no doubt in the things themselves, so to speak."[12] If, after Freud, it is hard not to see inconsistencies in any text as significant and therefore as interpretable, the question remains how contradictions within psychoanalytic theory itself should be understood. As I have suggested, Lacan and Laplanche interpret the vagaries of Freudian thought in terms of repression, seeing in Freud's conceptual turbulence an index of conflicts fundamental to psychic life. Laplanche's reading of Freud has been pursued in more overtly deconstructive terms by Leo Bersani, who, in *The Freudian Body,* takes the contradictions as fully constitutive, arguing that Freud conceptualizes precisely those mental forces that trouble any theoretical project and thereby prevent metapsychology from realizing its ambition. Brilliantly unpacking what he describes as "the operations of a psychoanalytic textuality in consciousness itself," Bersani reads Freud for those moments of textual collapse that indicate not so much signs of repres-

10

12. Derrida, " 'To Do Justice to Freud,' " 251.

sion as evidence concerning the impossibility of speculative closure.[13] In other words, for Bersani the vitality of psychoanalytic theory lies more in its internal disruptions than in its systematic conceptualization.

Much as I recognize the influence of Bersani's work on my own, I am also persuaded by Arnold I. Davidson's methodological approach to Freud, which implicitly dissents from Bersani's focus on textuality. In "How to Do the History of Psychoanalysis," Davidson provides an alternative explanation of the contradictions in Freudian thought by arguing that "[t]he hesitations and ambiguities of Freud's *Three Essays on the Theory of Sexuality* are not the result of some deconstructive indeterminacy or undecidability of the text but are rather the consequences of the dynamics of fundamental change."[14] Instead of emphasizing textual disruptions in Freud, Davidson constructs an archaeology of discourses concerning what we now call sexual desire. By showing how Freud's account of sexual instinct departed from the *functional* conception of instinct that governed nineteenth-century psychiatric approaches to sexuality, Davidson argues that Freud's *Three Essays* opens a radically new conceptual space. In this properly psychoanalytic conceptual realm the notion of sexual perversion makes no sense, because sexual instinct has no predetermined object or aim. In other words, the sexual instinct as theorized by Freud is originally dysfunctional, since underdetermined by nature.

However, Freud continued to employ the idea of sexual perversion inconsistently, as if his thinking were unable to accommodate the conceptual innovation that he himself had generated. Davidson illuminates Freud's apparent self-contradictions on this question by distinguishing between mentality and concept, two different dimensions of systems of thought. Citing developments in French historiography inspired by Foucault, Davidson explains:

> Automatisms of attitude have a durability, a slow temporality, which does not match the sometimes rapid change of conceptual mutation. Mental habits have a tendency toward inertia, and these habits resist change that, in retrospect, seems conceptually required. Such

13. Leo Bersani, *The Freudian Body: Psychoanalysis and Art* (New York: Columbia University Press, 1986), 6.

14. Arnold I. Davidson, "How to Do the History of Psychoanalysis: A Reading of Freud's *Three Essays on the Theory of Sexuality*," in *The Trial(s) of Psychoanalysis*, ed. Françoise Meltzer (Chicago: University of Chicago Press, 1988), 63.

resistance can take place not only in a scientific community but even in the individual who is most responsible for the conceptual innovation. Freud was a product of the old mentality that regarded perversions as pathological, a mentality whose first real signs of disintegration can be found at the beginning of the twentieth century. Freud's *Three Essays* ought to have stabilized the new mentality, speeding up its entrenchment by providing it with conceptual authorization. But given the divergent temporality of the emergence of new concepts and the formation of new mentalities, it is no surprise that Freud's mental habits never quite caught up with his conceptual articulations.[15]

This divergent temporality helps account for the dynamics of "fundamental change," dynamics that contextualize contradictions in Freudian theory without explaining them away or reducing them to a textual principle. I would like to see how Davidson's account of the complex dynamics entailed in a fundamental shift in sexuality's conceptualization may be applied to Lacan, as well as to Freud, since Lacan has not yet been read with anything like the sophistication devoted to Freud.

As with Freud, Lacan made conceptual innovations concerning sexuality of which he himself appears to have been only intermittently aware. Or, to adapt Teresa de Lauretis's phrasing and put the matter more pointedly, we might say that Lacan's most profound ideological and affective convictions sometimes run counter to his most brilliant critical and analytical insights.[16] In this book I am critical of Lacanian positions—as well as of psychologistic and explicitly antipsychoanalytic positions—because Lacan's followers have largely failed to clarify or develop his conceptual innovations on the question of sexuality. Such failure can be explained in several ways. In the first place, as has been suggested, Lacan's Anglophone reception—by aligning his emphasis on the signifier with the poststructuralist focus on textuality, on one hand, and the historicist focus on discursivity, on the other—has tended to obscure what's most interesting and valuable in his work. From my perspective, it is what differentiates his version of psychoanalysis from

15. Ibid. Davidson develops his archaeology of perversion in "Closing Up the Corpses: Diseases of Sexuality and the Emergence of the Psychiatric Style of Reasoning," in *Homosexuality and Psychoanalysis,* ed. Tim Dean and Christopher Lane (Chicago: University of Chicago Press, forthcoming).

16. Teresa de Lauretis, *The Practice of Love: Lesbian Sexuality and Perverse Desire* (Bloomington: Indiana University Press, 1994), 18.

the philosophical and semiotic theories emerging during the same period in France that lends Lacan his greatest command on our attention.

But the blame for domesticating Lacan does not reside with his English-speaking audience alone, as some Francophiles appear to believe. The Lacanian establishment in France also has stymied the development of his most radical ideas about sexuality, in part by trying to systematize what is not simply an unsystematic body of thought, but, more profoundly, an antisystematic one. Anglophone and Francophone normalizations of Lacan remain distinct, yet they overlap and subtly reinforce each other by imposing complementary forms of coherence on a fundamentally inchoate mode of thinking. It pays to bear in mind that for almost quarter of a century Lacan improvised seminars before a live audience; and so despite his baroque polemics and his ostensibly dogmatic manner, Lacan was never just presenting a theory or outlining a position. Even the most cursory inspection of his seminars reveals a highly mobile, dialogic mode of thinking in process—an intellectual style that we violently disrespect by making it into a theoretical edifice or system. To suggest that we pay attention to the conceptual mobility of Lacan's work—that we read him rather than translating him, irrespective of what language we're working in—doesn't mean that we cannot be lucid about psychoanalysis. On the contrary, we attain greater clarity in this matter when we attempt to follow Davidson's example and disentangle Lacanian concepts from Lacan's mentality.

Lacan's Competing Logics

In this book I draw out two different logics from Lacan's work, one associated with his concept of the phallus, the other associated with his concept of the object; and I try to exploit the tension between them rather than harmonizing them. In my view, feminist and deconstructive critiques of the Lacanian phallus remain limited by their failure to recognize that the alternative, counterheterosexist understanding of sexuality is already implicit in Lacan's own theory, in the logic of *objet petit a*. Valuable though feminist perspectives on Lacan have been, the critique of the phallus—together with the systematizing impulse that tends to accompany any mediation of French psychoanalysis—has prevented us from appreciating more fundamental and productive contradictions internal to Lacan's own thinking. It is not so much that the phallus is

13

really a penis—or, in Judith Butler's reading, a dildo—as it is a giant red herring.[17]

Yet lest I appear unsympathetic to feminist work on Lacan, let me make clear that the impulse to stabilize psychoanalytic concepts—which is, after all, a prerequisite for launching any critique—can be explained in terms of Lacan's own style, since his notorious verbal opacity virtually compels his audience to impose forms of coherence on what tend to appear as disturbingly incoherent or sibylline utterances. By disorienting us, Lacan's words encourage us to identify some authority that would provide the coordinates to orient his reader or listener. Another way of putting this would be to say that Lacan's verbal style produces an effect of the real, a kind of trauma within his own discourse, which prompts a set of characteristic responses, both positive and negative. The positive response to this confusion entails hunting for definitions, for stable meaning, and hence beginning the process of systematizing Lacan by introducing elements of coherence into his work. This approach locates the source of authority in Lacan himself and effectively treats him as a genius uncontaminated by the ideological or material constraints that hamper the rest of us. Hence this approach leads to the construction of a psychoanalytic orthodoxy and to the Lacanist dogmatism that deters so many otherwise curious people from engaging Lacan's texts.

The negative response to the disorientation accompanying any encounter with Lacan simply inverts what I've just characterized as the positive response. Faced with Lacan's difficulty, many readers respond by locating an authority outside his work by which to negate that work. As I elaborate in chapter 1 when discussing contextualist accounts of psychoanalysis, in this negative mode of response Lacan tends to be explained away as intellectually derivative or ideologically reprehensible (and often as both). I would diagnose these positive and negative responses as essentially defensive reactions to the epistemological difficulty and rebarbative rhetoric of Lacan's work; neither mode of response, whether idealizing or demonizing, does justice to the complexity of that work.

The time has come to cease presenting Lacan as a thinker one must

17. See Judith Butler, "The Lesbian Phallus and the Morphological Imaginary," in *Bodies That Matter: On the Discursive Limits of "Sex"* (New York: Routledge, 1993), 57–91. I discuss Butler's reading of Lacan in chapter 5.

either embrace or repudiate in his totality. In making this recommendation, I'm not suggesting a critically eclectic approach to psychoanalysis, one that would pick and choose among ideas and phrases, selecting those that conform to one's agenda and discarding the rest. Instead, I'm suggesting a reading strategy that patiently untangles the heterogeneous logics informing Lacan's work, and that—as far as possible—suspends prejudices and preconceived ideas about psychoanalysis while doing so. Perhaps this amounts to recommending that we treat Lacan psychoanalytically, reading the analyst in the way that he listens to his patients, prepared to encounter paradoxes and nonlinear forms of argumentation, without flattening his work under ready-made skepticism or unquestioning belief.

Having said that, I think we should recognize that psychoanalysis elicits such polarized responses of negation and assent partly because its epistemological status remains closer to that of religion than to science. The idea that psychoanalysis is a religion—the form of mystical authority to which a secular age prefers to devote its faith—is far from new. Even before Foucault characterized psychoanalysis as an updated version of the Catholic confessional, Philip Rieff elaborated the same connection, albeit in a different idiom; and many others have repeated the charge.[18] The fact that the unconscious is empirically unverifiable accounts for the peculiar epistemological status of psychoanalysis, since its most basic concept demands acceptance on grounds other than those we're accustomed to employing in a secular world. "I believe in the unconscious," we say, as if psychoanalysis entailed a doctrinal creed that one must either accept or reject wholesale. When asked by skeptics for evidence of the unconscious, we insist that it is visible or legible in its effects, and we refer to the everyday phenomena of dreams and parapraxes, slips of the tongue and bungled actions. But one cannot base a science on anything so resolutely subjective and shadowy as dreams,

---

18. See Foucault: "Perhaps some progress was made by Freud; but with such circumspection, such medical prudence, a scientific guarantee of innocuousness, and so many precautions in order to contain everything, with no fear of 'overflow,' in that safest and most discrete of spaces, between the couch and discourse: *yet another round of whispering on a bed*" (*History of Sexuality*, 1:5; emphasis added). See also Philip Rieff, *The Triumph of the Therapeutic: Uses of Faith after Freud* (New York: Harper and Row, 1966). Psychoanalyst François Roustang has devoted his career to demystifying French analytic institutions as structured according to ecclesiastical principles. See Roustang, *Dire Mastery: Discipleship from Freud to Lacan*, trans. Ned Lukacher (Baltimore: Johns Hopkins University Press, 1982); *Psychoanalysis Never Lets Go*, trans. Ned Lukacher (Baltimore: Johns Hopkins University Press, 1983); and *The Lacanian Delusion*, trans. Greg Sims (Oxford: Oxford University Press, 1990).

just as one cannot produce objectively sound theory from mistakes. Every effort to make psychoanalysis a science, to shore up its reputation in empiricist terms, negates the very thing it attempts to validate and ends up eliding the insight—that of the unconscious—on which psychoanalysis is founded. Hence the ineluctably precarious position of psychoanalysis, one that encourages the degeneration of conceptualization into declarations of faith, and leads ultimately to dogmatism.

Recognizing the lure of these tendencies, I try in this book to avoid pieties of both the intellectual and ideological sort by putting Lacan into dialogue with the contemporary theorists of sexuality whom he surely would have engaged had he survived for another generation. In many respects, *Beyond Sexuality* could be regarded as a sustained critical response to Judith Butler's work, which has attained such widespread influence in the humanities, social sciences, and even in clinical writing on psychoanalysis in the United States. Valuable though Butler's antifoundationalist approach to gender and sexuality has been, my critique is based on the conviction that Butler's appropriation of psychoanalysis for feminism and queer theory continues to obscure psychoanalysis's greatest potential for a progressive critique of sexuality. So many academics and clinicians today rely on Butler's work for their understanding of psychoanalysis that it is necessary to lay out as fully as possible exactly where Butler goes wrong. Though this approach might seem uncharitable or tantamount to breaking political rank, engaged autocritique in fact remains indispensable to the vitality of feminism and queer theory.[19] It is not so much a question of identifying Butler's errors (though this remains an important corrective to certain hagiographic strains in queer theory) as of showing how her style of thinking forecloses a more thoroughgoing antinormative critique of sexuality within psychoanalysis itself. I take up this issue most explicitly in chapters 2 and 5.

Although *Beyond Sexuality* develops the logic of a profoundly antinormative critique by way of a particular reading of Lacan, it would

---

19. For substantial critiques of Butler's work, see Amanda Anderson, "Debatable Performances: Restaging Contentious Feminisms," *Social Text* 54, vol. 16, no. 1 (1998): 1–24; Joan Copjec, "Sex and the Euthanasia of Reason," in *Read My Desire,* 201–36; Cynthia Dyess and Tim Dean, "Gender: The Impossibility of Meaning," *Psychoanalytic Dialogues,* forthcoming; Frances L. Restuccia, "The Subject of Homosexuality: Butler's Elision," *Clinical Studies* 5, no. 1 (1999): 19–37; Molly Anne Rothenberg and Joseph Valente, "Performative Chic: The Fantasy of a Performative Politics," *College Literature* 24 (1997): 295–304.

be naive or disingenuous to pretend that there remain no residues of heterosexism in Lacanian theory. Not only can we view attempts to systematize Lacan as distinctly normalizing, but we can also begin to see how these attempts dovetail all too neatly with certain normalizing mental habits discernible in Lacan and his followers. By *normalization* I'm referring to both the impulse to domesticate conceptual turbulence and the impulse to organize sexuality into categories of social identity, all the better to regulate erotic expression. While not identical, these twin impulses of normalization overlap and reinforce each other, to the degree that even progressive efforts to enlist psychoanalysis in the critique of sexual identity politics flatten out the most productive contradictions in psychoanalytic theory. Though far from homophobic, Lacanian speculation nevertheless bears the imprint of certain normative ideologies, such that it should be regarded as incoherent in the best possible sense. To consider briefly one example: Lacan's axiom that "there is no sexual relation" counters the heterosexist assumption of complementarity between genders; yet Lacan's explanations of this axiom are couched in terms of each gender's failure to relate to the other, rather than in terms of sexual relationality's failure as such, independent of gender. What Davidson says of Freud—that his mental habits never quite caught up with his conceptual articulations—is true also of Lacan. Nevertheless, what I find so valuable about Lacan's writing is that in its constitutive resistance to closure his speculative work bears witness to a fundamental antinomy between the unconscious and all techniques of normalization.

Beyond Sex

I want to contribute to a fundamental change in our thinking about sexuality by exploiting this antinomy and theorizing sexuality outside the realm of individuals—indeed, outside the realm of persons. We take it for granted that sexuality involves other persons; *Beyond Sexuality* attempts to undermine that assumption. I try to push the critique of sexual identity politics in another direction, toward an understanding of the radical impersonality of desire. Thus I develop an account of desire as coming into being as the consequence less of subjective identity—my own or the other's—than of an impersonal object. Once we escape an understanding of desire based on persons, our sexual politics may expand beyond the imaginary diversification and proliferation of sexual norms to which multiculturalism and the critique of identity politics has brought us. As I argue more fully in chapter 6, the problem with multiplying sexual norms is that this political strategy—no matter how well intentioned—simply enlarges the scope of normalization by treating desire as a question of the imaginary.

By contrast, Lacan's account of the symbolic order, which remains at best implicit in Freud, provides the conceptual ground from which to begin thoroughly depersonalizing or deindividualizing our understanding of sexuality.[20] Since the symbolic order denotes a transindividual aspect of subjectivity, this concept allows us to think about sexuality outside the realm of persons, as well as outside the confines of biology or nature. Hence the significance of Lacan's claim that his version of psychoanalysis does "not shrink from seeking the origins of symbolic behaviour outside the human sphere" (E 62). It is not simply that the symbolic updates our vocabulary for discussing human sexuality as a cultural rather than a natural phenomenon, but, more interestingly, that Lacan's theory of the symbolic shows how human sexuality involves persons only contingently. *Beyond Sexuality* develops the counterintuitive thesis that we misconstrue sexuality's functioning when we begin our analysis of it from the point of view of men and women, rather than from the perspective of language and its effects.

Some of the confusion about Lacan's reconceptualization of the unconscious in terms of symbolization stems from the failure to recognize that his theory of language takes account of a resistance or negation *within* language, which Lacan terms the real. As with the maxim that life is what happens when you're making other plans, the real is what interrupts every symbolic trajectory, spoiling our imaginary view of things. Since each chapter in this book approaches Lacan's concept of the real from a slightly different angle, I shall not attempt a definition here. Suffice to say that, as the third dimension in Lacan's triad of imaginary-symbolic-real, it remains the most underappreciated in Anglophone studies of French psychoanalysis. Indeed, in contemporary writing on Lacan one still comes across references to the imaginary

20. Since misconceptions abound concerning the conceptual and ideological status of the symbolic order, we should note that there are many symbolic orders, many interwoven networks of signifiers through which we move. Referring to these networks as a singular entity represents not so much insidious universalism as a form of shorthand.

and the symbolic unaccompanied by any reference whatsoever to the real.

The work of Slavoj Žižek and the Slovenian school of psychoanalysis has done much to redress this deficit by bringing the category of the real—along with the concepts of *jouissance,* drive, and object associated with it—to the fore.[21] Given the intimate connections between the dimension of the real and the place of sexuality in psychic life, one would have thought that the attention recently accorded this conceptual category would have generated a genuinely new perspective on sexuality, one able to account for new sexual practices and new conditions of sexual life, such as AIDS. Unfortunately—perhaps owing to Eastern European sexual politics—the question of sexuality is hardly a strong suit of the Slovenian school of psychoanalysis, in whose writing one often encounters the most banal heterosexism.[22] On the other hand, the vagaries of Lacan's Anglophone reception, together with the American mental health establishment's tradition of sexual conservatism, have forestalled queer theory's recognition of what Lacanian psychoanalysis has to offer a radically antinormative critique of sexuality. 19

Beyond Sexuality attempts to develop the category of the real in light of queer theory, in order to generate a new perspective on the manifestations of sexuality—particularly its unconscious manifestations—in our time. I began work on this book by trying to articulate two of my principal concerns, Lacanian psychoanalysis and AIDS, in order to see how each could help me think about the other. I've ended this book firm in the conviction that it is unethical to talk about contemporary sexuality without talking about AIDS, and that it is intellectually stunting to theorize sexuality without taking into account the unconscious. Chapters 3 and 4 of this book are devoted explicitly to thinking through psychoanalytically some of the issues surrounding the epidemic; yet the specter of AIDS hovers over every chapter and may explain their sense of urgency about theorizing sexuality in a different way than reigning academic models permit.

One of the hardest psychoanalytic ideas—hard to come to terms

21. See Slavoj Žižek, *The Sublime Object of Ideology* (New York: Verso, 1989). For a helpful and very judicious account of Žižek's work, see Robert Miklitsch, " 'Going through the Fantasy': Screening Slavoj Žižek," *South Atlantic Quarterly* 97 (1998): 475–507.

22. The principal exception to this general weakness is Parveen Adams, *The Emptiness of the Image: Psychoanalysis and Sexual Differences* (London: Routledge, 1996).

with both conceptually and emotionally—concerns sexuality's imbrication with a dimension of negativity that Freud called the death drive. AIDS gives a ghastly new life to this idea, literalizing longstanding connections (many of them purely mythic) between sex and death in a way that raises the stakes of our theoretical discussions about sexuality. While it remains necessary to distinguish the stakes of intellectual debates from the life-and-death stakes of contemporary sexual practices, it is also necessary to remember that how we talk about sex profoundly affects how we experience it. We live in a world of sexually transmitted diseases, a viral world where sexual intercourse can be lethal; but we also live in a symbolic world, where words can be as medicinal as they can be deadly. Hence it is in the interests of helping to create a healthier symbolic universe that I write about sexuality, having learned from psychoanalysis that talking about sex in the right way can in fact save lives.

Contemporary theories of language's power and efficacy, whether psychoanalytically derived or otherwise, have far more to say about language's power to harm than its power to heal or protect us.[23] This emphasis on the privative aspects of symbolic existence comports well with Lacan's description of the signifier's mortifying effects on human life. Yet the whole point of psychoanalysis as a talking cure is that the signifier can be good for your health, as well as detrimental to it. While no amount of discourse can redress certain basic losses, one doesn't have to resort to utopianism in order to recognize that a different discourse on sexuality holds open the possibility of less destructive sexual relations. Though Freudianism was caught up in the emergence of our modern understanding of sexuality, nevertheless a certain version of psychoanalysis retains the potential to push us beyond that epoch in the history of sexuality.

AIDS represents an especially crucial chapter in the history of sexuality, partly because it sharpens the question that Foucault identified in the opening volume of his *The History of Sexuality,* namely, whether sex is worth dying for. According to Foucault, the modern deployment of sexuality situates sex as so central to our self-understanding that we effectively become willing "to exchange life in its entirety for sex itself,

23. See, for example, Elaine Scarry, *The Body in Pain: The Making and Unmaking of the World* (New York: Oxford University Press, 1985), and Judith Butler, *Excitable Speech: A Politics of the Performative* (New York: Routledge, 1997).

for the truth and the sovereignty of sex."[24] Of course, Foucault was speaking in epistemic, not individual terms. Nevertheless, my point is that by dramatizing this symbolic pact—the exchange of life for sex—AIDS may push us beyond it, to a new chapter in the history of sexuality. It would be easy and perhaps comforting to misconstrue this claim as implying either that AIDS will unleash a backlash of puritanical moralism, returning us to the preliberation norms of abstinence, monogamy, and the closet; or that the horrors of the epidemic can be recast redemptively, such that those who have died can be viewed as martyrs for the weary enlightenment of those who survive. I'm not trying to make either of these points. Instead, I'm suggesting that a psychoanalytic understanding of contemporary sexuality and of AIDS may enable us to move beyond the intransigent, systemic assumption that sex confers the principal guarantee of subjective truth.

One of the implications of this possibility would be that gayness cease being defined primarily in terms of sex—not because anybody would necessarily have less sex or fewer sexual partners or different kinds of sex, but because sex would signify fundamentally differently. In such a world, one would be defined by one's sexuality no more than by any other contingent feature, because erotic desire would have been fully disarticulated from personhood. If the deployment of sexuality were to shift in this direction, "sexuality" could be reinserted between quotation marks, as Foucault recommended, and psychoanalysis might become obsolete. Then we would be truly beyond the couch. But in my view, such an outcome would represent the fulfillment, not the default, of Freud's radical promise.

24. Foucault, *History of Sexuality*, 1:156.

21

Chapter 1

How should we approach Lacan's work? I address this question here by assessing the various ways in which he has been read. Although it would seem incontestable that the way we read Lacan determines what ideas we get from him, many of his recent interpreters appear surprisingly unreflective about methodological approaches to psychoanalysis. In this respect, a professional training in something as ostensibly nugatory as *reading* represents the resource that a literary critic has to offer psychoanalytic theory. I am particularly concerned, in this chapter, with how various contextualist accounts of Lacan paradoxically obscure what is most distinctive about his work. Situating Lacan in different histories, these commentators intend to illuminate his work, yet in so doing they tend to overlook the complex history of concepts within Lacan's own thinking. In order to revitalize psychoanalytic conceptualization, I want to show how Lacan's reception has quashed the potential of his most far-reaching ideas. By charting the history of his concept of the object, I want to begin suggesting the multivalence and usefulness of this concept for cultural study.

Against Understanding

In the preface to his "Rome Discourse" of 1953—in a formulation that remains as cogent today as it was almost half a century ago—Lacan

himself suggested how we might approach psychoanalytic theory: "I consider it to be an urgent task to disengage from concepts that are being
deadened by routine use the meaning that they regain both from a re-
examination of their history and from a reflexion on their subjective
foundations" (*E* 33). One has only to consult contemporary humanistic
discourse or, further down the cultural food chain, peruse the self-help
section at the bookstore—or, further yet, turn on the television to one
of the many talk shows glutting the airwaves—to confirm that Freudian
concepts have become almost completely "deadened by routine use."
And by referring to "subjective foundations," I think Lacan is getting at
the basic epistemological idea that while concepts have a history through
which they come into being, their conceptual value exceeds the conditions and processes of their historical emergence. If it were not so, all
ideas would be subject to the relativizing introduced by historicism,
including the concept of historicization itself. Thus although in this chapter I focus on particularly egregious contextualist approaches to Lacan,
I want also to suggest the limits of historicizing psychoanalytic concepts
in general.[1]

23

It is significant for my purposes that Lacan specifies the project of
reexamining concepts' histories and reflecting on their subjective foundations as "the teacher's prime function," not that of the clinician. In
distinguishing between the role of the teacher and that of the analyst,
Lacan reminds us that in his seminars he fulfills a somewhat different
function than in the consulting room, one closer to what we do in the
classroom. Yet he also draws a useful analogy between analytic work
and professional reading:

> [T]he method of textual commentary proves itself fruitful. Com-
> menting on a text is like doing an analysis. How many times have I
> said to those under my supervision, when they say to me—*I had the
> impression he meant this or that*—that one of the things we must guard

---

1. Although my critique is far from limited to these examples, I focus on Mikkel Borch-Jacobsen,
Lacan: The Absolute Master, trans. Douglas Brick (Stanford: Stanford University Press, 1991); and
David Macey, *Lacan in Contexts* (New York: Verso, 1988). For a critical review of Borch-Jacobsen
that engages many of the issues I address here, see Shuli Barzilai, "Reading Lacan, or Harlaquanage:
An Essay Review," *American Imago* 52 (1995): 81–106. This chapter was first drafted in 1991, before
the appearance of Joan Copjec's *Read My Desire: Lacan against the Historicists* (Cambridge: MIT Press,
1994), which provides the most sustained psychoanalytic critique of historicism. Copjec's brilliant
critique notwithstanding, the fundamental problems of Lacan's Anglophone reception remain so
intractable that I considered it necessary to pursue these issues once more here.

most against is to understand too much, to understand more than what is in the discourse of the subject. To interpret and to imagine one understands are not at all the same things. It is precisely the opposite. I would go as far as to say that it is on the basis of a kind of refusal of understanding that we push open the door to analytic understanding. (*SI* 73)

Distinguishing between reading or textual commentary, on one hand, and understanding, on the other, Lacan aligns a kind of careful reading with what goes on in analysis. This kind of reading, for which so many of his critical commentators have no patience, is psychoanalytic in the sense that it resists understanding too quickly, since understanding, as a particular function of consciousness, concerns the precipitate satisfactions of the ego. The faculty of understanding and the agency of the ego are both structured according to the illusion of coherence; both operate like a perceptual gestalt, totalizing into a spurious unity what remains fragmented and heterogeneous. In other words, the problem with understanding as *connaissance* is that it is always founded on a *méconnaissance*, insofar as its formation of coherence constitutively misses something. Lacan articulates this principle most bluntly when he remarks that "[t]o think, it is often better not to understand" (*E* 252).

By assigning understanding to the domain of the imaginary and characterizing it as a function of the ego, Lacan suggests why psychoanalytic practice and, indeed, his own writing are designed to frustrate us, since his conception of analysis is based on a critique of the ego as the agent of misrecognition. Lacan's attitude also explains why any systematization of psychoanalytic thought, no matter how rigorous, necessarily reduces that thought to ego-reinforcing dogma, since systematization entails making theory falsely coherent. Indeed, at the beginning of his first seminar Lacan announces, "This kind of teaching is a refusal of any system. It uncovers a thought in motion—nonetheless vulnerable to systematisation, since it necessarily possesses a dogmatic aspect" (*SI* 1). This announcement comes just two months after Lacan delivered his "Rome Discourse," from which I quoted earlier in this chapter. Taken together, these lines suggest that at a crucial, semi-inaugural moment in his teaching Lacan attempted to forestall the systematization of psychoanalytic concepts—indeed, that he actively resisted previous systematizations of Freud. Hence we can see that Lacan's notorious critique of the ego is cognate with his less widely appreciated objection to systematization.

In consequence of his awareness that mobile speculation remains forever "vulnerable to systematisation," Lacan devised strategies for thwarting the imaginary lures of the intellectual ego, practicing techniques in his own discourse for inhibiting ready understanding. The assumption underlying such a rebarbative verbal stance is that we can think differently only once we learn to listen and read differently. And though Lacan's dense style makes more sense from this perspective, the content of his discourse is no more readily grasped in its totality. Thus while I try in this book to resist the temptation to systematize Lacan, I also want to be as clear as possible about what he offers, without underestimating the difficulties of both his conceptualization and the form in which it is presented.

In the seminar passage I'm discussing, Lacan continues by comparing his own teaching to Freud's: "Freud's thought is the most perennially open to revision. It is a mistake to reduce it to a collection of hackneyed phrases" (*SI* 1). A collection of hackneyed phrases or mantras describes perfectly the state into which Lacanian thought is constantly in danger of deteriorating—even though, more than Freud's, Lacan's thought is "perennially open to revision." Indeed, in his acknowledgments to the first seminar edited after Lacan's death, Jacques-Alain Miller proposed that the work of producing Lacan's seminars is one in which—because Lacan's conceptual development remains unclosed—the readers of his texts participate: "I thank in advance any reader who would like to collaborate in the revision of a text that is the object of continuing work" (*SVII* 326).[2] The seminar may have been provisionally interpreted between the time of its presentation and its publication, but this interpretation is merely preliminary.

It is this unfinished, unsettled aspect of Lacan's work that I find so exhilarating and intellectually productive. For me, Lacan's writing reads like poetry, not so much in its verbal complexity as in its potentiality, its incitement to further thinking. Despite the initial effect of a "closed book" that one tends to experience when first encountering Lacan, his work is profoundly open to what we make of it through our careful

25

---

2. I take Miller's statement to be offered in good faith, even though I remain skeptical about his role in posthumously systematizing Lacan.

reading. This is particularly the case with his seminars, which capture thinking quite differently than do published books, even books of essays (or *écrits*), since the latter undergo a greater degree of revision, interpretation, and systematization before publication. (Here we can see one major difference between Lacan and his academic contemporaries, the French structuralists and poststructuralists with whom he's often grouped.) It is because Lacan's principal intellectual work consisted in his bimonthly seminars, improvised before an audience, rather than because of uncritical reverence, that I refer to Lacan's "teaching."

Given that all reading occurs within some interpretive horizon that imposes a framework on the text in the interests of legibility, I want to evaluate the common hermeneutics through which Lacan gets read. In this chapter I focus on the historicist hermeneutic, and in subsequent chapters I assess the other principal framework—that of feminism—through which Lacanian psychoanalysis has been mediated in the English-speaking world. The influence of new historicism in contemporary literary studies has prompted me to think about the virtues and limits of contextualist approaches to both literary and psychoanalytic texts, even though the examples I discuss aren't, strictly speaking, new historicist.[3] I suggest that the historicist mode of reading Lacan—exemplified here by David Macey and Mikkel Borch-Jacobsen—gives us an account of Lacan that is not only inimical to the history of his work, but also profoundly ahistorical with respect to psychoanalytic concepts. Contending that we are served better by a periodized than a historicized Lacan, I outline an alternative, periodized paradigm, which I hope will yield more useful readings of Lacan. Unlike the historicists' Lacan, my periodized model has the flexibility of allowing for its own disintegration under the pressure of individual readings of specific texts.

Contextualizing Lacan

Historicist approaches to psychoanalysis may be distinguished according to whether they situate their object of study in relation primarily to intellectual influences (Borch-Jacobsen) or to a broader cultural milieu and its attendant prejudices (Macey). I want first to examine the latter,

3. I discuss this historicist epistemology at greater length in "Wanting Paul de Man: A Critique of the 'Logic' of New Historicism in American Studies," *Texas Studies in Literature and Language* 35 (1993): 251–77.

more culturalist approach because my argument thus far concerning systematization accords with Macey's critique, in *Lacan in Contexts,* of what he calls "final statism." I agree with Macey that the early Anglo-American reception of Lacan has tended to produce a final state or coherent theoretical edifice that leaves the reader in a disabling position of either embracing or rejecting wholesale that edifice. It is this position that turns Lacanian psychoanalysis into a kind of cult. However, I disagree with the solution that Macey proposes, because I see his remedy as leading to merely a different final state from the one he initially diagnoses. In other words, his solution repeats the problem.

Macey's remedy for final statism—"to place the master in a variety of contexts" (25)—represents a historicist solution to the problems involved in treating any artifact or text as transcending the cultural context that produced it. Arguing against the notion of transcendent creative genius by emphasizing a text's social embeddedness or cultural immanence has been a tremendously useful critical approach, since it provides a way of apprehending the multiple cultural voices circulating within a single text. This approach admirably demystifies genius by identifying the various social factors that constrain any thought or utterance, thereby rooting intellectual work in its proper milieus. However, applying this historicist contextualism to psychoanalysis limits the possibility that psychoanalytic concepts may have any purchase beyond the moment and circumstances of their historical emergence. Freud himself recognized this limitation, observing dryly that "[w]e have all heard of the interesting attempt to explain psychoanalysis as a product of the Vienna milieu" (*SE* 14:39). Nevertheless, historicism counters by objecting to what it views as psychoanalysis's failure to consider cultural and historical specificity in the formulation of psychic laws and models, such as the Oedipus complex—an objection that also forms part of feminist and queer critiques of psychoanalysis.[4] According to histori-

---

4. While the question of psychoanalytic universalism is too far-reaching to assess properly here, we might perhaps recall what Lacan means by the "universality" of the Oedipus complex. Responding to a lecture by Lévi-Strauss entitled "Kinship versus the Family," Lacan distinguishes universality from both necessity and the generic, asserting that "[w]ith respect to the introduction of the symbolic system, I think that the answer to the question raised by Lévi-Strauss yesterday, is that the Oedipus complex is both universal and contingent, because it is uniquely and purely symbolic" (*SII* 33). Hence Lacan conceives the universality of the Oedipus complex not anthropologically, in terms of the incest taboo, but symbolically, in terms of a signifying structure that predetermines an alienated symbolic identity for every subject. Another way of putting this would be to say that symbolic alienation is cultural, but universally so, since every culture depends on language. For further

cism, concepts have a history that renders them contingent; therefore concepts cannot be understood adequately without elaborating the histories through which they are produced and the contexts in which they come to wield explanatory power.

This notion of cultural immanence—as opposed to transcendence—derives in large part from Foucault's influential critique of the repressive hypothesis, by way of his argument that "[r]elations of power are not in a position of exteriority with respect to other types of relationships (economic processes, knowledge relationships, sexual relations), but are immanent in the latter."[5] By conceiving of power as productive rather than repressive—"Power is everywhere; not because it embraces everything, but because it comes from everywhere"[6]—and thus by making power coextensive with desire rather than opposed to it, Foucaultian discourse analysis foregrounds the material and discursive constructions of sexuality, subjectivity, gender, and suchlike as the primary focus of critical attention. Within this hermeneutic, psychoanalysis and literature tend to be treated as little more than homologous instances of the discourses (and practices) that construct, say, the bourgeois subject. Despite the various problems with this hermeneutic, some of which Lacan himself anticipated,[7] a certain historicist logic has become pervasive in the humanities, influencing the methods even of those who don't think of themselves as historicists.

Macey's account of Lacan is guided by exactly this logic. For example, he characterizes Lacan's work on feminine sexuality as derivative of and coterminous with various aesthetic tenets and icons of French surrealism. Macey's reading is governed by the historicist principle that converts every text into a historically determined cultural document, placing it on an equal footing with other contemporaneous documents: "Lacan is not influenced by surrealism, as though it were some external

psychoanalytic discussion of this issue, see Moustafa Safouan, "Is the Oedipus Complex Universal?" in *The Woman in Question: M/F*, ed. Parveen Adams and Elizabeth Cowie (Cambridge: MIT Press, 1990), 274–82, and, more recently, Jacqueline Rose, "On the 'Universality' of Madness: Bessie Head's *A Question of Power*," *Critical Inquiry* 20 (1994): 401–18.

5. Michel Foucault, *The History of Sexuality*, vol. 1, *An Introduction*, trans. Robert Hurley (New York: Random House, 1978), 94.

6. Ibid., 93.

7. The Foucaultian argument that the law produces desire, that sexuality and power are coextensive rather than opposed, fails to account for the production of neuroses, according to Lacan ("Names" 89).

factor impinging upon his subjectivity; his writing is part of the same web" (74). This form of reductionism eliminates the possibility of any discursive specificity whatsoever. Furthermore, Macey's contextualism remains vulnerable to the poststructuralist critique that charges historicism with failing to treat texts as textual, insofar as documents tend to be read thematically (that is, imaginarily) rather than textually (symbolically). For example, in his account of feminine sexuality Macey fails to consider the elementary differences between surrealist pictures and surrealist texts, thereby overlooking the fact that the surrealism he characterizes as an unequivocally sexist representational practice could produce only an *imaginary* theory of sexuality. Macey conflates the complex formulations of *Encore*—in which sexuality is theorized in terms of the symbolic and real—with Lacan's historical association almost forty years earlier with surrealist painters, such as Salvador Dalí, and the surrealist journal *Minotaure*. This conflation requires Macey to effectively reimaginarize both symbolic and real orders—to treat imaginary, symbolic, and real as indistinguishable—in order to sustain his argument that surrealist misogyny determines the theory of feminine sexuality in *Encore:* "the frequent but veiled references to convulsive beauty, and the iconography of both *Encore* and *Ornicar?* all combine to suggest that, for Lacan and his disciples, the riddle of femininity is basically a question of pussy" (195). Macey describes Lacan's theory of sexuality as if it involved only one register, the imaginary, when Lacan is quite emphatic about the necessity, when theorizing sexuality, of taking into account language and the dimension of trauma or impossibility that he calls the real.

Furthermore, in order to argue that Lacanian psychoanalysis has no contribution to make to feminism, Macey is compelled to basically ignore the long history of feminist appropriations of Lacan—from work by Juliet Mitchell and Jacqueline Rose to Jane Gallop, Joan Copjec, Parveen Adams, Kaja Silverman, and others. Although he is to some degree correct in his assessment that early feminist work on Lacan produced a "final state" of psychoanalytic theory that requires a major overhaul, it does not follow that rethinking Lacanian psychoanalysis will unmask it as thoroughly misogynist. Indeed, the burden of my argument in subsequent chapters is that although for various reasons feminist critiques have developed what I take to be less useful aspects of Lacan,

French psychoanalysis still holds many radical ideas that can be developed for feminism and queer theory.[8]

In the end, Macey's problem isn't just that he misinterprets Lacan and is unfair to certain feminists, but that in his zeal to contextualize he reproduces exactly the problem he initially diagnosed—the solidification of Lacanian theory into a system or orthodoxy, a set of judgments beyond dialectic. The question remains whether this is a necessary result of his approach or whether contextualism can maintain a dialectical openness with respect to psychoanalytic concepts.

Mastering Lacan

Since historicism isn't discredited in toto by Macey's shoddy contextualism, let us consider Mikkel Borch-Jacobsen's critique, in *Lacan: The Absolute Master,* of what he calls "the Lacanian system." As I have suggested, treating Lacan's teaching as a "system" projects it into the context of mastery, for there is no systematization without a master. The rub here is that Borch-Jacobsen wishes to invert, not merely subvert, the position of mastery by arguing that Lacan "never really had a thought of his own" (2).[9] We start to see that Borch-Jacobsen stands as Europe's version of Frederick Crews. Wishing to completely invert the position of mastery, Borch-Jacobsen forgets that an inversion in the imaginary is liable to effect an imaginary *identification,* since the imaginary is structured dyadically. Like Macey's, Borch-Jacobsen's account proceeds almost exclusively at the imaginary level—hence, for instance, the doubling phenomenon whereby Macey reproduces the problem he begins by diagnosing.

Borch-Jacobsen tries to demonstrate the historicist proposition that Lacan was "a son of his times," "rooted in his era by every fiber of his being" (1). "A son of his times," Borch-Jacobsen tells us, was—like "the absolute master"—a phrase of Hegel's favored by Lacan (and, we might note, favored by Borch-Jacobsen). Borch-Jacobsen situates Lacan in a very specific philosophical context, that of Alexandre Kojève's reading

---

8. See Mari Jo Buhle, *Feminism and Its Discontents: A Century of Struggle with Psychoanalysis* (Cambridge: Harvard University Press, 1998), for an admirably judicious historical account of what these two great theories of liberation still have to offer each other.

9. Subsequent to *Lacan: The Absolute Master,* Borch-Jacobsen's denunciations have become increasingly strident, anti-intellectual, and populist. See his *Remembering Anna O: A Century of Mystification,* trans. Kirby Olson (New York: Routledge, 1996).

of Hegel; implicitly he constructs a line of filiation that runs from Hegel to Kojève, through Lacan, and on to Borch-Jacobsen himself. The appellation "a son of his times" is "eminently applicable" to Lacan, according to Borch-Jacobsen; yet it is also applicable to the author of *Lacan: The Absolute Master*. Like François Roustang's *The Lacanian Delusion*, on which it often relies, *Lacan: The Absolute Master* is penned by a European who, "raised in an intellectual atmosphere dominated by Lacan," identifies negatively with the position he takes Lacan to represent.[10] Calling Lacan "a son of his times" is one sign of that identification.

Borch-Jacobsen foregrounds the Hegelian idiom because Kojève's Hegelianism is his principal intellectual context for situating Lacan—a context that, like Macey's emphasis on surrealism, reduces Lacan's thinking to the sum of his early influences. Thus Borch-Jacobsen's account cannot accommodate the Lacan for whom "Hegelian dialectic is false."[11] Lacan passes negative judgment on the Hegelian dialectic later in his career because he sees its impulse toward synthesis as confirming the ego's synthesizing tendency, a tendency Lacan considers fundamentally misguided and, indeed, destructively exclusionary. Beyond the ego or fully integrated self, Lacan is ultimately more interested in the undialectizable remainder that keeps desire in motion. He will call this remainder object *a*.

Another way of putting this involves pointing to Lacan's insistence

31

10. See François Roustang, *The Lacanian Delusion,* trans. Greg Sims (Oxford: Oxford University Press, 1990). I take the quotation characterizing Borch-Jacobsen from the cover of the paperback edition of *Lacan: The Absolute Master.* Roustang's critique also wishes to invert the mastery it imputes to Lacan, though differently than Borch-Jacobsen's: while the latter seeks via a philosophical historicism to deny Lacan credit for any innovation at all, Roustang projects onto the Lacanian canon a motivating principle of scientistic systematization in order to dismantle that alleged systematicity. Thus where Macey identifies a final state only to historicize and substitute for it an "origin state" of his own, Roustang imputes a final state that will, of course, collapse under extended critical scrutiny. Roustang's account is so intensely inscribed in a transferential relation to "the master" that he remains blind to how his emphasis on details—particularly details of Lacan's dress—situates "Lacan" as maleficent Other: "Lacan is a strategist who does not make a move without precise intentions" (16). For Roustang, Lacan's sartorial style, his discursive style, and his institutional style ("[h]e was always able to come up with a strategy *tailor-made* for each individual" [4; my emphasis]) are all cut from the same seamless cloth—a veil covering the noxious *jouissance* of the Other. In this respect Roustang's take on Lacan is eminently subject to the analysis developed by Joan Copjec in "The Sartorial Superego," in *Read My Desire,* 65–116.

11. "Whatever the prestige of Hegelian dialectic, whatever the effects, seen by Marx, through which it entered into the world, thus completing that whose meaning Hegel *was,* namely: the subversion of a political order founded on the *Ecclesia,* the Church, and on that score, whatever its success, whatever the value of what it sustains in the political incidences of its actualization, Hegelian dialectic is false and contradicted as much by the testimony of the natural sciences as by the historical progress of the fundamental science, mathematics" ("Names" 84).

that subjectivity must be theorized in several dimensions at once. This multidimensionality poses a problem for Borch-Jacobsen, who has to either ignore Lacan's quaternary models or convert them back into ternary or binary structures, since Hegelian dialectic is structured by a maximum of three terms. Early on Lacan argued against a "two-body psychology" (a term of John Rickman's popularized by Michael Balint) by insisting on the intervention of a third term—first the image and then the symbol: "If, as we must, we take speech as the central feature of our perspective, then it is within a three- rather than two-term relation that we have to formulate the analytic experience in its totality" (*SI* 11). Yet Lacan quickly acknowledges the necessity of a *fourth* term for his conceptual models, since "a quadripartite structure, given the unconscious, is always to be required in the construction of a subjective ordinance" ("Kant" 62). By this Lacan means that psychoanalytic interactions should be seen as not simply one person talking to another (a two-term relation), but a relation in which more entities—more complex structures of mediation—are involved. The unconscious is always a third party to any psychoanalytic exchange. Interpersonal relations are mediated by both discourse and the real (what discourse cannot accommodate).

However, Borch-Jacobsen's account of Lacan rarely proceeds beyond two-term formulations—as, for instance, in his claim that "[o]bviously, Lacan's whole complex reformulation of the Oedipus complex ultimately rests on the rigid 'dualist ontology' of Kojève" (225). Yet Lacan theorizes the Oedipus complex in terms of symbolic mediation and thus outside of any dualistic economy. In general, Borch-Jacobsen pursues binary logics, arguing in terms of affirmation and negation without grasping Freud's account of negation, whose importance lies in the discovery that negation isn't a function of binary oppositions. For Freud, negation also involves symbolic mediation and therefore depends on the intervention of a third term.[12]

12. See Jean Hyppolite, "A Spoken Commentary on Freud's *Verneinung*," appendix to *SI* 289–97. Hyppolite distinguishes between the symbol of negation used by the ego and the "concrete attitude of negation," which originates in unconscious destructiveness. This distinction enables him to identify an asymmetry between affirmation, as belonging to Eros, and negation, as belonging to Thanatos. From this it follows that negation constitutes the possibility-condition of symbolization as such, and that consequently negation, not affirmation, institutes the faculty of judgment. A primordial negation precedes any affirmation: "Why doesn't Freud say: the functioning of judgement is rendered possible by affirmation? Because negation has a role to play not as a tendency to destruc-

The main consequence of Borch-Jacobsen's binarism, which also governs his mimetic model of identification in *The Freudian Subject,* is that he remains unable to comprehend psychoanalytic concepts in anything but imaginary terms.[13] In his book's final chapter (on desire and sexuality), in which one would most expect to find him discussing symbolic and real orders, Borch-Jacobsen, like Macey, flattens concepts down to the imaginary level: "desire organizes itself into imaginary scenarios, where it imagines (itself in) an object" (204). Borch-Jacobsen's relentless Hegelianism prevents him from apprehending the elementary fact that Lacan situates desire at the level of the unconscious. This remarkable oversight also leads to his mistranslation of the ethic of psychoanalysis as "Do not give in to your desire," which reduces ethics to simple moralism and turns Lacan into Nancy Reagan.[14] Borch-Jacobsen defines even the object *a* in imaginary terms: "The *objet a* thus has the remarkable property of furnishing an image of the subject, *insofar as he is lacking in that image*" (232; original emphasis); and "[i]n phantasy, in other words, the subject imagines himself as the object that could fulfill the desire of the Other" (230). Although Lacan's earliest conception of the object sometimes described it in imaginary terms, the significance

33

tion, no more than within a form of judgement, but in so far as it is the fundamental attitude of symbolicity rendered explicit" (296).

13. Mikkel Borch-Jacobsen, *The Freudian Subject* [1982], trans. Catherine Porter (Stanford: Stanford University Press, 1988).

14. Lacan's phrase, "cédé sur son désir" (Jacques Lacan, *Le séminaire livre VII: L'éthique de la psychanalyse 1959–1960,* ed. Jacques-Alain Miller [Paris: Seuil, 1986], 368), is admittedly somewhat ambiguous. However, to render it as giving *in to* one's desire, rather than giving *up on* one's desire, promotes exactly the opposite meaning for the ethical imperative elaborated by Lacan, who repeatedly enunciates the matter in terms of a positive statement rather than in terms of a negative prohibition ("Thou shalt not"): "Je propose que la seule chose dont on puisse être coupable, au moins dans la perspective analytique, c'est d'avoir cédé sur son désir" (368); "Le seule chose dont on puisse être coupable, c'est d'avoir cédé sur son désir" (370). (This formulation is rendered by Dennis Porter, translator of Seminar 7, as "the only thing one can be guilty of is giving ground relative to one's desire" [*SVII* 321], which is more cumbersome, but remains faithful to the sense of Lacan's text.) Yet Borch-Jacobsen's account—by quoting out of context, by putting in quotation marks a paraphrased negative injunction rather than any actual line from Lacan's text, and by the placing of his own mischaracterization of the Lacanian concept of desire—manages to create the impression that Lacan's psychoanalytic ethic consists in the conventional negative prohibition: "Do not give in to your desire!" (Borch-Jacobsen, *Lacon: The Absolute Master,* 226). It is important to stress that this is a conceptual rather than a linguistic or translation error: the translator's note that prefaces *Lacan: The Absolute Master* assures us that "Thanks to Mikkel Borch-Jacobsen's extensive participation, the reader will be spared the translator's habitual complaints about inevitable unfaithfulness to the 'original,' since the present volume is more a cooperative rewriting than a translation. In fact . . . it could even be said that the 'translation' *precedes* the 'original' " (xiii). This conceptual mistranslation, attributable as much to Borch-Jacobsen as to his translator, stems from the former's failure to comprehend desire as "that which supports an *unconscious* theme" (*SVII* 319, emphasis added).

of object *a* lies in its nonspecularity and its function within a structure involving at least three dimensions. Object *a*—the object of unconscious fantasy—designates that which escapes the imaginary and the domain of the ego.

Like Macey's account of surrealism's influence on Lacan, Borch-Jacobsen's argument remains locked in imaginary terms, because it is only in the imaginary that the Other can be an other—that is, an image of another person.[15] Following his elaboration in Hegelian terms of Lacan's early theory of desire as desire of the other, Borch-Jacobsen fails to register the significance of Lacan's move beyond Hegel. Lacan moves beyond a Hegelian conception of desire by redefining it as desire of the Other—a shift that immediately removes desire from the imaginary register and into the symbolic. By claiming that for Lacan, "desire is a desire to be desired as a subject—that is, as a non-object" (208), Borch-Jacobsen conflates two incompatible accounts of desire. Lacan's early, neo-Hegelian account of desire saw it as a result of the intersubjective dialectic of speech, in which speech aimed at eliciting subjective recognition. But treating the Other as nonsubjective, as a domain of alterity irreducible to other persons, entails a conception of desire that isn't intersubjective. Instead, Lacan's later account of desire locates its origins in the objectal remainder—*objet petit a*—of the Other's action on my own body.

By discussing desire and the object as questions of intersubjectivity, Borch-Jacobsen reimaginarizes both the Other and the object, according them the status of non- or negated subjects. Yet Lacan implied as early as January 1955 that it is only in the imaginary that the Other is an other: "Hegel is at the limit of anthropology. Freud got out of it. His discovery is that man isn't entirely in man. Freud isn't a humanist" (*SII* 72). In contrast to Freud, Hegel remains a "humanist," because he sees the subject's ontology as constituted in its relation to an other subjectively conceived—that is, another person. As long as the other remains captive to the status of the subject, one is stuck in the imaginary domain of psychologized relations. However, by theorizing alterity impersonally—in terms of the symbolic Other, rather than the imaginary other—Lacan moves beyond psychology and hence beyond intersubjectivity.[16]

15. I elaborate this distinction in "Two Kinds of Other and Their Consequences," *Critical Inquiry* 23 (1997): 910–20.

16. This shift explains my methodological disagreement with the work of relational psychoana-

Yet *Lacan: The Absolute Master* treats Other and object in accordance with the dictates of Hegel's master-slave dialectic, in which the subject is defined in relation to an other subject. By viewing the other as the binary opposite of (or complement to) the subject, Borch-Jacobsen makes the subject-Other relation basically symmetrical. This symmetry prompts him to explain the concept of the gaze in Sartrean, rather than Lacanian, terms, since in Sartre's account of specular relations subject and other *are* symmetrical, and the visual field in which they confront each other (Sartre's famous park) conforms to the Euclidean conventions of perspectival space.[17] By contrast, Lacan's account of the gaze—which owes more to Merleau-Ponty's last, unfinished work than to Sartre—locates the gaze as object *a,* thereby situating it closer to the domain of the real than to that of the imaginary.[18]

Despite the longstanding availability in English translation of the seminar in which Lacan elaborates his theory of the gaze as object *a,* Anglophone accounts of Lacan repeatedly misconstrue this concept.[19] While neither Macey, Borch-Jacobsen, nor historicism can be held directly responsible for this problem, historicism's influence does account for the failure to comprehend the significance of object *a,* since this concept implies a certain notion of transcendence. The historicist rejection of transcendence, which is disallowed on other grounds by the deconstruction of metaphysics, promotes a critical emphasis on discursive constructions or linguistic constitutivity that tends to be regarded as fundamentally compatible with Lacan's insistence on the determining effects for the human subject of relations of signification. This tendency to extract the concept of the signifier as the sole basis of Lacan's rethinking of Freud—as if Lacan could be grasped by merely combining Freud, Saussure, and Lévi-Strauss—derives in part from the canonization of Lacan's "Rome Discourse" and has led to the bracketing of French psychoanalysis with a version of poststructuralism for which it is axiomatic

35

lysts whose primary concern lies in specifying more equitable intersubjective arrangements, particularly between the sexes, and who often rely on a Hegelian model of intersubjective recognition. See, for example, Jessica Benjamin, *Like Subjects, Love Objects: Essays on Recognition and Sexual Difference* (New Haven: Yale University Press, 1995).

17. Jean-Paul Sartre, *Being and Nothingness: An Essay in Phenomenological Ontology,* trans. Hazel E. Barnes (Secaucus, N.J.: Citadel, 1977), 230 and passim.

18. Jacques Lacan, "Of the Gaze as *Objet Petit a*" (*Four* 67–119). See also Maurice Merleau-Ponty, "The Intertwining—The Chiasm," in *The Visible and the Invisible,* ed. Claude Lefort, trans. Alphonso Lingis (Evanston: Northwestern University Press, 1968), 130–55.

19. On this misconstrual, Copjec, *Read My Desire,* chap. 2, is particularly helpful.

that "there is nothing outside the text."[20] Thus even though deconstruction and historicism remain vigorously opposed, both approaches—at least in their North American variants—have proven capable of assimilating a psychoanalysis that emphasizes the linguistically structured unconscious. As a result, the theoretical potential of psychoanalysis has been diluted. It may be restored by taking seriously Lacan's concept of the object. In order to do so, we need to see how this concept emerges in Lacan's own work.

Periodizing Lacan

The scheme I propose for periodizing Lacan involves bracketing his work after 1932 into four distinct stages: a "40s Lacan" of the imaginary, a "50s Lacan" of the symbolic, a "60s Lacan" of the real, and a "70s Lacan" of the *sinthome*. Each decade designation belongs in quotation marks insofar as this splitting of Lacan's work into discrete periods is necessarily artificial. Yet this kind of periodization serves heuristic purposes and helps to guard against final-statist kinds of systematization. Along with these four periods, each of which may be characterized by focus on a particular order, goes a conceptual element in relation to which Lacan maps the subject: the image or imago for the "40s Lacan" of the imaginary, the signifier for the "50s Lacan" of the symbolic, the object for the "60s Lacan" of the real, and the reconceived symptom for the "70s Lacan." In the interests of highlighting the significance of Lacan's reconceptualization of the object, I refrain from providing much account of the "70s Lacan" in this chapter.

20. Jacques Derrida, *Of Grammatology*, trans. Gayatri Chakravorty Spivak (Baltimore: Johns Hopkins University Press, 1976), 158. The "Rome Discourse" was canonized by Anthony Wilden's translation and presentation in 1968 of "The Function and Field of Speech and Language in Psychoanalysis" as Lacan, *The Language of the Self: The Function of Language in Psychoanalysis* (Baltimore: Johns Hopkins University Press, 1968). In his notes to a 1971 interview, Derrida used his famous formulation—"*Il n'y a pas de horstexte*"—to gloss the Lacanian formulation that repudiates the possibility of a metalanguage: "There is no Other of the Other" (Jacques Derrida, *Positions*, trans. Alan Bass [Chicago: University of Chicago Press, 1981], 111). This alignment suggests that if there *were* an Other of the Other, there would be a position outside the text from which the text could be judged without that judgment's being textually contaminated. This would be a transcendent position, which both Derrida and Lacan supposedly discredit. However, although there is no Other *(A)* of the Other, there is an object *(a)* of the Other that remains strictly unassimilable to any text. It is for this reason that Lacan includes an extradiscursive cause, *a*, in his discourse structures. The question then is not whether there is an outside to the text but how the relation between inside and outside is to be thought. "Transcendence" is one way of naming that relation, but only so long as transcendent relations are conceived topologically.

We should distinguish this method of periodizing Lacan from the tendency to locate epistemological breaks or ruptures in the history of his thought, since such breaks often impose a false homogeneity of "before" and "after" on concepts that mutate without necessarily developing teleologically. For example, Slavoj Žižek's commitment to treating the *Ethics* seminar of 1959–60 as just such a radical break—while it has undoubtedly revivified the psychoanalysis of ideology and popular culture—inserts the complex discontinuities of Lacanian thought into a conversion narrative characteristic of ego formations, producing a "before" that is implicitly repudiated and an "after" that is embraced as the desired theoretical identity.[21] Instead of a final state, the Bachelardian notion of epistemological rupture often produces two states, each of which is totalized by being contrasted with the other. An "after" Lacan does have the benefit of revealing a thinker who is more than the sum of his early influences. But the notion of a profound discontinuity between "early" and "late" Lacan leads to a repudiation of the "early" in the way that Macey and Borch-Jacobsen effectively repudiate the "late."

"40s Lacan"

Some early remarks about the mirror stage illuminate this issue of periodization:

> The mirror stage isn't a magic word. It's already a bit dated. Since I put it out in 1936, it's about twenty years old. It's beginning to be in need of a bit of renovation—which isn't always for the best, for in order to make progress, one should know how to go back

37

---

21. In "The Undergrowth of Enjoyment: How Popular Culture Can Serve as an Introduction to Lacan," *New Formations* 9 (1989): 7–29, Žižek refers to "the break marked by the seminar on *Ethics of Psychoanalysis* (1959–60), a break which radically shifted the accent of [Lacan's] teaching: from the dialectics of desire to the inertia of enjoyment *(jouissance)*, from the symptom as coded message to the *sinthome* as letter permeated with enjoyment, from the 'unconscious structured like a language' to the Thing in its heart, the irreducible kernel of *jouissance* that resists all symbolization" (7). Where Žižek treats Seminar 7 as the point of radical break, Jacques-Alain Miller has spoken of Seminar 11, *The Four Fundamental Concepts of Psychoanalysis,* as the break (in "Context and Concepts," in *Reading Seminar XI: Lacan's Four Fundamental Concepts of Psychoanalysis,* ed. Richard Feldstein, Bruce Fink, and Maire Jaanus [Albany: SUNY Press, 1995], 5). And in "Reading the Real in the Seminar on the Psychoses," in *Criticism and Lacan: Essays and Dialogue on Language, Structure, and the Unconscious,* ed. Patrick Colm Hogan and Lalita Pandit (Athens: University of Georgia Press, 1990), 64–83, Michael Walsh treats Seminar 3 as "a text which readily lends itself to nomination as a locus of the emergence of a more purely Lacanian contribution to psychoanalysis" (68).

over things. It isn't so much repeating it that is a bore, as not using it properly. (*SII* 102)

The "40s Lacan" (a period that conventionally begins in 1936) emphasizes the mediation of the imaginary register, using optical models to describe the specular formation of the ego. The famous mirror stage is one description of how narcissism works, but it is certainly not Lacan's only one, as his model of the inverted bouquet shows. This model derives from a classical experiment in which a stand is placed in front of a large spherical mirror. When one places an empty vase on top of the stand and suspends a bouquet of flowers beneath it, their reflection in the spherical mirror produces an image of the flowers in the vase. By showing how a mirrored surface can register on the same plane and in the same perspective visual phenomena from different planes, Lacan's experiment of the inverted bouquet shows how the imaginary involves techniques of trickery.[22] Imaginary identification forms the ego by means of a constitutive alienation in the specular other, for which the mirror is one classical, poetic figure. It is important to distinguish this specular other that founds the ego from the Other or object that founds the subject and its desire. Furthermore, we should not confuse the fascinating, seductive lure of the mirror—or the mythic jubilation encountered in the image—with desire (which is unconscious, not imaginary) or *jouissance* (which is real).

The mirror is a useful model for describing narcissism just so long as one bears in mind that its significance derives in large part from what cannot be seen in it. For centuries the technology of mirroring remained imperfect in one crucial sense, for the mirror was as likely to be the beloved's eyes or the aqueous surface in which one sought his own image as it was to be glass produced for purely reflective purposes: "In becoming fascinated by a mirror, and preferably by a mirror as it has always been since the beginning of humanity until a relatively recent period, more obscure than clear, mirror of burnished metal, the subject may succeed in revealing to himself many of the elements of his imaginary fixations" (*SII* 57). The mirror produces an ego by revealing what

---

22. A diagram of the inverted bouquet experiment may be found in *SI* 78. A more complex version of the diagram appears on 124, and a simplified diagram on 165. Lacan repeats the diagram in *SII* 109, referring to it as the "optical schema for the theory of narcissism." The classic discussion of this diagram appears in Jacqueline Rose, "The Imaginary," in *Sexuality in the Field of Vision* (London: Verso, 1986), 166–97.

cannot be "objectively" perceived—that which, though visual, cannot be registered independently by a material surface. This is why the domain of its effects is called imaginary. The experiment of the inverted bouquet produces an image of an object that has no objective existence outside the mirror, but nevertheless compels the viewer's conviction. The ego is just such an object, produced through identifications that, as a consequence of their illusoriness, are bound to be frustrating. It is for this reason that Lacan resituates a central component of ego psychology by observing that the ego "is frustration in its essence" (*E* 42).

Although the imaginary dimension of the subject is the ego, Lacan takes great pains to avoid collapsing the subject into the ego; after all, this is precisely what he accuses ego psychology of doing. "[T]he unconscious is the unknown subject of the ego," he maintains (*SII* 43). This claim should prompt us to question the relation between subject and ego—a question that also concerns the relation between imaginary and symbolic. This relation, which Lacan on one occasion describes as "excentric," is what his various models try to conceptualize (*SII* 44). Much of this excentricity has been lost in the application of Lacan's theory of imaginary identification to analyses of film and ideology. For example, Althusser's famous definition of ideology as "the representation of the imaginary relationship of individuals to their real conditions of existence" restricts ideological effects to the domain of the imaginary.[23] Yet it is already clear in the "40s Lacan" of the imaginary—specifically, in his 1948 paper on "Aggressivity in Psychoanalysis"—that there is a crucial distinction between subject and ego:

> [W]e call ego that nucleus given to consciousness, but opaque to reflexion, marked by all the ambiguities which, from self-satisfaction to "bad faith" *(mauvaise foi)*, structure the experience of the passions in the human subject; this "I" who, in order to admit its facticity to existential criticism, opposes its irreducible inertia of pretences and

23. Louis Althusser, "Ideology and Ideological State Apparatuses," in *Lenin and Philosophy and Other Essays,* trans. Ben Brewster (New York: Monthly Review, 1971), 162. See also Christian Metz, *Psychoanalysis and Cinema: The Imaginary Signifier* (London: Macmillan, 1982). The Althusserian formulation of ideology has been developed most rigorously by Michel Pêcheux, *Language, Semantics and Ideology: Stating the Obvious,* trans. Harbans Nagpal (London: Macmillan, 1982), and most influentially by Benedict Anderson, *Imagined Communities: Reflections on the Origin and Spread of Nationalism* (New York: Verso, 1983). The best psychoanalytic critique of ideology in nonimaginary terms may be found in Slavoj Žižek, *The Sublime Object of Ideology* (New York: Verso, 1989).

méconnaissances to the concrete problematic of the realization of the subject. (*E* 15)

Couched in the vocabulary of existential phenomenology, this distinction between ego and subject is so marked as to constitute an opposition ("this 'I' . . . *opposes* its irreducible inertia . . . [to] the subject"). Yet once Lacan moves beyond phenomenology, his account of the subject-ego relation becomes more complex and interesting. These shifts take us to the "50s Lacan."

"50s Lacan"

Throughout the 1950s Lacan moves from theorizing the imaginary to emphasizing the mediation of the symbolic register to focusing on the real Thing (*das Ding*). There is such conceptual productivity during this period that we might say that 40s, 50s, and 60s Lacans are actually all compressed into one historical decade—hence my effort to distinguish periods, theoretical emphases, and conceptual distinctions. The "50s Lacan" of the signifier, embraced by literary critics as part of a transatlantic wave of structuralism and poststructuralism, has been so approximately rendered that a number of elementary distinctions are in order.

The "50s Lacan" encompasses the famous "Rome Discourse" of 1953 and "The Agency of the Letter in the Unconscious, or Reason since Freud" (1957), the latter of which was the first *écrit* translated into English, in 1966. In these texts Lacan presented a theory of the linguistic unconscious by developing the rhetorical tropes of metaphor and metonymy, which he borrowed from Roman Jakobson's classic paper on aphasia (and which I discuss at greater length in chapter 5). In so doing, Lacan followed Freud's use of a classical literary narrative to theorize the principal unconscious formation—the Oedipus complex. As early as 1953, Lacan treats the Oedipus complex as a model, not as an unequivocal truth:

> When we get on the trail of the unconscious, what we encounter are structured, organised, complex situations. Freud gave us the first model of it, its standard, in the Oedipus complex. Those of you who have followed my seminar for some time have had the opportunity to see for themselves to what extent the Oedipus complex poses problems and to what extent it contains ambiguities, thanks to the

commentary I made on those cases least subject to reservations on account of their having been so richly sketched in by Freud himself, namely three of the five great psychoanalyses. In short, the entire development of analysis has resulted from showing to advantage, one after another, each of the tensions implied within this triangular system. This fact alone requires us to see in it something quite different from this solid mass summed up in the classic formula—sexual attraction for the mother, rivalry with the father. (*SI* 65–66)

That Lacan proceeds to reinterpret the triangulated relations of Oedipus in terms of his own tripartite scheme of imaginary, symbolic, and real should prevent us from too readily assigning the Oedipus complex solely to the domain of the symbolic. Although we have noted Lacan's observation that what makes the Oedipus complex both universal and contingent is its "purely symbolic" character, the meaning of this symbolic character shifts throughout the fertile period of the 1950s. Perhaps the best way to elucidate these changes is to follow Lacan's shifting descriptions of clinical technique. During his 1950s "return to Freud," Lacan devoted extensive attention to questions of technique, in part owing to the relative neglect and consequent ossification of technical theory after World War II.

41

Lacan begins his "Rome Discourse" with the following assertion, revealing both the underlying assumption of "50s Lacan" and the reason he's been mischaracterized as a theorist merely of the linguistic subject: "Whether it sees itself as an instrument of healing, of training, or of exploration in depth, psychoanalysis has only a single medium: the patient's speech" (*E* 40). Lacan emphasized the importance of speech in response to the abandonment of linguistic questions in psychoanalytic theory and practice—hence his "return" during this period to the founding works of psychoanalysis, in which Freud finds the unconscious interrupting ordinary discourse in ways that suggest an *other* discourse, speech on another scene *(ein andere Schauplatz)*.

If speech is the sole medium of psychoanalysis, then it follows that transference must be a symbolic, rather than a purely affective, phenomenon. One year later, however, Lacan describes transference in strictly imaginary terms: "When does transference really start? When the image which the subject requires becomes confused for the subject with the reality in which he is placed. The whole progress of the analysis is to show him the distinction between these two planes, to unstick the imaginary and the real" (*SI* 241). To suggest that the method of "unsticking" imaginary and real must be a symbolic method fails to mitigate the predominance of the imaginary relation in this description of transference. The "image which the subject requires" is the imago in which he narcissistically recognizes and identifies himself; the "reality in which [the subject] is placed" is that of the analytic situation; and the moment at which the subject's imaginary relation fastens onto the analyst as the objective correlative of his ego is the moment transference begins. In this description, the analyst occupies—at least initially—the position neither of Other nor of object *a*, but of imaginary other.

However, this scenario is complicated further when Lacan equates "the reality [*réalité*] in which he is placed" with "the real [*réel*]" from which the imaginary relation must be dissociated. Too much confusion stems from equating "reality" and the Lacanian real for me to pass this description without comment. "Reality" is not commensurate with the unsymbolizable real that forms one order in the triad imaginary-symbolic-real, since for Lacan what we call reality is closer to what he means by the imaginary. Nevertheless, all three registers are involved in transference and hence in the technique of analysis: "I am rather inclined to leave intact the empirical totality of the notion of transference, all the while remarking that it is plurivalent and that it acts in several registers at a time, in the symbolic, the imaginary and the real" (*SI* 112–13). While one's narcissistic identifications may be altered in analysis, this is not the primary goal of psychoanalysis—just as consolidating those identifications is also not the point of Lacanian technique, though it's often implicitly the aim of more ego psychology–based analyses.

This question of imaginary and symbolic relations in transference crystallizes in Lacan's 1951 reading of Freud's Dora case, "Intervention on Transference," in which his emphasis on the dialectical relation of speech goes hand in hand with his characterization of transference in imaginary terms. As a consequence of this early conception of analysis in terms of Hegelian dialectics, commentators such as Borch-Jacobsen have concluded that Lacanian theory may be described in primarily imaginary terms, as if Lacan offered nothing more than a revamped theory of narcissism. Thus although Lacan begins his account of Dora with a reference to the "immediate given" of analysis—"the self-evident fact that it deals solely with words" ("Intervention" 63)—the dialectical stages through which his interpretation moves culminate in his description of Dora's "imaginary matrix": "the original *imago* shows us that her only opening to the object was through the intermediary of the masculine partner, with whom, because of the slight difference in years, she was able to identify, in that primordial identification through which the subject recognises itself as *I*" ("Intervention" 68).

The confusion stemming from Lacan's early conception of transference in imaginary terms may be attributed to his emphasis on the *intersubjectivity* of speech, since the idea of intersubjectivity remains an imaginary rather than a symbolic one. That is, intersubjectivity pictures relationality as subject-to-subject, rather than subject-to-Other. In his "Intervention on Transference," Lacan emphasizes intersubjectivity in order to distinguish his version of psychoanalysis from "all psychology considered as the objectification of certain properties of the individual" ("Intervention" 62). But a decade later he begins his seminar on transference with a critique of intersubjectivity (*SVIII* 20–26). The problem with the idea of the intersubjective dialectic is, as Lacan noted of Hegel, that intersubjectivity remains at the limit of anthropology, in which the other always retains the status of subject. Thus intersubjective relations are, in principle if not in practice, symmetrical and reversible. But when Lacan reconceives the subject-other relation as a subject-Other relation, he insists that there cannot be an Other of the Other, since the Other's conceptual value—as it accumulated throughout the 1950s—is that it is strictly divested of subjective status. The subject-Other relation, which describes a fully *symbolic* subject, is definitively asymmetrical.

Unfortunately, there is no tidy progression from the other to the Other in Lacan's work. In this respect, Seminar 2, on the ego, seems more Lacanian than Seminar 3, on psychoses.[24] For example, in a very suggestive seminar session entitled "The Circuit" (by which he means the symbolic circuit of language), Lacan proposes a distinction between

24. In "Deux axiomatiques des psychoses," *Ornicar?* 44 (1988): 52–64, Dimitris Vergetis makes a fine argument for distinguishing between the account of psychosis given in Seminar 3, *Les psychoses* (1955–56), and that given in "On a Question Preliminary to any Possible Treatment of Psychosis" (1959), which *écrit* was supposed to summarize the findings of the seminar. Based on an analysis of the conceptual shift in schema L from seminar to *écrit*, Vergetis argues that in the seminar "the concept of the Other still remains a prisoner of the status of the subject" (53). It is for this reason that Lacan defines psychosis in terms of the *exclusion of the Other* in the seminar, while in the *écrit* he defines psychosis in terms of the *foreclosure of the Name-of-the-Father*. I discuss further these shifts in the conceptualization of psychosis in chapter 3.

other and Other: "the unconscious is the discourse of the other. This discourse of the other is not the discourse of the abstract other, of the other in the dyad, of my correspondent, nor even of my slave, it is the discourse of the circuit in which I am integrated. I am one of its links" (*SII* 89). The discourse of the other retains the structure of intersubjective communication, in which "the sender receives his own message back from the receiver in an inverted form" (*E* 85). But the discourse of the Other, the locus of the unconscious, comprehends speech within the field of discourse. In this view, the subject's communication partner is not the other but the signifying chain into which he or she is articulated.

This distinction between different modes of alterity holds crucial implications for Lacan's theory of desire, because his early conception of it as "desire of the other" maintains desire within a Kojève-Hegelian intersubjective dialectic, in which it is impossible not to reduce desire— and fantasy—to imaginary scenarios.[25] For example, in an early passage remarkable for its self-consciousness, Lacan refers to "the fundamental Hegelian theme—man's desire is the desire of the other," a theme he discusses in strictly imaginary terms via reference to "Jacques Lacan's classical mirror phase" (*SI* 146). In Hegel desire is the desire for recognition, a desire for the other to ratify my existence by means of affirmation; thus insofar as the imaginary is ordered by recognitions and especially by misrecognitions *(méconnaissances),* this Hegelian perspective reduces desire to the imaginary level.

Speech is implicated in this dialectical structure because speech implicitly includes a demand, for both recognition and love. Lacan's categories of "full" and "empty" speech depend on a distinction between speech that performs recognition and speech that does not: "Full speech is speech which aims at, which forms, the truth such as it becomes established in the recognition of one person by another" (*SI* 107). Because speech, conceived according to Hegelian dialectics, includes a demand for recognition, verbal utterance plays its part in the ordering of imaginary relations. And thus in the model of the inverted bouquet speech functions to skew the mirror. Lacan elegantly summarizes this

45. This can be seen in Lacan's early definition of the system of the ego as including "fundamental fantasies which orient and direct the subject" (*SI* 17), a definition that will be supplanted by the later formula for fantasy ($\mathcal{S} \diamond a$), which conjoins symbolic $\mathcal{S}$ and a ("remainder" of the real), rather than conceiving fantasy in imaginary terms.

way of picturing imaginary-symbolic relations: "In my little model [of the inverted bouquet], in order to conceive of the incidence of the symbolic relation, all you have to do is assume that it is the introduction of linguistic relations which produces the swings of the mirror, which will offer the subject, in the other, in the absolute other, the various aspects of his desire" (*SI* 157). Here Lacan's account of desire as unfolding within an imaginary-symbolic scheme must be distinguished from his subsequent account of desire as an unconscious effect of the cause he names object *a*. At this moment in Lacan's thinking, his notion of the object as something that can never appear in the mirror—and which therefore remains heterogeneous to the imaginary register—has not yet emerged.

45

Toward a Model for Desire

This notion of the object—the object *a* that causes desire—emerges fully in the "60s Lacan," even though an earlier seminar, *Le désir et son interprétation* (1958–59), is explicitly devoted to the question of desire. This transitional period, 1958–59, is to my mind the most problematic in Lacan's work. Not incidentally, it is also the period during which Lacan directly theorizes the phallus, a concept I want to resituate as provisional rather than foundational. I consider the phallus a provisional concept because so many of its functions are taken over by other concepts, in particular that of object *a,* which has no a priori relation to gender and, indeed, may be represented by objects gendered masculine, feminine, or neuter. To a certain extent, the logic of his concept of the object supersedes that of the phallus, even though Lacan continued to retain the term *phallus* throughout his career. For whatever reason, Lacan appeared not to realize that his own subsequent thinking makes the concept of the phallus largely obsolete; and his followers have done their best to obscure this obsolescence by continuing to insist that the phallus retain its status as an indispensable term within the Lacanian conceptual system.[26]

In order to make this argument, which amounts to dethroning a

26. I have since found confirmation of this thesis in the work of certain non-Millerian Lacanian analysts in Paris. See, for example, Michel Tort, "The New Testament of Lacan" (unpublished manuscript), which argues that Lacan's theory of the phallus is a phallic theory, a theory generated from within the phallic stage and therefore subject to supersession.

Lacanian shibboleth from a rather different vantage point from the customary attacks launched on it, I consider it necessary to elaborate a methodological qualification regarding the status of conceptual models in Lacan's work. As is well known, throughout his career Lacan borrows models, ideas, and terminology from other disciplines to theorize subjectivity in increasingly complex ways. These disparate models and their accompanying terminology come and go with such dizzying frequency in Lacan's work that we would be mistaken in too readily hypostasizing any one of them. For instance, when furnishing his seminar audience with an optical model for grasping the imaginary order's functioning, Lacan makes clear that this model of the inverted bouquet represents "a substitute for the mirror-stage" (*SI* 74). The model of the inverted bouquet offers a different way—perhaps at the moment it is introduced a better way—of explaining how the imaginary works and how the ego is formed.

46

When presenting this model, Lacan quotes a passage from *The Interpretation of Dreams,* in which Freud rationalizes his own use of analogical models, such as the compound microscope or the camera, to explain how the psychic apparatus works. Lacan cites the following to justify the introduction of his own new optical model:

> Analogies of this kind are only intended to assist us in our attempt to make the complications of mental functioning intelligible by dissecting the function and assigning its different constituents to different component parts of the apparatus. So far as I know, the experiment has not hitherto been made of using this method of dissection in order to investigate the way in which the mental instrument is put together, and I can see no harm in it. We are justified, in my view, in giving free rein to our speculations so long as we retain the coolness of our judgement and *do not mistake the scaffolding for the building* . . . [A]t our first approach to something unknown all that we need is the assistance of provisional ideas. (*SE* 5:536; quoted *SI* 75; my emphasis)

Freud's point is that thinking proceeds analogically, using what is known to get to the unknown, and that in this process we do well to remember that the analogies or models thus employed remain provisional, subject to supersession when other models come to hand. Following this elementary methodological qualification, I want to argue that when we insist on invoking the concept of the phallus to talk about desire, we're effectively mistaking the scaffolding for the building, forgetting the model's epistemological status as provisional.

In order to begin demonstrating this thesis, I turn to Lacan's essay on "The Signification of the Phallus" (1958), in which he elaborates his theory of the phallus for the purpose of generating a fully symbolic account of desire. Departing from his more Hegelian formulations concerning desire, Lacan describes desire in "The Signification of the Phallus" as "desire of the Other." Similarly, by 1958 the unconscious has become the discourse of the Other, and the Other is conceived in thoroughly linguistic terms as "the level of the chain of materially unstable elements that constitutes language" (E 285). In other words, his theory of desire has been detached from the category of the imaginary other as a causal explanation and resituated as an effect of language.

Consequent upon this depersonalized conception of the Other, Lacan's understanding of speech as always entailing a demand for love takes on a more symbolic character. This account makes desire unconscious, structured metonymically, yet it still does not postulate a nonlinguistic object *a* as the causal principle of desire. Hence the following well-known definition of desire:

> For the unconditional element of demand, desire substitutes the "absolute" condition: this condition unties the knot of that element in the proof of love that is resistant to the satisfaction of a need. Thus desire is neither the appetite for satisfaction, nor the demand for love, but the difference that results from the subtraction of the first from the second, the phenomenon of their splitting *(Spaltung)*. (E 287)

According to this definition, desire *resists* satisfaction and remains qualitatively distinct from biological need and from the Freudian notion of wish, since both needs and wishes can be satisfied, whereas it is in the nature of desire to be insatiable.[27] By this account, desire remains unconscious because it is articulated in the signifying chain without being fully articulable by the subject. In this respect Lacanian desire seems

47

---

27. For a meticulous analysis of these and related distinctions, see Charles Shepherdson, "The Epoch of the Body: Need and Demand in Kojève and Lacan," in *Perspectives on Embodiment: The Intersections of Nature and Culture*, ed. Gail Weiss and Honi Fern Haber (New York: Routledge, 1999), 183–211. See also Shepherdson, "The Gift of Love and the Debt of Desire," *Differences* 10, no. 1 (1998): 30–74.

conceptually proximate to what Freud meant by an unconscious wish, whose expression can be only ever indirect and disguised.

Having defined desire abstractly, Lacan gets more concrete, suggesting that the central problem in human sexual relations—one of the reasons sexual relations fail—is that "for both partners in the relation . . . it is not enough to be subjects of need, or objects of love, but that they must stand for the cause of desire" (E 287). The name Lacan gives this "cause of desire" in 1958 is *the phallus:* "The phallus is the privileged signifier of that mark in which the role of the logos is joined with the advent of desire" (E 287). In other words, the phallic signifier connects the function of signification to what causes desire—what it is outside the signifying chain that enables desire. That is to say, although desire is in language, it is not purely linguistic.

43 Why is the phallus given this causative role with respect to desire? Lacan explains:

> It can be said that this signifier is chosen because it is the most tangible element in the real of sexual copulation, and also the most symbolic in the literal (typographical) sense of the term, since it is equivalent there to the (logical) copula. It might also be said that, by virtue of its turgidity, it is the *image* of the vital flow as it is transmitted in generation. (E 287; emphasis added)[28]

As *image,* the phallus is not exactly a signifier or a real cause of desire. Lacan's recourse, in this passage, to an image of the phallus suggests just how hard it is to completely divest the phallic signifier of its imaginary trappings—and therefore how hard it is to generate a fully symbolic, nonimaginary account of desire using this concept. But irrespective of the problems in this passage, its complex rationale for adopting the phallus as "the privileged signifier of that mark in which the role of the logos is joined with the advent of desire" need not be embraced without question in order to justify a Lacanian theory of desire and sexuality. The great advantage of Lacan's theory of desire, as I develop it through-

28. This passage continues: "All these propositions merely conceal the fact that [the phallus] can play its role only when veiled, that is to say, as itself a sign of the latency with which any signifiable is struck, when it is raised *(aufgehoben)* to the function of the signifier" (E 288). Here the phallus functions as a metaphor by virtue of its potential for erection, in that Lacan compares the sublation, or raising up, to which entities become subject in language with the elevation of the penis during sexual excitement. The function of the phallic signifier thus depends for its intelligibility on an *image* of the penis.

out this book, lies in its resistance to normalization, since he consistently pokes fun at the heterosexist *idée reçu* that genital relations between the sexes represent an ideal for psychological maturity: "It has to be said here that the French analysts, with their hypocritical notion of genital oblativity, opened the way to the moralizing tendency, which, to the accompaniment of its Salvationist choirs, is now to be found everywhere" (*E* 287). In thus mocking the accepted norm of sexual life—including the norm as promulgated by psychoanalysis—Lacan undermines one of the principal assumptions buttressing the pathologization of same-sex erotic desire. That this antinormative remark should come in his article theorizing the phallus as signifier of signifiers indicates the degree to which conceptual and ideological tensions remain unresolved in this period of his work.

The extent of these tensions becomes even clearer in a contemporaneous *écrit*, "The Direction of the Treatment and the Principles of Its Power" (1958), in which Lacan reiterates his post-Hegelian definition of desire: "produced as it is by an animal at the mercy of language, man's desire is the desire of the Other" (*E* 264). Lacan pictures ever more starkly the nonreciprocity of the subject-Other relation when he describes desire as "the mark of the iron of the signifier on the shoulder of the speaking subject" (*E* 265). This vivid description continues:

> [Desire] is not so much a pure passion of the signified as a pure action of the signifier that stops at the moment when the living being becomes sign, rendering it insignificant.
>
> This moment of cut is haunted by the form of a bloody scrap—the pound of flesh that life pays in order to turn it into the signifier of the signifiers, which it is impossible to restore, as such, to the imaginary body; it is the lost phallus of the embalmed Osiris. (*E* 265)

Lacan often has recourse to the Shakespearean, potentially anti-Semitic figure of "the pound of flesh" to describe the toll exacted by symbolic alienation; however, he does not always specify the form of this "bloody scrap" in terms of the phallus. While he remains consistent in characterizing desire as consequent upon a forced separation or "cut," he figures the corporeal morsel that is lost thereby in a variety of ways. It is because any number of body parts can stand in for this "bloody scrap" that Lacan's catalogue of objects *a* contains so many examples and implies such varied possibilities for desire.

Since it is primarily the phallus's *imaginary* attributes that permit it to represent the signifier of signifiers, we must deduce that it is purely conventional and therefore, in the final analysis, arbitrary that the phallus should hold any indisputable priority in relation to the symbolic order's exigencies. Though Lacan never relinquished the phallus as a concept, his theory of object *a* makes clear that desire has multiple causes, many of which have no relation whatsoever to gender or sexual difference. Rather than trying to purify the phallus of its imaginary residue or, alternatively, showing the impossibility of any such purification, I want to suggest that the phallus as Lacan's model for the causal principle of desire may be bracketed once the full significance of object *a* comes into view. Such an appreciation enables us to move beyond interminable and increasingly sterile debates over the phallogocentric biases of Lacan's account of the phallus toward a more interesting "60s Lacan" of the object.[29]

"60s Lacan"

At the end of the 1950s, in his seminar *The Ethics of Psychoanalysis,* and throughout the 1960s, Lacan's emphasis shifts from the symbolic order to the nonsymbolic real. During this period Lacan qualifies the determinations of the signifier by another level of causality—that of the object as cause of desire. In other words, "60s Lacan" focuses on the limits rather than the omnipotence of the symbolic order. These limits can be deduced from the resistance to symbolization of elements that Lacan tends to describe in logical, rather than phenomenological, terms. His principal name for this limit is *the real.* In order to fully assess the sub-

29. The kind of debates I have in mind, most of which demonstrate familiarity only with the pre-60s Lacan, are represented in *Differences* 4, no. 1 (1992), special issue on "The Phallus." I find particularly helpful Parveen Adams's essay in that collection, "Waiving the Phallus" (76–83; reprint in Adams, *The Emptiness of the Image,* 49–56), since Adams recognizes that "[t]he concept of the phallus puts in play all three orders of the Imaginary, the Symbolic, and the Real and this is its complexity as a concept, a complexity rarely acknowledged" (82). More importantly, Adams acknowledges that the phallus is not the central component of Lacan's theory of desire, since phallic identification "produces the subject of the signifier and not the subject of desire" (ibid.)—which is why the phallus can, to some degree, be waived. In my reading of Lacan, any tenable distinction between the subject of the signifier and the subject of desire is rather difficult to maintain, since the former gives rise to the latter. We might say that the subject of the signifier and the subject of desire represent two sides of the same coin. Nevertheless, Adams is elaborating a version of the distinction I'm making between the phallus as cause of desire (in Lacanian doctrine, circa 1958) and the object as cause of desire. For her emphasis on the "phallic identification" that produces the subject of the signifier, I would substitute an analysis of *normative* identification.

ject's relation to language and representation, it makes sense that we take into account a logical limit internal to symbolization. And although in this respect it is defined wholly negatively, the real nonetheless has a positive role to play in subject formation, since it represents not only a barrier to subjective or symbolic realization, but also the impossibility against which symbolization is constantly being elaborated. In other words, the real is generative, not simply constraining.[30]

The difficulty with this concept—and surely the reason it has been so comparatively neglected in Lacan's Anglophone reception—is that it remains so abstract. Unfortunately, this nonsymbolic real cannot be pointed to, as a positivist inclination might prompt us to wish, since the real has no substance. Throughout this book, I rehearse different ways of describing the real, offering a range of examples to suggest the positive effects of its purely negative presence. At this point, let me just say that what Lacan calls the real can be inferred from trauma, whose effects are characterized by a recurring impossibility or blockage, a deep impact that calls out for—yet resists—symbolization. Understood in terms of trauma, the real designates not so much a zone of emptiness as of resistance. And thus it would be inaccurate to say that the real *precedes* language in any intuitive sense, since its temporality conforms to the deferred, nonlinear chronology of trauma, which is characterized by what Freud called *Nachträglichkeit,* or belatedness. Because the temporality of the real is *nachträglich,* this concept implies a different, more complex notion of causality than the linear, Newtonian understanding of causation with which we're generally familiar. Needless to say, different concepts of temporality and causality may help us formulate a different idea of history and historicity. Psychoanalytic concepts are not so much indifferent to the claims of historicity as they are grounded in an alternative understanding of it. And this distinction bears on the historicist commitment to a purely immanentist critique of history and causality.

30. One way of illustrating the generative effects of this negativity would have reference to John Forrester's intriguing thesis concerning the indispensable role in childhood development of mendacity. In his most recent book, *Truth Games: Lies, Money, and Psychoanalysis* (Cambridge: Harvard University Press, 1997), Forrester argues (following Freud) that the child's first lie to its parents is crucial for opening up the child's own subjectivity and desire, since by making itself opaque to its parents the child creates a symbolic world distinct from that of its caretakers. This insight may be rephrased in Lacanian terms by pointing to the dimension of duplicity inherent to language. Since whatever language says can be denied, a fundamental negativity inhabits linguistic subjects— a negativity Lacan calls the real.

As a consequence of the real's irreducibility to either symbolic structures or brute materiality—its immanence in neither language nor phenomena—the real can be conceived in terms of transcendence. Hence its foreignness to the logic of historicism.[31] Aligning the real with a certain notion of transcendence permits us to suggest that the real is like God in that it does not exist (it has no positive existential status), yet it obtains palpable effects nonetheless—effects rendered through the symbolic. Since both the real and the symbolic, defined as mutually exclusive, produce subjective effects, neither order should be considered a determinist concept. Their effects cannot be known in advance, but can be extrapolated only from the specifically differentiated relations among real, symbolic, and imaginary. The psychoanalytic subject is a product of these relations. Hence the subject in "60s Lacan" is mapped not topographically (as a position), nor temporally (as a moment of fading), nor even semiologically (as a linguistic differential). Rather, the psychoanalytic subject of the 1960s, defined by its relation to object *a,* is mapped topologically, its structure conceived in terms of non-Euclidean space.

Here we enter particularly difficult conceptual terrain. Mapped topologically, the psychoanalytic subject is so far from approximating any notion of the discrete individual person as to be virtually unrecognizable. And thus even without grasping the details of Lacan's shifting theoretical emphases, we immediately can see just how far he has gone beyond theorizing the subject psychologically. I think it is worth pursuing Lacan's increasingly abstract accounts of subjectivity, because his later formulations, alien though they may appear, offer a range of implications for rethinking interpersonal relations and, in particular, the relations between subject and society. It is perhaps only a topologically mapped subject whose relation to the object can be thought of as transcendent without at the same time lapsing into metaphysics, since—abstract and counterintuitive as it is—topology is not theology.[32] Indeed, it is this transcendent relation that Slavoj Žižek captures in his title *The Sublime Object of Ideology,* for the subject's *relation* to the object

52

31. As Copjec succinctly puts it, "some notion of transcendence is plainly needed if one is to avoid the reduction of social space to the relations that fill it" (*Read My Desire,* 7).

32. Useful accounts of Lacan's use of topology may be found in Jeanne Granon-Lafont, *La topologie ordinaire de Jacques Lacan* (Paris: Point Hors Ligne, 1985), and Johann Listing, *Introduction à la topologie,* trans. Claude Léger and Michael Turnheim (Paris: Navarin, 1989).

is what makes it sublime. Hence I persist with the notion of transcendence not in order to elude historical contingency, or the material grounding of social relations, or a sense of the subject's constructedness. Rather, I want to insist on those "subjective foundations" of object *a* that remain irreducible to these dimensions, and I want to describe them in terms of transcendence in order to designate a locus of conceptual value.

As a branch of modern mathematics, topology may help us rethink the subject's relation to its desire, because topological descriptions of space formulate relationality in radically new ways. For example, finding a rational way to describe how the "outside" functions as the subject's innermost core permits us to redescribe the subject of the unconscious, since, according to Freud, the unconscious knows no contradiction. A theory that provides logical means for overcoming spatial and propositional contradictions offers extremely useful tools for describing the psychoanalytic subject. By reformulating—not simply deconstructing—the relation between inside and outside, a topological account holds the potential for engendering new theories of social relations.[33] Hence, for instance, the possibility of rethinking the public-private distinction so central to social theory, jurisprudence, and ethics, to name a few.

From a psychoanalytic perspective, it is not so much a question of "blurring the boundaries" between inner and outer as it is of revealing how the outside—an alien alterity—inhabits the subject's most intimate inwardness. Lacan coined a neologism for this reconception of the inside-outside relationship, and his reference to *extimité*, or "extimacy," has been developed into a full-blown theory by his son-in-law, Jacques-Alain Miller (whose seminars on Lacan have taken the place of Lacan's seminars on Freud, in the Parisian psychoanalytic milieu, since Lacan's demise).[34] Whereas contemporary critiques of the public-private distinc-

53

33. For an interesting consideration of the sexual politics of reconceiving the relation between inside and outside, see Diana Fuss, "Inside / Out," in *Inside / Out: Lesbian Theories, Gay Theories,* ed. Diana Fuss (New York: Routledge, 1991), 1–10. Fuss's meticulous deconstruction of the inside / out opposition, on which so many other oppositions are based, almost moves beyond deconstruction with her recognition that, conventionally speaking, Lacan's topological structures have neither inside nor outside. The choice of a figure akin to a Borromean knot as the illustration for the cover of this anthology of gay and lesbian theory points to a conjunction between the topological Lacan and queer theory that remains to be realized.

34. In a pattern reminiscent of Lacan's, Miller devoted his seminar for the 1985–86 academic year to the topic of extimacy and then published a redaction of that work in article form. See

tion tend to focus on how the boundary between public and private is constructed in the service of social regulation, especially the social regulation of sexuality, a psychoanalytic critique of privacy might show not that privacy is a pernicious legal fiction so much as its connection to the public realm of language and convention is structured and produced differently. The kind of protection that privacy entails has less to do with personal intimacy than with one's relations to social institutions (grouped by Lacan under the rubric of "the big Other"), since, from a psychoanalytic point of view, interpersonal intimacy is predicated on impersonal, public relations, rather than the reverse. In other words, the subject's relation to the Other provides the basis for his or her relations—social, legal, sexual, ethical—with other people. Rethinking the relation between subject and society in this way has wide-ranging implications, especially for recent debates about public sex within queer theory, some strands of which I take up in chapter 4.

I've been suggesting that subjective relations require rethinking in more complex ways because our customary psychological, philosophical, and sociological models tend to reduce relationality to two or, at most, three dimensions. From Lacan's perspective, even the subject-object relation always involves more than two elements. And therefore his increasing interest in topology stems in part from his quaternary models of subjectivity, since as soon as the dialectic's tripartite structure reaches its conceptual limit, quadripartite structures become increasingly difficult to formalize without a different idea of relationality.[35] Indeed, topological mappings of space may be especially appropriate for theorizing psychic space. As Victor Burgin has pointed out in a remarkably suggestive essay, space has a history, the most recent chapter of which marks the demise of the anthropocentric certainties of Euclidean geometric space. Arguing that twentieth-century technology has effectively converted space into time, Burgin reproaches theorists of repre-

---

Jacques-Alain Miller, "Extimité," in Lacanian Theory of Discourse: Subject, Structure, Society, ed. Mark Bracher, Marshall W. Alcorn Jr., Ronald J. Corthell, and Françoise Massardier-Kenney (New York: New York University Press, 1994), 74–87.

35. This connection between topology and quaternarity supports my hypothesis that topology is not tainted by theology, that its conception of relations is far from metaphysical, because Lacan's topological models distance his 1960s work from what might otherwise be considered troubling forms of trinitarianism. Not only is the topologically conceived real-symbolic-imaginary triad (RSI) of "70s Lacan" supplemented by the fourth order of the *sinthome*, but the Borromean knot structure of RSI is more accurately conceived as a chain made up of any number of elements. That is, the Borromean knot is tied with a *minimum* of three loops.

sentation for clinging to outmoded assumptions of Euclidean geometry, which maps space perspectivally and therefore centrically, rather than excentrically, as Lacan will map the subject. Although Burgin's argument moves toward a topological consideration of Kristeva's abject rather than Lacan's object, one of his central questions, premised on the historicity of space, remains highly pertinent for us here: "[w]hy should we suppose that the condensations and displacements of desire show any more regard for Euclidean geometry than they do for Aristotelian logic?"[36] In order to take seriously psychoanalysis's resituating desire at the level of the unconscious, I think it's worth pursuing Lacan's forays into topology, no matter how eccentric or abstract they may appear on first encounter.

Mapping the Object Topologically

The most obvious benefit of theorizing objects of desire from such a decentered perspective lies in how this approach gets us beyond an imaginary conceptualization of desire. Such a move enables us to think about desire outside the appropriative and incorporative vectors of the ego. Indeed, situating desire in terms of the unconscious separates desire from narcissism and its ills. Yet any move beyond imaginary conceptions of desire remains cognitively challenging, since topological mappings cannot be pictured intuitively, only mathematically. A further problem with topological formalizations of subjectivity is that they're cognate with the impulse to systematize psychoanalytic theory.[37] Given this problem, it seems to me a virtue rather than a deficit that Lacan's use of topology remains as haphazard as it does, since his only rudimentary grasp of advanced mathematics makes it that much harder for us to systematize his thinking.

36. Victor Burgin, "Geometry and Abjection," in *Abjection, Melancholia, and Love: The Work of Julia Kristeva*, ed. John Fletcher and Andrew Benjamin (New York: Routledge, 1990), 111.

37. In an updated edition of her *Psychoanalytic Politics*, Sherry Turkle argues that Lacan turned to mathematical models and formal logic only under the influence, toward the end of his life, of his philosopher son-in-law: "While Lacan produced concepts that were deliberately ambiguous and open to multiple interpretations, Miller sought to rationalize them in the direction of greater logical coherence and uniformity. This 'corrected,' more 'coherent' version of Lacan facilitated attacks on now more easily identifiable theoretical enemies" (Turkle, *Psychoanalytic Politics: Jacques Lacan and Freud's French Revolution* [New York: Guilford, 1992], 253). Her book's second edition provides a useful account of the origins of doctrinal intolerance among Millerians—an intolerance in which mathemes certainly play a role.

We may begin to see how Lacan derives his concept of the object from topology rather than from psychoanalytic object-relations theory by considering an important footnote added, in 1966, to his 1959 article on psychosis. As I elaborate at length in chapter 3, this article, "On a Question Preliminary to any Possible Treatment of Psychosis," contains Lacan's first development of properly quadripartite schemas, which map the psychoanalytic subject "over the four corners of the schema: namely, S, his ineffable, stupid existence, *o,* his objects, *o',* his ego, that is, that which is reflected of his form in his objects, and O, the locus from which the question of his existence may be presented to him" (*E* 194). (It helps to bear in mind, when considering this quadripartition of the subject, that Lacan's translator, Alan Sheridan, has put into English what conventionally is left in French: the phrase "*o,* his objects" refers to those *objets petit a,* where *a* stands for *autre.*) What Lacan means by referring to the subject's "ineffable, stupid existence" is the subject's being in the real. He describes it as ineffable because, at this point in his thinking, Lacan lacks the conceptual and terminological means for articulating this dimension of subjectivity.

However, the crucial footnote appended seven years later retroactively confers on this schema a topological dimension that helps account for his derivation of object *a:*

> The mapping in this schema R of the object (*objet* a) is interesting for the light it sheds on the field of reality (the field that bars it).
>
> I have since laid great stress on the need to develop it—by stating that this field functions only by obturating itself [*s'obturer*] from the screen of phantasy—but this still requires a good deal of attention.
>
> There might be some point in recognizing that, enigmatic as it may then have seemed, but perfectly legible for anyone who knows the outcome, as is the case if one claims to use it as a support, what schema R shows is a projective plan.
>
> In particular the points . . . are those that frame the only valid cut in this schema . . . [and] are sufficient indication that this cut isolates a Moebius strip in the field.
>
> To say this is to say all, since this field will now be merely the representative of the phantasy of which this cut provides the entire structure.
>
> I mean that only the cut reveals the structure of the entire surface

from being able to detach from it those two heterogeneous elements (represented in my algorithm ($ \cancel{S} \, \lozenge \, a $) of the phantasy . . .).

It is as the representative of the representation in phantasy, therefore, that is to say as the originally repressed subject that $\cancel{S}$, the barred S of desire, here supports the field of reality, and this field is sustained only by the extraction of the object a, which, however, gives it its frame.

. . . Whoever has followed my topological expositions (which are justified by nothing but the structure of the phantasy to be articulated) must know very well that in the Moebius strip there is nothing measurable to be retained in its structure, and that it is reduced, like the real with which we are concerned here, to the cut itself.

This note is indicative for the present stage of my topological elaboration (July 1966). (E 223–24 n. 18)

57

This footnote gives us Lacan at his most elliptical and abstract. But it is worth pursuing him here because he's getting at the problem of how to specify a relationship between heterogeneous elements.

Lacan begins this note by distinguishing "the field of reality" from "the screen of phantasy" in a manner quite different from the conventional distinction between fantasy and reality. Not only is the object a—the object of fantasy, as well as of desire—nowhere to be found in "the field of reality," but it is also not to be found in the imaginary register. In contrast to our usual view of the matter, Lacan suggests that fantasy and desire don't concern imagined, hallucinatory objects as distinct from actually existing objects. Rather, objects of fantasy (objects a) are forever lost—even from the visual projections of the imagination—thanks to their cutting away from the subject that they thereby bring into being.

Here Lacan is trying to specify the relation between the subject of desire ($\cancel{S}$) and the object-cause of its desire (a), since this relation describes the structure of fantasy, which he writes using the formula ($\cancel{S} \, \lozenge \, a$). Once subject and object are conceived as radically heterogeneous, formulating the mode of relationship between them poses a distinct problem. Lacan's schema R suggests a solution to this problem—though it took Lacan himself quite some time to figure it out—because cutting along this schema's axes produces the elementary topological form of a Möbius strip. This is why Lacan says that schema

R shows "a projective plan," since, in mathematical terms, the projective property of a geometrical figure remains unchanged when the figure undergoes projection. And by producing a surface whose geometrical properties remain inconceivable in Euclidean terms, a Möbius strip demonstrates the heuristic potential of a form whose inside and outside are continuous, indivisible, though not identical. This form provides an unusual way of relating heterogeneous elements, and Lacan maintains that "there is nothing measurable to be retained in its structure," since it partakes only of the negativity of the "cut."

It is through this notion of the cut that Lacan most directly theorizes object *a*—object *a* is produced by cutting away something from the subject. Whereas earlier Lacan described this cut in fairly conventional terms, insisting that "[t]his moment of cut is haunted by the form of a bloody scrap," which he then identified with the phallus, now he describes it differently, in topological terms, as an *internal* cut, the "extraction" of some element from a domain that thereby constitutes that domain and, indeed, "gives it its frame." Hence the sentence asserting that "[i]t is as the representative of the representation in phantasy, therefore, that is to say as the originally repressed subject[,] that $\mathcal{S}$, the barred S of desire, here supports the field of reality, and this field is sustained only by the extraction of the object *a,* which, however, gives it its frame." The kind of cut that produces object and subject both is not a border separation, a more or less culturally regulated division between domains or acceptable objects of desire. Instead, this is an internal cut, one that constitutively ensures the separation of subject and object by making the subject's reality and its desire depend on the object's never coming into view, never entering the field of reality or of imaginary relations. Hence the frustrating sense, in this passage, that the objects of desire we picture to ourselves are merely substitutes, doubly mediated promises of fulfillment that sustain—while never satisfying—desire. Lacan is getting at this notion that the subject remains separated from its objects by a complexly doubled mediation when he refers to "the representative of the representation in phantasy." Another way of putting this would be to identify the three different modes of alterity— corresponding to the three registers of imaginary, symbolic, and real— that constitute the subject.[38]

38. In "Two Kinds of Other and Their Consequences," I distinguished between imaginary and symbolic modes of alterity. In this book I am concerned more with the third mode of alterity that

The agent of the cut that produces both subject and object is, of course, language. According to Lacan, symbolic networks dissect the human body, producing leftovers that cause desire. He explains that the psychoanalytic subject "thinks as a consequence of the fact that a structure, that of language—the word implies it—a structure carves up his body, a structure that has nothing to do with anatomy. Witness the hysteric" (*Television* 6). The ill fit between language and the body introduces wrinkles and gaps that generate desire. We might say that the unconscious and desire exist only as a consequence of this disharmony between the structures of language and those of the body. Since there are certainly better and worse fits between bodies and symbolic networks, the category of hysteria was invented to describe a particularly bad fit, a subjective wrinkle so pronounced as to disfigure the body itself. And if we accept that the symbolic order causes illness, it follows that language also can alleviate it—hence the idea of a talking cure. Yet we would be mistaken in assuming that the body could be made to conform perfectly to the structure of language. No amount of talking—or of cutting, augmenting, scarring, tattooing, starving, or exercising the body—can alleviate completely the disjunction of the unconscious.

Language and the body are permanently out of synch, though not always in the same way. Bodies change over the course of a lifetime and over longer time spans too, as aesthetic fashions, sexual ideals, nutrition, diet, and styles of living mutate. Over longer periods we also would have to consider evolutionary changes in the human form. Symbolic networks are constantly mutating too, though we would be falling into linguistic determinism if we suggested that corporeal changes corresponded to, or followed directly, symbolic shifts. My point here is that given these changes—and therefore the changing configurations by which the body could be said to be out of synch with language— psychoanalytic diagnostic categories require a flexibility that can take full account of such shifting configurations. Retaining nineteenth-century nosological terms such as *hysteria,* no matter how one redefines their meaning, inhibits rather than enhances diagnostic flexibility.

If Lacan's theory that language carves up the body implies a gloomy

constitutes the subject, the real mode. To the distinction between imaginary other and symbolic Other, we add that mode of alterity designated by the formula *objet petit a.*

prognosis by pointing to a rift that nothing can heal, its happier implication is that anatomy is not destiny. Since the hysteric bears witness to
an effect of symbolic networks on the body that "has nothing to do with
anatomy," it follows that the desire borne by language need not be
heterosexual at all. Throughout this book I argue that, in Lacanian theory, desire remains independent of heterosexuality. Hence the significance of Lacan's account of object *a* for contemporary sexual politics.
His concept of the object recognizes the diversity of forms that erotic
desire may take, as he points out in a seminar of 1963: "The *a,* the
object, falls. That fall is primal. The diversity of forms taken by that
object of the fall ought to be related to the manner in which the desire
of the Other is apprehended by the subject" ("Names" 85). Acknowledging the plurality of forms in which human desire originates, Lacan never
developed this insight in the direction of a radical sexual politics. In the
rest of this book I hope to do so. Yet I want to make clear that Lacan's
pluralization of desire does not imply that genders and sexualities may
be reconfigured in line with ideological demands, since the pluralization
of desire stems from a symbolic fissuring of anatomy that gives rise to
both the unconscious and the death drive. In the next chapter, I introduce these sobering constraints into the ostensibly psychoanalytic theory
of gender performativity, showing how Lacan's pluralization of desire
differs from recent accounts of gender and sexuality with which it has
been associated.

TRANSCENDING GENDER

Chapter 2

Drag is as American as apple pie.

—Esther Newton,
Mother Camp: Female Impersonators in America

We Are All Transgenderists Now

On the contemporary scene of sexual politics transgenderism reigns supreme. In practical terms, transgendered people insist more vociferously than ever on being included in the rainbow coalition of lesbian and gay national politics; in conceptual terms, various transgender phenomena exemplify our most avant-garde theories of gender and sexuality. For instance, in her book *Vested Interests,* Marjorie Garber identifies cross-dressing as not only central to U.S. culture, but as constitutive of culture as such, in that the "category crisis" induced at all levels by transvestism is "not the exception but rather the ground of culture itself."[1] Toward the end of her book Garber intensifies this claim, arguing that "there can be no culture without the transvestite, because the transvestite marks the entry into the Symbolic" (354). Before considering fully such claims, I want to register that transgenderism encompasses

---

1. Marjorie Garber, *Vested Interests: Cross-Dressing and Cultural Anxiety* (New York: Routledge, 1992), 16. Subsequent page references are in main text.

far more than cross-dressing. It is not only drag queens and transsexuals who fall under the rubric of transgender, but in fact all "gender outlaws," all those who remain unwilling or unable to conform to the norms attendant on either side of the gender divide. This definition of transgenderists as gender outlaws—which comes from transsexual lesbian performance artist Kate Bornstein—has the capacity to bring within its purview anybody who does not completely "pass" as a regular heterosexual member of the male or female sex, anyone who expresses dissatisfaction with the normative exigencies of masculinity or femininity.[2] Membership in this transgenderist category thus expands almost infinitely, encompassing feminists as well as lesbians, gays, bisexuals, transgendered, the intersexed, and their political supporters. We are all potentially transgenderists now.

I have chosen to begin with this generous understanding of transgenderism not because it furnishes us with an undisputed definition (far from it), but because it suggests some implications of conceiving cross-dressing and transsexuality in primarily political terms. As will become clear, transgenderism stands in relation to transsexuality as queer stands in relation to homosexuality: both transgender and queer designate political identities that have more to do with ideological allegiances than with actual sexual practices. Just as many lesbians and gay men don't consider themselves queer and, in fact, continue to resent the term, so also many transsexuals don't consider themselves transgendered, insisting instead that they "really" belong to one sex and just happen to have been born into the wrong biological category. The majority of transsexuals struggle to conform rigorously with the normative demands of the opposite sex; indeed, far from being gender outlaws, "many transsexuals are, in fact, 'more royalist than the king' in matters of gender," says anthropologist Judith Shapiro.[3] And male-to-female transsexual lesbian feminist Sandy Stone, in a critique that laid the conceptual groundwork for transgenderism, claims that "[t]he highest purpose of the transsexual is to erase him/herself, to fade into the

2. Kate Bornstein, *Gender Outlaw: On Men, Women, and the Rest of Us* (New York: Routledge, 1994).

3. Judith Shapiro, "Transsexualism: Reflections on the Persistence of Gender and the Mutability of Sex," in *Body Guards: The Cultural Politics of Gender Ambiguity,* ed. Julia Epstein and Kristina Straub (New York: Routledge, 1991), 253.

'normal' population as soon as possible."[4] Hence the paradox in which transgender represents not so much the preferred term for transsexual phenomena as the rubric encompassing almost everybody *except* certain transsexuals.

This paradox brings into focus two sets of questions that permeate all the literature on transsexuality, including statements by transsexuals and the transgendered themselves. The first set of questions concerns the political implications of transgenderism—how subversive or conservative it is with respect to gender norms. The distinction between transsexuality and transgenderism offers a ready template for adjudicating this issue, since the recent terminological shift from transsex to transgender bespeaks a movement from gender essentialism to gender constructionism that lies at the heart of contemporary sexual politics. In other words, if transsexuals in their "more royalist than the king" commitment to polarized gender norms appear conservative, then transgenderists in their bodily commitment to the artifactuality—even arbitrariness—of sex and gender appear radically progressive. Yet debates over the political implications of transgender phenomena are far more complex than this schematic distinction allows and cannot be settled by terminological discriminations alone.

The second set of questions relates to the first and asks in what register transgenderism should be primarily conceived: political or psychological. This kind of question, more fundamental than the first, is crucial for any psychoanalysis of sexual politics, especially given the way that transgender phenomena have come to stand in contemporary theory for antiessentialist accounts of identity—that is, the academic consensus that gender and sexual identities are socially constructed rather than inborn. In order to assess fully the place of drag and transsexuality in psychoanalytically inflected gender theory, I think it necessary to turn the tables and consider psychoanalysis from the transgender perspective.

As with homosexuality, the history of transgenderism has been closely intertwined with that of psychoanalysis, particularly in the United States, where the availability of what is known as sex-reassignment surgery (SRS) remains connected to psychiatric diagnoses, treatment,

63

4. Sandy Stone, "The *Empire* Strikes Back: A Posttranssexual Manifesto," in *Body Guards,* ed. Epstein and Straub, 295. Stone's term "posttranssexual" prefigures the currently preferred alternative, "transgender."

and recommendations. The current edition of the American Psychiatric Association's *Diagnostic and Statistical Manual of Mental Disorders, DSM-IV,* still lists transsexualism as a mental disorder; it entered *DSM* in 1980 and vigorous efforts to remove that diagnosis have been under way for some time. In *DSM* transsexuality falls under the rubric of "gender identity disorders," a category that was introduced shortly after the manual's elimination of homosexuality as a mental disease, following the APA's decision to declassify it in 1973. The problem with "gender identity disorder" as a pathological category lies in its potential for casting all dissatisfaction with normative gender arrangements in terms of psychological sickness. The diagnosis of gender identity disorder can be used not only to retain the pathologizing perspective on homosexuality that was officially outmoded in 1973, but also to defang political resistance to sex-gender norms. Gender identity disorder is always a potentially depoliticizing diagnosis, a way of suggesting that feminists and their ilk might have something wrong in the head. By making unhappiness about the state of sex-gender arrangements a psychological problem, such diagnoses obscure the extent to which sex-gender arrangements are a sociopolitical problem too.

According to *DSM,* the triggering diagnosis for transsexuality is "gender dysphoria," a term that refers to persistent anxiety, depression, and distress concerning one's gender identity. Once we accept that gender acquires its meaning socially as well as individually, however, we begin to see the impossibility of drawing a hard-and-fast line between distress over one's own gender and distress at the sex-gender system. Any political questioning of power disequilibriums organized along gender lines cannot help but prompt a questioning of—and perhaps some anxiety, even depression over—one's own participation in such gender arrangements. To concede to feminist critiques of the social organization of gender the slightest legitimacy whatsoever is to court at least mild gender dysphoria. And while this pervasiveness of gender dysphoria need not completely invalidate gender identity disorder as a diagnostic category, it does suggest some of the difficulties involved in making a diagnosis that stands as one prerequisite for sex-reassignment surgery.

Persons who desire this surgery are intensely aware of these difficulties. In order to qualify for sex-change surgery, the transsexual has to be diagnosed as mentally ill. The problem here lies not only in the pathologizing of what may be understood as at least partly a political desire, but also in the paradoxical assumption that a subjective disorder should be treated through surgery. Whether we conceive of transsexuality as primarily psychological or political or a complex combination thereof, it remains highly questionable that the issue should be resolved with a surgeon's knife.[5] Yet this is the solution preferred by both medical experts and most transgender political organizations. Indeed, the new Health Law Standards, adopted in 1993 by the Second International Conference on Transgender Law and Employment Policy, explicitly assert that "many, if not most, of the patients doctors see for gender medical services (hormones; surgery) do not require any psychological services."[6] This assumption is articulated also in the International Bill of Gender Rights, which elaborates a "right to freedom from psychiatric diagnosis or treatment" in the following terms: "Given the right to define one's own gender identity, individuals should not be subject to psychiatric diagnosis or treatment solely on the basis of their gender identity or role."[7] While this impulse to remove the stigma of psychiatric pathologization from transsexuality is politically laudable, it nevertheless implies that psychoanalysis, the practice of effecting change through discourse, has nothing to offer transsexuals or the transgendered. While we should acknowledge that some transgendered persons have experienced only grief on their psychoanalysts' couches, the recent political effort to foreclose psychoanalysis altogether—and, by extension, to foreclose an experience of symbolic subjectivity—remains a problem.[8]

5. A version of this point was made some time ago by two Marxist sociologists, Billings and Urban, who argued that the surgical response to gender dysphoria depoliticizes a gender consciousness that otherwise might lead to revolution. See Dwight B. Billings and Thomas Urban, "The Socio-medical Construction of Transsexualism: An Interpretation and Critique," *Social Problems* 29 (1982): 266–82. Judith Shapiro puts the point this way: "addressing gender issues through sex change surgery is a bit like turning to dermatologists to solve the race problem" (Shapiro, "Transsexualism," 262).

6. International Conference on Transgender Law and Employment Policy, *Health Law Standards of Care for Transsexualism* (1993), cited in James L. Nelson, "The Silence of the Bioethicists: Ethical and Political Aspects of Managing Gender Dysphoria," *GLQ* 4 (1998): 221.

7. International Conference on Transgender Law and Employment Policy, *The International Bill of Gender Rights* (1993), cited in Martine Rothblatt, *The Apartheid of Sex: A Manifesto on the Freedom of Gender* (New York: Crown, 1995), 169. Rothblatt's book includes the complete Bill of Gender Rights in an appendix.

8. In her autobiography, *Second Serve: The Renée Richards Story* (New York: Stein and Day, 1983), the eponymous author, a professional tennis player who also maintained the successful ophthalmologist career begun while she was Richard Raskind, relates her disappointing experiences with various psychoanalysts over the course of almost a decade. While I do not doubt the veracity of Richards's

65

This is a problem in which medical science colludes with the transsexual's demand for surgery, as if little more than surgical technology and individuals' ability to pay for the operations were at stake. As Charles Shepherdson observes in his discussion of transsexuality, "this focus on the body as material substance coincides with a shortcircuit of the symbolic order, which brings the entire medical apparatus, in spite of its cultural centrality, into close proximity with psychosis."[9] Shepherdson's claim refers to Lacan's redefining psychosis in terms of language and the symbolic order, a theory that I elaborate more fully in the next chapter. The point I want to emphasize here is that although we have grounds for skepticism regarding the psychiatric conception and treatment of transsexuality, we also have grounds for considerable skepticism about transsexuals' demands for surgery and surgeons' readiness to accede to those demands. It is far from the case that language is irrelevant to transgenderism; furthermore, its relevance isn't reduc-

---

anecdotal evidence, I also would counsel caution about accepting at face value everything that appears in transgender autobiographies and testimonies. The transgendered author's status as oppressed minority should not grant his or her utterances an unquestionable truth-value. Indeed, as Judith Shapiro suggests:

> [O]ne cannot take at face value transsexuals' own accounts of a fixed and unchanging (albeit sex-crossed) gender identity, given the immense pressure on them to produce the kinds of life histories that will get them what they want from the medico-psychiatric establishment. To take the problem one step further, the project of autobiographical reconstruction in which transsexuals are engaged, although more focused and motivated from the one that all of us pursue, is not entirely different in kind. We must all repress information that creates problems for culturally canonical narratives of identity and the self, and consistency in gender attribution is very much a part of this. (Shapiro, "Transsexualism," 251)

Bernice L. Hausman makes a similar point in greater detail in *Changing Sex: Transsexualism, Technology, and the Idea of Gender* (Durham: Duke University Press, 1995), chap. 5. The question of what kind of authority should be granted to transsexuals' autobiographies is part of a larger problem concerning authoritative discourse on transgender phenomena. This problem appears in baldest form on a website detailing "Suggested Rules for Non-Transsexuals Writing about Transsexuals, Transsexuality, Transsexualism, or Trans_" (http://www.actlab.utexas.edu/sandy/hale.rules.html). Composed by a professor at the University of Texas, the fifteen rules appeal to the authority of experience in a quite breathtakingly essentialist way, as if feminist theory had never problematized the authority of experience. Rule number 1 advises: "Approach your topic with a sense of humility: you are not the experts about transsexuals, transsexuality, transsexualism, or trans_ Transsexuals are." While one may appreciate transsexuals' frustration with all the misinformation disseminated about their lives, this effort to restrict all discursive authority to those who speak from the lived experience of transsexuality hardly seems like a viable solution. At the very least we should recall how the unconscious qualifies any authority one might claim when speaking of his or her own experience. Indeed, from a psychoanalytic perspective the blatant attempt to police what can and cannot be said—on whatever topic—appears suspect in and of itself.

9. Charles Shepherdson, "The *Role* of Gender and the *Imperative* of Sex," in *Supposing the Subject*, ed. Joan Copjec (New York: Verso, 1994), 171.

ible to terminological questions or debates over the most appropriate vocabulary for discussing transgender phenomena. In this chapter I want to suggest an alternative to thinking of these phenomena in primarily psychological terms, on the one hand, or primarily political terms, on the other, since depsychologizing transgenderism does not reveal it as a purely sociopolitical problem. I would like to shift the terms of these debates by arguing for a completely different psychoanalytic conception of transgenderism, one based on the Lacanian category of the real.

Realness

The distinction between transsexualism and transgenderism hinges on a relation to reality as that term is commonly understood in everyday usage. Whereas "[t]he essence of transsexualism is the act of passing" as a normal member of the opposite sex, transgenderism entails a resistance to passing, a refusal to conform with the appearance or reality of *either* sex.[10] The assumption behind the transgenderist's refusal is that gender nonconformism disrupts social reality as we know it, opening up possibilities for other ways of inhabiting our bodies and, indeed, inhabiting the world. As transgender activist Leslie Feinberg succinctly puts it, "I was born female, but my masculine gender expression is seen as male. It's not my sex that defines me, and it's not my gender expression. It's the fact that my gender expression appears to be at odds with my sex . . . It's the social contradiction between the two that defines me."[11] Central to Feinberg's theory and practice of sexual politics is the status of social reality: transgenderism wishes to call into question nothing less than reality itself.

Besides the commonsense meaning of this term *reality*—the way in which it is used by people who rarely enclose the word in quotation marks—there are several other meanings that I will attempt to distinguish. The philosophical sense of reality concerns existences whose status is necessary and essential rather than contingent or accidental. Freud uses the term in this standard philosophical sense, with the crucial qualification that most of psychic life remains disconnected from reality—that is, from the necessities imposed by external constraints. Since he

10. Stone, "The *Empire* Strikes Back," 299.

11. Leslie Feinberg, *Transgender Warriors: Making History from Joan of Arc to RuPaul* (Boston: Beacon, 1996), 101.

maintains that unconscious processes "pay . . . little regard to reality" (*SE* 14:187), Freud is obliged to introduce the dimension of psychical reality, a concept that Lacan develops in terms of the real. And in contradistinction to both the commonsense and the philosophical sense of reality, what Lacan means by the real has more to do with contingency and accident than with essential existence. I want to get at Lacan's concept of the real and its implications for an account of transgenderism by considering a fourth sense of reality—what drag queens calls *realness*.

The notion of realness came to prominence in 1991, thanks to Jennie Livingston's documentary film *Paris Is Burning,* which focused on the lives of various gay men and transsexuals of color in Harlem, particularly their culture of drag balls and voguing—the catwalk-style posing that participants in the balls made into a dance form and Madonna mainstreamed in the video for her 1990 hit single "Vogue." *Paris Is Burning* achieved considerable popularity with gender critics and was almost immediately taken to exemplify the theory of gender performativity put forth in Judith Butler's *Gender Trouble* (1990), even though Butler didn't discuss the film until her subsequent book, *Bodies That Matter* (1993). *Paris Is Burning* and *Gender Trouble* helped canonize each other, disseminating a version of Continental feminist theory far beyond the academy and shoring up Butler's political credibility by virtue of its association with minority street culture, while at the same time intensifying academic attention to issues of transsexualism, cross-dressing, and nonwhite gay identities.[12]

12. The critical debate surrounding *Paris Is Burning* began with a review of the film by bell hooks, "Is Paris Burning?" (reprinted in hooks, *Black Looks: Race and Representation* [Boston: South End Press, 1992], 145–56), which faulted the director, Jennie Livingston, for not making explicit in the film her stakes as a white lesbian filming a racial minority subculture. Demurring from hooks's racial essentialism, Judith Butler, *Bodies That Matter: On the Discursive Limits of "Sex"* (New York: Routledge, 1993), chap. 4, used the film to qualify her theory of gender performativity and to argue that parodying dominant norms remains insufficient to effect real change. Phillip Brian Harper, in " 'The Subversive Edge': *Paris Is Burning,* Social Critique, and the Limits of Subjective Agency," *Diacritics* 24 (1994): 90–103, took Butler's qualification one step further to argue that the subversiveness some critics have attributed to *Paris Is Burning* paradoxically is constrained by the very medium through which the drag balls became widely known. Pointing to the failure of the film's subjects to gain further monetary compensation for its success, Harper distinguishes between different public arenas—the ballroom, in which the drag queens have agency, and the courtroom, in which they don't (their lawsuits against Livingston all were dismissed). Arguing that the film's intelligibility depends upon the public arena in which its subjects have least agency, Harper suggests that the very terms through which the drag balls make sense are what deprive their participants of agency and hence of subversiveness. Harper's implausible subthesis, in an otherwise persuasive account, involves his attempt to rescue Butler's theory of gender performativity from the many charges of voluntarism leveled against it: what's most bizarre about Harper's article is its situating Butler's

For the characters in *Paris Is Burning* realness is the ultimate accolade, since this term denotes the degree of successful imitation produced by a gender performance. As an effect of scrupulously accurate mimesis, realness is in some sense the social or subcultural equivalent of the aesthetic category of realism. Literary critics such as Roland Barthes have argued for the concept of a "reality effect" as undercutting the aesthetic of realism by showing how prerepresentational reality—to whose faithful imitation the transparency of realist representation aspires—is itself the effect of highly complex and artificial rhetorical codes. Similarly, gender critics such as Butler argue that drag realness undermines the ontological or existential status of every identity, especially gender identity, by showing the imitative and fictive structure of identity—and thence of everyday reality. Realness reveals social reality as a construct, something fabricated.[13]

Drag's potential for undermining naturalized gender identities depends on an important, if somewhat hazy, distinction between drag as realness and drag as parody. To take two more examples from popular culture: the force of Jaye Davidson's character, Dil, in Neil Jordan's 1992 movie, *The Crying Game,* depends entirely on Dil's realness—and hence Fergus's belief that Dil is a real woman. By contrast, the camp effect of pop culture drag icons—such as seven-foot-tall, blonde-wigged African American entertainer RuPaul and cabaret monologist Lypsinka (a.k.a. John Epperson)—depends on recognizing their femininity as hy-

69

---

theory as the solution rather than the problem. By contrast, in *The Ethics of Marginality: A New Approach to Gay Studies* (Minneapolis: University of Minnesota Press, 1995), chap. 4, John Champagne views Butler's work as symptomatic of the larger problem of conceiving sexual politics in terms of style. Champagne also takes issue at great length with hooks's account of the film, particularly her recourse to a politics of experience, which, like a politics of style, he considers insufficiently responsive to the material realities of poverty and exploitation that also are represented in *Paris Is Burning.*

13. Butler summarizes her position thus:

[D]rag is not an imitation or a copy of some prior and true gender . . . drag enacts the very structure of impersonation by which *any gender* is assumed. Drag is not the putting on of a gender that belongs properly to some other group, i.e. an act of *expropria-tion* or *appropriation* that assumes that gender is the rightful property of sex, that "mascu-line" belongs to "male" and "feminine" belongs to "female" . . . Drag constitutes the mundane way in which genders are appropriated, theatricalized, worn, and done; it implies that all gendering is a kind of impersonation and approximation. If this is true, it seems, there is no original or primary gender that drag imitates, but *gender is a kind of imitation for which there is no original;* in fact, it is a kind of imitation that produces the very notion of the original as an *effect* and consequence of the imitation itself.

Judith Butler, "Imitation and Gender Insubordination," in *Inside/Out: Lesbian Theories, Gay Theories,* ed. Diana Fuss (New York: Routledge, 1991), 21; original emphases.

perbolic, purely parodic. Whereas *The Crying Game*'s Dil is trying to pass, RuPaul and Lypsinka are not.[14]

This distinction between trying to pass as the real thing and mocking the notion of the real thing can be restated in terms of our earlier distinction between transsexualism as a commitment to passing and transgenderism as resistance to passing. Restating the distinction in these terms clarifies the murky issue of appropriation, since transgenderists, understood as gender outlaws, are trying neither to appropriate the privileges of the opposite sex nor yet to parody the opposite sex. Instead, transgenderists can be seen as questioning the very idea of gender. In this respect, transgender solves a nagging problem faced by proponents of drag, namely, the difficulty in distinguishing between parodies of femininity and mockery of actual women. Although feminist theory now embraces drag, twenty years ago it did not, and for just this reason. Janice Raymond put the feminist critique of transsexualism most polemically when she asserted that "[a]ll transsexuals rape women's bodies by reducing the real female form to an artifact, appropriating this body for themselves."[15] Nowadays, however, it is *because* transsexuals reduce "the real female form to an artifact" that feminist theorists praise them.

According to Butler, it's not just gender identities but all identities that drag reveals as artifactual. The drag balls filmed in *Paris Is Burning* showed drag realness not only in the relatively conventional form of female impersonation, but also in the form of college-student impersonation, bank-executive impersonation, military-officer impersonation, and "banjee girl" impersonation, as well as more glamorous categories of female impersonation. Almost every conceivable kind of identity can be a form of drag insofar as, being imitable, identity is revealed to be itself imitative. We are all in drag, whether or not we're aware of it, and one purpose of the drag balls is to make us aware of it. RuPaul's aphorism—"You're born naked, and the rest is drag"—also insists on

14. Late capitalism absorbs these distinctions perfectly well: both Davidson (photographed bare-chested by Annie Leibovitz) and Lypsinka have been featured in magazine advertisements for Gap clothing, the hallmark of sartorial normativity. More recently, RuPaul has starred in magazine advertisements for equally mainstream men's shoes: wearing a man's suit, shirt, and tie while sporting a goatee and shaved head, RuPaul displays sensible Rockport men's shoes, hyped for their comfort. Since the figure in the ad bears no resemblance to the glamorous blonde on MTV, he is directly named—"RuPaul, drag superstar." This disjunction between image and name is made into a joke by the ad's punch line legend: "I'm comfortable being a man."

15. Janice Raymond, *The Transsexual Empire: The Making of the She-Male* (Boston: Beacon, 1979), 104.

making us aware of it. Drag's deconstruction of gender identity has made it central to popular academic theories of sex and gender identification; the drag queen and the transsexual are the social constructionist's friends. Transsexuals "make us realize that we are all passing," notes Shapiro.[16] And while Garber suggests that cross-dressing accomplishes a significant amount of "cultural work," I must emphasize that drag also performs a good deal of *theoretical* work. As Carole-Anne Tyler wryly observes, "[t]he controversy over the meaning of camp reveals as much about the fears and desires of theorists of drag as it does about the fears and desires of impersonators themselves."[17]

There is something quite appropriate, indeed unremarkable, about a bunch of English professors arguing over transsexual phenomena, insofar as the central concept at stake is imitation—an aesthetic, philosophical, and social problematic that long antedates the more local aesthetic of realism. As an aesthetic problematic, imitation goes under the name *mimesis,* and connects to sociopolitical questions of gender identity via the politics of mimicry. It poses no threat to disciplinary boundaries for literature professors, trained in theories of representation, to debate the politics of gender mimesis much as we might debate the politics of aesthetic mimesis in a poem or a novel. While the object of attention has shifted, the methodological approach remains largely unchanged—despite what both the proponents and the detractors of cultural studies often claim.

The psychoanalytic challenge to this business-as-usual lies in the contention that theories of mimesis or imitation represent the wrong approach to gender altogether, because formulating questions of gender and sexuality in terms of the mimetic or imitative generation of reality effects restricts vital political questions to the arena of ego identifications. In Lacanian terms, the concept of mimicry situates identification at the level of imaginary representations, excluding the real from consideration. By factoring the Lacanian real back into an account of transsexuality, I want to argue against the mimeticist understanding of transgender phenomena and suggest that what motivates identifications across gender is not so much the visible or imagined attributes of the other

16. Shapiro, "Transsexualism," 257.

17. Carole-Anne Tyler, "Boys Will Be Girls: The Politics of Gay Drag," in *Inside/Out,* ed. Fuss, 33.

71

sex or of more socially privileged racial groups. Instead, Lacan's concept of the real can help us grasp that cross-gender identifications are motivated by something that cannot be seen or imagined—a place beyond sexual difference where gender would not be simply questioned or subverted but completely transcended. Paradoxical though it may sound, transsexualism's obsession with gender norms represents an attempt to escape sexual difference altogether. Transsexual identification occurs not with the opposite sex, but with a position outside sex. Clearly this thesis cannot be argued from a theory of identification that remains centered on mimesis and thence on the imaginary. Lacanian psychoanalysis offers a nonmimetic account of identification based on the concept of the real.

72

The Real as an Effect

In order to grasp how drag and transgender phenomena have achieved such a prominent place in contemporary gender theory, we must go back to Esther Newton, whose work on female impersonation Butler describes as a formative influence on her theory of gender performativity.[18] Researching female impersonation before Stonewall and essentially prefeminism, Newton viewed drag through a functionalist anthropological paradigm and interpreted it as a cultural expression of the contradictions generated by the social stigma of homosexuality.[19] This functionalist approach perceives conflict in socially expressive, purely epiphenomenal terms and therefore considers conflict eradicable. The psychoanalytic idea of an *ineradicable* conflict structuring subjectivity has no place in the functionalist framework—a distinction that will be important as we investigate the theory of gender performativity that grows out of Newton's functionalism. Sociological functionalism perceives social deviance, exemplified by cross-dressing, as the social expression—

18. Judith Butler, *Gender Trouble: Feminism and the Subversion of Identity* (New York: Routledge, 1990), 136–137. See also Butler, "Imitation and Gender Insubordination," 21: "I remember quite distinctly when I first read in Esther Newton's *Mother Camp: Female Impersonators in America* that drag is not an imitation or a copy of some prior and true gender; according to Newton, drag enacts the very structure of impersonation by which *any gender* is assumed" (original emphasis).

19. Esther Newton, *Mother Camp: Female Impersonators in America,* 2d ed. (Chicago: University of Chicago Press, 1979 [1st ed. 1972]). Subsequent references provide pagination in main text. I refer to Newton's work as prefeminist because, on her own account, the research for and writing of *Mother Camp* were completed before her own feminist politicization. Her feminist revision of *Mother Camp* is inscribed in the second edition's preface and many footnotes.

and, indeed, resolution—of individual deviance. By socializing deviance, cross-dressing serves society like the symptoms of illness serve a biological organism: they are part of the natural process that helps rid the organism of foreign bodies and maintain its homeostasis. Hence Newton's reference to the "fact that the effect of the female impersonator subculture is to socialize individual deviance so that it is brought under group control and legitimized" (51).

Despite the limitations of her functionalist paradigm, Newton's argument that "homosexuality is symbolized in American culture by transvestism" (3) remains largely valid for U.S. culture even today. For example, the persistent misidentification of homosexuality with transvestism led to charges of homophobia against Jonathan Demme's 1991 Oscar-winning movie, *The Silence of the Lambs,* in which a man named Jame Gumb/Buffalo Bill—who has been refused sex reassignment surgery by the world-famous Gender Identity Clinic at Johns Hopkins University—sets about making his own bodysuit from the human skin of his female victims.[20] Gay activists charged the film and its director with homophobia for representing a homosexual man as a transvestite killer, and thus for identifying homosexuality with pathology, transvestism, and homicidal compulsions. The activists were not implying that transvestism or transsexualism are pathologies, although they were objecting to the identification of homosexuality with transvestism. Yet the movie represents not so much a sick homosexual as a sick transsexual. Jame Gumb's/Buffalo Bill's desire for men is not gay male desire but straight female desire; he desires from within a fantasy of himself as a heterosexual woman and commits murder in the service of literalizing this heterosexual fantasy. Hence the critical charge of homophobia, rather than transphobia, unwittingly repeats the film's—and our culture's—misidentification of transvestism with homosexuality.

This persistent misrecognition of transvestism prompts Newton to claim that "[p]rofessional drag queens are, therefore, professional homosexuals; they represent the stigma of the gay world" (3). I would not

73

20. The movie was based on Thomas Harris's 1988 novel of the same name. In 1966, the Johns Hopkins Hospital performed the first ever clinic-based sex-reassignment surgery in the U.S., beginning a revolution that helped make Baltimore a haven for transsexuals. However, in 1979, under rather questionable circumstances, Hopkins's Gender Identity Clinic abruptly stopped performing sex-reassignment surgery. For an excellent investigative report on the clinic's decision to terminate its surgical option, see Ogi Ogas, "Spare Parts," *City Paper* (Baltimore), March 9, 1994, 10–15.

want to convey the impression that Newton endorses the cultural mis-identification of transvestism with homosexuality or that her account should be deemed homophobic. But I do want to emphasize one implication of her functionalist argument, namely, that if no social stigma were attached to homosexuality, then transvestism—and transsexuality—simply would not exist. *Mother Camp* includes an implicit account of causation that sees transvestism as stemming from social contradictions about polarized sex-gender roles. The most important social contradiction to which drag responds is the contradiction between what sociologists call "ascribed" and "achieved" roles—or between what we might call "essential" and "constructed" identities.

The meritocratic foundation of U.S. society treats almost all identities as achieved: they are something one earns rather than something with which one is born. Yet gender is considered an *ascribed* identity that, says Newton, "radiates a complex and ubiquitous system of typing *achieved* roles" (102). Drag's most significant effect on what Newton calls "the sex-role system" is that drag

> questions the "naturalness" of the sex-role system *in toto;* if sex-role behavior can be achieved by the "wrong" sex, it logically follows that it is in reality also achieved, not inherited, by the "right" sex. Anthropologists say that sex-role behavior is learned. The gay world, via drag, says that sex-role behavior is an appearance; it is "outside." It can be manipulated at will. (103)

What could be more democratic, more essentially American, than a gender that "can be manipulated at will"? Drag turns out to be as American as apple pie.

This idea of gender as fully manipulable informs most transgender political theory. Within North America's dominant political system the expressivist model of gender, which underlies Newton's functionalist account, quite logically gives rise to demands for freedom of gender expression. Freedom of expression is a fundamental political right in the United States, and transgender activists argue that gender expression should be included under this right. As transsexual activist Nancy Nangeroni claims, "[e]nding gender oppression means encouraging our children to experiment with alternative gender expressions; ending the segregation of boys from girls; encouraging kids to choose their own clothes, hairstyles, interests—in short, their own gender—and supporting their choices."[21] When gender difference is described in terms of segregation—or, even more polemically, apartheid—any right-thinking person would be inclined to subscribe to this doctrine of freedom of gender expression.[22]

The utopian implications of Newton's account of female imperson-ation survive not only into transgender theory, but also into Butler's theory of gender performativity. Butler finds *Mother Camp* enabling be-cause it shows how "[i]n imitating gender, drag implicitly reveals the imitative structure of gender itself—as well as its contingency" (*Gender Trouble* 137). Hence in *Gender Trouble* the imitative structure of drag becomes the model according to which gender identity is radically de-naturalized. This theory is valuable for, among other things, undermin-ing the notion of "core gender identity" that rationalizes gender dyspho-ria as a diagnostic category. Indeed, the idea of gender as performance opens the political possibility for performative "resignification" of gender categories—if not for the voluntarist manipulation of gender "at will." Butler's feminist "subversion of identity" concludes: "That gender reality is created through sustained social performances means that the very notions of an essential sex and a true or abiding masculinity or femininity are also constituted as part of the strategy that conceals gender's per-formative character and the performative possibilities for proliferating gender configurations outside the restricting frames of masculinist domi-nation and compulsory heterosexuality" (141). Gender *reality,* by which Butler means a gender identity bearing the force of ontology, essence, and inwardness, is demystified by drag and shown to be the effect of performances at once gestural and discursive—both acts and speech acts. In line with *Paris Is Burning,* realness emerges as the effect of a signifying performance; both the real and the gendered subject can be conceived as effects of discourse. Indeed, Butler suggests that the very idea of the prediscursive should be understood as just one more discur-sive effect of masculinist regulatory regimes.

Impersonating Lacan

Butler's deconstruction of gender reality purportedly derives from a Lacanian theory of subjectivity, as well as from Newton's theory of

21. Cited in Feinberg, *Transgender Warriors,* 163.

22. On the conception of gender difference as a form of apartheid equivalent to racial apartheid, see Rothblatt, *The Apartheid of Sex: A Manifesto on the Freedom of Gender.*

drag. And though she makes different claims than Butler, Marjorie Garber's account of transvestism also purports to be based on Lacan. In order to argue that Lacan actually offers a completely different account of gender and of transsexuality than Butler and Garber, I want to show how these critics have misconstrued—or simply ignored— Lacan's concept of the real. This problem concerns the Anglo-American reception of Lacan, particularly the influential part played by Jacqueline Rose's mediating between French psychoanalysis and Anglo-American academic feminist discourses during the 1980s. Let me quote Butler quoting Rose quoting Lacan to show one crux of this misunderstanding. Butler says: "Rose writes compellingly that 'for Lacan, as we have seen, there is no pre-discursive reality ("How return, other than by means of a special discourse, to a prediscursive reality?", SXX, p. 33), no place prior to the law which is available and can be retrieved.'"[23] Rose's interpretation prompts Butler to conclude that "[t]he rendition of Lacan that understands the prediscursive as an impossibility promises a critique that conceptualizes the Law as prohibitive and generative at once" (*Gender Trouble* 55). What's really going on here is Butler's assimilating Lacan to Foucault, for whom power operates generatively rather than repressively with respect to sexuality. The problem lies in Butler's failure to distinguish prediscursive reality *("une réalité prédiscursive")* from the real *("réel")*. As I shall elaborate, while for Lacan there is indeed no prediscursive reality, nevertheless he maintains that the real is always *extra*discursive.

This problem crops up again in Butler's essay on Douglas Sirk's 1959 movie *Imitation of Life,* in which she quotes Lacan and Rose's interpretation of Lacan to support her argument that "[t]he subject is founded as a speaking agent who requires the exclusion and, hence, creation of a domain of language—and, hence, linguistically constituted sexual-

23. Butler, *Gender Trouble,* 55, quoting Jacqueline Rose, "Introduction II," *Feminine Sexuality: Jacques Lacan and the école freudienne,* ed. Juliet Mitchell and Jacqueline Rose, trans. Jacqueline Rose (New York: Norton, 1982), 55. The passage from which Rose quotes has been rendered more recently by Bruce Fink as follows:

> How is one to return, if not on the basis of a peculiar *(spécial)* discourse, to a prediscursive reality? That is the dream—the dream behind every conception *(idée)* of knowledge. But it is also what must be considered mythical. There's no such thing as a prediscursive reality. Every reality is founded and defined by a discourse.

Jacques Lacan, *The Seminar of Jacques Lacan,* Book 20: *On Feminine Sexuality, The Limits of Love and Knowledge, 1972–1973,* ed. Jacques-Alain Miller, trans. Bruce Fink (New York: Norton, 1998), 32.

ity—that consistently threatens that subject's claim to coherence."[24] Referring to "the exclusion and, hence, creation of a domain of language" that founds the subject, Butler is attempting to characterize the Lacanian real. But the real is not "a domain of language"; on the contrary, it is what resists and limits language. Not only does she fail to distinguish between the real and prediscursive reality, but Butler also mistakenly attributes performativity to the real, alluding to "the performative and, finally, gestural quality of the real."[25] By making the real performative, Butler treats it as essentially linguistic, claiming the attribute of "substitutability as the indeterminate site of the real."[26] Yet Lacan characterizes the real in completely opposite terms, describing it as that which always returns to the same place. Substitutability is the property of the signifier, and is what makes discourse and the real mutually exclusive. The real always returns to the same place, in Lacan's gnomic formulation, because it remains heterogeneous to the displacements of language.

The problem here isn't merely that Butler misconstrues Lacan, but that from this misconstrual she produces a one-dimensional theory of sexed subject formation, in which discourse comprehends everything and knows no logical limit. Ignoring the limit to language that Lacan calls the real, Butler's account of subversive performative practice— what in the "Lana" essay she calls "parodic repetition"—relies on an untenable discursive idealism, since no motivation (other than a discursive one) is adduced for the production of discourse.[27] Butler's model

24. Judith Butler, "Lana's 'Imitation': Melodramatic Repetition and the Gender Performative," *Genders* 9 (1990): 12. Given my contention that Butler relies on a questionable version of Lacan, it seems appropriate that when she subsequently cites this essay, "Lana's 'Imitation,'" Butler refers to it as "Lacan's 'Imitation'" (Judith Butler, "Critical Exchanges: The Symbolic and Questions of Gender," in *Questioning Foundations: Truth / Subjectivity / Culture,* ed. Hugh J. Silverman [New York: Routledge, 1993], 269 n. 1). It is indeed a fake Lacan that Butler offers her readers. I have more to say about Butler's symptomatic parapraxes in chapter 5 of this book.

25. Butler, "Lana's 'Imitation,'" 7.

26. Ibid., 14.

27. In their critique of Diana Fuss's reliance on performativity theory, Molly Anne Rothenberg and Joseph Valente make a similar point, arguing that this theoretical model fails to account for motivation, that it contains no conceptual space for any coherent notion of causality:

> The specific incoherence of Fuss's model . . . marks its adherence to the performative school of gender studies. The central concept of this school, "primary mimetism," holds that acts of identification precede and constitute the economies of desire that have generally been taken to animate them. In executing this reversal of commonsense logic, primary mimetism can rightfully pretend to be a fully and distinctively postmodern theory of gender development, perhaps the first such theory. But that by itself is no warrant

frees discursive effects from any extradiscursive constraints, thus generating an idealistic and ultimately voluntaristic sense of subversive potential.

I am struck by the similarity between Butler's repudiation of the real, in her account of gender performativity, and the transsexual subject's repudiation of the real. The classic Lacanian account of transsexuality comes from psychoanalyst Catherine Millot, who contends that "[t]ranssexuality is a response to the dream of forcing back, and even abolishing, the frontiers of the *real*."[28] Millot suggests that this dream of abolishing the real often is shared by nontranssexuals. Perhaps we could say that philosophical voluntarism—the theory that reality "can be manipulated at will"—has something basic in common with transsexuality. Where gender performance theory describes the real and the gendered subject as effects of discursive performance, psychoanalysis argues precisely the opposite, namely, that discourse—and hence the subject—appear as effects of the real. In this context it seems important to emphasize that Butler's position on subject formation is not overly Lacanian, as many of her readers seem to think. Instead, her position, despite its reliance on Lacanian vocabulary, runs contrary to Lacan's most basic ideas.

Garber's account of transsexuality also misses the point of the Lacanian interpretation of transsexuality, though differently than Butler's. Garber is interested in transsexualism because "transsexual surgery literalizes the constructedness of gender" (117).[29] What for Newton, Butler,

---

of its viability. For the mimetic account cannot tell us what, in the absence of desire as such, could motivate identification in the first place, nor how identification would determine its object, directionality, or telos, nor even where the object or motive of identification could be located if not in an a priori structure of identity, an inference that ties this most postmodern of gender narratives to its premodern antitypes.

Molly Anne Rothenberg and Joseph Valente, "Fashionable Theory and Fashion-able Women: Returning Fuss's Homospectatorial Look," in *Identities,* ed. Kwame Anthony Appiah and Henry Louis Gates (Chicago: University of Chicago Press, 1995), 416.

28. Catherine Millot, *Horsexe: Essay on Transsexuality* (1983), trans. Kenneth Hylton (New York: Autonomedia, 1990), 15; original emphasis. An earlier Lacanian work on transsexuality—which I find somewhat less persuasive on account of its barely concealed normalizing impulse—may be found in Moustapha Safouan, "Contribution to the Psychoanalysis of Transsexualism" (1973), in *Returning to Freud: Clinical Psychoanalysis in the School of Lacan,* ed. and trans. Stuart Schneiderman (New Haven: Yale University Press, 1980), 195–212. This essay offers a reading of cases of transsexual children described in the first volume of Robert Stoller's *Sex and Gender,* vol. 1, *The Development of Masculinity and Femininity* (New York: Science House, 1968). Regrettably Safouan never addresses the methodological problems involved in analyzing another clinician's cases.

29. Similarly, Newton notes in her preface to the second edition of *Mother Camp* that she considers "the transsexual phenomenon as a variant of this struggle . . . within the gay male community

and Garber was merely figured by drag—the artifactuality of gender—
is literalized by transsexuality and by the sex-change doctor, who ostensibly can make you any body you wish. It is not only "the gay world,
via drag" that says that gender "can be manipulated at will"; it is also
the hubris of modern science, in the figure of the gender dysphoria
specialist, that claims to be able to manipulate gender at will. Both
Millot, from a Lacanian perspective, and Bernice Hausman, from a Foucaultian vantage, point out that transsexuality depends upon the surgeon
and the endocrinologist.[30] The way in which a feminist critique of gender
as constructed falls into line with modern endocrinological and surgical
"technologies of gender" leads to the paradox that, in her effort to dismantle the binary opposition essential/constructed, Garber formulates
thus: "The phenomenon of transsexualism is both a confirmation of the
constructedness of gender and a secondary recourse to essentialism—   79
or, to put it a slightly different way, transsexualism demonstrates that
essentialism *is* cultural construction" (109).

The logic that authorizes this claim involves seeing transvestism and
transsexuality on a continuum, as both Garber and Newton do. Garber's
interest in these figures stems from her conviction that they disrupt
cultural and conceptual binaries, that the cross-dresser "offers a challenge to easy notions of binarity, putting into question the categories
of 'female' and 'male,' whether they are considered essential or con-

---

to come to terms with the stigma of effeminacy" (xiii). Although forms of transsexual surgery have
been available since the 1920s, it was not until the Christine Jorgensen case of 1953 and Harry
Benjamin's 1954 coinage of the term *transsexualism* (in "Transvestism and Transsexualism," *American
Journal of Psychotherapy* 8 [1954]: 219–30) that the phenomenon gained substantial notice. Benjamin
subsequently published *The Transsexual Phenomenon* (New York: Julian Press, 1966); but it was not
really until Stoller's work later in the 1960s and early 1970s—culminating in Robert J. Stoller,
Sex and Gender, vol. 2, *The Transsexual Experience* (New York: Jason Aronson, 1975)—that the term
became at all widely disseminated in the United States. Thus it was not until the second edition
of *Mother Camp,* in 1972, that Newton mentioned transsexualism. A somewhat different account
of this history is provided in Joanne Meyerowitz, "Sex Change and the Popular Press: Historical
Notes on Transsexuality in the United States, 1930–1955," *GLQ* 4 (1998): 159–87, which argues
that transsexual identity emerged decades before Benjamin's coinage of the term, thanks to sex-
change narratives circulated in the popular media during the 1930s and 1940s. Meyerowitz uses
Janice Radway's reader-response theory to suggest that marginalized subjects appropriated these
stories in order to invent transsexual identities *avant la lettre.* Meyerowitz's history provides a useful
counterbalance to Bernice Hausman's strictly Foucaultian thesis, in *Changing Sex,* that transsexual
subjectivity did not exist until developments in medical technology permitted its emergence.

30. Millot, *Horsexe,* 17. Similarly, Hausman argues that the development of medical technologies
for treating babies born intersexed also laid the groundwork for the emergence of transsexualism.
But she also argues that these technologies contributed to current meanings of gender as a concept—
that medical technology helped bring about the sense of gender as denoting an individual's sociosexual identity.

structed, biological or cultural" (10). In typographical terms, the cross-dresser overdetermines the virgule in that unpronounceable, yet common, pronoun blend *s/he*. And as a disturbing challenge to binary thinking, the transvestite is identified by Garber with "thirdness," with a third term that is not a third sex, but what she describes as "a mode of articulation, a way of describing a space of possibility" (11). Garber acknowledges that psychoanalysis provides the vocabulary for this mode of articulation, because it offers a theory neither of gender essence nor yet of gender construction. Hence Garber describes her conceptual paradigm of thirdness in terms of the symbolic order, even going so far as to identify the transvestite with the symbolic. She insists that the Lacanian model is

> not just [an] analogy, but [is] also *inextricable* from the functioning of transvestism as such. In fact, the very example Lacan uses to demonstrate his notion of the Symbolic, of the signifying chain, is an example which is directly pertinent to transvestite / transsexual experience as well as to the cultural construction of gender difference. (13; original emphasis)

And later Garber reminds us that "the transvestite is the equivalent of Lacan's third term" (121).

Yet perhaps there is a disjunction rather than a continuum between transvestism and transsexualism in this regard. Garber identifies the transvestite with the symbolic order as a third term that disrupts binary relations, and at one point she identifies this third term with the phallus (121). By contrast, Millot argues that the transsexual identifies with the phallus as a way of *escaping* the symbolic—specifically, escaping the division and, hence, desire that accompanies symbolic subjectivity. As I indicated at the beginning of this chapter, Garber claims that "there can be no culture without the transvestite, because the transvestite marks the entry into the Symbolic." However, for Millot the transsexual marks the *exit* from the symbolic—and herein lies the problem. To paint this contrast in its starkest hues, we could say that whereas for Garber the cross-dresser is a hero(ine), for Millot the transsexual certainly is not. Yet there is a more subtle distinction here, one that is crucial for both this chapter's argument and the thesis of this book as a whole. Because she sees cross-dressing and transsexualism on a continuum, Garber misses this distinction. And although her theoretical model in *Vested Interests* is ostensibly Lacanian, Garber makes no reference to the Lacanian theory of transsexuality as put forth in Millot's *Horsexe,* despite her encyclopedic research on the topic.

Horsexe is a work of clinical and cultural theory. Millot wants to explain why some transsexuals are appropriate candidates for sex-reassignment surgery, while others are not. By conceiving of trans-sexualism in other than imaginary terms, Millot shows how transsexual phenomena involve forms of identification that aren't simply cross-gendered. The transsexual subject does not always identify with the opposite sex, but sometimes with a position outside sexual difference—hence her book's title, *Horsexe,* which requires the portmanteau word "outsidesex" to be rendered into English.[31] Millot suggests that the subject whose identification is outsidesex will not be served well by sex-reassignment surgery, since this subject is likely to discover postoperatively that s/he has not achieved the position beyond lack and desire that s/he fantasized.[32] Given this problem, Millot wants transsexuals to be treated as subjects, each with his or her own unique subjective particularity, rather than as generic candidates for surgery who, if they measure up to an imaginary norm predetermined by Harry Benjamin, will be admitted to the operating theater. Thus Millot refuses to take the demand for sex-reassignment surgery at face value; from her perspective the demand for surgery comprehends a quite disparate range of motivations, which must be interpreted before being actualized:

> The feeling of being a woman trapped inside a man's body (or
> *vice versa*) admits of radically different interpretations, depending on
> the context. In the same way, the demand for sex-change, which in
> itself is a symptom, may also emanate from a woman hypochondriac

31. Lacan coins the neologism *horsexe* (*SXX* 78–79). Rose translates *horsexe* as "outsidesex"; Fink translates it as "beyondsex." In this case I follow Rose's translation, because Fink's makes it harder for me to distinguish between an impossible identificatory position and the epistemological shift "beyond sexuality" for which I'm arguing in this book.

32. In an interesting recent article on transgenderism, two feminist theorists take issue with this aspect of Millot's argument. Undertaking a discussion of queer politics and embodiment that remains strongly committed to a role for psychoanalysis in theorizing body politics, Patricia Elliot and Katrina Roen qualify their otherwise wholly enthusiastic engagement with Charles Shepherdson's reading of Millot (in "The *Role* of Gender and the *Imperative* of Sex") by suggesting that transsexuals' identification "outsidesex" is "often given up after the surgery fails to realize it but that in the process one gains a body and a relationship to sexual difference that the fantasy had precluded. On this issue we disagree with Shepherdson and Millot, who fear that surgery for this group of transsexuals is necessarily dangerous." Patricia Elliot and Katrina Roen, "Transgenderism and the Question of Embodiment: Promising Queer Politics?" *GLQ* 4 (1998): 261 n. 40.

(this has been encountered) who claims to be a transsexual in order to have her breasts removed because she is afraid that they may be affected with cancer, or from a hysteric who sacrifices herself to the power-drive of the doctor who is willing to perform the operation. (26)

When confronted by a subject claiming to be a transsexual, Millot wants to know what that claim means for the subject enunciating it. She suggests that often, though certainly not always, transsexual identification involves a fantasy about escaping sexual division altogether. Sex-reassignment surgery invariably fails to realize such a fantasy.

There is a fundamental paradox, not to mention considerable pathos, in the male-to-female transsexual's undergoing orchiectomy—surgical removal of the testes—in order to elude castration. Millot equates an identification "outsidesex" with an identification with the phallus, and hence the transsexual who makes this identification does so in order to escape castration. This identification is with an impossible state, a position no person can actually occupy; and this impossibility points to the function of the unconscious in identification, a function that makes identification much more than a question of imitation or of the imaginary. What does it mean to identify with the phallus? And why should identification with the phallus count as identification "outsidesex," with a position beyond sexual difference? I argued in the previous chapter that the phallus is not an indispensable psychoanalytic concept, that it represents no conceptual linchpin, and that in fact it is superseded by Lacan's theory of the object. I want to develop that argument here by exploring what Millot means by "identification with the phallus" and suggesting how we might retain the central insights of her account without relying on the concept of the phallus to do so. Given transsexualism's genital preoccupations, it makes a certain kind of sense to think about the phallus for a bit longer, even if in the end we decide that it's dispensable.

The Phallus: Imaginary, Symbolic, Real

Perhaps it is because Lacan's *"La signification du phallus"* has been available in two English versions that feminist appropriations of psychoanalysis have relied so heavily on this brief essay.[33] While Millot concedes

33. Jacques Lacan, "The Signification of the Phallus," *E* 281–91; "The Meaning of the Phallus," trans. Jacqueline Rose, in *Feminine Sexuality,* ed. Mitchell and Rose, 74–85.

that the phallus "admits of at least two different readings" (33), I think it safe to say that it admits of at least three different readings—imaginary, symbolic, and real. These three different readings of the phallus suggest that a single conceptual term has been asked to perform an extraordinary amount of theoretical work. Since "the phallus" names various functions and structural elements that may be substituted with alternative conceptual terms, it may be time to retire the phallus and, in so doing, clear up some of the consternation that this concept provokes.

At the imaginary level, the phallus is the penis and women are perceived as castrated. This reading of the phallus indicates that in the imaginary the phallus is eminently detachable and amenable to circulation. As detachable, the imaginary phallus implies that men, as well as women, are subject to the threat of castration, while also suggesting, correlatively, that women may gain the phallus just as much as men. Though she never makes this clear, it is the *imaginary* phallus that Butler is describing in her famous article on the lesbian phallus.[34] Butler's critique of the Lacanian phallus remains limited to this imaginary level, and while that is useful as far as it goes, I want to take critiques of the phallus much further.

At this imaginary level the phallus is associated with what can be exchanged—feces, babies, gifts—and therefore with what can be lost. It is only in the imaginary domain that one situates him- or herself in relation to the phallus as "appearing to have" or "appearing to be." In this reading of the phallus there is no sexual relation because each subject relates to either the feminine masquerade (appearing to be the phallus for the one who lacks it) or the masculine parade (appearing to have the phallus). And with respect to the masculine parade, Lacan insists that "virile display in the human being itself seem[s] feminine" (*E* 291). At the imaginary level there is no sexual relation because persons connect with each other only by way of mediating images, illusions of gender, irrespective of whether the sexual relationship in question is heterosexual, homosexual, or of some other kind.

Since the imaginary is a dualistic economy, gender identity and sexual relations appear to be organized in terms of oppositions when viewed imaginarily. Yet the very structure of the imaginary renders these oppositions and identifications inherently unstable, such that it

83

34. See Butler, *Bodies That Matter,* chap. 2.

should come as no surprise that gender binaries and the opposition between straight and gay identities readily admit of deconstruction. The instability of imaginary gender and sexual identities helps explain the massive cultural efforts undertaken to secure them, as well as the violence and aggressivity that tend to be unleashed when this instability becomes too evident. The paradox here is that despite this instability one's own imaginary gender and sexual identities often feel very secure, since these ego identifications provide the basic coordinates with which we negotiate the external world. Yet the mechanism by which the ego is formed renders these identifications structurally precarious, and this is why any uncertainty regarding one's own sense of gender or sexuality can feel so threatening.

Culturally normative gender identifications help keep any such threat at bay. The symbolic—as distinct from the imaginary—phallus comes into play here. At the symbolic level the phallus is designated the primary signifier because "it is the signifier intended to designate as a whole the effects of the signified, in that the signifier conditions them by its presence as a signifier" (E 285).[35] As a special kind of signifier, the symbolic phallus holds meaning in place, and hence it helps to secure imaginary identifications. However, on this score critical suspicion erupts vis-à-vis the relation between language and gender, as well as the role of the phallus in stabilizing normativity. Calling the signifier meant to signify the overall effects of the signified "the phallus" depends upon the meaning of the imaginary phallus as connoting loss. As suggested in the previous chapter, Lacan figuralizes the imaginary phallus in order to make the phallic signifier stand for a more general, abstract loss occasioned by linguistic existence. Since signification often exceeds expressive intention and consciousness, we are in a sense linguistically castrated, deprived of mastery. We are never fully in control of language, because words carry more associations than human intentionality can manage. Sometimes Lacan refers to this condition of subjectivity as symbolic alienation; sometimes he calls it castration. The idea of symbolic *castration* is simply a metaphor, based on the resonance of the imaginary phallus. There are other perfectly serviceable terms for

35. In the Rose translation this crucial sentence includes a notable typographical error: "For it is to this signified [signifier; *signifiant*] that it is given to designate as a whole the effect of there being a signified" (80).

34

describing the subjective division imposed on us by symbolic existence—*alienation* is one of them.[36]

If for the moment we stick with the vocabulary of castration—
keeping in mind its provisionality—we can see that it is because we
are subject to the signifier rather than its being fully subject to us that
the phallus can count as a signifier. Yet by reversing this relation and
making the signifier subject to us through its notion of "resignification,"
gender performance theory implicitly refuses the psychoanalytic idea of
symbolic alienation. Whereas Lacan defines a signifier as "what represents a subject for another signifier," gender performance theory defines
a signifier as what represents a subject for another subject (this conception conforms to Lacan's definition of the *sign*). From this distinction
it follows that there is no sexual relation at the symbolic level because
each subject couples with the signifier of the Other, rather than with
another subject. In other words, at the symbolic level sexual relationality is linguistically mediated and subject to the displacements of
language. At this level one's partner is the impersonal, abstract Other
as much as it is the individualized, personal other who ostensibly is
loved or desired.[37]

85

36. Since the phallic signifier organizes any subject's symbolic universe by knotting signifying
chains into meaning, we could describe this function in terms of the Name-of-the-Father. When,
later in his work, Lacan pluralizes the Name-of-the-Father he displaces emphasis from the father
to the proper name. He thus develops a fully symbolic account of paternity based on his inflection
of the name as *the name in which one speaks*. The Names-of-the-Father thus determines a subjective
structure of enunciation. Because the proper name is "read identically in all languages," it constitutes
a special class of signifier—a signifier of primary identification that is not subject to substitution
in the way other signifiers are ("Names" 88). Referring to Bertrand Russell, Lacan reminds us that
a name does not necessitate a subject, something that speaks, for anything can be given a name (a
chalk dot on the blackboard, in Russell's example), but nomination alone does not personify sufficiently to produce speech. By developing this analysis of the proper name via the example of the
Hebrew God, who has many names but whose name cannot be pronounced, Lacan argues for a
concept of the name as a *nonsignifiable identity* that produces self-symbolization. It is as this nonsignifiable identity that the phallus or the Name-of-the-Father constitutes a primary signifier. And as
Millot points out, this primary signifier cannot be gendered in the way the phallus is charged to
be gendered (when the charge is phallogocentrism) because "The Woman is one of the Names-of-
the-Father" (*Horsexe* 43). Thus we arrive at the apparently paradoxical conclusion that the phallus
is ungendered and outside sexual difference—precisely, *horsexe*. To push this point one step further,
a final revision of the paternal metaphor reveals that the object *a* (remainder of *jouissance*, and cause
of desire) can function in the place of the Names-of-the-Father. This revisionary theorization is
confirmed by Lacan's inclusion of the phallus in his list of objects *a* (breast, feces, phallus, urinary
flow, phoneme, gaze, voice, the nothing). See Ellie Ragland-Sullivan, "The Paternal Metaphor: A
Lacanian Theory of Language," *Revue internationale de philosophie* 46 (1992): 49–92.

37. I think Butler is mistaken in her judgment that the failure of sexual relationality is "implicitly
lamented as a source of heterosexual pathos" in Lacan (Butler, "Imitation and Gender Insubordina-

Because at the symbolic level the phallus is considered ungendered, it represents the signifier that accomplishes what Lacan calls "the installation in the subject of an unconscious position without which he would not be able to identify himself with the ideal type of his sex" (*E* 281). Or as Millot puts it, "[w]hatever one's biological sex, it is one's position relative to the phallus that determines whether one is a man or a woman" (38). It is important to register that this conception of gender views it as neither anatomically nor culturally determined. Instead, at the symbolic level gender concerns the unconscious, which invariably complicates matters, not least because the unconscious has no knowledge of sexual difference.

It's worth pausing here to consider some implications of this idea. Following Freud, Lacan maintains that there is no signifier for sexual difference in the unconscious. Hence the phallus cannot be a signifier of sexual difference; instead, it counts as a signifier of the total effects of the signified—that is, of meaning. If there is no signifier for sexual difference in the unconscious, then as far as the unconscious is concerned heterosexuality does not exist.[38] To Freud's list of the characteristics of primary process thinking—the unconscious knows no negation, no contradiction, nothing of time—we now can add that the unconscious knows nothing of heterosexuality. This is a remarkable idea, though it's not one that queer theorists have developed.

The absence of sexual difference—and hence of heterosexuality—in the unconscious throws into relief the incommensurability between conscious and unconscious mental processes. It also suggests the heterogeneity of imaginary and symbolic orders to each other, and therefore how misleading it can be to picture the symbolic order as some sort of extension of the imaginary.[39] Despite the abundance of cultural representations of differences between the sexes, the unconscious just doesn't get it. What can this mean but that sexual difference should be understood as a real rather than a symbolic difference? To claim that there is no signifier for sexual difference in the unconscious is to point to the traumatic aspect of sexual difference, its existence in the real. Whereas

tion," 31 n. 14). Rather, the sexual nonrelation tends to offer an occasion for comedy, as Lacan's remarks in *Television* make clear.

38. This is the idea behind *L'inconscient homosexuel,* a special issue of *La cause freudienne* 37 (1997), published by Lacan's École de la Cause Freudienne.

39. Some feminist critics claim that the symbolic order is "really" nothing more than a masculine imaginary. See, for instance, Tyler, "Boys Will Be Girls," 41.

the unconscious endlessly proliferates meaning, the dimension of the real points to an impossibility of meaning, a fundamental resistance to sense. It is within this aporia that Lacanian psychoanalysis situates sexual difference.[40] And it is because Lacan's conception of sexual difference explains it in terms of neither nature nor culture that psychoanalysis offers ways of conceptualizing gender and sexuality that remain irreducible to the now-sterile essentialism-constructionism debate.

The idea that there is no sexual difference in the unconscious also helps explain Freud's notorious axiom that there is only one kind of libido, the masculine kind. "[I]f we were able to give a more definite connotation to the concepts of 'masculine' and 'feminine,'" suggests Freud, "it would even be possible to maintain that libido is invariably and necessarily of a masculine nature, whether it occurs in men or in women and irrespectively of whether its object is a man or a woman" (*SE* 7:219). Rather than trying to delineate a feminine form of libido to counter Freud's apparent sexism, I think we could interpret this axiom as a way of suggesting that libido or desire finds gender fundamentally irrelevant. I pursue the implications of this contention further in chapter 6, but I would like to emphasize at this point that the obliviousness of the unconscious to sexual difference should not be taken as justification for completely disregarding sexual difference. We live in a social world where there is more than one sex. Nevertheless, the bizarre fact of there being no signifier for sexual difference in the unconscious means that *sexual difference does not organize or determine sexual desire.* This fundamental psychoanalytic insight is in danger of evaporating every time we suspend consideration of the unconscious in our hypotheses about gender and sexuality.

Allow me to make my argument completely clear on this point. Following Millot, I am suggesting that there is a problem with foreclosing sexual difference by trying to occupy a position "outsidesex." No matter what one does or says, there is a sense in which transcending gender remains impossible. This does not mean that social gender norms cannot or should not be changed—far from it. But there is an aspect of gender—the real dimension—that cannot be transcended. At the same time I'm arguing that sexual difference cannot determine sexual

87

---

40. For an elaboration of this point, see Cynthia Dyess and Tim Dean, "Gender: The Impossibility of Meaning," *Psychoanalytic Dialogues,* forthcoming.

desire, because desire originates in the unconscious and the unconscious knows nothing of sexual difference. The point here is simply that desire is originally independent of heterosexuality, so that Lacanians' insistence on an ethics of sexual difference with respect to desire misses Lacan's radical insights about desire entirely. Therefore I'm suggesting that we move beyond sexual difference as the principal explanatory framework for theorizing desire. Certainly I'm arguing for moving beyond hetero-sexuality as the grid through which we make sense of subjectivity and desire. But ultimately I'm arguing also for a shift beyond sexuality as the primary register in which we make sense of ourselves at all. I want to clarify and emphasize the distinction between transsexualism's para-doxical foreclosure of sexual difference and my suggestion that we qual-ify sexual difference as the prime mover of desire.

88   This distinction may become clearer by recalling that transsexualism concerns subjective identity far more than it concerns desire. According to Millot, the "outsidesex" identification characteristic of transsexualism involves escaping desire by forestalling subjective division. What distin-guishes this kind of identification is its status as neither an imaginary nor a symbolic identification, but a real identification. This distinction brings us to a third reading of the phallus. At the level of the real the phallus stands for castration as loss of *jouissance*. Symbolic castration, as I have described it, should not be located *in* the real, because the real lacks nothing (it is devoid of signifiers). This is why Lacan characterizes the real as always returning to the same place, for the signifier as a principle of substitutability remains foreign to the real. Hence the real can be defined only negatively, as a zone of impossibility. Yet far from its negativity rendering it conceptually redundant, the real's impossibility is what renders it constitutive. That is, the real represents the condition of possibility for both the subject and discourse, insofar as the real is what must be excluded for the subject as a speaking being to constitute itself. The real is not an effect of symbolic or imaginary orders; at most it is a theoretical construct that explains negatively the function and limits of these other two orders.

The way in which the real functions as a logical limit prompts Lacan to speak of a real phallus, for *jouissance* is real, and the phallus signifies a limit to the *jouissance* we can access. Since this limit to *jouissance* is embodied in a range of mythic figures whose *jouissance* is unlimited, the function of the real phallus also is covered by other conceptual terms.

In Freudian theory, the father of the primal horde and the phallic mother are both conceived as all-enjoying and lacking nothing. In Lacanian theory, ~~The~~ Woman and the *père-jouissant* occupy this position of plenitude, beyond division. As their mythic status suggests, and as Lacan's famous pronouncements concerning ~~The~~ Woman indicate, none of these figures actually exists. But this fact of nonexistence does nothing to diminish the effectiveness of their functioning. Because these figures possess or embody the phallus in the form of unlimited *jouissance,* they are ungendered in the sense of their not being subject to sexual division.

Effects of the Real

Possessing "the phallus," these mythic figures generate powerful identificatory effects—both positively and negatively—based on *jouissance.* Slavoj Žižek's description of the *père-jouissant* as "the anal father" suggests that this level of real identification may be useful for theorizing gay sex and the excessive social responses to it.[41] As I argue in the next chapter, the common supposition that gay men somehow have access to extra— even unlimited—*jouissance* often leads to homophobic violence, since the prospect of such excessive enjoyment is hard to tolerate. Hence recent efforts to increase the stringency of sodomy legislation, regarding which I would suggest that it is ultimately this "anal father" against which such legislation and social hysteria tend to be mobilized.

Since both the anal father and ~~The~~ Woman embody the real phallus, they are beyond gender in the usual sense. In other words, they are beyond division. Another way of putting this is to say that to embody the phallus—to have access to enjoyment without limit—would be to have no unconscious, to remain exempt from subjective disunity. Millot contends that transsexualism involves identifying with this impossible position. According to this view, transsexualism would be motivated by identification in the real, at the level of *jouissance,* rather than by imaginary or symbolic identifications. Hence the paradox in which the transsexual identifies not with the other sex but with what is beyond gender, "outsidesex."

We see a good example of this kind of identification in *Paris Is*

---

41. Slavoj Žižek, "Grimaces of the Real, or When the Phallus Appears," *October* 58 (1991): 53–57.

Burning, in the figure of the black transsexual model, Octavia Saint Laurent, whose apartment wall is covered with pictures of her ego-ideal, Estée Lauder supermodel Paulina Porizkova. From what she says in the movie, it seems that Octavia identifies not with Paulina Porizkova, but with "Paulina," the advertising construct of ~~The~~ Woman. Although advertisements construct an impossible ideal of femininity that is racially, sexually, and often nationally marked, as well as distinctly classed, I'm suggesting that Octavia's identification "outsidesex" is not an identification across gender and racial lines, even though it very clearly appears to be a case of an African American man wanting the privilege that comes with being a rich, European, white woman. "I want to be a spoiled, rich white girl," says a Latina/o transsexual, Venus Xtravaganza, in *Paris Is Burning.* Similarly, Newton's subjects, in *Mother Camp,* generally wish to incarnate the ideal woman embodied in, for example, Hollywood's representation of Marilyn Monroe. Although transsexual identification gives rise to quite spectacular imaginary effects that are hard to ignore, this kind of identification is not at base mimetic. Octavia identifies with the impossible position "outsidesex" not in order to be a perfect woman, as critiques of transsexuality generally assume, but in order to secure *jouissance,* the perfect enjoyment that remains the prerogative of ~~The~~ Woman (who does not exist). The impossibility of this fantasy motivating many of the demands for sex change should make us pause before automatically supporting political campaigns for equal access to surgery on behalf of all those who claim transsexual status.[42]

We might also register the poignance of those whose belief in the real phallus is so great that they insist on sacrificing their own genitals in order to attain it. If the phallus is only one figure for unlimited enjoyment at the level of the real, then we do not have to accept the Lacanian theory of the phallus wholesale in order to find Millot's critique viable. Her account of *horsexe,* an identification "outsidesex," is simply a way of talking about eluding symbolic alienation and subjective division. Psychoanalysis is a way of coming to terms with this alienation

90

42. It would be preposterous to claim to know the fantasy underlying every demand for sex-reassignment surgery. I do not think this fantasy identification "outsidesex" motivates all transsexuals, though I suspect it motivates a considerable number of subjects who express the fantasy in other, nontranssexual forms. The fantasy may be far more common than the comparatively small number of transsexuals would lead one to believe.

and division. It may even be a less expensive way than sex-reassignment surgery. While Lacanian psychoanalysts tend to describe this process as coming to terms with *castration,* I think we can see now that castration—and its correlate, the phallus—is simply one metaphor for characterizing this process.

However, the problem with some critiques of the psychoanalytic rhetoric of castration lies in their tendency to view "castration" as nothing more than the alibi of an oppressive, yet contestable, heteronormative regime. There remains deep resistance in queer theory to conceding any ineluctable limit, especially if that limit involves sexual expression or sexual pleasure. Lacan's concept of the real concerns limits that have no predetermined content—the real is not about prohibitions—but that nevertheless guarantee a measure of subjective deprivation and hence desire. Lacan sums it up like this:

> If the living being is something at all thinkable, it will be above all as subject of the *jouissance;* but this psychological law that we call the pleasure principle (and which is only the principle of displeasure) is very soon to create a barrier to all *jouissance.* If I am enjoying myself a little too much, I begin to feel pain and I moderate my pleasures. The organism seems made to avoid too much *jouissance.* Probably we would all be as quiet as oysters if it were not for this curious organization which forces us to disrupt the barrier of pleasure or perhaps only makes us dream of forcing and disrupting this barrier. All that is elaborated by the subjective construction on the scale of the signifier in its relation to the Other and which has its root in language is only there to permit the full spectrum of desire to allow us to approach, to test, this sort of forbidden *jouissance* which is the only valuable meaning that is offered to our life. ("Of Structure" 194–95)

I will return to the ideas in this dense passage in subsequent chapters; for now I want to emphasize the point that it is barriers or limits to *jouissance* that "permit the full spectrum of desire." Although Lacan does not say so, I think logically we should read "the full spectrum of desire" as encompassing all those nonnormative manifestations of desire grouped under the rubric of *queer.* In other words, it is a barrier to *jouissance,* not unlimited access to *jouissance,* that permits queer desire to flourish.

In this passage Lacan describes the limit to *jouissance* in terms of the pleasure principle, a designation that immediately points to the fundamental psychoanalytic distinction between pleasure and *jouissance* that is at the heart of my argument about gay sex, in chapter 4. More generally, however, Lacan theorizes constitutive limits in terms of the real. The real has no predetermined content because it is always in some sense contingent: it comes as a surprise. In this respect, Lacan's real differs considerably from the philosophical sense of the real as necessary. Yet, on the other hand, the real is also Lacan's way of conceptualizing necessity—that is, an insuperable barrier that cannot be overcome. It is easiest to explain the real in paradoxical terms, though this is not always the most helpful route to take. Nevertheless, formulated paradoxically, Lacan's real indexes a *necessary contingency*.

By contrast, political theories often prefer to picture limits the other way around—as contingent necessities, evils that may be eliminated. Lacan insists that our existence as creatures of language incurs an intractable limit. Of course, intractability is just what the transsexual and his or her medical partners refuse. It is also what gender performance theory refuses in its effort to assimilate the real to the symbolic by making the real performative and gestural. Without a nonsymbolic real as limit, discursive gendering cannot amount to more than a particularly sophisticated form of voluntarism—Butler's protestations to the contrary notwithstanding. I would suggest that any queer or feminist political theory that refuses to acknowledge intractability will remain less effective than it otherwise might be, because it will ceaselessly encounter the real as an unfathomable blockage of its political aims. Here I find Leo Bersani's emphasis on intractability helpful. In his critique of various forms of idealization prevalent in gay politics, Bersani refers to "the beginning of an important new political critique, one that would take intractability into account in its rethinking and remodeling of social institutions."[43] It is perhaps testimony to the persistent failure to acknowledge intractability that such a political critique is only just beginning.

In this chapter, I have dwelt on Millot's account of transsexual identification because it shows that race and, especially, gender cannot be treated as comprehensively motivating in the way that many accounts would have them be. More than imaginary relations of identification,

43. Leo Bersani, *Homos* (Cambridge: Harvard University Press, 1995), 90.

opposition, power, and mimicry are at stake in transgender phenomena. These overtly political relations involve the real as well as realness. It is because the real functions as an ineluctable limit that, like death, it bears political consideration. And, like death, no performance can overcome it. In the next chapter, I try to factor death and the real back into queer politics by way of a psychoanalytic consideration of AIDS.

THE PSYCHOANALYSIS
OF AIDS

Chapter 3

Would it not be better to give death the place in reality and in our thoughts which is its due, and to give a little more promi-nence to the unconscious attitude towards death which we have hitherto so carefully suppressed?

—Sigmund Freud, "Thoughts for the Times on War and Death" (1915)

The Scope of AIDS

Twice as many Americans were killed by AIDS in the first nine years of the epidemic (June 1981 to June 1990) as were claimed as casualties in the nine years of the Vietnam War (1964–73). When I first drafted this chapter in the summer of 1991, after the first decade of the epidemic, over 110,000 Americans had died as a consequence of AIDS; as I revise this chapter seven years later, the number of AIDS deaths in the United States has exceeded 417,000. This figure does not take into account the thousands more who are HIV-positive and whose lives have been extended thanks to drug combination therapies, let alone the millions worldwide who are infected with HIV but have no access to the drugs that middle-class gay men in the United States have been taking to fight the disease.

AIDS was first identified among North American gay men, yet

quickly was discovered to be a global disaster, a worldwide plague that—despite medical advances—shows little sign of abating. What can psychoanalysis, which works on the human subject in his or her particularity, say or do in the face of such pandemic dimensions? I try to answer that question by suggesting a different way to think about AIDS, developing in this and the following chapter an approach that makes clearer how widespread fantasies about AIDS and about homosexuality affect everybody's experiences of AIDS—the experiences of those who are HIV-positive, as well as of those who are HIV-negative.

In addressing itself to the subject of speech, psychoanalysis recognizes that every body, including the sick body, is caught in a network of signifiers, a network that mortifies all bodies, albeit in various ways, by precluding access to either one's own *jouissance* or any knowledge of the body outside of symbolic structures. Insofar as AIDS represents a crisis in medical knowledge and treatment of the body, it also concerns a crisis in the body's symbolization, which renders AIDS in part a question of the signifier. The politicizing of this symbolization makes AIDS a sociopolitical question as well. And since, as I have suggested, neither the political nor the social should be considered independently of psychical processes, a psychoanalysis of AIDS entails the widest scope of investigation and the broadest range of implication, including the question of how psychoanalysis theorizes the social.

Yet AIDS is not only a sociopolitical phenomenon, and its theorization cannot remain restricted to the level of symbolic analysis alone, whether that analysis proceeds from a psychoanalytic understanding of the operations of the signifier, or—as has largely been the case so far—from a Foucaultian model of discursive construction that anatomizes the sociosymbolic "invention of AIDS."[1] Beyond the effort to provide an enabling psychoanalytic vocabulary with which to diagnose more accurately the pathology of the social and cultural responses to AIDS, this chapter tries to think psychoanalytically about sexual desire while keeping AIDS central, rather than peripheral, to that broader project. The significance of AIDS for the psychoanalytically conceived subject of the unconscious goes beyond its social dimension, because the suffering as-

95

1. See, for example, Cindy Patton, *Inventing AIDS* (New York: Routledge, 1990); Simon Watney, *Policing Desire: Pornography, AIDS, and the Media* (Minneapolis: University of Minnesota Press, 1987); and the essays collected in Douglas Crimp, ed., *AIDS: Cultural Analysis / Cultural Activism* (Cambridge: MIT Press, 1988).

sociated with the disease finds its exclusive origin in neither an external nor an internal source. I contend that psychoanalysis can help us conceptualize AIDS beyond the politically debilitating inside / outside or us / them polarities that govern thinking on this topic. In particular, Freud's notion of the death drive—which remains quite distinct from the homophobic suggestion that gay men have "brought AIDS on themselves,"[2] yet is also irreducible to the various phenomena of material discrimination perpetrated by a hostile society against gay people and people with AIDS—provides a new way of understanding AIDS.

The Society of AIDS

My first suggestion is that a psychoanalytic perspective on AIDS must begin by acknowledging that *each of us is living with AIDS:* we are all PWAs (Persons with AIDS) insofar as AIDS is structured, radically and precisely, as the unconscious real of the social field of the United States. We encounter AIDS not only as the discourse of the Other, in a return of the repressed that constitutes the repressed as such (the structure by which we understand a *neurotic* subject), but also in the real, as a consequence of its wholesale repudiation by a society that refuses to admit a signifier for AIDS. In this way, the social response to AIDS is analyzable according to the structure by which we understand a psychotic subject. Let us approach this paradoxical formulation of an "unconscious real" by considering what is at stake in the idea that we understand society on the basis of a psychoanalytical model.

Although any psychoanalysis of society may rest on an analogy, this analogical relation is far more complex than thinking of the social as the mirror image of a psychoanalytical unit such as the family, the individual, or even the subject. Psychical elements and social structures inform each other, although never directly or homologously. The relationship between psyche and society should be understood as intimate and yet mediated.[3] In a Lacanian analysis of political formations, neither the psychical nor the social acquires the status of first cause, because

2. This widespread reactionary sentiment was enunciated publicly by Massachusetts state senator Edward Kirby, May 25, 1991, while watching AIDS activists protest AIDS funding cuts.

3. See Joan Copjec, *Read My Desire: Lacan against the Historicists* (Cambridge: MIT Press, 1994), chap. 4, for a convincing account of the relation between the psychic and social as linked by the Lacanian real and dominated by the death drive.

neither one wholly or unidirectionally determines the other. In order for psychoanalysis to gain conceptual leverage upon political analysis, it is necessary to acknowledge the epistemological limits of a rationalist political analysis and to insist, along with Jacqueline Rose, that the socio-political domain cannot "continue to be analyzed as if it were free of psychic and sexual processes, as if it operated outside the range of their effects."[4]

The initial model through which I propose we reconsider social responses to AIDS is that of Lacan's theory of psychosis, particularly because, in his 1959 article on the topic, Lacan makes provision for the concept of *social psychosis* (E 216). I want to argue that the public response to AIDS can be characterized as psychotic in a clinically precise way, and in order to make this argument I shall disentangle two distinct formulations about psychosis in Lacan's work. The advantage of this approach over those common among critics who discuss the socio-symbolic "invention of AIDS" lies in how psychoanalysis offers a more nuanced account of the relation between the symbolic and the real.

The idea of a psychotic society seems especially pertinent with respect to AIDS because received psychoanalytic wisdom characterizes psychosis as a defense against homosexuality. Yet it is just such post-Freudian dogma that Lacan's work repeatedly challenges. And hence, in his article on psychosis, he follows Ida Macalpine in relegating homosexuality from the etiological level of causal determinant to the epiphenomenal level of symptom (E 190). This designation of homosexuality as a symptom rather than the cause of psychosis is less homophobic than it might appear, because it is part of Lacan's effort to shift emphasis away from the facile understanding of psychosis as "loss of reality"—a reality defined in practice as heterosexual, indeed, heteronormative. By substituting for the defense against homosexuality as determinant of psychosis the "determinants of the relation of man to the signifier," Lacan promulgates a nonnormative, nonadaptive psychoanalysis:

> That such a [social] psychosis may prove to be compatible with what is called good order is not in question, but neither does it authorize the psychiatrist, even if he is a psychoanalyst, to trust to his own compatibility with that order to the extent of believing that he is in

4. Jacqueline Rose, "Margaret Thatcher and Ruth Ellis," in *Why War? Psychoanalysis, Politics, and the Return to Melanie Klein* (Oxford: Blackwell, 1993), 41.

possession of an adequate idea of the *reality* to which his patient appears to be unequal. (*E* 216; original emphasis)

Social reality, defined as the social norm and therefore implicitly as heterosexual, is not what the psychotic subject is lacking. Rather, the psychotic subject lacks a signifier, specifically the signifier of paternity, what Lacan calls the Name-of-the-Father. Consequently, psychosis is not a question of maladjustment to reality, a reality from which the psychotic subject has taken too great a distance. It is rather a question of the real that is too proximate, a real from which sufficient distance has not been obtained.

As I began suggesting in the previous chapter, psychosis names a primordial disturbance of the subject's relation to language such that the paternal metaphor does not become part of the subject's symbolic universe because it is foreclosed from the Other and therefore from the unconscious. Lacan summarizes thus: "It is in an accident in this register and in what takes place in it, namely, the foreclosure of the Name-of-the-Father in the place of the Other, and in the failure of the paternal metaphor, that I designate the defect that gives psychosis its essential condition, and the structure that separates it from neurosis" (*E* 215). Since "foreclosure" (French: *forclusion*), which is Lacan's translation of the Freudian term *Verwerfung* (also translatable as "rejection," "repudiation," or "exclusion"), remains distinct from repression, a structural—as opposed to phenomenal—distinction exists between neurosis and psychosis. In contrast to the neurotic subject, who experiences a return of the repressed in the symbolic (the discourse of the Other), the psychotic subject experiences a return in the real of what has been foreclosed of the symbolic.

How is U.S. society psychotic about AIDS? Recall that the *S* in the acronym *AIDS* stands not for "signifier" but for "syndrome," and that AIDS is to be understood not as a specific disease—it is not in itself contagious or communicable—but rather as a condition of the body, an index of the body's vulnerability to disease, to its environment, and to itself. The analogy of social psychosis enables us to understand AIDS as a condition of the body politic, an index of the socialized body of the U.S. subject caught in a network of signifiers that renders it vulnerable to AIDS because, by refusing a truly meaningful signifier for AIDS, we face the prospect that what is foreclosed in the symbolic will return

in the real. By persistently representing itself as having a "general population" that remains largely immune to incidence of AIDS, the United
States pushes AIDS—and the social groups seen as representing AIDS—
to the outside of its psychic and social economies, treating them exactly
like shit.[5] For example, in New York City alone, by 1991, thirteen
thousand PWAs had been literally "put outside," made homeless by a
sociopolitical system that refused to shelter its sick.[6] "Testing is more
cost-effective than treatment," said George Bush before his election to
the presidency.[7]

Following such a lead, emphasis has been placed not on care (who
tends their shit?), but on properly identifying the "outside"—hence calls
for mandatory HIV testing—so that it may be excluded all the more
thoroughly—hence calls to quarantine all persons who test positive for
HIV antibodies. However, as Lacan notes in his essay on psychosis, "It
is not his rags, but the very being of man that takes up its position
among the waste matter in which his first frolics occur" (E 225).[8] The

5. See Michael Fumento, *The Myth of Heterosexual AIDS* (New York: Basic Books, 1990), which
concludes that to the extent that an insufficient number of decent heterosexuals are dying from
AIDS, too much federal money is being apportioned to AIDS research and treatment. As Simon
Watney, among others, has argued, the notion of a "general population" of heterosexuals obtains
as its corollary the notion of a "disposable population" of homosexuals (*Policing Desire,* 135). In
subsequent essays Watney's argument is pushed almost to the point of inverting its categories: the
heterosexual population's self-perception of immunity is precisely what threatens it with extinction.
See, for instance, Watney, "Psychoanalysis, Sexuality, and AIDS," in *Coming On Strong: Gay Politics
and Culture,* ed. Simon Shepherd and Mick Wallis (London: Unwin Hyman, 1989), 22–38:

> For centuries homophobia has hurt and wounded and even killed us. Now it seems
> that it is turning back on heterosexuals themselves, in their refusal and inability to
> acknowledge the reality of HIV disease. At this moment in time there seems little to
> prevent a major HIV epidemic among heterosexuals, unless they can identify and over-
> come their own self-destructive homophobia. That is the underlying tragedy of AIDS
> today, a tragedy which most heterosexuals seem totally unable to comprehend (37).

6. This figure, like other statistics in this chapter, was taken from Larry Kramer, "Ten Years
of Plague: 110,530 Deaths . . . and Counting," *Advocate,* July 2, 1991, 62–63. Unfortunately,
statistics on homeless PWAs are inevitably approximate. ACT UP's PWA housing committee esti-
mated eight thousand homeless PWAs in New York City in spring 1989; the projected estimate
for 1991 was thirty thousand. See "Housing Now" in *AIDS Demo Graphics,* ed. Douglas Crimp and
Adam Rolston (Seattle: Bay Press, 1990), 122–29. See also Catherine Saalfield and Ray Navarro,
"Shocking Pink Praxis: Race and Gender on the ACT UP Frontlines," in *Inside/Out: Lesbian Theories,
Gay Theories,* ed. Diana Fuss (New York: Routledge, 1991), 341–69, esp. 352. We should note
that these statistics reflect not so much the rate at which the homeless recklessly indulge in unsafe
sex and drug practices as the systematic discrimination against PWAs and those identified as HIV-
positive in terms of housing, employment, and insurance.

7. Crimp and Rolston, *AIDS Demo Graphics,* 12.

8. Lacan leaves the reader in no doubt that he is talking here about "the act of shitting" by
poking fun at analysts for whom "the anal phase" is merely a figurative abstraction: "It would be
good to see the analyst's face if the patient suddenly defecated, or even slobbered, on his couch"

issue here is not one of a developmental phase ("anal") in the history of the subject, but concerns the status of the subject in its very existence. One way of encapsulating Lacan's complicated theorizing on the topic of psychosis, which spans more than a decade's work, would be to say that the being of the subject is not where it thinks it is; rather, the subject's being is located at the heart of what it excludes. AIDS constitutes an American "symptom" insofar as the *jouissance* of AIDS forms one of the strongest bonds of social cohesion.[9] To fully argue that thesis, it is necessary to elucidate further the discontinuities of Lacan's theory of psychosis. Here I'm trying to do two things: contribute to the kind of periodizing of Lacanian thought for which chapter 1 argues; and explain how thinking about AIDS in terms other than either the cultural construction of disease or biomedical realities provides a different perspective on how AIDS functions socially.

Although the article from which I have been quoting, "On a Question Preliminary to any Possible Treatment of Psychosis," ostensibly represents the distillation of Lacan's yearlong (1955–56) seminar *Les psychoses* (according to his own headnote appended to the article on its first publication, in 1959), the formulas for psychosis presented in each text differ significantly.[10] For example, the definitive axiom concerning

---

(*E* 225). To complete the quotation about the subject's being inhabiting his waste matter is to recognize an early adumbration of the concept of object *a*:

> It is not his rags, but the very being of man that takes up its position among the waste matter in which his first frolics occur, much as the law of symbolization in which his desire must operate catches him in its net by the position of the part-object in which he offers himself on arrival in the world, in a world in which the desire of the Other lays down the law.

The relation between the analyst and the turd as object *a* is prefigured early in the Third Seminar, in which Lacan proposes an analogy between the analyst and a *dépotoir*—a container for night soil, a kind of cesspit (*Le séminaire, livre III: Les psychoses (1955–1956)*, ed. Jacques-Alain Miller, Paris: Seuil, 1981, 39). The excremental resonance of this analogy is diluted in the English translation: "The comparison that can be made between the analyst and a rubbish dump is justified" (*SIII* 29). As object *a* in the transference, it is this difficult place that the analyst must occupy.

9. The etymological link between "symptom" and "syndrome" reinforces the implications of this notion of a social "symptom": in a profound way, AIDS names the condition of contemporary U.S. society. I should perhaps add that my use of the term *symptom* at this point accords with Lacan's later, more radical conceptualization of the symptom as *sinthome*, the "fourth order" that grounds imaginary, symbolic, and real in their Borromean structure, thereby giving consistency to the subject's being through *jouissance* (see Jacques Lacan, "Les paroles imposées," in Johann Listing, *Introduction à la topologie*, trans. Claude Léger and Michael Turnheim [Paris: Navarin, 1989], 83–91). Slavoj Žižek summarizes Lacan's development of the concept of the symptom in Slavoj Žižek, *The Sublime Object of Ideology* (New York: Verso, 1989), 55–84.

10. It is his failure to consider this crucial discrepancy that mars the otherwise useful account provided in Michael Walsh, "Reading the Real in the Seminar on the Psychoses," *Criticism and Lacan:*

the foreclosure of the Name-of-the-Father remains unformulated in the Third Seminar, and is hardly even implied in the earlier parts of the seminar from which Lacan's headnote claims the article derives. Conversely, the familiar maxim that "what is foreclosed in the symbolic returns in the real," which is repeated in the seminar, is itself foreclosed from the forty-five-page article. The significance of the difference between the formulas for psychosis presented in the seminar and the article may be grasped by considering the fact that the tendency for psychotic hallucinations to assume *verbal* form—witness the exemplary psychotic patient, who hallucinates her neighbor calling her "Sow!"—poses a theoretical problem with respect to the seminar maxim, since the real is defined by its *resistance* to symbolization. The real lacks nothing precisely because it is wholly devoid of signifiers. Yet the psychotic phenomenon of verbal hallucination suggests that what is foreclosed returns in *the discourse of the Other,* which rather undermines the structural distinction between psychosis and neurosis. To try to resolve this problem by suggesting that the foreclosed returns in the symbolic *and* the real simply implies that the real is, after all, partly symbolizable. This conceptual impasse has not gone completely unnoticed, at least by Dimitris Vergetis, who, writing in the Lacanian journal *Ornicar?,* indicates that this impasse concerns the very definition of psychosis, and that it is soluble by reference to "the evolution of the concept of the subject in Lacan."[11] The only addition I would make to Vergetis's perceptive treatment of the topic is to note that the paradoxes of the theory of psychosis also may be solved by reference to the evolution of the concept of the real in Lacan—a suggestion that ends up revealing the further difficulty of a subject of the real.

Lacan appeals to the real in his yearlong seminar on psychosis in order to characterize the hallucinatory phenomena encountered in psychosis. Yet his doing so often amounts to little more than an attempt to stress the radical exteriority in which hallucinations are experienced: it's a way of saying that hallucinations are experienced as coming from outside. However, although not experienced as such thanks to repression, exteriority is as much a property of the symbolic Other as it is of the real, since alienation names the subject's insertion into a field

101

Essays and Dialogue on Language, Structure, and the Unconscious, ed. Patrick Colm Hogan and Lalita Pandit (Athens: University of Georgia Press, 1990), 64–83.

11. Dimitris Vergetis, "Deux axiomatiques des psychoses," *Ornicar?* 44 (1988): 52–64.

"beyond" itself, a register of alterity that precedes, succeeds, and exceeds the subject. The subject in the Other therefore houses the "outside" at its very heart—a condition Lacan calls *extimacy*. Perhaps the distinction between the real and the symbolic as realms of the foreclosed's return depends upon the difference between exteriority and alterity. Yet the absence of the seminar maxim ("what is foreclosed in the symbolic returns in the real") from the article suggests Lacan's awareness of the dubious status of this distinction and thus reveals the real as not only a stumbling block for the subject of psychoanalysis, but also a problem for the theory of psychoanalysis.[12]

This concept of a primordially real subject, together with the concomitant notion of an unconscious real (to which I referred a few pages ago), becomes more comprehensible when we reconsider Lacan's theorization of the real in his article "On a Question." My suggestion is that our appreciation of Lacan's extensive reformulation of psychosis in terms of signification rather than reality has allowed his equally crucial conceptual development of the real to be obscured. I'm claiming that Lacan redefines psychosis in terms of the loss of a signifier, rather than the loss of "reality." Yet I'm also claiming that in order to understand

12. Vergetis formulates the shift from seminar to article slightly differently, focusing on the subject's relation to the Other (formalized in schema L), rather than on the conceptual modulations of the real. Investigating why the seminar produces an "axiomatic" for psychosis based on the *exclusion* of the Other when Lacan "already has at his disposal the terms of the Other and the Name-of-the-Father in its essential relation to the Law, terms necessary for forging the definition that he will perfect in his *écrit*," Vergetis argues that the later axiom of psychosis is impossible to formulate in the seminar because the operative "notion of the Other still remains a prisoner of the status of the subject" (52–53). In other words, Lacan characterizes the subject's relation to the Other, particularly in the earlier parts of his seminar, as a subject-to-*subject* relation—this being a consequence of his theorizing the subject in terms of speech, rather than in terms of discourse. Speech *(parole)* is famously defined as a structure in which "the subject receives his message from the other in an inverted form" (*SIII* 36), a definition that provides elsewhere for such misleading notions as "the Other subject" ("Desire" 13). Therefore, according to Vergetis, "[t]he exclusion of the Other implies the rupture of the subject-subject axis, followed by the collapse of the subject into the ego" (55).

Vergetis identifies a crucial distinction here, one that Lacan himself approaches toward the end of his seminar on psychosis when he undertakes pronomial analysis to elaborate the distinction between *je* (subject) and *moi* (ego) via the grammarian's phrase "I'm much more myself [*Je suis beaucoup plus moi*]" (*SIII* 271). This analysis anticipates Emile Benveniste's distinction between subject of enunciation and subject of the statement that Lacan invokes in a later seminar to characterize the divided subject of the unconscious, while the phraseology anticipates the "in you more than you" that Lacan employs to describe object *a* as cause of desire (*Four* 44 and 268, respectively).

Vergetis proceeds to argue not only that Lacan finds schema L, which formalizes the subject-Other relation, insufficient by the time he composes his article (hence his devising schemas R and

what this means we need to look at what Lacan does with the theory
of the real—that which designates not reality but the point at which
the signifier fails. Concluding his analysis of the verbal hallucination
"Sow!" reported by his psychotic patient, Lacan says:

> I have referred to this example here only to show in living, con-
> crete detail that the function of irrealization is not everything in the
> symbol. For, in order that its irruption into the real should be beyond
> question, it has only to present itself, as it usually does, in the form
> of a broken chain. (E 183)

The "chain" to which Lacan refers is, of course, the signifying chain of
language, which is disrupted by the unsymbolizable real. The locus of
the signifying chain is the Other, where the subject appears. Yet the
subject's being is real, for which reason it is mortified by, precisely
nonexistent in, the Other. The subject as an "answer of the real" is the
symbolic subject, a response to the trauma of being; yet the broken
chain as mark of the real is *also* the space of the subject—an empty space
whose symbolic failure registers the strictly negative identity proper to
subjectivity. It is this constitutive lack of identity that makes identification literally vital for the subject, who must identify itself with a master
signifier in order not to remain completely foreclosed from the symbolic
order.[13] This brings us to the question of an identificatory signifier for
AIDS.

103

I), but also that schema L in the seminar and schema L in the article remain conceptually nonidentical.
Their difference is a consequence of how Lacan modifies the status of the subject, transforming it
from subject of speech to subject of discourse. Hence his subsequent characterization of schema L:
"This schema signifies that the condition of the subject S (neurosis or psychosis) is dependent on
what is being unfolded in the Other O. What is being unfolded there is articulated like a discourse"
(E 193). To this Vergetis helpfully adds: "The term discourse . . . permits the installation of speech
in the field of language," which allows him to conclude that the signifying chain thereby takes
theoretical precedence over the intersubjectivity of speech (59).

I think these distinctions may be elaborated further, since Lacan's characterization of schema
L continues by designating S, the first point of the schema over whose four corners the subject is
stretched, as the subject in "his ineffable, stupid existence" (E 194). This designation should be
understood as descriptive rather than evaluative, since it points to the primordial status of the
subject as outside the symbolic *(hors symbolique)*. It is crucial not to interpret this primordial subject
as presymbolic (or pre-Oedipal), for its inscription is formal and its mapping topological, rather
than chronological. Neither subject of speech nor of discourse, the subject in its primordial existence
is real (S rather than $), As Vergetis concludes, "It can no longer be a question of the exclusion
of the Other, for what is primordially excluded, foreclosed, is the subject himself" (63).

13. See Slavoj Žižek, *Looking Awry: An Introduction to Jacques Lacan through Popular Culture* (Cambridge: MIT Press, 1991), 163.

The Language of AIDS

It is wholly in keeping with a psychotic social response to AIDS that linguistic systems have been plunged into crisis, since, from a Lacanian perspective, profound linguistic disturbance is the primary symptom of psychosis. Yet in view of persistent condemnations of any attempt to theorize AIDS and its effects, it is still necessary to insist that "theory," certainly psychoanalytic theory, does not reduce the "realities" of AIDS (tenaciously held to be prediscursive) to a question of language.[14] This is the case for several reasons.

In the first instance, although psychoanalytic theory emphasizes the determining effects of the signifier upon the human subject, Lacan also takes into consideration the domain of extradiscursivity—the real—in his account of subjective causality. However, the concept of object *a*, which represents a cause outside of—but not preceding—language, has, as I've suggested, been almost completely lost in the assimilation of Lacan as merely one among many versions of French structuralism or poststructuralism.

Second, the AIDS epidemic has been from its very beginning a source of linguistic crisis. The rapid transformations of nomination, the proliferation of acronyms, euphemisms, and metaphors, plus the birth of whole new social and scientific discourses, together with the emergence of strategies of discursive censorship, attest to a characteristically postmodern linguistic formation in which language itself, let alone sex, seems unsafe. The very term *AIDS*—whose connotative ironies have become so naturalized that many of us find its enunciation routine, while for others it remains so alarmingly new and volatile that they find it impossible to let the term pass their lips—is mutating once more: *HIV disease* may be establishing itself as the preferred, more accurate term.[15]

14. See the widely disseminated cover article by Daniel Harris, "AIDS and Theory," *Lingua Franca*, June 1991, 1, 16–19, which takes a thoroughly anti-intellectual, reactionary stance in order to argue that any theorizing about AIDS is worse than useless. Harris's crude logic, mobilized principally against what he sees as the influence of deconstruction on ACT UP, opposes thought to action, and argues for the latter at the expense of the former: a counsel to thoughtless action. On this issue, see also Paula A. Treichler, *How to Have Theory in an Epidemic: Cultural Chronicles of AIDS* (Durham: Duke University Press, 1999).

15. On the case for renaming the syndrome *HIV disease*, see Simon Watney, "Taking Liberties: An Introduction," *Taking Liberties: AIDS and Cultural Politics*, ed. Erica Carter and Simon Watney (London: Serpent's Tail, 1989), 14–17. See also Simon Watney, " 'AIDS' or 'HIV Disease'?" in *Practices of Freedom: Selected Writings on HIV/AIDS* (Durham: Duke University Press, 1994), 76–78. The independent, nonprofit AIDS service, HERO (Health Education Resource Organization), for which I was working, in Baltimore, at the time I first drafted this chapter, was one example of a

If the steady proliferation of neologistic acronyms marks linguistically the cogency of the social, scientific, and political struggles toward specifying the problem, we might note that the production of neologisms is characteristic of psychosis too. The intimate link between language and disease revealed by any examination of AIDS provokes the suspicion that language itself is diseased, or is a form of disease. Thus, for instance, Paula Treichler has discussed the tropology of biomedical discourse vis-à-vis AIDS under the rubric of "an epidemic of signification," suggesting that not only is AIDS essentially unnatural but that it is so because language itself is unnatural: "the very nature of AIDS is constructed through language and in particular through the discourses of medicine and science."[16] The notion of "epidemic" in Treichler's argument reaches beyond the commonplaces of metaphor (in which one can speak of "an epidemic of signification" in relation to AIDS as a consequence of the rapid spread of new words and an extended usage of old ones) to such a degree that language and AIDS are made to appear homologous:

105

> The epidemic of signification that surrounds AIDS is neither simple nor under control. AIDS exists at a point where many entrenched narratives intersect, each with its own problematic and context in which AIDS acquires meaning. It is extremely difficult to resist the lure, familiarity, and ubiquitousness of these discourses. The AIDS virus [sic] enters the cell and integrates with its genetic code, establishing a disinformation campaign at the highest level and ensuring that replication and dissemination will be systemic. We inherit a series of discursive dichotomies; the discourse of AIDS attaches itself to these other systems of difference and plays itself out there.[17]

At this homological level, one of whose rhetorical costs consists in the failure to resist the disinformation ("AIDS virus") of which it speaks, it becomes increasingly hard to distinguish between illness as a metaphor and metaphor as a kind of illness, a disabling condition of the subject of discourse.

---

group that substituted "HIV disease" for "AIDS" in all its printed material. Although in 1991 it looked as though this new name might supersede *AIDS*, it has not done so.

16. Paula A. Treichler, "AIDS, Homophobia, and Biomedical Discourse: An Epidemic of Signification," in Crimp, *AIDS: Cultural Analysis / Cultural Activism*, 31.

17. Ibid., 63.

The notion of illness as metaphor derives from the work of Susan Sontag, whose book *AIDS and Its Metaphors* has been wholeheartedly denounced, in terms self-consciously drawn from the medical discourse on AIDS, as "opportunistic," because of its heterosexist, homophobic "silence about people with AIDS" and its denial of "the specifically gay bearings of AIDS metaphors."[18] There are many points one could raise for and against both Sontag's book and D. A. Miller's critique—points concerning the misogyny and homophobia that often inform relations, including discursive relations, between women and gay men; points about the inextricability of language from metaphor such that even the most self-conscious critiques of metaphorical language end up inscribing figures divergent from their professed polemical stance. For now, however, I will confine my discussion to suggesting how discourses on AIDS and metacritical discourses about those discourses seem unable to avoid terms of disease. These discourses are themselves diseased, contaminated, in the sense that their distanced metacritical purity is impossible to maintain, and the language of AIDS thus appears as part of its discursive object.[19]

I would like to propose an alternative approach to that implied by the deconstructive emphasis of this part of my argument by suggesting that it is the *subject* of discourse who is "diseased," rather than language itself. The radical dis-ease to which the subject is introduced via the signifier is in fact part of Lacan's account of psychosis, for the dilemma of the psychotic patient throws into relief our common malaise as linguistic subjects: "How do we not sense that the words we depend upon are imposed on us, that speech is an overlay, a parasite, the form of cancer with which human beings are afflicted?"[20] Lacan's question is rhetorical because it is precisely our routine failure to fully "sense" speech as imposed that prevents us from succumbing to psychosis. If Lacan had survived to witness the ravages of the AIDS epidemic, would his question formulate AIDS, rather than cancer, as figure for the affliction particular to subjectivity? And would such a formulation, in its

18. Susan Sontag, *AIDS and Its Metaphors* (New York: Farrar, Straus and Giroux, 1989). The critique comes from D. A. Miller, "Sontag's Urbanity," *October* 49 (1989), 91–101.

19. Lee Edelman makes a similar argument in "The Plague of Discourse: Politics, Literary Theory, and 'AIDS,' " in *Homographesis: Essays in Gay Literary and Cultural Theory* (New York: Routledge, 1994), 79–92.

20. Cited by Jacques-Alain Miller, "Teachings of the Case Presentation," in *Returning to Freud: Clinical Psychoanalysis in the School of Lacan,* ed. and trans. Stuart Schneiderman (New Haven: Yale University Press, 1980), 49.

ostensible generalization of AIDS at the price of gay specificity, count merely as one more "opportunistic" relation to AIDS?

The struggle to speak or remain silent about AIDS is certainly in large measure a struggle, as another commentator has put it, "to say or not to say the word 'gay.' "[21] But to argue that AIDS has unleashed an epidemic of signification is not tantamount to claiming that American society's symbolization—of the deaths, of the personal and political struggles of gay men—has been in any way adequate. Since symbolization is defined in a Lacanian perspective by its failures, such inadequacy is in one sense inevitable. However, the symbolization of AIDS hinges upon a political failure, or a series of political failures, of particular specificity. Those in power have made every effort to prevent the establishment of any identificatory signifier by which the suffering and deaths of hundreds of thousands of gay men, nonwhites, and other socially marginalized groups could achieve positive significance. There has been an epidemic of signification without any officially affirmative "S1" for gay men. It is this foreclosure of any such signifying possibility that leads me to characterize the American response to AIDS as psychotic. Before outlining the valuable counterattempts by AIDS activists to produce an S1, let us consider briefly the Lacanian theory of discourse in which this concept of an identificatory signifier finds its place.

In his seminar *L'envers de la psychanalyse,* Lacan elaborates four discursive structures—those of the master, the university, the hysteric, and the analyst—using combinations of four algebraic units: S1, S2, $, and a. These units have the following denotations: S1 is the master signifier, the signifier of primary identification; S2 represents knowledge *(savoir),* and the movement S1 $\rightarrow$ S2 represents unconscious interpretation as a shift along the signifying chain; $ is the subject in its division, subject of the unconscious as an effect of the signifier; a represents the remainder or leftover of *jouissance,* and while object a is understood as strictly unsymbolizable, it nevertheless stands in a causal relation to the subject. It should be clear from the beginning that the combination of these units in specific discursive structures distinguishes Lacan's theory of discourse from other theories. As in Foucaultian theory discourse is seen as constitutive; but the Lacanian concept of discourse includes an extradiscursive cause—object a—within its structure, thereby provid-

107

21. Helena Michie, "A Few Words about AIDS," *American Literary History* 2 (1990): 328.

ing for subjective inscription as the effect of desire beyond the pleasure principle *(jouissance)*.

The particular discourse structure with which I'm concerned here is that of the master, which Lacan writes thus *(SXVII* 105):

$$\frac{S1}{\cancel{S}} \to \frac{S2}{a} \qquad \frac{\text{master signifier}}{\text{subject}} \to \frac{\text{knowledge}}{\textit{jouissance}}$$

This discourse structure is significant because it is the characteristic political discourse, and is invoked by the seminar's title: *"l'envers de la psychanalyse, c'est cela même que j'avance cette année sous le titre du discours du maître"* ("the converse of psychoanalysis: it is just that which I have advanced this year under the title of the discourse of the master") *(SXVII* 99). Thus the analytic discourse is formulated by inverting the structure of the master discourse:

$$\frac{a}{S2} \to \frac{\cancel{S}}{S1}$$

and Lacan introduces this analytic discourse under the rubric of "The Castrated Master," declaring that "the psychoanalytic discourse finds itself very precisely at the opposite pole of the discourse of the master" *(SXVII* 100). Since *L'envers de la psychanalyse* represents Lacan's seminar work for the 1969–70 year, its reference to the master discourse as the discursive structure of politics, made in the aftermath of May 1968, may be read as implying that what is contrary to psychoanalysis is precisely the hegemonic ideological formation against which political struggles were being actively waged. Psychoanalysis is political precisely to the extent that the position of the analyst diametrically opposes that of the master, for the latter of which all division is repressed by the oneness or unity of certainty:

$$\frac{S1}{\cancel{S}}$$

Indeed, *all* discourse is political from a Lacanian viewpoint, "discourse being that which determines a form of social tie" *(SXX* 76).

The master discourse functions politically in two ways: first, in relation to subjective identification; and second, in relation to occulted *jouissance*. Because the subject, $\cancel{S}$, is subject to division, S1 offers a symbolic consistency to hide this division: a fantasy of oneness provides the illusion of identity, as well as reassurance that the traumatic real of sex can be rehabilitated to a sexual *relation*—a fantasy image of sexual completion, the copulatory couple. The price of such identification with S1 in a master discourse is precisely the repression of division ($ below the "bar"), the mechanism by which political discourse itself functions repressively and by which it displaces division to its outside in the form of externalized *agents* of division. Thus, for example, a certain concept of the nuclear family functions in contemporary Anglo-American political discourse as an S1, operating as the fundamental social unit to which political discourse addresses itself.[22] Like the Holy Family (and the doctrine of the Trinity) that still sanctions it, this mythic family is sacred; as a unit denoting unity, oneness, it figures the social bond by repressing divisions of gender, sexuality, and the sexual nonrelation, while giving rise to the routine domestic violences of incest, rape, and battering as symptomatic returns of the repressed.

A further consequence of the constitutive repression entailed by any S1 in the master discourse is that division is understood as having only an external source, such that the family is perceived as threatened from without by forces such as feminism, homosexuality, and "coloration" (these last two being combined in recurring debates on immigration and travel restrictions for those testing positive for HIV antibodies). So elevated an S1 status does the mythical family hold that its corruption—or even acknowledgment of its illusory, purely symbolic status—tends to be interpreted by the most extreme proponents of the master discourse (for example, religious fundamentalists) as the ruinous destruction of society itself.[23]

109

22. Although it would be correct to argue that the Enlightenment philosophy from which the American political tradition derives enshrines the *individual* in his autonomy (rather than the family) as the fundamental unit of social address, my suggestion is that the master discourse on *sexuality* addresses the family insofar as the individual accedes to his or her sociopolitical "rights" only in a familial context: persons achieve "individual" status only by fulfilling certain ideological prerequisites which are historically variable. Thus although "the individual" (and "whiteness," for example) operates as a powerful S1 in political discourse, when the issue is an even remotely sexual one "the family" is S1.

23. Hence, for example, in Britain the passage, in 1988, of Clause 28 of the Local Government Bill, which prohibits local authority funding of any teaching that promotes "the acceptability of homosexuality as a pretended family relationship." The Thatcher government's explicit refusal to sanction with family (S1) status any lesbian or gay relationship formed part of a trend toward recriminalizing what is viewed as a potent threat to the social fabric. Yet the arguments offered in support of the bill during the hotly contested political debate were based on a fundamental ideologi-

From this it should be apparent that discourse establishes "a form of social tie" not directly with other members of society, and certainly not with one's neighbor, but with a collective identificatory signifier. Yet symbolic or imaginary identification alone remains insufficient to establish social cohesion, since both the subject and the social cohere, such as they do, around real *jouissance,* for which Lacan's theory of discourse makes provision within its structure by reference to object *a.* An appreciation of *jouissance* reveals that there is indeed "a form of social tie" with the noxious neighbor, although not a happy one.[24] But before examining the crucial role played by homosexual *jouissance* in U.S. society, let us consider the symbolic dimension of national politics.

In June 1991, when I first started thinking about the issues this chapter addresses, the identificatory signifier "Vietnam" had just been eclipsed—or rather *interpreted*—for the U.S. subject by the signifier "victory" in the Gulf War.[25] Both wars were symbolically impelled, governmentally orchestrated because human sacrifice on behalf of national signifiers—the stars and stripes of the U.S. flag, the signifiers of democracy, freedom, the West—produces and maintains social subjectivity. The past decades have witnessed an outpouring of discourse and imagery about Vietnam, an enormous and sustained effort at cultural symbolization of national trauma, in relation to which the Gulf War may be merely another symptom. Death opens a hole in the real that symbolization must supply if mourning is to succeed.[26] Yet, until recently, no

cal contradiction: homosexuality should not be "promoted" because it is unnatural, and even social organizations of sexuality remain grounded in nature; if homosexuality is "promoted" we will be inundated by people, especially children, turning gay. The constant appeals to laws of nature revealed just how unnatural is "human nature," and how tenuously connected to nature is human sexuality.

24. Lacan's discussion of the "noxious neighbor" may be found in *SVII,* chap. 14. If I may be permitted a Žižekian moment here, I would propose the best embodiment of Lacan's "noxious neighbor" in popular culture to be Dennis Hopper's character in David Lynch's 1986 movie, *Blue Velvet,* psychotic Frank: during a joy ride that we must interpret as a *jouissance* ride in the sense of a "death drive," Frank consistently addresses the horrified Kyle McLachlan character, ingénu Jeffrey, as "Neighbor."

25. Here we recall Lacan's definition of a signifier as that which represents a subject for another signifier.

26. Following William Haver's critique of mourning as a redemptive process that occludes—by making sense of—the traumatic materiality of death and, indeed, of the erotic, I wish to qualify my reference to successful mourning. Mourning is necessary, yet also necessarily incomplete, since its successful completion involves creating an imaginary unity with violent implications of its own. As Haver explains:

> The refusal of the historicizing work of mourning is at the same time the refusal of the redemptive consolations of every humanism. These refusals give the lie to the logic of integration that is the ideological ground of humanism and, indeed, humanitarian-

comparable cultural effort had been made to symbolize the greater loss caused by AIDS. Rather, the reverse is true: Ronald Reagan, for example, refused to enunciate the word "AIDS" in public until late 1987, by which point over twenty-five thousand U.S. citizens had already died in the epidemic.

Instead, the work of symbolization has been largely relegated to the private domain, from which it has been taken up by volunteers and activists of various kinds, who have struggled to force AIDS back into the public realm, since "the public" is the only realm in which the signifier signifies. One notable instance of this effort has consisted in taking a traditionally private, domestic, feminized form of artistic practice and converting it into public spectacle. If we follow Laclau and Mouffe in using Lacan's term *point de capiton* to denote the retroactive ordering and fixing—or *quilting*—of signification via a certain S1 within a given ideological field, then we may press the translation of the term *point de capiton* in order to understand the symbolic functioning of the NAMES Project AIDS Memorial Quilt.[27] Begun by Cleve Jones in 1987, after six years of presidential silence about AIDS, and influenced by a long native tradition of folk art, the Quilt modifies and extends that tradition by the semiosis with which it is imbued and the discursive political field within which it is displayed.

Although cultural traditions make available a repertoire of institutions of mourning, in the current sociopolitical context the religious institution of the funeral and the literary institution of the elegy have been deemed inadequate for the performance of mass symbolization required in the work of mourning AIDS deaths.[28] Neither the funeral

111

---

ism. For humanism projects an Imaginary totality—the human community—within which the essentially erotic abject is reintegrated *only on condition that that abjection is accepted or in fact affirmed.* One is accepted into the community of the "we" only insofar as one accepts one's essentially passive objectness (as the abject object of a proleptic work of mourning), only insofar as one rejects one's difference, one's singular otherness.

William Haver, *The Body of This Death: Historicity and Sociality in the Time of AIDS* (Stanford: Stanford University Press, 1996), 19, original emphases.

27. Ernesto Laclau and Chantal Mouffe, *Hegemony and Socialist Strategy: Towards a Radical Democratic Politics,* trans. Winston Moore and Paul Cammack (London: Verso, 1985). Lacan's concept of *point de capiton,* or quilting point, is introduced in *SIII,* chap. 21.

28. There is, nevertheless, a significant body of testimonial literature that performs various elegiac functions in relation to AIDS and forms part of the history of both the elegy as a genre and the subgenre of what I would call the literature of homosexual testimony. Despite the importance of literary texts, perhaps the most widely encountered medium of contemporary testimony is video. See, for instance, Tom Kalin's video elegies discussed in Jeff Nunokawa, " 'All the Sad Young Men':

nor the elegy constitutes a native U.S. tradition (elegy is a genre associated in the United States more with death by assassination), whereas quilting and civil rights activism have specifically native histories.

As textile, the Quilt is also text, each grave-sized panel inscribed with the name of somebody who has died from AIDS, ranging from the famous—Rock Hudson, Michel Foucault, Perry Ellis, Keith Haring, Robert Mapplethorpe—to those "ordinary people" famous only to those who knew them. As a multimedia elegy and a public artwork, the Quilt can be understood as a contemporary genre of testimony, testifying that even though quilters may remain anonymous (this text bears no signature), many of those who have died will not. When it was displayed in Washington, D.C., in October 1989, in view of the White House and the Capitol Building, the Quilt covered the full fourteen acres of the Ellipse and comprised almost eleven thousand panels—a metonymic pile of dead bodies arranged outside the metonymic body of the president (the White House), and symbolizing by its flatness profound governmental neglect, in comparison with which the adjacent Vietnam Memorial, nationally funded and endorsed, testifies according to a very different code. The signifying structure of the Quilt is ordered according to the metonymic logic of substitution: panel for grave (a substitution based also on morphological resemblance), grave for body, house for body (metonymies of container-for-contained), and the linked metaphors of quilt for shroud, quilt for wall (the Vietnam Memorial), quilt for page. It is by means of this series of metonymic substitutions that the bodies of the dead are textually inscribed and lent a minimal symbolic identity—and, indeed, through this same structure that a text functions testimonially.

This testimonial structure operates also at the micro-level of the individual quilted panel, for each section combines disparate media, heterogeneous signifying systems (images, names, words), and different perspectives in a single grave-sized plane. Pieces of the dead person's clothing, locks of hair, photographs, other objects invested with memory and desire, and metonymic shreds of various kinds are quilted via the S1 of the proper name. Perhaps we could say that these material shreds represent objects a, since anything that "falls" from the body, bearing thereby a purely metonymic relation to it, is capable of becom-

---

AIDS and the Work of Mourning," in *Inside/Out,* ed. Fuss, 311–23, and the essays by Gregg Bordowitz, Douglas Crimp, and Martha Gever in Crimp, ed., *AIDS: Cultural Analysis/Cultural Activism.*

ing such an object ("Names" 85). The object *a* as "cause of desire" enters the signifying chain in the form of an interruption, which prompts a signifier of demand as the only substitute for that which is lost, and which in this instance is articulated by that special class of identificatory signifier making up the proper name of the deceased.

That the Quilt functions as a potent identificatory signifier in American society is left in no doubt by the testimonies of those quilters who have produced panels for people they never met or whom they knew only slightly. Inspired by a photographic "quilt" published by *Newsweek* in 1987 ("The Face of AIDS" profiled 302 people dead from AIDS in the year ending July 1987), many readers felt compelled to symbolize their identification with the chronic loss occasioned by AIDS. As one such reader, "just a housewife," put it: "I felt bad about all the people who die of AIDS that nobody knows."[29] The Quilt's testimonial power—the power of a homemade S1—was officially recognized by the collective decision to show it in the nation's capital even after the acknowledgment at its full showing in Washington, D.C., in 1992, that it had grown too large ever again to be displayed there in one piece. Hence the more than forty thousand panels simultaneously displayed October 11–13, 1996, in Washington, D.C.

But the Quilt functions as more than a site of mourning, testimony, and commemoration. It is also a prophylactic artwork dedicated to harnessing the power of images and symbols to save lives. In other words, the Quilt isn't simply retrospective, engaged in the redemptive project of making meaningful lives lost to AIDS; it is also prospective, engaged in the ongoing educational project of bringing home the proximity and pervasiveness of HIV.[30] There is an important distinction here between the liberal-humanist view of art as culturally redemptive—as that without which human life is essentially meaningless—and a more radical

113

29. Cindy Ruskin, Matt Herron, and Deborah Zemke, *The Quilt: Stories from the NAMES Project* (New York: Simon and Schuster, 1988), 61.

30. The Quilt has inspired other public art projects, such as the AIDS Bottle Project, initiated in 1990, and sponsored by the Santa Monica–based Institute of Cultural Inquiry. This ongoing project collects glass jars, each of which is marked with the surname of someone dead from AIDS. Under the lid of each jar is a brief biography, and the jars are left open so that visitors to the institute may place symbolic objects inside them. On December 1 each year, International AIDS Day and the Day without Art, the jars are sealed and distributed to the public in order "both to remember those who have died and to emphasize the responsibility of each member of the community to resist complacency about this ongoing crisis" (Deborah Cullen, ed., *Bataille's Eye and ICI Field Notes 4* [New York: Studley Press, 1997], 94).

understanding of art that recognizes the central place of images and signifiers in forming human subjectivity. In this respect, I must disagree with William Haver who, in his important study *The Body of This Death,* claims that "[n]o text, about AIDS or anything else, has ever saved a single life."[31] If the materiality of human life were as removed from signification as this claim implies, then subjectivity simply would not exist. But human life, even in its brute materiality, remains so bound up with images and signifiers that "art *does* have the power to save lives," as Douglas Crimp argues.[32] And although Crimp refers not to the Quilt but to more explicitly activist aesthetic practices, in fact the Quilt implicitly recognizes the signifier's ineluctable potential—its life-giving as well as its mortifying power—in human lives. We may assess this paradoxical power by considering further the credo of AIDS activism.

114

In March 1987, three months before the first Quilt panel was sewn and with presidential silence on the topic of AIDS still unbroken, another native tradition was revived for symbolic purposes: civil rights activism. Founded by Larry Kramer, the "direct-action group" ACT UP (AIDS Coalition to Unleash Power) took as its rallying slogan "Silence = Death." This austerely brief text, "Silence = Death," is typically set beneath the figure of a pink triangle for which it functions as legend (a pink triangle being the symbol appended to gay men in Nazi death camps), and the whole thus intensifies its rhetorical urgency via allusion to the Holocaust as the contemporary signifier of absolute horror. Unsurprisingly, the slogan has itself generated much discourse and many competing interpretations of its significance and effectiveness, not least because its structure dramatically conflates a causal relation with an identic relation.[33] First, the equation points to the perpetuation of AIDS deaths as a direct consequence of governmental silence and inaction. Silence as a refusal of symbolization also functions as a disavowal of death, a refusal to allow AIDS deaths to signify; silence thus performs a kind of second death on top of the first, physical death by forestalling the mourning that allows the dead to achieve their proper relation to the living. The double logic of the slogan therefore points in two direc-

31. Haver, *The Body of This Death,* xvi.

32. Douglas Crimp, "AIDS: Cultural Analysis / Cultural Activism," in *AIDS,* ed. Crimp, 7.

33. Besides Harris's article and Edelman's, see Patton, *Inventing AIDS,* 126–30, Crimp's introduction to *AIDS: Cultural Analysis / Cultural Activism,* 3–16, and his response to Edelman's argument in Douglas Crimp, "Mourning and Militancy," *October* 51 (1989): 3–18.

tions at once: on the one hand, it implies that if Silence = Death, then speech equals life, in the sense of lives saved by a discourse of AIDS education and an official mandate for AIDS research; while on the other hand, it implies that symbolization = death in the sense of conferring proper dignity on the dead. I will have more to say shortly about these implications of the ACT UP slogan in relation to a psychoanalytic theory of symbolization and mourning, but for now let us consider the paradox of a slogan that places such emphasis on the life-and-death stakes of symbolization for a group whose manifest commitment is to "direct action."

What rhetorical or semantic function does the adjective *direct* in the phrase *direct action* serve? Is it not the case that *in*direct action would be tantamount to *symbolic* action, and that therefore the emphasis on *direct* action rather dilutes the urgency of symbolization implied in the slogan? Although it is necessary to acknowledge that ACT UP's actions are in fact largely symbolic, the incalculability of those actions' effects is in large measure a consequence of the attempt to circumvent symbolic structures by intervening directly in the real. Let me make clear that our only possible access to the real outside of symbolization is psychotic access. Furthermore, the qualitative incalculability of the effects of symbolic action is a consequence of the signifier's status as not fully masterable. The paradox of the signifier for ACT UP resides in the disjunctive effect obtained by the breaking of silence, for speech divides its speaker such that the subject's every effort at representation is, in part, a failure—indeed, it is this very failure that constitutes the subject.

This psychoanalytic premise remains unpalatable to ACT UP supporters, not because it represents a slight modification of activist theory, but because it diametrically opposes activist theory and points to a contradiction at the heart of activist practice. The second edition of the *Oxford English Dictionary* (1989)—which includes a remarkably sensitive and accurate entry under *AIDS* (denotatively qualifying the "always fatal" connotation of the term)—offers its primary definition of *activism* in philosophical terms by reference to a twentieth-century "philosophical theory which assumes the objective reality and active existence of everything." Thus, even semantically, activism refers to theory before practice. The *OED*'s second definition speaks of a doctrine or policy advocating energetic action, and its subdefinition of *activist* (which seems not to merit a separate entry of its own) identifies the latter simply as an

115

advocate of activism in either the primary or secondary sense. What must be added is that logically one cannot be an activist in the second sense (advocate of energetic action) without also being an activist in the first sense. Now of course there are many ACT UP supporters who explicitly subscribe to philosophical theories incompatible with the dictionary definition. Douglas Crimp, for example, takes a standard Foucaultian line in introducing the *October* dossier on AIDS when he writes, "I assert, to begin with, that 'disease' does not exist . . . AIDS does not exist apart from the practices that conceptualize it, represent it, and respond to it."[34] No practice conceptualizes, represents, or responds to anything without the intervention of the signifier and the consequent installation of "practice" within the field of discourse. Yet there remains a tendency to consider the signifier's intervention as an *avoidable* barrier to effective political intervention, and to consider the "talking cure" no real cure at all.

This paradoxical tendency, which is one of the greatest stumbling blocks for any political program centered on "direct action," is caught in the title of a collection of ACT UP documents and archival material coedited by Crimp: *AIDS Demo Graphics*. AIDS demography, the study of population statistics with respect to AIDS, is achieved in this book by presenting *graphic* images—photographs and posters—that function *demo*nstratively as examples (the book presents itself in the classic American genre of the handbook) and as actual, active interventions. The prefix *demo-* is inflected according to its "proper," etymological (Greek) meaning, "people," but also according to its colloquial meaning, as an abbreviation of *demonstration* (whose Latin root has nothing to do with the word for "people"). The titular *demo* thus signifies people acting, intervening symbolically via organized public demonstrations in the political spheres that affect their lives: "This book . . . is meant as direct action, putting the power of representation in the hands of as many people as possible."[35] Yet this book is precisely demo-graphy, people *writing*, people caught in a signifier whose defining characteristic is displacement of the subject elsewhere than the place of his or her conscious intention, for which reason representative power is displaced and deferred at the moment of its dissemination—a qualification that never-

---

34. Crimp, *AIDS: Cultural Analysis / Cultural Activism*, 3.
35. Crimp and Rolston, *AIDS Demo Graphics*, 13.

theless should not discourage the effort. Recognition of language's non-transparency does not eliminate that opacity; however, eliminating a naive conception of representational power may indeed help us engage more accurately the very significant power that representation and rhetoric hold over our lives.

But what about ACT UP's implicit recognition in its slogan of the signifier's power in relation to life, the power of silence to cause death? In one sense, the implication of the slogan—that if silence = death, then speech = life—runs directly against the Lacanian thesis that speech mortifies the subject, that the signifier itself entails a certain death. However, in another sense, the assumption behind both activism and the Quilt that symbolization of AIDS deaths has been institutionally insufficient is a potentially psychoanalytic assumption, one that is consonant, moreover, with my characterizing the social response to AIDS as psychotic. Lacan defines mourning in his seminar on *Hamlet* as a question of symbolization: "What are these rites, really, by which we fulfill our obligation to what is called the memory of the dead—if not the total mass intervention, from the heights of heaven to the depths of hell, of the entire play of the symbolic register[?]" ("Desire" 38). I am interested here in Lacan's interpretation of the Freudian paradigm of mourning, which is based on an *object* relation, in terms of a model of mourning based on a *signifying* relation. Yet as with his effort to redefine psychosis as a question of the subject's relation to language rather than its relation to reality, so too here Lacan's effort to conceptualize mourning as a symbolic economy leads to his characterizing psychosis in a formulation that reverts to an earlier theoretical moment:

> Where is the gap, the hole that results from this loss and that calls forth mourning on the part of the subject? It is a hole in the real, by means of which the subject enters into a relationship that is the inverse of what I have set forth in earlier seminars under the name of *Verwerfung* [repudiation, foreclosure].
>
> Just as what is rejected from the symbolic register reappears in the real, in the same way the hole in the real that results from loss, sets the signifier in motion. This hole provides the place for the projection of the missing signifier, which is essential to the structure of the Other. This is the signifier whose absence leaves the Other incapable of responding to your question, the signifier that can be purchased

only with your own flesh and your own blood, the signifier that is essentially the veiled phallus. ("Desire" 37–38)

That this seminar, dated April 29, 1959, should revert in its formula for psychosis to a moment preceding the insights of the psychosis article composed early in 1958 confirms that any periodization of Lacan's teaching cannot proceed adequately by linear chronology. I don't think it coincidental that Lacan's theoretical regression in this passage is accompanied by reference to the phallus as ultimate explanatory term. Nevertheless, his notion that psychosis and mourning are connected in a relation of structural inversion supports our thesis that the social relation to AIDS is properly psychotic as a consequence of its refusal of a signifier for AIDS that would provide for mourning: silence = death.

It is worth recalling that *Hamlet* is a play about failed mourning, a *dearth* of mourning, which anticipates our social condition with respect to AIDS. When Freud discusses mourning, he speaks of its failure in precisely opposite terms: melancholia is an *excess,* rather than a dearth, of mourning. So long as U.S. society refuses a signifier to make positively meaningful the deaths of thousands of gay men,[36] there is danger that the work of mourning undertaken by activists may tip into melancholic excess. The Freudian theory of mourning revises, among other things, Freud's theory of identification, insofar as the defining characteristic of melancholia—which Freud also compares to psychosis because of the excessive distance taken by the subject from "reality"—as pathological mourning is its proclivity to replace an object cathexis (love for the lost object) by an identification with that object (*SE* 14:249). This is dangerous because the ego takes the object with which a part of it has identified and chastises it with the viciousness of a hatred that is the underside of any love relationship having the status of ambivalence. From this Freud develops one version of his concept of the superego, which Lacan reformulates in his *Ethics* seminar through the concepts of the noxious neighbor and *jouissance.*

What about those of us so torn by grief at the losses occasioned by AIDS that our acts of mourning the objects of love are transformed into identification with the cause of loss? I am thinking here of a comment

---

36. Although society remains perfectly willing to render meaningful the deaths of those perceived through a disavowed tautology as "innocent victims"—for example, children—on condition that the latter maintain a nonsexual status.

by Larry Kramer, who, recounting the conditions under which he founded ACT UP and responding with justifiable ire to President Bush's denunciations of AIDS activism, declared: "ACT UP is impolite, abrasive, rude—like the virus that is killing us."[37] Identification with the cause of loss only unleashes an aggressivity whose ultimate aim, no matter against whom or what it is directed, is death. Hence Freud's point that the melancholic's desire for suicide is simply a displacement onto his own ego of the murderous wishes toward the loved object held in the unconscious. Ambivalence toward the object of love may be endemic to any love relation, yet Freud emphasizes ambivalence as one of the prerequisites for mourning's transformation into melancholia. How much more ambivalent must gay love be in a homophobic culture, and therefore how much more prone to melancholic identification—and the subsequent unleashing of murderous aggression—must gay men be in the age of AIDS?

In an essay remarkable, among other things, for its willingness to engage with psychoanalysis and for its emphasis on the unconscious, Crimp expresses the ambivalence of gay people toward those living and dying with AIDS: "we must recognize that our memories and our resolve also entail the more painful feelings of survivor's guilt, often exacerbated by our secret wishes, during our lovers' and friends' protracted illnesses, that they would just die and let us get on with our lives."[38] There are many startling confessions in "Mourning and Militancy," none of which should be accorded an unquestioned truth value just because it deidealizes the psychic difficulties that are usually so utopianly purified out of existence in explicitly gay-identified writing and criticism. What seems to me particularly useful about Crimp's admission is that it allows for consideration of the death drive not as something inflicted from the outside by a homophobic culture, but, as Crimp says, "the result of psychic as well as of social conflict."[39] The death drive is a notoriously difficult concept, and neither Crimp nor Jacqueline Rose (from whose essay on the topic he derives much of his argument) gets far enough with it.[40] However, by conceptualizing the death drive in terms of *jouis-*

37. Kramer, "Ten Years of Plague," 62.

38. Crimp, "Mourning and Militancy," 10.

39. Ibid., 16.

40. Jacqueline Rose, " 'Where Does the Misery Come From?'—Psychoanalysis, Feminism, and the Event," in *Why War?* 89–109.

sance Lacan makes the idea more accessible, because *jouissance* suggests that there is a certain kind of satisfaction in death, that death itself is actually something one might, at some radical level, want—if not desire.

Crimp's terms in the quotation above—"survivor's guilt," "secret wishes"—resonate with the kind of pop psychology against which Lacanian psychoanalysis so firmly sets itself. Indeed, the concept of the death drive is perhaps the one that most clearly distinguishes psychoanalysis from psychology, for the death drive is reducible neither to the level of consciousness or the unconscious, nor to the popular notion of self-destructiveness that has been leveled at gay men with renewed homophobic vigor in the wake of AIDS. In its positivization of pure negativity, the death drive is literally unthinkable for traditional psychology, which, as Joel Fineman once put it, "can only understand desire, that is, that which motivates an action, as an impulse or a pulsion toward the good."[41] However, I would like to consider briefly one fictional treatment of "survivor's guilt," by a consciously gay-identified writer, which does come close to dramatizing the death drive as it is conceived by Lacan. David Leavitt's short story "Aliens" (1984) is not about AIDS; neither does it contain any character identified as gay. As the title suggests, though, the story thematizes monstrosity and abnormality through each of its familial characters, the point being that abnormality, deformity, and crisis are not contingent accidents that befall the typical, suburban, middle-class, American nuclear family, but are rather its essential condition.

Like other stories in *Family Dancing,* the narrative is told from the first-person point of view of the mother, who, we learn, survived relatively intact the automobile accident a year earlier that crippled her husband: "Alden lost half his vision, much of his mobility, and the English language." The story thematizes language in relation to crisis as a limit point: trauma is unsymbolizable, words fail, but the one who survives crisis is the one who must testify: "Earlier, during the argument, he had said that seatbelts do more harm than good, and I had buckled myself in as an act of vengeance. This is the only reason I'm around to talk about it." The other characters are the narrator's two children,

---

41. Joel Fineman, "The Sound of O in *Othello*: The Real of the Tragedy of Desire," in *The Subjectivity Effect in Western Literary Tradition: Essays toward the Release of Shakespeare's Will* (Cambridge: MIT Press, 1991), 147.

Charles and Nina, and the narrator's mother, the grandmother, who assumes the form of a superegoic voice by communicating only via the technological Other—"her new cordless electric telephone" and mimeographed Christmas "family report" letters she begins preparing (gestating) in March, nine months early. From this technological Other comes the truth of the family's condition: their status as survivors and their *jouissance* in monstrosity.

It is not possible to delineate here the complex interweave of fantasized identifications with the alien and the monstrous in this story. Suffice it to indicate the condensed effect of *survival* as the defining element in the characters' familial identifications. This is a consequence of the metonymic relation between loss and survival that enables survival to function as object *a* in the family's collective fantasy of itself. It is, finally, not "survivor's guilt" of which the narrator is accused by her mother's allegory of the Holocaust, so much as survivor's *jouissance*. Speaking of a "study" reminiscent of that conducted by the satirized Dr. Tree in Cynthia Ozick's story "Rosa,"[42] the narrator's mother in "Aliens" reads over the phone:

121

> "There is a man who is studying the Holocaust," she says. "He makes a graph. One axis is fulfillment / despair, and the other is success / failure. That means that there are four groups of people—those who are fulfilled by success, whom we can understand, and those who are despairing even though they're successful, like so many people we know, and those who are despairing because they're failures. Then there's the fourth group—the people who are fulfilled by failure, who don't need hope to live. Do you know who those people are?"
>
> "Who?" I ask.
>
> "Those people," my mother says, "are the ones who survived."[43]

It is this fiction's thematizing the notion of fulfillment in failure—the idea that there might be something at the heart of the subject that wishes

42. Cynthia Ozick, *The Shawl* (New York: Vintage, 1990). Dr. Tree pursues Rosa, "a madwoman and a scavenger," in order to subject her to his study of Holocaust survivors, based on a theory entitled—in a perfect amalgam of Freud and Disney—"Repressed Animation."

43. Leavitt, *Family Dancing,* 88. In "Some Character-Types Met with in Psychoanalytic Work" (*SE* 14:309–33), Freud speaks of "those wrecked by success." Freud's explanation is that people fall ill after achieving some cherished ambition because this success reawakens in them oedipal ambition, and therefore arouses a psychical conflict that engenders neurosis. Rewriting Freud's master narrative of the Oedipus complex, Lacan interprets "those wrecked by success" in terms of an overridden internal barrier to *jouissance*.

it harm yet which it clings to as the very ground of its being and the source of its satisfaction—that seems to me insightful, because this idea counters the psychological notion that the human subject automatically pursues its own happiness and its own good.

This insight dispenses immediately with the simplistic notion, prevalent in so many studies of homophobia, that the harm done gay people has a purely external source, to the extent that even gay self-hatred, internalized homophobia, is conceived according to this model—the dictates of a homophobic society being internalized by the gay subject who necessarily also identifies as a social subject.[44] Consideration of the death drive allows us to conceptualize a nonexternal force that works against the subject (that is, against the subject's well-being), yet which cannot be characterized as the effect of any internalization. When we try to conceive the death drive—or psychic negativity—in terms of inside / outside (an essentially topographical model), our theorization runs into problems. I think we should acknowledge that the death drive is not merely an effect of the violence of the inside / outside dichotomy, and that "the ambiguity of the concept" is *not* "the concept itself."[45] As I suggested in chapter 1, it was to circumvent such impasses of conceptualization that Lacan developed a theory of the subject mapped topologically, substituting for the notion of an individual with a psychic interiority partially independent of the outside world the notion of a subject in the Other. For this subject the relation between inside and outside is thinkable only by the counterintuitive topological model of the Möbius strip, which gives rise to new conceptual terms, such as *extimité* or extimacy.[46]

---

44. See, for example, Nunokawa, " 'All the Sad Young Men,' " which, despite its sophistication, still pictures death as something that comes from outside—in this case, from the "lethal culture" that defines the homosexual in terms of his youthful fatality: "The gay community is thus taxed during its sad time by a double burden: the variegated regime of heterosexism not only inhibits the work of acknowledging the loss of a gay man, it also exacts the incessant reproduction of this labor, by casting his death as his definition" (319).

45. Rose, " 'Where Does the Misery Come From?' " 95.

46. See Jacques-Alain Miller, "*Extimité*," in *Lacanian Theory of Discourse: Subject, Structure, Society,* ed. Mark Bracher et al (New York: New York University Press, 1994), 74–87, which argues the necessity of the term and its conceptual referent "in order to escape the common ravings about a psychism supposedly located in a bipartition between interior and exterior" (75). It follows, therefore, that "extimacy is not the contrary of intimacy," but rather that "extimacy says that the intimate is Other" (76). Among other things, Miller uses the concept in relation to *jouissance* to adumbrate a psychoanalytic theory of racism. I wish to adapt the concept for a psychoanalytic theory of homophobia.

The impatience of many critics, particularly so-called political critics, with sustained theorization makes it necessary to emphasize that
conceptual impasses concerning AIDS and homophobia imply that new
terms and idioms may help to make certain phenomena accessible to
thought. Just as a new biomedical nomenclature for AIDS has been
necessary, so too is new terminology to describe the subject of AIDS
and of post-AIDS gay desire. In my view, the discourses of philosophy,
linguistics, and sociology must be supplemented in a fully psychoanalytic
account of AIDS by concepts drawn from the discourse of mathematics,
principally post-Euclidean geometry, which provides for topological
mappings based on a non-Euclidean conception of space. Topology—
"without which all the phenomena produced in our domain would be
indistinguishable and meaningless" ("Desire" 11)—is the theoretical
model that Lacan employs to map the subject of his later work, a subject
defined as much by its relation to an object as by its relation to a signifier. I want to try to get at the effects of AIDS by way of the concepts
named by two virtually untranslatable terms—*jouissance* and *extimité*.
The way that AIDS represents death as a signifier of sexuality forces a
confrontation with the death drive, insofar as "the drive," according to
Lacan, "the partial drive, is profoundly a death drive and represents in
itself the portion of death in the sexed living being" (*Four* 205).[47]

123

The *Jouissance* of AIDS

> It is always possible to bind together a considerable number of
> people in love, so long as there are other people left over to
> receive the manifestations of their aggressiveness.
>
> —Sigmund Freud, *Civilization and Its Discontents* (1930)

Perhaps the greatest psychic horror of AIDS for a society that always
segregates and shifts death elsewhere lies in how AIDS intertwines death
with life—and with what is generally assumed to be the life force: the
sex drive. In its combination of sex and death, *jouissance* is like AIDS
in this respect. However, the hardy resistance of *jouissance* to translation,
together with its appearance in French theoretical discourses—principally Barthes's—that were effectively assimilated by the academy prior

---

47. In an *écrit* from the same period, Lacan concludes that "every drive is virtually a death
drive" ("Position" 275).

to, and more easily than, the quasi assimilation of Lacan, means that the term *jouissance* and Lacan's usage of it to revise the Freudian death drive must be unpacked carefully.

If for Barthes in 1973 the relevant distinction is between the text of pleasure and the text of bliss *(jouissance)*, this is because Lacan has already formulated *jouissance* as the beyond of Freud's pleasure principle.[48] In Freudian terms the relevant distinction involves distinguishing between an unconscious wish for somebody else's death *(Todeswunsch)* and the death drive, or pulsion toward one's own death *(Todestrieb)*. This distinction translates approximately into Lacanian terms as the difference between unconscious desire and *jouissance*. Let me elaborate.

In the second part of his 1915 essay "Thoughts for the Times on War and Death"—an essay that, contra Sontag, is particularly pertinent because the psychic consequences and implications of the wartime conditions it describes can be read profitably as analogous to social and psychic conditions in the age of AIDS—Freud discusses the disturbance in our relation to death that war brings. War and AIDS force a confrontation not only with death but also with its place in the unconscious, and hence its relation to desire. Rehearsing the theme he would develop fifteen years later in *Civilization and Its Discontents*—namely, that an instinctual renunciation is demanded as the price of culture, and that there is therefore an incurable malaise intrinsic to culture itself—Freud argues that a historically cumulative series of repressions exacted by culture has modified our attitude to death. Hence, in the unconscious we not only wish for the deaths *(Todeswunsch)* of our enemies, but often desire the speedy elimination of our nearest and dearest too, as a consequence of the ambivalence that infects all love.[49] From this counterintuitive proposition—that (unconsciously) we would like to see those we love dead—it seems but a small step to suggesting that we desire our own deaths, that there is something at the heart of the human subject that wishes it ill. Yet since one of the properties of the unconscious is that, existing atemporally, it knows neither contradiction nor negation, there is no provision for the subject's own death, no signifier for self-annihilation, registered in the unconscious: "It is indeed impossible

48. Roland Barthes, *The Pleasure of the Text,* trans. Richard Miller (New York: Hill and Wang, 1975).

49. Sigmund Freud, "Zeitgemässes über Krieg und Tod," *Gesammelte Werke (1913–1917)* (London: Imago, 1946), 10:351.

to imagine our own death; and whenever we attempt to do so we can perceive that we are in fact still present as spectators" (*SE* 14:289). Therefore the death drive cannot be conceptualized at the level of unconscious desire; it is not part of the Other's discourse (the unconscious is the discourse of the Other), but an effect of the Other's *jouissance*.

Jouissance belongs to the order of the real and hence can be understood as extradiscursive. However, as Lacan remarks, "nothing is more burning [*brûlant*] than what, in discourse, makes reference to *jouissance*" (*SXVII* 80). The straight way to read this statement would be to understand that any discursive reference to *jouissance* makes the discourse itself torrid—or, as Jane Gallop once put it, "talk about sex is sexy."[50] Yet we could also read the sentence in that philosophical context that takes the figure of fire as paradigmatic of an effect requiring some causal explanation.[51] In this second reading, *jouissance* would appear as an enigmatic discursive effect whose cause remains extradiscursive. Hence the familiar Lacanian formula that says "*jouissance* is forbidden to him who speaks as such" (*E* 319)—a version of Freud's thesis in *Civilization and Its Discontents,* namely, that subjectification is achieved at the price of *jouissance,* a forced exchange of a portion of being, "a pound of flesh," for participation in the signifying systems of culture. *Jouissance* designates the ontological element in Lacanian theory and constitutes the only substantive dimension allowed to being.

Jouissance and the subject (of speech, of discourse, of desire, of the unconscious) are basically incompatible. Furthermore, *jouissance* remains so far beyond the pleasure principle that it works against the subject's well-being, as the Sadian text, for instance—which is about *jouissance* as opposed to pleasure—illustrates. Apropos of Sade as the truth of Kant, Lacan characterizes the pleasure principle as "the law of the good which is the *wohl,* let us say well-being [*bien-être*]" ("Kant" 56), while *jouissance* he characterizes as evil, insofar as it implies "precisely the [subject's] acceptance of death" (*SVII* 189). Since, as we have noted, the acceptance of one's own death is completely unthinkable in the unconscious, *jouissance* is therefore impossible *for the subject.* But not for the Other.

Sade's value for Lacan resides in his propensity for making himself

125

---

50. Jane Gallop, *Thinking through the Body* (New York: Columbia University Press, 1988), 86.

51. The possibility of this interpretation was suggested by Copjec, *Read My Desire,* 245 n. 32.

the *object* of the Other's *jouissance,* and in his formulating a "right to *jouissance*" that bears the same status as Kant's categorical imperative. As Lacan remarks in "Kant with Sade":

> The right to *jouissance,* were it recognized, would relegate the domination of the pleasure principle to a forevermore outdated era. In enunciating it, Sade causes the ancient axis of ethics to slip, by an imperceptible fracture, for everyone: this axis is nothing other than the egoism of happiness. ("Kant" 71)

The Sadian maxim, the universal law of *jouissance,* is enunciated thus: "I have the right of enjoyment over *[le droit de jouir de]* your body, anyone can say to me, and I will exercise this right, without any limit stopping me in the capriciousness of the exactions that I might have the taste to satiate" ("Kant" 58). This law can be conceived of as a universal—and hence ethical—law in the Kantian sense because it takes no account of specific, individual good or subjective interest; it is nonutilitarian and nonreciprocal.

Since there is no danger that this "right" to *jouissance* will make you happy, we could add that it is also a particularly un-American right—were it not for the anomaly of one of America's most visible cultural icons, Madonna, taking for the text and spectacle of one of her commercial exploits rather precise Sadian imagery and the approximate Sadian motto, "Poor is the man whose pleasures depend upon the permission of another" (a nice perversion of the Christian Beatitudes). We can see from the fact that it was banned that Jean-Baptiste Mondino's 1990 video for Madonna's "Justify My Love" was perceived as exhibiting the obscene, excessive, worse-than-useless *jouissance* of the Other. Staging its scene in a sort of hôtel de Sade, the video is replete with stylized gestures representing the whole catalogue of perverse activity: lesbianism, fetishism, voyeurism, transvestism, troilism, and the ritual accoutrements of sadomasochism. I remain unpersuaded that the video was banned because of its depiction of lesbianism, as some critics suggested, because Madonna had already represented lesbian voyeurism in the video for "Open Your Heart." However, there is something about the Other's *homosexual jouissance* that makes it particularly intolerable today, in the age of AIDS.

Its genital nonreciprocity with the opposite sex, together with its overt antiutilitarian—that is, nonreproductive—pleasure, plus its association with fatality and self-destruction (for which AIDS is the current, most intensified figure), makes homosexuality appear as an especially noxious form of the Other's *jouissance*. Only in the context of this understanding of homosexuality can the statement about HIV transmission made by Dr. Opendra Narayan of Johns Hopkins Medical School make any sense:

> These people have sex twenty to thirty times a night . . . A man comes along and goes from anus to anus and in a single night will act as a mosquito transferring infected cells on his penis. When this is practised for a year, with a man having three thousand sexual intercourses, one can readily understand this massive epidemic that is currently upon us.[52]

This fantasy is clearly Sadian, inhuman, delineating an impossible, Other *jouissance*. Gay sex in Narayan's scenario is beyond bestial, it is entomial, sex in the service of nothing but the absolute worst, namely, mass death. From this obscene image it should not be difficult to grasp how the *jouissance* of the Other operates as a mechanism of social exclusion, fueling homophobic recoil from gay people in the society of AIDS. I am not saying that gay men are the Other, but that the Other's noxious *jouissance* has become associated with gay sex. In this context, we may supplement Lacan's aphorism about transference and the *sujet supposé savoir*—"he whom I suppose to know, I love" (*SXX* 64)—with the following formulation: *he whom I suppose to know how to enjoy, I hate.*

In the course of formulating an ethic of psychoanalysis, Lacan makes clear that the evil obscenity from which we shrink in our neighbor is in fact the expression of our own *jouissance*. As cultural subjects, our desire is produced as the desire *not* to enjoy, thus rendering *jouissance* Other:

> [E]very time that Freud stops short in horror at the consequences of the commandment to love one's neighbor, we see evoked the presence of that fundamental evil which dwells within this neighbor. But if that is the case, then it also dwells within me. And what is more of a neighbor to me than this heart within which is that of my *jouissance* and which I don't dare go near? For as soon as I go near

52. Cited by Leo Bersani, "Is the Rectum a Grave?" in *AIDS: Cultural Analysis / Cultural Activism*, 197.

it, as *Civilization and Its Discontents* makes clear, there rises up the unfathomable aggressivity from which I flee, that I turn against me, and which in the very place of the vanished Law adds its weight to that which prevents me from crossing a certain frontier at the limit of the Thing. (*SVII* 186)

The insufferability of one's own *jouissance* prompts fury and hatred against anyone who seems to have access to the enjoyment he is denied. Indeed, homophobic recoil from the specter of gay *jouissance* also can be appreciated in the context of Freud's pronouncement that "all human beings are capable of making a homosexual object-choice and have in fact made one in their unconscious" (*SE* 7:144), since the maintenance of heterosexual identity is dependent upon active avoidance of that psychic reality.[53]

However, sexual antagonism is present not only between straight-identified and gay-identified people, but is internal to every person as an effect of every subject's constitutive *sexual* dependence upon the Other. Social antagonism based on different modes of sexual enjoyment—as that conflict is manifested directly and obliquely in various forms of homo- and heterophobia—should be understood as an effect of self-antagonism. In a sense similar to that of Laclau and Mouffe's when they argue that "society does not exist" as a totality because society is structured around a central antagonism that ideology operates to conceal, we could suggest that neither heterosexuality nor homosexuality exists, because every sexual identity is self-antagonistic, not merely at war with its opposite, but constituted through the repression of its opposite and thence actively at war with itself. This is simply another way of saying that there is no sexuality without the unconscious, no desire that does not have conflict already built into it.

In this regard we should not be surprised to encounter *gay* recoil from homosexual *jouissance*. One well-known example of this revulsion is expressed by Randy Shilts in his fantastic portrayal of "Patient Zero," Gaetan Dugas, whose "voracious sexual appetite" was mythologized by Shilts as the origin of North American AIDS, a mythology that too

---

53. In chapter 6 I launch a critique of this Freudian axiom from the perspective of queer theory, arguing that Freud's notion of object-choice remains captive to an understanding of sexual difference that his own theory ultimately discredits.

readily determines cause from effects (sex = death).[54] However, if, for Shilts, Dugas embodies the destructive *jouissance* of the Other, prompting censure, other gay commentators have deemed it politically expedient to embrace such an embodiment. I am thinking here of two opposing yet related positions vis-à-vis gay sex articulated by Douglas Crimp and Leo Bersani in their respective contributions to the 1987 *October* special issue on AIDS. Crimp concludes his essay thus: "Having learned to support and grieve for our lovers and friends; having joined the fight against fear, hatred, repression, and inaction; having adjusted our sex lives so as to protect ourselves and one another—we are now reclaiming our subjectivities, our communities, our culture . . . and our promiscuous love of sex."[55] In direct contrast to that positive closing note, Bersani's remarkable essay "Is the Rectum a Grave?" begins: "There is a big secret about sex: most people don't like it."[56] Between promiscuity and aversion, loving sex and disliking it, lies the meaning of *jouissance* and the concept of the death drive, for naming it *jouissance* is a way of "tinting" the drive with both erotophilia and erotophobia.

Crimp's argument in "How to Have Promiscuity in an Epidemic" is erotophilic and dismisses erotophobia (and, along with it, anything approximating the death drive) as a form of homophobia; Crimp lambastes Shilts, Kramer, and many others for whom "sex has been the real culprit all along."[57] Following Cindy Patton's analysis of erotophobia, Crimp argues that because "gay people invented safe sex," the recoil from gay sex as embodiment of the Other's noxious *jouissance* is "perversely distorted"; this explains "why [Shilts and Kramer] insist that our promiscuity will destroy us when in fact *it is our promiscuity that will save us.*"[58] Shilts's tacit slogan, sex = death, is inverted by Crimp— (safe) sex = life—thereby providing his erotophilic rationale for the

54. Randy Shilts, *And the Band Played On: Politics, People, and the AIDS Epidemic* (New York: St. Martin's Press, 1987), 22. Shilts quotes a line from *Faggots*, which he describes, without a trace of irony, as the climax of Larry Kramer's famous 1978 novel; this line—"It all needs to change . . . before you fuck yourself to death" (27)—is proffered as the truth of his cautionary tale, *And the Band Played On*.

55. Douglas Crimp, "How to Have Promiscuity in an Epidemic," *AIDS: Cultural Analysis / Cultural Activism*, 270.

56. Bersani, "Is the Rectum," 197.

57. Crimp, "How to Have Promiscuity," 238.

58. Ibid., 253; original emphases. See also Cindy Patton, *Sex and Germs: The Politics of AIDS*, Boston: South End Press, 1985.

promotion of, not merely apology for, promiscuity: "Gay male promiscuity should be seen instead as a positive model of how sexual pleasures might be pursued by and granted to everyone if those pleasures were not confined within the narrow limits of institutionalized sexuality."[59]

I shall have considerably more to say in my next chapter concerning the mythology of gay promiscuity; but for now I want simply to indicate how Crimp's erotophilic model of sexuality provides a prime target for Bersani's critique of "the *redemptive reinvention of sex,*"[60] an enterprise so broadly encompassing as to include in its adherents, besides Crimp, such widely disparate figures as Andrea Dworkin and Catherine MacKinnon (feminist antipornographers), Pat Califia and Gayle Rubin (feminist proponents of lesbian sadomasochism), Simon Watney and Jeffrey Weeks (propornography gay Foucaultians), and Michel Foucault himself. Like Lacan in his appreciation of Sade, Bersani rejects the illusory, redemptive version of sex in favor of "the inestimable value of sex as—at least in certain of its ineradicable aspects—anticommunal, antiegalitarian, antinurturing, antiloving."[61] Thus in a completely opposite way to Crimp, Bersani embraces a certain image of the Other's noxious *jouissance* as it is associated with gay sex.

Bersani's position depends, however, upon a certain conflation of sex with fucking—in this case, buttfucking. Anal penetration is indeed the prototypical act associated with the Other's *jouissance,* as Lacan enigmatically suggests, in "Kant with Sade," by referring to "spintrian *jouissance*" (*jouissance* of the sphincter, defined as "pertaining to [male prostitutes and] those who seek out, or invent new and monstrous forms of lust" ["Kant" 67, 95]). This connection also is illustrated by the fate of Sade's Justine, who, during her interminable submission to every whim of sexual caprice, following the "right to *jouissance,*" is buttfucked countless times, but only once, symbolically, is she vaginally raped.[62]

Bersani pictures the rectum as a grave "in which the masculine ideal of proud subjectivity is buried," an ideal that he unmistakably identifies with the ego. It is thus the ego-shattering *jouissance* of receptive rectal

---

59. Ibid.

60. Bersani, "Is the Rectum," 215; original emphases.

61. Ibid.

62. For Justine's spintrian fate, see "Justine, or Good Conduct Well Chastised" (1791), in the Marquis de Sade, *Justine, Philosophy in the Bedroom, and Other Writings,* trans. Richard Seaver and Austryn Wainhouse (New York: Grove, 1966), 447–743.

sex that leads him to characterize sexuality as "a tautology for masochism."[63] My only reservation concerning this fascinating psychoanalytic argument has to do with its appeal to the gay ego as an agent of mastery, for in the face of AIDS Bersani recommends "an arduous representational discipline," which involves "the pain of embracing, at least provisionally, a homophobic representation of homosexuality" in order to make the gay man's rectum a metaphorical grave for "the sacrosanct value of selfhood, a value that accounts for human beings' extraordinary willingness to kill in order to protect the seriousness of their statements."[64] Recent U.S. foreign and domestic policies, including the political responses to AIDS, must compel increasingly vigorous assent to Bersani's characterization of the fatal dangers of upholding "the sacrosanct value of selfhood." However, in appealing to the ego to solicit its own shattering, Bersani's recommendation implies a redemption of subjectivity—if not of selfhood—as such. Hence the crucial distinction we were able to make earlier, with the help of Vergetis, between a subject founded in the *ego* (the subject of speech, presented in the psychosis seminar) and a subject founded in—and therefore split by—the *unconscious* (the subject of discourse, presented in the psychosis article) disappears. Owing to Bersani's reliance on Freudian psychoanalysis and his deriving the term *jouissance* from Bataille rather than Lacan, our complex distinction between subject and ego tends to gets lost in his account. This is not so much an issue of theoretical purity as of the attempt to cure subjectivity itself.[65]

131

A Cure?

The problem of bypassing the difficulties of the unconscious by appealing to the ego devolves upon the question of the possibility of political change: Bersani's appeal is motivated by his desire to substitute psychic violence (sexual self-shattering) for social violence. Although there

63. Bersani, "Is the Rectum," 217. This idea is developed in Bersani, *The Freudian Body: Psychoanalysis and Art* (New York: Columbia University Press, 1986), in order to argue that masochism nevertheless "serves life" rather than death, since "[i]t is perhaps only because sexuality is ontologically grounded in masochism that the human organism survives the gap between the period of shattering stimuli and the development of resistant or defensive ego structures" (39).

64. Bersani, "Is the Rectum," 209, 222.

65. Bersani's account is worked out somewhat differently in *Homos* (Cambridge: Harvard University Press, 1995).

CHAPTER THREE

is not yet any cure for AIDS, we write in an effort to contribute toward a cure for sociosymbolic ills. This chapter—and, indeed, this whole book—bears a complex political intention and addresses a heterogeneous audience. In response to various impasses of conceptualization brought about by reliance on a Foucaultian, implicitly antipsychoanalytic, paradigm in gay studies and queer theory, I have tried to develop a specifically psychoanalytic perspective on AIDS and its effects. In response to a relative neglect of gay questions and an avoidance of the overwhelming cultural import of AIDS by psychoanalytically oriented thinkers, including Lacanian critics, I have tried to analyze AIDS, while at the same time reassessing the place of psychoanalysis in contemporary cultural theory. Subsequent chapters attempt to consider further the challenges of safe-sex education in relation to the death drive, and to provide a post-AIDS psychoanalytic account of same-sex desire. And, indeed, Lacan's ethic of psychoanalysis—"don't give up on your desire"—acquires special poignancy for gay men in the age of AIDS and the pernicious moralism of "just say no."

I have taken the Lacanian theory of psychosis as a model to analyze the U.S. social response to AIDS, suggesting that an identificatory signifier for AIDS has been socially foreclosed and that therefore mourning—whose psychic structure is the inverse of psychosis—remains incomplete in a particularly troubling way. Examining the compensatory efforts at social symbolization of AIDS—by ACT UP and the makers of the Quilt—I have tried to generate a new discourse for symbolizing AIDS. Against Foucaultian accounts of the "discursive constructions" of AIDS, I have argued for Lacan's theory of discourse because it takes account of the extradiscursive (the real) by inclusion within its structures of object *a* as "cause of desire." In an attempt to modify the Anglo-American misreception of Lacan as theorist of the signifier, which leads to overemphasizing the symbolic order, I have stressed his development of the concept of the real and suggested its necessity for theorizing the death drive.

My argument is that in a psychotic society we are all PWAs. The question remains: is there a cure for this, if not yet a cure for AIDS? One of Lacan's many revisions of the orthodox theory of psychosis involved demonstrating that psychosis is not untreatable via the talking cure (*E* 214). However, Lacanian psychoanalysis offers nobody a cure for subjectivity. Rather, it insists upon a confrontation with the very condition

132

of subjectivity: that the death drive inhabits our being, that death is at the heart of life, and that there is therefore something fundamentally incurable in being human. Because AIDS has become a figure for death in life, we may say that although the acronymic S stands for syndrome, a condition of the body, it stands also for the subject of the signifier, $. Living with language, we are also now, as a consequence of the political specificities of U.S. society, living with AIDS. If ACT UP sometimes made its point by writing AID$, my final suggestion must be that we are subjects of AID$.

SAFE-SEX EDUCATION
AND THE DEATH DRIVE

In recent years it has become disturbingly apparent that safe-sex education programs need all the help they can get, simply because they aren't working as effectively as they once seemed to be doing. After an initial decline in transmission rates during the eighties, the rate of infection has been climbing steadily in the very population group—urban gay men—that pioneered safe-sex education in the first place.[1] With the advent of protease inhibitors, a class of new drugs that block an enzyme crucial to viral replication, AIDS may have become—for those lucky few who can afford and tolerate the drugs—a chronic rather than terminal condition, a manageable disease rather than a death sentence. And

1. In this chapter I focus primarily on gay men's responses to safe-sex education, not because other demographic groups remain unaffected by the issues I discuss (far from it), but because the problem is most acute for gay men and most demonstrably involves complex psychical factors. For an analysis of safe-sex education differently factored by gender, race, and class, see Elisa Janine Sobo, *Choosing Unsafe Sex: AIDS-Risk Denial among Disadvantaged Women* (Philadelphia: University of Pennsylvania Press, 1995). Sobo conducted anthropological work with straight African American women in Cleveland, between 1991 and 1993, finding that the majority of these women "usually chose to forgo condoms. They did so because they did not think that they could 'catch AIDS.' Most participants believed, as do most U.S. adults, that they were simply not at risk for AIDS. Most said that AIDS is a disease that only other people get" (2–3). Transmission rates among men who have sex with men are also higher among racial and ethnic minorities; for an analysis of unsafe sex among Latino gay men, see Rafael M. Diaz, *Latino Gay Men and HIV: Culture, Sexuality, and Risk Behavior* (New York: Routledge, 1997). For a discussion of lesbians' responses to safe sex, see Sue O'Sullivan and Pratibha Parmar, *Lesbians Talk (Safer) Sex* (London: Scarlet, 1992). For one heterosexual white woman's conflicted response to safe-sex education, see Meghan Daum, "Safe-Sex Lies," *New York Times Magazine,* January 21, 1996, 32–33.

so as the interval lengthens between HIV infection and the likely onset of illness, gay men's principal deterrent for unprotected sex recedes, with potentially catastrophic implications. In this era of accelerating AIDS science and the resurgence of unsafe sexual practices, I'd like to suggest how thinking psychoanalytically about the epidemic can help us grasp both the necessity for maintaining safer sex and some new strategies for doing so.

While it is notoriously difficult to generate accurate statistics about the rate of unsafe sex among gay men, the figure *one-third* has been repeated as axiomatic since the early 1990s—"one third of gay men are having buttsex without condoms."[2] What makes such estimates so striking is that even those who "know the facts" about HIV transmission continue to become infected with the virus that causes AIDS. Much of the evidence of escalating unsafe sex has been anecdotal, circulating privately, but also publicly in the form of third-person and, more remarkably, first-person accounts in the mainstream—as well as gay— media. When, in 1994, leading gay journalist Michelangelo Signorile and then, in 1995, prominent queer theorist Michael Warner both wrote about their own recent unsafe sexual encounters, these revelations highlighted the extent to which safe-sex education was failing.[3] The problem penetrated mainstream national consciousness in 1996, thanks to a controversial *New York Times Magazine* cover story on Mark Ebenhoch, a thirtysomething, white gay man, who became HIV-positive for reasons other than simple lack of knowledge.[4] Such high-profile accounts of individual cases dramatized what epidemiological data on sero-

2. Dan Savage, "Life after AIDS," *The Stranger* (Seattle), January 16, 1997, 11. Some studies show an even higher incidence of unsafe sex—up to 50 percent—among gay men. For discussion of unsafe sex statistics, see Edward King, *Safety in Numbers: Safer Sex and Gay Men* (New York: Routledge, 1994), chap. 4; and Gabriel Rotello, *Sexual Ecology: AIDS and the Destiny of Gay Men* (New York: Dutton, 1997), chap. 5. Unsafe sex is hard to quantify, in part because the comparative safety of different sexual acts varies and therefore what counts as "unsafe" remains disputed; particular ambiguity persists concerning the relative safety of unprotected oral sex. For recent reports of escalating unsafe sex, see John Gallagher, "Slipping Up," *Advocate*, July 8, 1997, 33–34.

3. Michelangelo Signorile, "Unsafe like Me," *Out*, October 1994, 22–24, 128; Michael Warner, "Why Gay Men Are Having Risky Sex," *Village Voice*, January 31, 1995, 32–37.

4. See Jesse Green, "Flirting with Suicide," *New York Times Magazine*, September 15, 1996, 39–45, 54–55, 84–85. However, as early as April 1994, *The New York Times Magazine* had run a first-person account by an HIV-positive Generation Xer, who didn't describe unsafe sex but did announce himself as part of the "second wave" of gay seroconversions, about whom he wrote, "At this point, let's face it, we're the least innocent of 'victims'—we have no excuse, the barrage of safe sex information, the free condoms, blah blah blah . . ." See Stephen Beachy, "20+, HIV+," *New York Times Magazine*, April 17, 1994, 52–53.

conversion rates in the United States had been indicating since the early nineties—that basic information about AIDS, though indispensable, is nonetheless radically insufficient to stopping the epidemic.

Michael Warner's *Village Voice* account of anal sex without a condom threw into stark relief the degree to which intellectual sophistication and an openly gay identity are less likely to ensure the consistently successful practice of safe sex than one might have imagined. When juxtaposed with Warner's case, the various demographic strikes against Mark Ebenhoch—his disadvantaged working-class background, his lower level of formal education, the fact that he'd remained closeted for most of his life, his nonurban residence and thus his only peripheral participation in the highly developed gay subcultures that characterize major metropolitan areas in the United States—all appear less significant risk factors than safe-sex educators usually assume. Although such demographic considerations are far from negligible, they index only what one knows consciously, whereas gay men's unsafe sex has as much to do with what one actively wishes *not* to know, irrespective of education, access to information, or intellectual sophistication. This chapter attempts to clarify exactly what's at stake in recognizing that gay men's unsafe sex has less to do with lack of education than with the unconscious; that is, it has to do with not only a passion for sex, but also a passion for ignorance.[5] Before going any further, however, I should reemphasize that I understand the unconscious to be an effect of the symbolic order—a precipitate of those networks of signifiers that are culturally determined but also always inflected by subjective particularities. Thinking about AIDS in terms of the symbolic order rather than in terms of individual risk promises to illuminate how social fantasies about erotic *jouissance* guarantee safe-sex education's failure.

---

5. Explaining how the unconscious may be understood in terms of motivated nonknowledge, Lacan characterizes "ignorance as a passion" (*SI* 271). For a useful gloss on this idea, see Ellie Ragland, "The Passion of Ignorance in the Transference," in *Freud and the Passions,* ed. John O'Neill (University Park: Pennsylvania State University Press, 1996), 151–65. In an extremely interesting account of sex education in primary and secondary schools, gay teacher Jonathan Silin analyzes the education system's tacit commitment to actively producing ignorance, rather than knowledge, about sexuality and AIDS. This system churns out young people who don't simply lack information concerning sexuality but instead are predisposed to resist confronting the difficulties sexuality entails—a resistance that helps account for both their unsafe sex and their confounding response to gay safe-sex educational material, which comes at a tertiary stage, after a certain dynamic of motivated ignorance has been established. See Jonathan G. Silin, *Sex, Death, and the Education of Children: Our Passion for Ignorance in the Age of AIDS* (New York: Teachers College, 1995).

Dying for It

Sex without barriers is important to gay men even if it threatens our lives.

—Tony Valenzuela

In view of statistics on new seroconversions, some AIDS educators have begun to acknowledge that, unlikely though it may seem, remaining HIV-negative in fact poses significant psychological challenges to gay men. For example, a newspaper advertisement for the San Francisco AIDS Foundation explicitly addresses HIV-negative gay men presumed to be putting themselves at risk. Headlined *"Sex"* and picturing a rueful-looking black bodybuilder, the text of the ad runs:

> You don't know how or why it happened again, but it did and it does. And then you wake up and the anxiety starts in on you. The realization that you didn't catch his name, let alone a detailed description of his past. The fleeting recollection that any idea of protection was most likely lost to desire. And without someone to talk to, this seesaw struggle between passion and prudence is all you have to look forward to.

This ad could not have been produced earlier in the epidemic, during the eighties, because it explicitly assumes that gay men still are having anonymous, unprotected sex on a regular basis and, furthermore, that they don't really know why they're doing it ("You don't know how or why it happened again"). While the reference to "fleeting recollection" might allude to the fact that most unsafe sex happens under the influence of alcohol or drugs, it also acknowledges that not only one's motives for risking unprotected sex but also the event itself remain barely accessible to consciousness.[6] Given such circumstances, the ad accurately assumes the futility of mandating condom use for every sexual encounter, which was the standard message of earlier safe-sex education. Instead,

137

6. To the fact that perhaps the majority of unsafe sex occurs under the influence of alcohol and other drugs should be added the qualification that it occurs also under the influence of the unconscious. For a report on the relationship between unsafe sex and drugs, see David Heitz, "Men Behaving Badly," *Advocate,* July 8, 1997, 26–29. In his blistering critique of monogamy, writer Edmund White refers to "the fact that the leading cause of unsafe sex was the 25% rate of alcoholism among gays"; see White, "What Century Is This Anyway?" *Advocate,* June 23, 1998, 58. For a useful account of the role of drugs, especially crystal-methamphetamine, in unsafe sex, see Douglas Sadownick, *Sex between Men: An Intimate History of the Sex Lives of Gay Men, Postwar to Present* (New York: HarperCollins, 1996), esp. 229–34.

recommending only that its addressee "begin a dialog," this ad comes close to implying that psychoanalysis really can help safe-sex education, since blanket admonitions to "Just Say No" or "Use Condoms Every Time" are impossibly idealistic and therefore remain ineffective.

Given that moralizing slogans have failed to achieve their ostensible aims, it may be useful to distinguish psychoanalytic from pedagogic techniques, in order to make clear that a psychoanalytic account of safe-sex education does not entail advocating a Lacanian version of social engineering. Although Freud linked psychoanalysis with education as one of the "impossible professions," he also stressed crucial differences between the two. Warning prospective analysts about the "temptation aris[ing] out of the educative activity which, in psychoanalytic treatment, devolves on the doctor without any deliberate intention on his part," Freud insisted that "educative ambition is of as little as therapeutic ambition" (SE 12:118–19). Both therapeutic and educative ambitions are incompatible with psychoanalysis, as Freud conceived it, because both substitute an imposition of the analyst's norms for any engagement with the analysand's unconscious. As Lacan points out, those who conceptualize analysis in terms of "an emotional re-education of the patient" "end up forcing [psychoanalysis] in the direction of the exercise of power" (E 226; 250). To treat psychoanalysis as simply a special kind of education would be to reduce analysis to suggestion in an ethically suspect manner that would justify the otherwise misguided critiques of psychoanalysis by commentators such as Mikkel Borch-Jacobsen, whose work is devoted to demolishing any tenable distinction between psychoanalysis and suggestion or hypnotism.[7]

On the contrary, it is precisely what distinguishes psychoanalysis from any psychology of education—its account of the unconscious—that enables psychoanalysis to help safe-sex education. AIDS educators are confronting the life-and-death stakes of Freud's insight that "the sexual instincts . . . are peculiarly resistant to external influences" (SE 18:40). This difficulty doesn't simply entail the psychological problem of subjective desire resisting external constraints—which is, after all, a familiar enough story. Rather, the peculiarity of this difficulty lies in

138

---

7. Mikkel Borch-Jacobsen, The Emotional Tie: Psychoanalysis, Mimesis, Affect, trans. Douglas Brick (Stanford: Stanford University Press, 1993); and Borch-Jacobsen, Remembering Anna O: A Century of Mystification, trans. Kirby Olson (New York: Routledge, 1996). On Borch-Jacobsen's tendency to reduce all phenomena to the imaginary level, see my critique in chapter 1.

the resistance internal to desire itself. As I began to explain in the previous chapter, this internal resistance stems from intolerance for one's "own" excess *jouissance* in the Other. Yet owing to the implicit psychological assumption that resistance is always only external—it comes from malignant others rather than from the self-division introduced by the Other—safe-sex education remains ill equipped to deal with the ways in which people often fail to act in their own interests. Divorcing an account of sexual practices from the unconscious and the death drive leaves you with merely a commonsensical, conflict-free notion of pleasure and desire.[8]

Returning to Unsafe Sex

People always lie to themselves about this disease.

—Hervé Guibert

Most people can't comprehend why anyone would risk death for a good fuck. From a certain viewpoint, unsafe sex appears as inconceivably self-destructive behavior. Indeed, while such health-threatening practices as smoking, drinking, and drug abuse must be indulged repeatedly over a substantial period before they are likely to cause harm, HIV infection can result from a single unprotected encounter. Casual, anonymous sex without a condom seems suicidal—hence the title of Jesse Green's *New York Times Magazine* article on the issue, "Flirting with Suicide."

However, from another perspective the risk of unprotected gay sex is minimal. Far less addictive than smoking, drinking, or drugs, unsafe sex actually carries a low risk of HIV infection in any given encounter, even if your partner is seropositive. The blood-borne human immunodeficiency virus is so comparatively difficult to transmit from one person to another that you can have unprotected anal sex dozens of times—and oral sex even more frequently—before there is an overwhelming

---

8. It is necessary to reiterate this distinction between the psychical and psychological because the term *unconscious* commonly designates so many incompatible ideas as to be virtually useless without further conceptual specification. For example, in his otherwise insightful account of contemporary gay sexual practices, *Sex between Men,* Douglas Sadownick routinely notes that "[s]ex often is a matter for the unconscious" (5) and "desire is an unconscious manifestation" (216); yet what he means by *unconscious* turns out to be a thoroughly psychological notion involving inner depth, shadowy doubles, and archetypes. Similar problems abound in the ostensibly psychoanalytic account of contemporary gay sexuality provided in Guy Kettelhack, *Dancing around the Volcano: Freeing Our Erotic Lives: Decoding the Enigma of Gay Men and Sex* (New York: Crown, 1996).

risk of becoming infected.[9] Furthermore, an HIV-positive diagnosis today is much less likely to be a death sentence than previously. Although in the early years of the epidemic most people with AIDS died fairly rapidly, usually only months after diagnosis, these days one can expect a decade—possibly two or three—to elapse before a newly infected man in North America becomes symptomatic for AIDS. And even before protease inhibitors, there was evidence of people with AIDS surviving many years longer than the typical, short-term prognosis.[10] In his memoir, porn actor–turned–writer Scott O'Hara estimates that he became infected with HIV around 1981, at the very beginning of the epidemic; yet "I'm in pretty good health fifteen years later," he claims.[11] Thus from the perspective of a young gay man aged, say, twenty-five today, the prospect of chronic or even terminal illness at, say, age forty-five can appear so remote as to offer no deterrent to unsafe sex at all, especially given his individual odds against infection. And in view of American culture's emphasis on youthfulness, which gay subculture reinforces, the prospect of not having to endure middle age thanks to AIDS may positively encourage sexual recklessness. As one seropositive gay man put it, "I may die at a younger age than my gay brothers who are more cautious, who limit the number of their sexual contacts, and than my straight brothers who, presumably, are rigidly monogamous. And you know something? I decided a long time ago that it is worth it."[12]

Unfortunately, this kind of implicit cost-benefit analysis completely misses the point that unsafe sex is a social activity as well as a question of individual decision making. Unlike other risky behaviors such as smoking, drinking, and substance abuse (which arguably can be indulged as solitary pursuits), unsafe sex always directly involves somebody else. The problem with unsafe sex—as Gabriel Rotello's important book, *Sexual Ecology,* makes clear—is not only that people often fail to act individually in their own interests, but also that gay men practicing unsafe sex are failing to act collectively in the interests of gay men as

9. See Rotello, *Sexual Ecology,* 240.

10. See Michael Callen, *Surviving AIDS* (New York: HarperCollins, 1990).

11. Scott O'Hara, *Autopornography: A Memoir of Life in the Lust Lane* (New York: Harrington Park, 1997), 129.

12. Scott O'Hara, "Safety First?" *Advocate,* July 8, 1997, 9. In fact, O'Hara died on February 18, 1998, age thirty-six, from AIDS-related lymphoma, in San Francisco.

a group. *Sexual Ecology,* a controversial study of sexual politics and AIDS epidemiology, has become something of a litmus test for members of the gay community. Though I discuss Rotello's work in greater detail below, for now I would like simply to register that in Lacanian terms gay men's unsafe sex had been considered only imaginarily, in individual terms, until Rotello came along. But his idea of "sexual ecology" enables us to grasp unsafe sex *symbolically,* in terms of the complex web of relations that mediate any sex act.

Rotello's controversial discussion broadens the perspective on unsafe sex in such a way that the function of the Other in this problem can be taken into account. In other words, *Sexual Ecology* provides the means whereby we may appreciate the truly psychoanalytic, rather than psychological, dimension of unsafe sex. However, as I elaborate at the end of this chapter, Rotello's solution to the problem is limited by his biologically derived notion of "cultural adaptation," which reobscures the dimension of the Other and therefore prevents Rotello from fully realizing the radical potential of his own account. By way of Lacan's distinction between the Other's *jouissance* and others' pleasure, I shall suggest some alternative solutions to the difficulties of practicing safe sex. Given the extreme reactions to *Sexual Ecology,* especially in the gay community, I should perhaps make clear at this point that I neither embrace nor reject wholesale Rotello's account. The normalizing implications of his proposed solutions, though meriting critique, unfortunately do not invalidate Rotello's analysis of the problem of unsafe sex—a distinction that many queer theorists seem unable to make.

In order to see just how novel Rotello's approach is, we need first to consider the paradox that although most cultural-studies work on AIDS is framed in explicitly social and political terms, such analyses tend to remain at the imaginary level. Theoretical accounts of unsafe sex by progressive critics such as Edward King, Cindy Patton, and Simon Watney unwittingly repeat—albeit in inverted form—the binary polarization of innocence and guilt that has typified public discourse on AIDS since the epidemic began. From a Lacanian perspective, this style of attributing responsibility for AIDS primarily to *either* gay men *or* the powers-that-be is imaginary and therefore dangerously delusive. For example, King argues that "gay men's practice of unsafe sex is best understood not from the individualistic perspective of 'relapse' theory, but by an attention to the actions—or inactions—of AIDS educators.

Any 'relapse' which has occurred has, ironically, been on the part of those charged with responsibility for HIV prevention, who have largely neglected their duties to gay men during the AIDS crisis."[13] Writing from London, King accuses the British government of genocidal neglect in much the same way as Patton's latest account of unsafe sex blames the U.S. government and mainstream media, which she claims together generated an insidious "national pedagogy."[14] Although the record on AIDS of both nations' ruling parties, especially Thatcher's and Reagan's, was nothing less than appalling in ways that cultural-studies analyses have helped us fully appreciate, the inversion of responsibility and blame that typifies such analyses is profoundly unhelpful. To see how this pervasive rhetoric of blame misrecognizes—and thus obscures—the interconnecting web of sociosymbolic relations within which unsafe sex occurs, we need only respond to King's contention by asking: Aren't gay men "AIDS educators" and among those "charged with responsibility for HIV prevention" too?

While most of the discussion in cultural studies about AIDS has focused on the ideological roadblocks that impede frank, socially aware safe-sex education programs, much less attention has been given to what makes safe sex psychically difficult. Thinking about AIDS psychoanalytically doesn't involve conceptualizing unsafe sex in individual rather than social terms, or treating the social on the model of the individual, as some critics charge. Instead it requires us to acknowledge that social relations cannot be grasped without taking psychical processes into account, and vice versa. In this context, the problem with conceiving subjectivity either psychologically or sociologically is that unsafe sex ends up being explained primarily as a function of homophobia. For example, Patton's new book, *Fatal Advice: How Safe-Sex Education Went Wrong,* theorizes subjectivity as an effect of membership in any number of overlapping and mutually exclusive social categories. When subjectivity becomes a question of "subject-positions," psychic life inevitably gets reduced to an epiphenomenon of social and cultural dictates, with gay men's failure to consistently practice safe sex being rationalized in terms of the discrimination we face from a profoundly normalizing society.

13. King, *Safety in Numbers,* 163.

14. Cindy Patton, *Fatal Advice: How Safe-Sex Education Went Wrong* (Durham: Duke University Press, 1996).

This position was articulated most dramatically by the late gay film critic Vito Russo, in a speech he gave at an ACT UP rally in May 1988:

> I'm here to speak out today as a PWA who is not dying *from*— but for the last three years quite successfully living *with*—AIDS . . . If I'm dying from anything it's from homophobia. If I'm dying from anything it's from racism. If I'm dying from anything it's from indifference and red tape. If I'm dying from anything I'm dying from Jesse Helms. If I'm dying from anything I'm dying from Ronald Reagan. If I'm dying from anything I'm dying from the sensationalism of newspapers and magazines and television shows.[15]

Russo's powerful rhetoric points to the epidemic's intense politicization in the United States, making clear that AIDS involves far more than complex biomedical issues. While it was crucial in the eighties to emphasize how social forces such as homophobia and racism exacerbated the epidemic, it is foolhardy now to maintain that prejudice represents the principal impediment to effective AIDS prevention. Yet this assumption continues to pervade virtually all progressive discourse on safe-sex education, generating the fantasy that once we fine-tune educational techniques to take exhaustive account of the multiple demographic variables involved, then—together with adequate funding and thorough dissemination of this finely calibrated educational material—the safe-sex message will take hold and the epidemic can be eradicated. And while it isn't hard to see how the intense desirability of ending AIDS encourages commentators to convert critical analysis into wish fulfillment, this well-meaning educational fantasy amounts to little more than a sophisticated form of denial when put in the context of rising sero-conversion rates.

However, there is a more psychoanalytic way of reading Russo's rhetoric, one that would emphasize how cultural, inorganic phenomena can increase one's vulnerability to illness. As one of safe-sex education's

143

15. Vito Russo, "A Test of Who We Are as a People," in *Democracy: A Project by Group Material,* ed. Brian Wallis (Seattle: Bay Press, 1990), 299. A 1987 British pamphlet made the same point almost as baldly as Russo: "The climate of guilt, secrecy, and fear that surrounds much homosexual activity in Britain creates the conditions in which the AIDS virus can flourish. It is the *oppression of homosexuals* that allows HIV infection to spread among gay men. Hence, the way to stop the spread of AIDS is neither to pretend that it is a threat to heterosexuals, nor to make futile exhortations to gays, but rather to challenge *every* act of discrimination or harassment directed against homosexuals." See Michael Fitzpatrick and Don Milligan, *The Truth about the AIDS Panic* (London: Junius, 1987), 36.

originators put it, "The children's rhyme is wrong: Just like sticks and stones, words *can* harm us."[16] The symbolic order impacts human bodies both positively and negatively—albeit never directly or with a one-to-one correspondence. Indeed, Lacanian clinical practice is based on the insight that since the symbolic order can literally make you sick, words—or the right combination of signifiers—can also make you well. Lacanian psychoanalyst Luce Irigaray has pointed out that this is particularly the case for disorders such as AIDS that affect the immune system (even though it would be misleading to characterize acquired immunodeficiency syndrome as a strictly psychosomatic illness):

> [P]eople don't just become ill out of the blue. For the whole of a body to be affected, its equilibrium must have already been disrupted. That's true for all illnesses. It's painfully obvious for illnesses said to be of the immune system. But all illnesses are, in fact, since being ill comes down to being unable to distance oneself from pathogenic agents.
>
> So why do we have this proliferation of terminal illnesses at a period of civilization as developed as ours? My hypothesis is that it's this very civilization that continuously submits our minds and bodies to stresses and strains and thus gradually destroys our immune systems. I'm surprised doctors aren't saying this.[17]

What psychoanalysis adds to an anthropological understanding of the cultural construction of disease is an account of the unconscious that explains how the repertoire and arrangement of signifiers within any given culture—particularly the identificatory potency with which these signifiers are invested—affects not only the body politic but human bodies too. In the previous chapter, I suggested that despite what Paula Treichler calls "an epidemic of signification" surrounding the biomedical epidemic, we have not seen an identificatory signifier, or S1, by which the suffering and deaths of hundreds of thousands of gay men, non-whites, and other socially marginalized groups could achieve positive significance. Indeed, I argued that such a signifier remained forcibly foreclosed from the national symbolic and that therefore the United

144

16. Callen, *Surviving AIDS*, 52.

17. Luce Irigaray, *Je, Tu, Nous: Toward a Culture of Difference,* trans. Alison Martin (New York: Routledge, 1993), 62.

States' response to AIDS could be characterized clinically as psychotic, with all the pathological implications of collective psychosis.

However, the course of the biomedical epidemic and of the discourses surrounding it have not remained constant. It is very much to the credit of Quilt makers, ACT UP, and other kinds of AIDS activists that U.S. discourse on AIDS has changed and that the range of identificatory signifiers available within public discourse has expanded. Yet so much effort has been invested in changing the meaning of disease, of seropositivity, and of latex that in some quarters—that is, within some symbolic universes—PWA (Person with AIDS) has become a *desirable* identity, as if it were part of one's political obligation as a gay man to join the ranks of the HIV-positive. Hence by this point in the history of the epidemic it is crucial to examine the identificatory signifiers available within gay subculture to understand why safe-sex education isn't working as intended. This may be hard to do without appearing to embark on one more round of "blaming the victim." But I consider that risk preferable over the risks gay men continue to take during unprotected sex.

Insofar as gay AIDS-prevention education has focused primarily on "eroticizing safer sex" (by representing condoms as arousing rather than inhibiting), we have been reluctant to admit that death holds an erotic lure too. As Stephen Beachy, speaking for the "second wave" of gay seroconversions, commented, "Maybe the image of death, a dark, sexy man in black, is something we find exciting."[18] It has been very tough for safe-sex educators to acknowledge that the process of eroticizing condom use as a technique of disease prevention inadvertently connects condoms with death—an association that not only may discourage their use but also may shroud AIDS-related death in an erotic patina.[19] In the process of transforming latex from a heterosexual to a homosexual symbol, we have also transformed some of our fear of death into desire, such that the enormous social problem of "denial" surrounding AIDS is now exacerbated by positive identification with—even idealiza-

18. Beachy, "20+, HIV+," 52.

19. For an example of this new genre of AIDS erotica, in which the thrill depends on having completely unsafe sex in a hospital bed with somebody very close to death from AIDS, see the story "How Scott O'Hara Fucked Me . . . and Vice Versa . . . ," in *Black Sheets* 13 (1998): 14–15. *Black Sheets* is a San Francisco queer sex 'zine whose issue number 13 is titled "Unsafe!" and explores various forms of risky sex.

tion of—seropositivity.[20] The gay community's insistence on producing "positive images" of people with AIDS in order to counter the mainstream media's circulation of homophobic stereotypes has had the unforeseen consequence of lending seropositive gay bodies a certain glamour. And everybody knows that glamour, no matter how improbable its source, is almost as important to gay men as sex.

AIDS as an Identity

> Now more than ever seems it rich to die.
>
> —John Keats

Consider the case of the late Pedro Zamora, a very young, good-looking Latino gay man who first came to prominence on MTV's *Real World* and who, during the course of that television show, came out not only as gay but also as HIV-positive. Zamora quickly became a spokesman, a role model, an accomplished educator, and a poster boy for AIDS within the gay community. Akin to what Magic Johnson represents for many young African American men, Pedro Zamora became a subcultural hero, an ego ideal, someone with whom to identify. As one twentysomething, HIV-negative gay man reported after reading an interview with Zamora in a gay magazine on which he was the cover model:

> Matt and I were sitting around reading the interview with him, and talking about how hot he is. And Matt said to me, "I'd like to be exactly like him—he's got everything a queer queen could want. He's got it made." And I said, "Yeah, but he's got AIDS too." And Matt said, "So what? A lot of guys have AIDS. I mean, he wouldn't

20. Clinical psychologist Walt Odets observes that "[i]n the AIDS epidemic we find not only gay men identified with people with HIV. We also find lesbians and large numbers of heterosexual health care providers whose personal sacrifices are so great that we must assume some psychological identification, perhaps unconscious, with gay men" (*In the Shadow of the Epidemic: Being HIV-Negative in the Age of AIDS* [Durham: Duke University Press, 1995], 207). For one lesbian caregiver's narrative of identification with PWAs, see Rebecca Brown, *The Gifts of the Body* (New York: HarperCollins, 1994). Since no identity—least of all a nonheterosexual one—is pregiven but instead entails dynamical processes of identification, the psychical function of idealization in gay subculture warrants further investigation. For an extensive critique of current gay ideals, see Michelangelo Signorile, *Life Outside: The Signorile Report on Gay Men: Sex, Drugs, Muscles, and the Passages of Life* (New York: HarperCollins, 1997). For a powerful account of idealization, see Kaja Silverman, *The Threshold of the Visible World* (New York: Routledge, 1996).

be where he is if he didn't have AIDS. He'd be hot, but that's a dime a dozen. Guys who have AIDS get a lot more attention."[21]

In Matt's articulation of incompatible ideas that "exist side by side without being influenced by one another, and are exempt from mutual contradiction," we can see evidence of the unconscious (*SE* 14:186). Zamora's serostatus doesn't qualify his ego-ideal status, according to Matt, because "[a] lot of guys have AIDS"—it's too common to make any difference. But then he suggests the opposite: since good looks are too common a distinction, it's only the seropositive men who "get a lot more attention." On one hand, I needn't worry about AIDS because it's now so endemic as not to stigmatize me; while on the other hand, having AIDS is sufficiently uncommon as to set me apart in a positive light. Matt's reasoning is unsettling not only because of its inconsistent logic, but also because he appears oblivious to the real consequences of seroconversion. Yet this too registers his words' unconscious determination, since the unconscious "does not believe in its own death; it behaves as if it were immortal" (*SE* 14:296).[22]

147

One way of accounting for gay men's willingness to experiment with unsafe sex is to examine how AIDS has become a new cultural identity. Although "coming out" as a person with AIDS entails considerable costs, it nonetheless earns you a quite prominent place in the symbolic order. Acronyms such as *PWA, HIV+,* and *HIV–* now designate highly charged sociosymbolic identities; indeed, AIDS has become so associated with gay identity in the West that HIV-positive men tend to be considered gayer than their seronegative counterparts. Unfortunately, seropositivity has become the final ingredient in a complete gay identity. As Jesse Green reported in the *New York Times Magazine,* several young men "expressed to me the feeling that they would get AIDS no matter what they did; why even try to be safe? For them, ghoulish as it sounds, contracting the disease seemed almost like a rite of initiation into the gay community."[23] This fatal identification ignores the slogan activists

---

21. Cited in Odets, *In the Shadow of the Epidemic,* 223.

22. Freud continues by explaining that the disbelief in death and the exemption from mutual contradiction stem from the same primary process characteristic: "What we call our 'unconscious' . . . knows nothing that is negative, and no negation; in it contradictories coincide. For that reason it does not know its own death, for to that we can give only a negative content. Thus there is nothing instinctual in us which responds to a belief in death" (*SE* 14:296).

23. Green, "Flirting with Suicide," 43.

tirelessly reiterated throughout the eighties—*AIDS is not a gay disease,* in that you don't have to be gay to get it and being gay won't make you sick (gayness makes homophobes, not homosexuals, sick). However, it has become increasingly clear that AIDS *is* a gay disease in the Western world, insofar as gay men continue to be hardest hit and the heterosexual epidemic that was predicted for the West has not materialized.[24]

The consequences of AIDS becoming so central to gay identity have been investigated by clinical psychologists such as Walt Odets, a charismatic therapist who works primarily with gay men in Berkeley, and who has become notorious for insisting that safe-sex education should stop addressing seropositive and seronegative gay men in the same breath, as if both groups occupied indistinguishable or interchangeable positions. Diagnosing a psychic malaise that remained largely hidden behind the biomedical construction of the epidemic, Odets points out that "being gay and being uninfected is now *a condition,* not the absence of one."[25] One legacy of Odets's work is the San Francisco AIDS Foundation advertisement I described above, which specifically addresses seronegative gay men. Putting a sexually attractive man in this ad is part of the new effort to convert being an HIV-negative gay man into a desirable rather than a deficient identity, to wrench it from the register of cultural oxymoron.

What makes this task so unexpectedly strenuous is not simply glamorized images of seropositive men such as Zamora, but also the imaginary lure of guaranteed closure that death offers. Any identity that confers certitude—the less doubt the better—is narcissistically very appealing, as Andrew Sullivan acknowledged when describing his struggle to resist both "the emotional satisfaction of being cured and the emotional closure of death itself."[26] In fact, the imaginary satisfaction

24. Some left-wing gay commentators have acknowledged that Michael Fumento's right-wing critique of predictions about a major epidemic among non-IV-drug-using heterosexuals in the West, in *The Myth of Heterosexual AIDS* (New York: Basic Books, 1990), turned out to be accurate—at least in its epidemiological analysis, if not in its politics (see King, *Safety in Numbers,* 237–41, and Rotello, *Sexual Ecology,* chap. 7).

25. Odets, *In the Shadow of the Epidemic,* 15; original emphasis. For one East Coast therapist's account of the psychological processes through which HIV-positive men negotiate identifications with AIDS, see Steven Schwartzberg, *A Crisis of Meaning: How Gay Men Are Making Sense of AIDS* (New York: Oxford University Press, 1996). See also the roundtable discussion led by New York therapists Michael Shernoff and Steven Ball, "Sex, Secrets, and Lies," *Out,* April 1997, 104–6, 144–47.

26. Andrew Sullivan, "When Plagues End: Notes on the Twilight of an Epidemic," *New York Times Magazine,* November 10, 1996, 52–62, 76–77, 84.

of death may outweigh that of cure, since in many respects death's script is far less equivocal than the myriad possibilities opened up by protease inhibitors. These new drugs promise dramatically improved prognoses for those who are HIV-positive, but they also threaten the subjective identities that AIDS has conferred on gay men; they therefore have considerable *psychical* side effects. What Seattle sex columnist Dan Savage dubs the Lazarus Syndrome—"Men and women who were near death just a few short months ago are now running marathons, dumping boyfriends, being dumped by boyfriends who'd been quietly looking forward to being widows, and checking out of hospices"—is profoundly destabilizing.[27] Hence Sullivan's reaction to learning about protease inhibitors: "When you have spent years girding yourself for the possibility of death, it is not so easy to gird yourself for the possibility of life."[28] Discussing this new chapter in the history of the epidemic, Savage acknowledged that "[a]nticipating grief—fantasizing about your own death, or the death of a loved one—has an element of heady pleasure to it. I walked home absorbed in a fantasy about [my lover's] death."[29]

27. Savage, "Life after AIDS," 8.

28. Sullivan, "When Plagues End," 76. Sullivan also describes the range of subjective responses to this morphing AIDS tempo:

> And even now, among friends, there are those who refuse to be tested for a virus that, thanks to the new treatments, might be eliminated from the bloodstream. And there are those who are HIV-positive who are still waiting to take the drugs and are somehow unable to relinquish the notion that being positive is a death sentence that they can endure only alone. And there are those many who, having taken all the drugs they can, have found that for some reason the drugs will not work for them and watch as their friends recover while they still sink into the morass of sickness made all the more bitter by the good news around them. And those more who, sensing an abatement of the pressure, have returned, almost manically, to unsafe sexual behavior, as if terrified by the thought that they might actually survive, that the plague might end and with it the solidarity that made it endurable. (58)

29. Savage, "Life after AIDS," 9. Commenting on the resistance to relinquishing fatal identifications, Savage adds:

> Change is scary, and we are entering a period of change that involves not just the facts of this particular virus, or of one particular sex act, but the identities gay men have constructed around AIDS in order to survive: HIV-negative, HIV-positive, PWA, AIDS activist, AIDS educator, service provider, fundraiser. What do these roles mean anymore? Are they still relevant? What does it mean to be a "Person with AIDS" who isn't sick, or to be HIV-positive when no trace of virus can be found in your blood? What does it mean to have "unsafe" sex if you're not risking death? How are these new realities going to affect not just our sex lives, but every other aspect of our lives? (11)

These are exactly the right questions to be asking, since their subjective effects are widely discernible—even though few gay men are confronting them as frankly as Savage and Sullivan. Refusing to either endorse wholesale or demonize these critical voices, I should add that I'm in substantial sympathy with at least one queer critique of Sullivan, which reads his "When Plagues End" rather

The way in which death's terminus can provide a stable point of identification and thus function as a gay ego-ideal helps explain the relief so many men express upon learning they have seroconverted. "I felt better the moment I learned I had AIDS," declares Hervé Guibert's protagonist, anticipating more recent interview findings among U.S. gay men.[30] Mark Ebenhoch echoed this counterintuitive response when he discovered he'd tested positive:

> In a way it's a relief . . . I don't have to wonder anymore. That awful waiting is gone. So now, if I do find someone, the relationship can be 100 percent real with nothing in the way. That's what I want: 100 percent natural, wholesome and real. Maybe now that I'm HIV-positive, I can finally have my life.[31]

150

Ebenhoch's dream of a relationship "with nothing in the way" ostensibly alludes to both latex barriers and the problem of "serodiscordant" relationships, in which only one partner is HIV-negative.[32] I think the widespread antipathy toward condoms is not fully explicable by reference only to the differences in physical sensation that a latex barrier introduces. Indeed, aversion to condoms suggests that the physical barrier may stand for other obstacles to connection. The condom becomes the synecdoche for all the forms of mediation and incommensurability implied in Lacan's axiom that "there is no sexual relationship"—hence the pervasive fantasy that imaginary, symbolic, and real

differently than I do. See Phillip Brian Harper, "Gay Male Identities, Personal Privacy, and Relations of Public Exchange: Notes on Directions for Queer Critique," *Social Text*, 52/53, vol. 15, no. 3/4 (1997): 5–29.

30. Hervé Guibert, *To the Friend Who Did Not Save My Life*, trans. Linda Coverdale (New York: High Risk, 1994), 37. Guibert—writer, artist, and photographer—was France's foremost AIDS novelist at his death in 1991. His roman à clef *To the Friend Who Did Not Save My Life* (1990) tells the story of its author's life with AIDS via the screen of Foucault's experience with AIDS. Much of what we know about the end of Foucault's life comes from this powerful and scandalous book, whose motivating conceit—"that I would become, by an extraordinary stroke of luck, one of the first people on earth to survive this deadly malady" (1)—reads even more poignantly in the age of protease inhibitors. For a good account of Guibert's significance, see Emily Apter, "Fantom Images: Hervé Guibert and the Writing of 'Sida' in France," in *Writing AIDS: Gay Literature, Language, and Analysis*, ed. Timothy F. Murphy and Suzanne Poirier (New York: Columbia University Press, 1993), 83–97. See Schwartzberg, *A Crisis of Meaning*, 48–51, for testimony by U.S. gay men concerning similar relief upon discovering their own seropositivity.

31. Green, "Flirting with Suicide," 85.

32. On serodiscordant relationships, see Dudley Clendinen, "When Negative Meets Positive," *Gentlemen's Quarterly*, October 1994, 236–39, 265.

impediments to relationship may be overcome by fucking without protection.

This dangerous fantasy has become a staple element of much phone sex in a way that suggests the psychical importance of overriding barriers through sex:

> I have talked to other men through phone sex lines who have also eroticized unprotected anal sex. By this I do not mean that they simply like to talk about having anal sex and don't include the ritualistic putting on of the condom as part of the fantasy. I am speaking about men who find it exciting to consciously not use protection, and to articulate, often repeatedly, that condoms are not going to be used and that sperm is going to enter the anal tract. One man shared his fantasies, which focus on forcing me to have unprotected intercourse: he likes me to beg him to use a condom and then he refuses. Sometimes he enjoys telling me that he will use one and then not following through on his promise. I find this exciting as well.[33]

It is certainly the case that fantasy and phone sex represent the safest kinds of sex available and, moreover, that fantasies regularly involve scenarios their fantasists wouldn't necessarily want to enact. Yet by confirming the degree to which all sex is a question of fantasy as well as of practices, Eric Rofes's testimony suggests the limits of technological solutions (such as latex barriers) to unsafe sex, since these address sexual practices without fully taking account of sexual fantasy. Phone sex represents a different kind of technological solution to the danger of exchanging bodily fluids, in that the phone line serves as both a means of access and a barrier—one that the fantasy of abandoning condoms is designed to overcome. And so while phone sex is certainly safe sex in every isolated instance of its practice, I nevertheless remain troubled by this fantasy's projecting onto condoms the mediation that symbolic existence necessitates in all human relationships, since symbolic mediation may be circumvented only in the real—a risky venture in the age of AIDS.

One proposed solution to this problem is seroconcordance—having

---

33. Eric Rofes, *Reviving the Tribe: Regenerating Gay Men's Sexuality and Culture in the Ongoing Epidemic* (New York: Harrington Park, 1996), 170.

sex only with partners of the same HIV status. This idea gave rise to the Australian doctrine of "negotiated safety," in which you abandon latex only after a series of timed HIV tests, when you're sure your partner is seronegative.[34] But this idea also plays into the fantasy of overcoming all barriers to sexual relationship—or, more precisely, the fantasy of *using sex* to overcome constitutive barriers to intimate relations. Since negotiated safety attempts to eliminate or minimize uncertainty, its logic may prompt the ostensibly counterintuitive conclusion that seroconversion itself represents a solution to the difficulties of practicing safe sex—"In a way it's a relief . . . I don't have to wonder anymore. That awful waiting is gone . . ."[35]

The elimination of uncertainty—and hence anxiety—that seroconversion brings may be understood psychoanalytically as reducing the traumatic threat of the real, since the prospect of death narrows the real to a single, identifiable point on the horizon. While this prospect may itself be regarded with anxiety, many find comfort in the constraints imposed by a strictly measured death narrative, which evacuates living of its contingencies. As Guibert's narrator muses:

> I was afraid this new pact with fate might upset the slow advance—which was rather soothing, actually—of inevitable death. Jules had once said to me, at a time when he didn't believe we were infected, that AIDS was a marvelous disease. And it's true that I was discovering something sleek and dazzling in its hideousness, for though it was certainly an inexorable illness, it wasn't immediately catastrophic, it was an illness in stages, a very long flight of steps that led assuredly to death, but whose every step represented a unique apprenticeship. It was a disease that gave death time to live and its victims time to die, time to discover time, and in the end to discover life, so in a way those green monkeys of Africa had provided us with a brilliant modern invention.[36]

34. For an analysis of safe-sex education in Australia, see B. R. Simon Rosser, *Male Homosexual Behavior and the Effects of AIDS Education: A Study of Behavior and Safer Sex in New Zealand and South Australia* (New York: Praeger, 1991). For descriptions of negotiated safety procedure, see Rotello, *Sexual Ecology,* 190–92, and Signorile, *Life Outside,* 313–15.

35. Green, "Flirting with Suicide," 85. See also O'Hara, *Autopornography,* 129–30.

36. Guibert, *To the Friend,* 164.

By conferring a "death sentence," AIDS paradoxically provides its sub-jects with a life story, a symbolic narrative in several versions.[37] And by altering one's relation to time, seroconversion promises a subjective transformation analogous to those held out by other conversion narra-tives, whose before-and-after dichotomies imaginarize symbolic tem-porality.[38]

Here we should distinguish the conversion narrative—which speed-ily replaces your ego with an updated one—from the more arduous process of subjective change that psychoanalysis offers. Although the crisis status of HIV prevention has encouraged us to slot AIDS into conversion narratives that promise quick-fix, imaginary solutions, AIDS activists are beginning to realize that halting the epidemic may necessi-tate more thoroughgoing social changes than were previously antici-pated. The kind of social transformation required resembles more the hard-won change psychoanalysis brings than the polarized before-and-after shots we find so seductive in myths of conversion. Thus having examined the imaginary and symbolic identifications that make one more liable to practice unsafe sex, I want now to consider Gabriel Ro-tello's thesis that stemming the epidemic requires fundamental alter-ations in the very definition of what it means to be gay. Although Rotello provides no fully satisfactory solutions to the problem he diagnoses, *Sexual Ecology* does point in the direction of more thoroughgoing changes

153

---

37. Guibert confirms the power of this symbolic narrative when, toward the end of *To the Friend,* he declares:

> I've decided to be calm, to follow to the end this novelistic logic that so hypnotizes me, at the expense of all idea of survival. Yes, I can write it, and that's undoubtedly what my madness is—I care more for my book than for my life, I won't give up my book to save my life, and that's what's going to be the most difficult thing to make people believe and understand. (237)

His "novelistic logic" is that of the symbolic order, which confers not only a "second death" but also a second life beyond that of the body. This second life is in some sense more precious than biological survival, because although organic death is guaranteed to everyone, symbolic life isn't.

38. The relation between the biomedical and subjective temporalities of AIDS deserves more extensive consideration than I'm able to provide here. Further investigation would need to take account of the important philosophical (primarily Heideggerean) meditation on the temporality of AIDS provided by Alexander García Düttmann, *At Odds with AIDS: Thinking and Talking about a Virus,* trans. Peter Gilgen and Conrad Scott-Curtis (Stanford: Stanford University Press, 1996), which explores how HIV introduces temporal disjunctions that might guide our political resistance to the epidemic: the out-of-synch-ness implied by dying before one's time suggests also a specific, nonimaginary mode of being "at odds with AIDS."

than those usually proposed—by either the political left or the right—
for halting the epidemic.

Gay Ecology

> To create a sustainable gay culture requires a paradigm shift in
> many of the most basic aspects of the way gay men relate to
> each other and the world.
>
> —Gabriel Rotello

Rotello offers a compelling argument for substantially changing the institutional bases of gay subculture; so historian Martin Duberman is correct when, in his review of *Sexual Ecology,* he characterizes it as the best
and most important book about AIDS yet written.[39] Although ecological
theory originates in mid-nineteenth-century biology, Rotello makes evident how this "science of connections" is as much a philosophy of relationality as it is a Darwinist hangover (11). Ecological thinking consists
in discerning the complex web of interdependence that links us to each
other and to our environment. To put it slightly differently, ecological
thinking consists in grasping the radical limits of individual autonomy,
since the way in which a largely invisible network enmeshes all social

154

39. Martin Duberman, "Epidemic Arguments," *Nation,* May 5, 1997, 27–29. Duberman's judgment about this controversial book is far from shared by many on the gay left. For dissenting views,
see Joshua Oppenheimer, " 'Sexual Ecology' = Sexual Apartheid," *Harvard Gay and Lesbian Review*
5, no. 2 (1998): 15–18; and the articles referenced at note 44 below. Rotello responds to many
of the critiques of his analysis in his afterword to the 1998 Plume edition of *Sexual Ecology,* 293–
302. Along with Signorile's *Life Outside,* Rotello's *Sexual Ecology* provided the impetus for a new
grassroots activist organization, Sex Panic!, formed in New York City during the spring of 1997.
Sex Panic! advertises itself as exemplifying queer theory, and many of its leaders are academics:
historian Allan Bérubé, art critic Douglas Crimp, literary critics Ann Pellegrini and Michael Warner.
The group's name is taken ironically from a term historians use to describe periods of government
enforced crackdown on public morals and sexual expression; see Allan Bérubé, "Prophesy, 1984,"
Harvard Gay and Lesbian Review 5, no. 2 (1998): 10. The members of Sex Panic! have connected
Rotello's critique of gay sexual culture with mayor Rudolph Giuliani's attempts to clean up New
York City and the Disneyfication of Times Square. For a useful account of this new activist group
and its origins, see Caleb Crain, "Pleasure Principles: Queer Theorists and Gay Journalists Wrestle over the Politics of Sex," *Lingua Franca,* October 1997, 26–37; see also Michael Bronski, "Behind the Sex Panic! Debate," *Harvard Gay and Lesbian Review* 5, no. 2 (1998): 29–32. For an account
of this group by two of its members, see Eva Pendleton and Jane Goldschmidt, "Sex Panic!—Make
the Connections," *Harvard Gay and Lesbian Review* 5, no. 3 (1998): 30–33, which announces the
group's mission statement thus:

> Sex Panic! is a pro-queer, pro-feminist, anti-racist direct action group. Our multi-
> issue agenda aims to defend public sexual culture and safer sex in New York City from
> police crackdowns, public stigma and morality crusades. We are committed to HIV

inhabitants means that changes in one part of this "vast web of interrelationships" (11) necessarily affect others.

From a psychoanalytic viewpoint, thinking ecologically is tantamount to thinking in terms of the symbolic order and acknowledging that human subjectivity remains so ineluctably relational that the idea of subjective independence from the claims of others is nothing more than an individualist myth, albeit occasionally a necessary one. Furthermore, the ecological idea of an ecosystem (denoting an environment and the populations that inhabit it) illuminates Lacan's conception of the symbolic order, since, as with ecosystems, there are in fact many symbolic orders, different networks of signifiers that enmesh us as we move around, though these remain largely invisible to the untrained eye, just like ecosystems. This aspect of subjective existence is obscured when "the symbolic order" gets reduced to the purely linguistic register or explained in terms of language as such.

Rotello's contribution lies in his conceptualizing AIDS and safe sex symbolically rather than imaginarily. One of the principal problems of analyzing AIDS in imaginary terms is that, in line with the binarist aggression that typifies imaginary thinking, such analyses end up polarizing innocence and blame, thereby repudiating the connections that confer a measure of ethical responsibility on every member of society suffering an epidemic. If, as I argued in chapter 3, we are all living with AIDS, then we are all also ethically responsible for the epidemic, whether we like it or not, and regardless of our HIV serostatus. By speaking of *responsibility* for the epidemic, I do not mean responsible for the origins or the past history of AIDS, but rather responsible simply for its future. The politics of blame that characterizes so many cultural debates about AIDS may be interpreted as a symptom of just how hard it is to face our mutual and varied implications in the epidemic. That is to say, the politics of blame—an imaginary politics whether it's gay men, intravenous-drug users, and other minorities being blamed, or government officials and mediahounds who are the objects of censure—amounts to little more than "othering" AIDS by making it somebody

155

---

prevention through safer sex, sexual self-determination for all people, and democratic urban space. (30)

Though its critique of Rotello and Signorile seems utterly confused and defensive, Sex Panic!'s emergence is significant for its refueling the exhausted energies of AIDS activism and reinvigorating the separatist-assimilationist debate among gays at a crucial historical moment.

else's fault. A central paradox of this epidemic is that AIDS is nobody's fault, and yet its existence lends every member of the human community a measure of responsibility for AIDS.

This fundamentally ethical paradox has been missed by most of Rotello's critics, who remain unable to distinguish a rhetoric of blame from an analysis of our mutual responsibility for the epidemic's future. It's because his notion of sexual ecology operates at the symbolic rather than the imaginary level that Rotello is able to discuss gay subculture's role in the emergence of AIDS without blaming gay men for the epidemic. By "sexual ecology" Rotello refers not to any supposedly biological determinants of sexuality but to the constellation of historically specific sexual practices that gay men developed after Stonewall and that continue to define gay communities. Discussing these practices, particularly what he calls the "multipartnerism" so central to gay liberation, Rotello acknowledges that AIDS is neither a gay nor a straight disease. But he thoroughly discredits the claim, held to be axiomatic by AIDS activists and many progressive academicians, that the epidemic's emergence in the gay community was accidental. Until I'd read *Sexual Ecology,* I too was one of those for whom, as Rotello puts it, "the fact that AIDS in the world is largely a heterosexual disease has seemed comforting proof that the epidemic in the gay population was a fluke" (182). Building on AIDS epidemiology, Rotello argues to the contrary that gay men's sexual practices in the seventies created optimum ecological conditions for viral emergence and epidemic amplification. As two Columbia University epidemiologists explain in the canonical article on this topic, "[s]eroconversion rates depend on three basic factors: the rate of sexual contact (new partner acquisition rate), the prevalence of infection (the likelihood of selecting an infected partner), and the infectivity of the disease (the probability of disease transmission per partnership)."[40] Criticizing as myopic safe-sex educators' emphasis on latex, Rotello points out that "[t]he condom code seeks to curtail transmission by lowering the level of infectivity per sexual contact, but it ignores the enormous role played by the contact rate itself" (194).

The full significance of sexual contact rate for epidemic transmission becomes clear when one takes into account HIV's comparatively low

40. Martina Morris and Laura Dean, "Effect of Sexual Behavior Change on Long-Term Human Immunodeficiency Virus Prevalence among Homosexual Men," *American Journal of Epidemiology* 140 (1994): 218.

infectivity: as a blood-borne pathogen it is difficult to pass from one person to another through sexual contact. Although intravenous injection represents a far more efficient way to transmit any blood-borne virus, certain sexual practices innovated by gay men after Stonewall— versatile buttfucking, fistfucking, punchfucking, rimming, and so-called blood sports—also make unusually efficient routes for viral transmission.[41] However, in accordance with global epidemiology, Rotello views sexual contact rate as the most significant factor in the AIDS epidemic. Thus his argument is mounted against what he calls the "multipartnerist ethic" on which gay liberation is founded. When it comes to HIV, Rotello maintains, "numbers are the name of the game" (202).

Fortunately the Columbia epidemiologists have done some of the math for us, with startling results. Using data from the New York Longitudinal AIDS Impact Project (LAIP), Morris and Dean analyzed changes in the rate of unprotected anal sex among gay men since 1981. They discovered that by the early nineties the rate of unsafe sex had declined to just below the epidemic threshold, the quantitative tipping point at which an epidemic moves from decline to growth. Their most striking finding was that "[s]mall changes, as little as one additional partner per year on average, would be enough to push transmission above threshold, and the disease would instead become endemic."[42] In other words, if New York gay men's rate of unsafe sex remains as low as it became in the late eighties, the disease will gradually die out in this population (that is, within the sexual ecosystem LAIP surveyed) and the beginning

157

41. "Versatility" is North American gay argot for one's willingness to take both insertive and receptive roles in anal sex. According to Rotello, "versatility" became valorized and widespread in gay subculture beginning only in the seventies; it contributed significantly to epidemic amplification because viral transmission occurs primarily unidirectionally in anal sex, from the insertive to the receptive partner. In mathematical terms, sexual versatility compounds the rate of viral transmission to epidemic dimensions (*Sexual Ecology*, 77–78).

For an account of the practices of fisting and punchfucking, which were basically unknown before Stonewall, see O'Hara, *Autopornography*, 139–43. Blood sports is a sexual practice with even more recent origins, invented in response to the increasing danger associated with blood since the discovery of HIV. Its name derives from "water sports," a sexual practice involving urination (see O'Hara, *Autopornography*, 153–57). "Blood sports" eroticizes the drawing of blood, usually with a knife or scalpel, and like much S/M tends to be heavily ritualized. I suspect this sexual practice shares cultural roots with the recent explosion of interest in tattooing, piercing, branding, and scarification. For an interesting psychoanalytic interpretation of contemporary cutting practices as various attempts to maintain a subjective boundary against the real, see John P. Muller, *Beyond the Psychoanalytic Dyad: Developmental Semiotics in Freud, Peirce, and Lacan* (New York: Routledge, 1995), esp. 85–89.

42. Morris and Dean, "Effect of Sexual Behavior Change," 229.

of the end of AIDS will come into view. But all it takes to make HIV *endemic* to this population—that is, sufficiently prevalent to maintain the epidemic with no end in sight—is an average of one extra unsafe encounter per year. Morris and Dean's account has become renowned for demonstrating the validity of this unlikely thesis.

Evidently the problem with epidemic amplification is that "the inconsistency between individual and aggregate risk provides little direct incentive for individuals to maintain low contact rates, and even small increases in their behavior can tip the average over threshold levels."[43] Rotello's ecological analysis is devoted to helping us grasp the significance of this disparity between personal and collective risk, since thinking about unsafe sex in individual terms—that is, imaginarily—is terribly misleading. Preventing HIV from becoming endemic to gay populations would benefit all gay men, insofar as it would dissociate homosexuality from its longstanding connotations of disease and pathology, which AIDS has revived and, indeed, threatens to consolidate. Yet this kind of symbolic thinking about the collective consequences of unsafe sex is particularly difficult to pursue in a society based on the ideology of individualism—an ideology that also predicates gay liberation. Nevertheless, this is what Rotello struggles to achieve by way of his notion of "sexual ecology"; from a position he identifies as the gay left, he seeks to dislodge the cornerstone of gay libertarianism's ideological edifice—sexual promiscuity.

Promiscuity's centrality to gay libertarianism may be gauged from its status as one of the few remaining taboo subjects in contemporary gay subculture, and even Rotello refers to it euphemistically most of the time. Although the principal discourse on promiscuity proceeds from the religious right, this fact no longer represents sufficient reason to avoid theorizing it. It is extremely difficult to talk rationally about promiscuity, in part because the word itself carries so much moralistic baggage: discourse on promiscuity reeks of prejudice. And this explains the tendency for Rotello's critics to deem him a gay reactionary and to dismiss his analysis as the product of neoconservatism.[44] Indeed, in

43. Ibid., 230.
44. See Michael Warner, "Media Gays: A New Stone Wall," *Nation*, July 14, 1997 (also available as "The Bloodless Revolution of the New Gay Right" on the Sex Panic! website, http://www.geocities.com/~sexpanicnyc/revo.htm). On the same website, see also Jim Eigo's lengthy "Sexual Ecology: An Activist Critique."

queer circles it is considered ideologically suspect to adopt any position except that of denunciation with respect to Rotello.

Yet from a psychoanalytic perspective the very difficulty of speaking about promiscuity suggests all the more reason for doing so, since the topic's volatility indicates its proximity to something psychically fundamental, something that gets to the heart of the matter. My contention is that the comic folklore definition of who's promiscuous—anyone having sex with more people than you are—points to the function of *jouissance* in both the AIDS epidemic and its persistence in gay populations through unsafe sex. In short, promiscuity, the secret subject of *Sexual Ecology,* concerns *intolerance for one's own excess jouissance in the Other.* As I shall try to explain, this intolerance—not of the Other but of one's own excess *jouissance*—represents the greatest impediment to AIDS prevention, since unsafe sex involves trying to access through the sexual other (that is, your partner) something he does not have. Indeed, as I suggested in the previous chapter, intolerance for one's own excess *jouissance* also impedes AIDS prevention measures insofar as conservatives fear that by funding AIDS education they will somehow be bankrolling the extreme pleasures of homosexuals and drug addicts, who get to have all the fun while more restrained citizens foot the bill. Yet this dynamic concerning excess *jouissance* motivates gay men as well as their enemies.

One paradox of promiscuity is that while it tends to be discussed in absolutist terms, sexual promiscuity is necessarily a relative concept. As June Osborn, one of the leading national specialists in infectious diseases, remarked in 1980, after investigating STD rates in various urban gay communities throughout the United States: "Every time we do an NIH site visit the definition of 'multiple sex partners' has changed. First, it was ten to twenty partners per year. That was 1975. Then in 1976 it was fifty partners a year. By 1978 we were talking about a hundred sexual partners a year and now we're using the term to describe five hundred sexual partners in a single year."[45] Although such figures may seem derived from fantasy as much as from anybody's experience, they point to the post-Stonewall development of gay institutions, such as bathhouses and sex clubs, that provide opportunities for multiple sexual contacts on a scale previously unknown.

159

45. Laurie Garrett, *The Coming Plague: Newly Emerging Diseases in a World out of Balance* (New York: Penguin, 1995), 271.

Reviewing Osborn's figures, the reader is likely to wonder how even the most single-minded man could have more sexual partners than there are days in the year. But consider, for example, the testimony of Eric Rofes, a widely published gay critic, who, in his recent book *Reviving the Tribe,* describes in some detail his visit to the well-known San Francisco sex club Blow Buddies, which is dedicated to fellatio. "As my eyes adjusted [to the dim light]," notes Rofes, "I recognized more and more people—colleagues from political work, neighbors from my apartment building, friends from the gym."[46] Blow Buddies is a gay institution, a place where all kinds of men go, most of them ordinary. Rofes records that during his evening there he had sexual contact with ten different men.[47] A weekly visit to such an institution would readily enable any man's contact rate to reach or exceed five hundred partners per year without anything like superhuman sexual athleticism. In the seventies, gay subculture developed around such institutions, though you didn't have to go to the baths to end up in bed with somebody who did.[48]

160

46. Rofes, *Reviving the Tribe,* 193.

47. Ibid., 195.

48. Compare Michael Callen's testimony: "It wasn't until I was officially diagnosed with AIDS [in 1982, at age twenty-seven] that I faced squarely just how much sex, and how much disease, I'd had. With the gentle prodding of a doctor who was filling out my CDC AIDS case report form, I calculated that since becoming sexually active in 1973, I had racked up more than three thousand different sex partners in bathhouses, back rooms, meat racks, and tearooms" (*Surviving AIDS,* 5). Although the rate of various sexually transmitted diseases skyrocketed among North American gay men during the sixties and seventies, most of these diseases were bacterial and therefore curable with antibiotics—until drug-resistant strains developed in response to the use of penicillin as a widespread technological quick fix for gay men's health. Gay sexual ecology during this period also provided ideal conditions for the emergence and spread of viral diseases such as herpes and HIV, for which, as is well known, there is yet no cure. In her excellent history of recent microbial epidemics, *The Coming Plague,* Laurie Garrett makes clear how important it is to think in terms of transmission prevention rather than cure, a distinction Rotello also emphasizes. Examining viral emergence and epidemic amplification in as broad a perspective as possible entails considering AIDS from the viewpoint of viruses as well as of susceptible populations; Jaap Goudsmit's discussion, in *Viral Sex: The Nature of AIDS* (New York: Oxford University Press, 1997), of how retroviruses reproduce both sexually and asexually is useful for illuminating the role of viral evolution in the current pandemic. After genetic sequencing of different strains of HIV and the closely related simian immunodeficiency viruses (SIV), it was calculated that HIV is evolving or mutating at an overall rate of 1 percent per year, "one of the highest [annual rates] seen in any viral species" (Garrett, 664), though not as high as the influenza virus, whose mutation rate is so rapid that we require a different vaccine annually. Not only has HIV already mutated into drug-resistant strains that leave protease inhibitors ineffective, but its evolution is guided by adaptation to varying transmission routes. This is significant because, genetically speaking, the virus responsible for the AIDS pandemic is not simply HIV-1 but a number of subtypes of HIV-1: subtype D, one of the most lethal, is the virus strain responsible for the epidemic in Zaire, Uganda, and Rwanda, whereas subtype B is the primary strain found in North America (Garrett, 378). Subtype B is especially adapted to

Gay sexual ecology differs from straight sexual ecology not because gay people are essentially different from our straight neighbors, but because gay subculture has historically been constructed around different institutions and thus different modes of relating to others. While these institutions enabled HIV and other sexually transmitted diseases to become epidemic in the gay community, the different relational modes these institutions established may yet provide the basis for a different understanding of sex that—by locating our most intense experiences elsewhere than in men's bodies—would make it immeasurably easier for safe sexual practices to flourish, thereby dramatically reducing the rate of gay seroconversions. In the interest of constructing what Rotello calls "a sustainable gay culture," I'd like in the remainder of this chapter to suggest exactly what such a project entails.

Following the sexual liberation of the sixties and seventies, gay institutions were founded on an ideology of promiscuity that still largely defines what it means to identify as gay. Or to be more precise, increasingly the term *queer* is coming to stand for this seventies liberationist ideal, such that to identify as queer paradoxically entails identifying with a nostalgic vision of the sexual moment immediately after Stonewall. As Michael Callen explained, "seventies gay liberationist rhetoric proclaimed that sex was inherently liberating; by a curiously naive calculus, it seemed to follow that *more* sex was *more* liberating."[49] This libertarian ideology persists into academic gay studies and contemporary queer theory, in part because it's associated with the sexual avant-garde, so that even happily married college professors identify with the ideology of promiscuity. Thus another paradox of promiscuity is that you can identify with it as an ego-ideal while in practice remaining sexually monogamous. As critic Douglas Crimp formulates the ideological position, "Gay male promiscuity should be seen instead as a positive model of how sexual pleasures might be pursued by and granted to everyone if those pleasures were not confined within the narrow limits of institutionalized sexuality."[50] When sexual promiscuity is framed in these

---

penetrate the cells lining the rectal wall, which is partly why oral sex is so much safer than anal sex. But the emergence of subtype E, in northern Thailand, which is better adapted to infect the cells lining the mouth and vagina, indicates that a rise in unprotected oral sex with multiple partners (as at Blow Buddies) optimizes ecological conditions for another epidemic (see Rotello, chap. 11).

49. Callen, *Surviving AIDS*, 4.

50. Douglas Crimp, "How to Have Promiscuity in an Epidemic," *AIDS: Cultural Analysis / Cultural Activism*, ed. Crimp (Cambridge: MIT Press, 1988), 253.

terms, who but the most puritanical conservative could resist such a beneficently democratic extension of pleasure to the masses? Characterized as politically progressive, even radical, this extension of pleasure facilitates easy imaginary identifications. According to this view, promiscuity is simply one term for democratic sexual freedom, "the pursuit of happiness" that modern individualism guarantees its subjects. Psychoanalytically speaking, however, pleasure is nowhere near as straightforward or benign as individualism, libertarianism, and psychology assume, since pleasure is always complicated by *jouissance.*

The Paradox of Pleasure

The pleasure principle—the principle of pleasure—is that pleasure should cease.

—Jacques Lacan

Near the beginning of *Beyond the Pleasure Principle,* Freud reminds us that "the pleasure principle long persists, however, as the method of working employed by the sexual instincts, which are so hard to 'educate,' and, starting from those instincts, or in the ego itself, it often succeeds in overcoming the reality principle, to the detriment of the organism as a whole" (*SE* 18:10). It would be plausible, though simplistic, to view the pleasure principle's overriding the reality principle every time men fuck without a condom. Yet Freud's concept of the unconscious helps us see that pleasure is more complex than this:

> It is clear that the greater part of what is re-experienced under the compulsion to repeat must cause the ego unpleasure, since it brings to light activities of repressed instinctual impulses. That, however, is unpleasure of a kind we have already considered and does not contradict the pleasure principle: unpleasure for one system and simultaneously satisfaction for the other. (*SE* 18:20)

This psychoanalytic paradox reaches back to Freud's observation, in *The Interpretation of Dreams,* that "the mind has wishes at its disposal whose fulfillment produces unpleasure. This seems selfcontradictory; but it becomes intelligible when we take into account the presence of two psychical agencies and a censorship between them" (*SE* 4:235). If one agency or system within the psyche achieves pleasure or satisfaction at the expense of another, then we can begin to see how hard it is to predict what kind of pleasure anybody may be seeking in sex—including a certain satisfaction in one's own unpleasure, one's own danger. As Michael Warner reported in *The Village Voice*, "I had to think about why I wanted risky sex, knowing that the danger was part of the attraction."[51]

The Lacanian concept of *jouissance* moves this familiar idea of pleasure-in-danger out of the realm of individual psychology into the field of social relations. Lacan does this by showing how pleasure always bears some relation to the Other's *jouissance*. In his seminar *The Ethics of Psychoanalysis*, Lacan clarifies why people do in fact risk death for a good fuck. Considering an example provided in the *Critique of Practical Reason*, where Kant discusses the individual cost-benefit analysis undertaken by a man who may have intercourse only on pain of death with a woman he desires unlawfully, Lacan paraphrases, "For the sake of spending a night with a woman, no one would be mad enough to accept an outcome that would be fatal to him, since it isn't a question of combat but of death by hanging. For Kant, the answer to the question is not in doubt" (*SVII* 189). However, Lacan demurs from Kant's assessment of the situation, arguing that "one only has to make a conceptual shift and move the night spent with the lady from the category of pleasure to that of *jouissance*, given that *jouissance* implies precisely the acceptance of death—and there's no need of sublimation—for the example to be ruined" (*SVII* 189). And one has only to make Kant's example a homosexual rather than a heterosexual example to see how dramatically Lacan's reading of it illuminates the attraction of unsafe sex.

When one thinks about sex in terms of *jouissance*, it becomes clear that death represents not the penalty but the payoff for a good fuck, in that death confers an absolute quiescence, literalizing the *petit mort* of orgasm. Lacan thus develops the concept of *jouissance* to theorize the death drive, arguing that *jouissance* lies beyond the pleasure principle. Rather than *jouissance* designating simply an especially intense form of pleasure, "it is pleasure that sets the limits on *jouissance*, pleasure as that which binds incoherent life together" (*E* 319). Limits to *jouissance* are vital owing to what Lacan calls its "infinitude"—an idea that psychoanalyst André Patsalides, in a particularly helpful essay on the topic, glosses by indicating that "[i]t is the longing for infinitude in *jouissance* that con-

163

51. Warner, "Why Gay Men Are Having Risky Sex," 33.

stitutes a threat to the subject's life itself."[52] Thus we might say that promiscuity consists in testing the barriers to *jouissance* that pleasure establishes.

Jouissance may be understood as "self-destructive" insofar as it overwhelms the ego or coherent self. In a different psychoanalytic register, Leo Bersani pursues this idea, deriving masochism as a tautology for sexuality by arguing that the human subject is originally "shattered" into sexuality. Following the work of Jean Laplanche, Bersani finds sexuality's origins in the unmasterable excess of stimulation that parental care visits on the child, overwhelming the child's ego boundaries, whose defenses are weak or only partially formed. In other words, the premature emergence of sexuality in humans, prior to biological maturation, makes sexuality initially inassimilable to the self and thence inseparable from the unconscious.[53] In this view, the capacity inherent in sexual *jouissance* to undo the coherent self means that there is something *psychically* dangerous about sex as such. If sexuality's subjective origins involve overcoming the boundaries of the ego, we may begin to appreciate the fantasmatic significance of overriding latex barriers in sex. Indeed, once sexuality is understood in terms of what shatters the self, then the very notion of safe sex becomes oxymoronic.

It is troubling to find a version of this psychoanalytic conception of sex being advanced by the self-styled "king of unsafe sex," Scott O'Hara, who claimed that "[s]ex is not, cannot be, and *should not be* 'safe.' Neither should life be safe . . . Anytime you get intimately involved with another human being, there is risk."[54] For O'Hara, as for Bersani, sex and safety are fundamentally incompatible; indeed, sex is defined by its incommensurability with safety. In other words, these men conceive

---

52. André Patsalides, "*Jouissance* in the Cure," *Anamorphosis: Journal of the San Francisco Society for Lacanian Studies and the Lacanian School of Psychoanalysis* 1 (1997): 5.

53. See Leo Bersani, *The Freudian Body: Psychoanalysis and Art* (New York: Columbia University Press, 1986); and Bersani, *Homos* (Cambridge: Harvard University Press, 1995). In his justly celebrated essay "Is the Rectum a Grave?" (*AIDS*, ed. Crimp, 197–222), Bersani began working out this psychoanalytic argument explicitly in relation to AIDS.

54. O'Hara, "Safety First?" 9. O'Hara develops this position elsewhere:

I look at the HIV-negative people around me, and I pity them. They live their lives in constant fear of infection: mustn't do this, mustn't do that, mustn't take risks. They can't see past that simple "avoidance of infection," which has come to be their ultimate goal. They believe that AIDS = death sentence . . . I guess life in a prison of negativity sounds a lot worse. My life is so much more carefree than theirs, so much more "considered," that I shake my head and count myself lucky to have been infected. Risk taking

sex more in terms of *jouissance* than pleasure. From the perspective of AIDS education, it is imperative to distinguish what's *psychically* dangerous from what's *physically* dangerous—a difficult distinction to maintain when one is engaged in a encounter that is, after all, always physical, whatever else it may be. To complicate matters further, a considerable amount of energy in academic feminism and queer theory has been devoted to demolishing this distinction between the physical and the psychical, based on the hypothesis that, as Elizabeth Grosz puts it, "all the effects of subjectivity, all the significant facets and complexities of subjects, can be as adequately explained using the subject's corporeality as a framework as it would be using consciousness or the unconscious."[55] If the commitment to practicing safe sex depends in part on the capacity to distinguish what's psychically dangerous from what's physically dangerous, then critical attempts to invalidate the distinction between physical and psychical seem politically unhelpful at best.

One way to reinforce this vital distinction is by emphasizing the question central to negotiated safety—*How much risk do you consider acceptable?* Even though such a formulation leaves inexplicit the crucial difference between individual and aggregate risk, it is exactly the kind of psychoanalytic question that could be put in even the most elementary safe-sex educational material and printed on every condom packet. The psychoanalytic dimension of this question says, in effect, "This is what you're doing, but what do you want?" What do you imagine sex is going to do for you? As one of Walt Odets's patients wondered, "Is it true . . . that this expression of intimacy, love, and connection is as important or more important than survival itself?"[56] The limitation with

---

is the essence of life, and people who spend their entire lives trying to eliminate risk from their lives are . . . well, they're not my kind of people. (*Autopornography,* 129)

Since the pronouncements of a porn actor–turned–writer may appear to be dubious evidence, I should register that the character who emerges from *Autopornography* is surprisingly intelligent, literate, articulate, and engaging. While his former profession makes O'Hara appear thoroughly unrepresentative of gay men, my research suggests that he is simply more candid about his motives for pursuing unprotected sex.

55. Elizabeth Grosz, *Volatile Bodies: Toward a Corporeal Feminism* (Bloomington: Indiana University Press, 1994), vii. Work in feminism and queer theory on corporeality and the bodily ego usually takes off from Freud's point, in *The Ego and the Id,* that "[t]he ego is first and foremost a bodily ego; it is not merely a surface entity, but is itself the projection of a surface" (*SE* 19:26). As the latest chapter in a long tradition of normalizing the unconscious out of existence, this kind of work invariably reduces subjectivity to the ego and therefore cannot be called psychoanalytic work, despite what its practitioners sometimes claim.

56. Odets, *In the Shadow of the Epidemic,* 199.

this strategy, however, lies in the fact that while one may attempt to answer such a question honestly for himself, one cannot answer it for others. And every sexual encounter involves another. To this common-sensical qualification we add the psychoanalytic observation that every sexual encounter also involves the Other.

Unsafe sex holds many different subjective meanings, one of the most common being that unprotected anal sex represents the most intense experience attainable. As HIV-positive activist Tony Valenzuela recently affirmed, "The level of erotic charge and intimacy I feel when a man cums inside me is transformational, especially in a climate which so completely disregards its importance."[57] Unsafe sex is experienced as amazingly intense not simply because of the physical involvement but because of the explosive significance attached to it. As Scott O'Hara says, "[b]eing fucked, contrary to what most porn videos try to tell you, is not about being fucked. I suspect I could be fucked quite satisfyingly by a man who had no dick at all, if he were truly into it. It's a psychological sense of possession that is important, of surrender."[58] O'Hara's formulation makes clear that sex is often less about bodies or physicality than about fantasy, about accessing the disincarnate form of the Other's *jouissance* through someone else's body. This can feel like "possession" in both subjective and objective genitive senses: possessing the Other's *jouissance* by becoming the Other's possession—that is, by surrendering to the Other's alien *jouissance*. In this sense, there can be no intimacy without extimacy. Thus while Rotello is undoubtedly correct in observing that as far as HIV is concerned numbers are the name of the game, when it comes to sex, *fantasy* is the name of the game. It is the larger import of sex—the "in-you-more-than-you" that I imagine in my sexual partner—that makes safe-sex guidelines so difficult to follow.

Thus despite the popular conception that gay men treat sex too casually, all the recent research on unsafe sex suggests to the contrary that gay men place extraordinary expectations on sex. Indeed, those men whose multipartnerism makes them appear to take sex lightly are, from a psychoanalytic perspective, men whose approach to sex is deadly

57. Tony Valenzuela, "Let's Talk about Sex without Condoms," manifesto on the webpage of New York activist group Sex Panic! (http://www.geocities.com/~sexpanicnyc), a sequel to Valenzuela's notorious speech at the National Gay and Lesbian Task Force's Creating Change Conference, in San Diego, November 1997.

58. O'Hara, *Autopornography*, 73.

serious. To make screwing the basis for an identity, much less a politics, is to demand much more from sex than simply sex. By seeking recognition, narcissistic gratification, community membership, and even ideological affiliation through sex, we use sex as a medium for accessing what we're having difficulty obtaining elsewhere—the Other's love. As with anything else, sex can be used as a medium for acting out. Indeed, building gay life around sex makes erotic relations the most readily available medium for acting out one's relation to the Other. Let me make clear that I'm suggesting not that straight people don't also use sex as an arena for acting out (they certainly do), but rather that gay subculture has more fully sanctioned sex as such an arena via the ideology of promiscuity.

This is more than a question of looking for love in all the wrong places. Rather, the fantasy structure that makes sex mean so much entails discerning the lineaments of the Other in others' bodies. What is promiscuity if not the constantly thwarted attempt to access the *jouissance* from which I'm separated as the price of symbolic existence? As a consequence of life in the symbolic order—that is, subjectivity as such—my own excess *jouissance* resides in the Other, forever alienated and inaccessible. But misrecognizing the Other in my partner promotes the fantasy that *jouissance* may be regained through sexual relations. This fantasy finds support in the democratic ideal of individual liberty (freedom from the Other) and the pursuit of happiness that accompanies it. A psychoanalytic perspective on unsafe sex suggests that this fantasy should be worked through in encounters other than the explicitly sexual, instead of being acted out repeatedly through erotic encounters with other people. If I could accept the constitutive inaccessibility of the Other's *jouissance,* I'd be less inclined to imagine that overcoming latex barriers would enable me to reach nirvana. That is, if I could appreciate the psychical necessity of barriers regulating access to *jouissance,* I'd be more likely to appreciate the importance of physical protection during sex too. And if I could learn to distinguish my sexual partner (an other) from the alterity of the signifier, I might intuit that sexual relations offer only one medium through which to approach my *jouissance* in the Other.[59]

---

59. I elaborate this distinction between others and the Other in "Two Kinds of Other and Their Consequences," *Critical Inquiry* 23 (1997): 910–20.

Demeaning Sex

> *Sex is. There is nothing more to be done about it. Sex builds no*
> *roads, writes no novels and sex certainly gives no meaning to*
> *anything in life but itself.*

—Gore Vidal

So why is sex still apparently so popular? Why does fucking mean so much? In his *Introduction* to *The History of Sexuality,* composed before AIDS had been recognized as such and therefore before he was aware of his own destiny with the disease, Foucault wrote:

> The Faustian pact, whose temptation has been instilled in us by the deployment of sexuality, is now as follows: to exchange life in its entirety for sex itself, for the truth and the sovereignty of sex. *Sex is worth dying for.* It is in this (strictly historical) sense that sex is indeed imbued with the death instinct. When a long while ago the West discovered love, it bestowed on it a value high enough to make death acceptable; nowadays it is sex that claims this equivalence, the highest of all.[60]

Foucault's observation is even more pertinent to gay men today than it was when he originally wrote it. Sex has become literally "worth dying for," because the deployment of sexuality scripts sex as the ground of our ontological identities. Nowhere is this pernicious effect more demonstrable than in gay subculture. Thus while many cultural commentators consider gay promiscuity to have demeaned sex, I would argue that the reverse is true. Gay men haven't demeaned sex enough: sex still remains to be drained of its meaning as our source of ultimate value. In Lacanian terms, Foucault is pointing to the historical reduction of *jouissance* to sex; or, rather, the production of sex as the arena through which *jouissance* may be most directly approached.

Whereas psychoanalysis reveals that *jouissance* remains irreducible to fucking and orgasm, gay activists and queer theorists continue to mystify sex by drastically overestimating its potential.[61] In this respect, many queer theorists are far less Foucaultian than they imagine them-

---

60. Michel Foucault, *The History of Sexuality,* vol. 1, *An Introduction,* trans. Robert Hurley (New York: Random House, 1978), 156; emphasis added.

61. The most recent example of this queer mystification of sex is Michael Bronski's *The Pleasure Principle: Sex, Backlash, and the Struggle for Gay Freedom* (New York: St. Martin's Press, 1998).

selves to be. For example, Cindy Patton concludes her book on safe sex with a polemic on behalf of *"saving* sex," offering redemptive formulas such as: "The next step may be to stop using the term 'safe—even safer—sex' and to reject any idea of a wholesome 'gay lifestyle.' Instead, we must think about sex as the form of power that makes and saves queer lives."[62] While I appreciate that such romanticizing of queer sex is meant to contest the normalizing construction of sexuality that pervades American society, I would argue that when sex is idealized as "the form of power that makes queer lives" it is least likely to save lives. New seroconversions among queers are making amply evident that sexual relations cannot sustain the fantasmatic burden with which rhetoric such as Patton's imbues them. And though she announces her project as Foucaultian, we may regard her cant as perhaps the last, most extreme gasp of that deployment of sexuality about which Foucault was so scathing and that crystallizes in the formula "sex is worth dying for." Against Patton's sexual fundamentalism, I would adduce Bersani's more nuanced view of queer sex's redemptive potential: "the value of sexuality itself is to demean the seriousness of efforts to redeem it."[63]

169

Bersani points us toward a new realism concerning sex, one that would take fantasy fully into account rather than idealizing it out of existence when constructing theories of sexuality. A new realism about sex has nothing to do with the panoply of sociosexual norms that are palmed off as reality; instead it involves coming to terms with the function of the Other in sexual relations and thus rethinking relationality in toto. By conceptualizing AIDS and unsafe sex in terms of the symbolic order, I am arguing the following: First, in light of Rotello's valuable extrapolation from AIDS epidemiology, I've suggested that the disjunction between individual and aggregate risk must be represented. In the construction of a sustainable gay culture, collective risk should be taken into account.[64] Following this vital distinction, I've argued that fantasy must be conceived in symbolic rather than imaginary terms—that is,

---

62. Patton, *Fatal Advice,* 140 and 155, respectively.

63. Bersani, "Is the Rectum a Grave?" 222.

64. I am grateful to Phillip Brian Harper for reminding me that a sustainable gay culture must be based on something more than the gay identity inherited from gay liberation, not least because so many other sexual and racial minorities remain excluded from or marginalized within "gay identity" as it is currently conceived. My call for a collectivist ethic that takes into account aggregate as well as individual risk could not succeed if it interpellated uniformly all those whose sexual activity places them outside sexual norms.

in terms of the Other's *jouissance* rather than individual pleasure or satisfaction.

Thinking symbolically entails consequences for gay identity, since it may prove unworkably anachronistic to continue defining gayness in terms of the libertarian ideal of sexual freedom. "There have to be things in men's lives that are worth more than absolute sexual freedom," argues Rotello, referring to the multipartnerist ethic that founds gay libertarianism (223). "Sexual freedom" may need to be reconceived in terms of freedom from disease—and thus emancipation from the cultural logic associating homosexuality with pathogenesis. Whereas the libertarian ideal of sexual freedom is predicated on the assumption that my body and its pleasures are mine to dispose of as I please, the psychoanalytic idea of symbolic mediation (that is, the unconscious) makes clear that it is only in an excessively individualistic—even atomistic—society that one may imagine his life is wholly his own, exempt from multiple relations of interdependence and thence responsibility. Furthermore, the nostalgia expressed by queer theorists such as Douglas Crimp and Michael Warner for the post-Stonewall days of political activism organized around sexual liberation appears astonishingly naive, since such sentimental effusions forget completely Foucault's extensive critique of the very idea of "liberating" sexuality.[65] And as Michelangelo Signorile points out, there is something profoundly conservative in these ostensibly radical critics' wish to preserve an older gay culture, as if any change in seventies gay social organization were automatically a sign of backlash and regression rather than of progress.[66]

In this respect, Rotello is right to argue that our culture requires alternative institutions that would take interdependence and mutual responsibility into account; but he is wrong, or insufficiently imaginative, to propose gay marriage and monogamy as our best alternative to the

170

65. The latest round of calls for renewed sexual liberation coming from queer theorists seem especially ironic in view of Foucault's comments in *The History of Sexuality:*

> [T]he sexual cause—the demand for sexual freedom, but also for the knowledge to be gained from sex and the right to speak about it—becomes legitimately associated with the honor of a political cause: sex too is placed on the agenda for the future. A suspicious mind might wonder if taking so many precautions in order to give the history of sex such an impressive filiation does not bear traces of the same old prudishness: as if those valorizing correlations were necessary before such a discourse could be formulated or accepted. (6)

66. Michelangelo Signorile, "Nostalgia Trip," *Harvard Gay and Lesbian Review* 5, no. 2 (1998): 25–28.

bathhouse. He's wrong not because gay marriage represents the co-optation of subversive queer energies by a heterosexual institution, as the standard objection to his critique would have it. Rather, Rotello's proposed solution is inadequate because the problem is less that gay men are having too much sex or too many partners, than that—implausible though it may initially sound—gay men's sexual imagination remains too limited. Here I must emphasize the distinction between sexual promiscuity and the fantasies associated with it, since it is these fantasies that make safe sex so hard to sustain. Thus rather than advocating either promiscuity or monogamy, I am advocating taking seriously sexual fantasy, as both an explanatory concept and a range of instances. One cannot bring about social change in gay culture without engaging the fantasies underlying sexual practices.

Thinking about sex in terms of the symbolic order enables us to extend Rotello's account of sexual ecology in a different direction, since gay culture already has developed alternate modes of relationality. Rather than redeeming sex through gay marriage, sex should be completely demeaned, depersonalized to such a degree that the fundamental impersonality of sexual relations becomes evident. The fact of symbolic mediation means that each subject's primary relation is with the Other, and it's because this relation is not only linguistic but also corporeal—concerning the Other's *jouissance*—that erotic relations aren't strictly personal. Recognizing interpersonal relations as predicated on an impersonal relation to the Other enables us to grasp how *jouissance* remains irreducible to sex, since although the Other has your *jouissance,* it has no genitalia. I take this to be O'Hara's radical insight when he avows that he "could be fucked quite satisfyingly by a man who had no dick at all." Lacan's distinction between the Other's *jouissance* and the other's sexual pleasure may be illustrated by picturing the Other as a man without a dick.

This distinction provides a different way of thinking about sex, in that genital intercourse and orgasm represent only one way—perhaps the least imaginative—to approach what Lacan calls "this sort of forbidden *jouissance* which is the only valuable meaning that is offered to our life" ("Of Structure" 195). To suggest that we approach *jouissance* via routes other than the genital or corporeal need not amount to recommending that gay men stop screwing and start sublimating. Rather, I am interested in how alternative cultural practices may be inferred from

171

this irreducibility of *jouissance* to sex, and, furthermore, how gay culture's potential for devising new modes of relationality might be enlisted in this project. In a discussion of Bersani's *Homos* and David Halperin's *Saint Foucault,* I began considering what it might mean for gay men to locate our most intense experiences and highest values in realms other than the genital.[67] Many critics view this attempt as a betrayal of the ideals that founded gay liberation—and so do I. However, such a betrayal is necessary if we are to move beyond the limiting conceptions of sexuality and identity that came out of Stonewall. To continue to enshrine one historical moment as the touchstone for our political identities inhibits historical progress on the project of building a queerer world. At present queer theory is caught uncomfortably between its commitment to expanding identity categories to the point of incoherence, on one hand, and its insistence on the specificity of genital contact as the basis for all political work, on the other.

172

However, not only was there plenty of same-sex erotic activity before Stonewall, but there were also less genitally oriented traditions of identifying as queer. I am particularly interested in various commitments to aestheticism that marked men as deviants from norms of heterosexual masculinity—commitments that nevertheless cannot be understood in terms simply of sublimation or the distortions of the closet. In this respect, I wish to exploit Bersani's thesis that certain aesthetic practices reproduce a form of intensity or *jouissance*—a syncope—that is not secondary or sublimated, but is in fact identical to the self-shattering intensity of primary masochism. As Lacan noted in his disagreement with Kant, "there's no need of sublimation" when sex is rethought in terms of *jouissance.* What a certain psychoanalytic tradition makes available through the concept of *jouissance* is what Bersani calls the "peculiar idea of a sexuality independent of sex," or "sexual activity no longer attached to particular acts."[68] As I suggest in this book's conclusion, we might specify this idea further by focusing on forms of sexual intensity detached from genital activity. Hence, far from being antisex or "sex-negative," this project takes a more expansive view of sex, insisting along with Freud that what we mean by *sexual* might not conform to commonsensical, implicitly heteronormative ideas con-

67. Tim Dean, "Sex and Syncope," *Raritan* 15 (1996): 64–86.
68. Leo Bersani, *The Culture of Redemption* (Cambridge: Harvard University Press, 1990), 32.

cerning sex. By finding more sex rather than less, a psychoanalytic per-spective suggests how sexual satisfaction may be attained without genital stimulation. And thus to begin to see how *jouissance* may be approached without sexual acts—that is, by way of the Other without a dick—helps divest sexual acts of the redemptive significance that makes unsafe sex so hard to renounce. Such an effort would contribute toward ending not only the AIDS epidemic but also the deployment of sexuality that was the object of Foucault's critique and that cost him his life. In that case we really would be doing justice to Foucault, as well as to Freud.

Chapter 5

Modernism is an age not of rhetoric, but of rhetoricality, the age, that is, of a generalized rhetoric that penetrates to the deepest levels of human experience.

—John Bender and David E. Wellbery, "Rhetoricality: On the Modernist Return of Rhetoric"

Poststructuralist thought is in its operation a rhetorical machine: it systematically asserts and demonstrates the mediated, constructed, partial, socially constituted nature of all realities, whether they be phenomenal, linguistic, or psychological.

—Stanley Fish, "Rhetoric"

Rhetorical Machines

Contemporary rhetoric teachers commonly assign students the task of analyzing a magazine advertisement because—as even the most old-fashioned "modern" rhetoric manuals recognize—"Ad-writers are some of the most skillful rhetoricians in our society."[1] The pedagogical advantage of such an assignment lies in its capacity to help students connect the otherwise dry study of rhetoric to the study of social and sexual

1. Edward P. J. Corbett, *Classical Rhetoric for the Modern Student,* 3d ed. (Oxford: Oxford University Press, 1990), 5.

relations, for if ads use rhetoric to help sell products, they also—students are keen to insist—use sex. And ads (such as Volvo's) that do not substitute pounds of flesh for their products nevertheless appeal to "sex" in the form of *sexuality*—that is, the network of institutions (such as the family) that sanctify sexual relations as social relations. In the terms of this chapter's first epigraph, we might say that the rhetorical analysis of advertisements converts rhetoric into rhetoricality, defined further by Bender and Wellbery as "the new conditions of discourse in the modern world and, thus, the fundamental category of every inquiry that seeks to describe the nature of discursive action and exchange."[2] Indeed, by converting rhetoric into rhetoricality, such analysis also converts sex into sexuality, disclosing sex as socially situated. Rhetorical analysis of advertisements thus can unfold the full range of demographic differentials—of gender, race, class, sexuality, ethnicity, age—that, we maintain, are rhetorically, discursively, and culturally constructed (advertising and mass media playing a crucial role in this process of construction).

175

If it is easy to persuade students that ads sell forms of sexual and social relations rather than simply selling products, one cannot help wondering why the demystification of this process through rhetorical— or, in Roland Barthes's influential terms, *semiological*—analysis seems to leave advertising's suasive power spectacularly undiminished. Why does one form of persuasion—the rhetorical effect that disrupts conviction in the ad's promise—not cancel the opposing persuasive form— the rhetorical effect that convinces me this product will change my life? My suggestion is not that demystification or critique is pointless, but that rhetoricalist analyses, for all their suave power, are not persuasive enough. The poststructuralist "rhetorical machine" is faulty. Actually, its fault lies in our own readiness to be persuaded that sex is fully mediated, our eagerness to think of sex as constructed in—or materialized through—the imaginary and symbolic systems that permeate mass culture. For if student analyses of advertisements sometimes seem overenthusiastic in their assimilation of rhetoric to sex, their tendency to talk about body parts rather than, say, synecdoche, then critical analyses of rhetoric and sexuality exhibit the inverse problem of too quickly

2. John Bender and David E. Wellbery, "Rhetoricality: On the Modernist Return of Rhetoric," in *The Ends of Rhetoric: History, Theory, Practice*, ed. Bender and Wellbery (Stanford: Stanford University Press, 1990), 25–26.

assimilating sex to rhetoric. These critical analyses too readily assume, as Lee Edelman puts it, "that sexuality is constituted through operations as much rhetorical as psychological—or, to put it otherwise, that psychological and sociological interpretations of sexuality are necessarily determined by the rhetorical structures and the figural logics through which 'sexuality' and the discourse around it are culturally produced."[3]

The common assumption that sexuality is rhetorically or discursively constituted explicitly grounds some of the most sophisticated lesbian and gay theories of sexuality, as exemplified by Edelman's *Homographesis* and Judith Butler's *Bodies That Matter*. It is owing to this work's importance and influence that I devote so much space to criticizing it in this chapter. Whether we label the assumption poststructuralist, constructionist, or, for present purposes, rhetoricalist, this idea that sexuality is a product of rhetoric, discourse, culture, history, and social relations is widely held as the only viable alternative to the conservative notion that sex is grounded in nature. If, in Barthes's terms, myth "transforms history into nature," the contemporary rhetoricalist demystification of "natural" sexuality transforms sex back into history, culture, discourse, rhetoric.[4] So widely accepted is one or another version of this rhetoricalist position that we might even say rhetoricalism has naturalized itself in contemporary theory.

" 'Are bodies purely discursive?' " Butler inquires in *Bodies That Matter,* framing the question in quotation marks to signal her appropriation of one of the most cogent objections to her earlier account of gender as performative.[5] This question leads Butler to theorize bodily materiality in terms of materialization; that is, as an enforcement of bodily norms whose normative status depends upon a reiteration or citation wherein lies the possibility of disruption or "resignification." "Matter is always materialized," Butler argues, converting noun into verb, essence into performance, the pregiven into the yet-to-be-given or the to-be-given-again (9). Showing how materiality is always necessarily materialized introduces the linked notions of temporality and repetition, which Butler counterposes to what she repeatedly characterizes as the "stasis"

3. Lee Edelman, *Homographesis: Essays in Gay Literary and Cultural Theory* (New York: Routledge, 1994), xiv. Subsequent page references are in main text.

4. Roland Barthes, *Mythologies,* trans. Annette Lavers (New York: Hill and Wang, 1972), 129.

5. Judith Butler, *Bodies That Matter: On the Discursive Limits of "Sex"* (New York: Routledge, 1993), 67. Subsequent page references are in main text.

of "heterosexist structuralism" (90). Repetition in Butler's poststructuralist model is not necessarily repetition of the same; instead, repetition or citation is always potentially repetition with a difference—hence the possibility for resignifying and subverting identities.

Are bodies purely discursive? Or, to rotate the question slightly into Edelman's terms, is sexuality purely rhetorical? The problem with framing the inquiry this way is that such questions are themselves rhetorical, instances of the trope of erotema, which subtly biases what answers are more and less plausible in response to the question. These kinds of questions are posed strategically in opposition to an essentialism or foundationalism that would ground bodies and sex in nature or biology, would position bodies and sex as pregiven or prediscursive. The foundationalist position thus opposes the rhetoricalist one, just as essentialism opposes constructivism.[6] As Stanley Fish's brief history of rhetoric (from which this chapter's second epigraph is drawn) implies, most contemporary theories assume that critical thinking on corporeality and sexuality is fully exhausted by the coordinates these competing positions set. Fish maintains that "[t]he quarrel between rhetorical and foundational thought is itself foundational; its content is a disagreement about the basic constituents of human activity and about the nature of human nature itself."[7] Thus the figure whom Butler refers to as "the moderate critic" is situated somewhere within this conceptual field, on some middle ground between essentialism and antifoundationalism, conceding that—as Butler characterizes the moderate position she's arguing against—"some part of 'sex' is constructed, but some other is certainly not" (11; original emphasis). I leave this moderate critic to Butler and intend to take on the stronger position exemplified by Butler's own account. This chapter aims to outline a theory of rhetoric, sexuality,

177

6. Since foundationalism opposes rhetoricalism, Butler's explicitly antifoundationalist polemics warrant my assimilating her work to the rhetoricalist position with which Edelman's work is more obviously identifiable. See, for example, Butler, "Contingent Foundations: Feminism and the Question of 'Postmodernism,'" in *Feminists Theorize the Political*, ed. Judith Butler and Joan W. Scott (New York: Routledge, 1992), 3–21; and Butler, "Critical Exchanges: The Symbolic and Questions of Gender," in *Questioning Foundations: Truth / Subjectivity / Culture*, ed. Hugh J. Silverman (New York: Routledge, 1993), 134–49.

7. Stanley Fish, "Rhetoric," in *Critical Terms for Literary Study*, ed. Frank Lentricchia and Thomas McLaughlin (Chicago: University of Chicago Press, 1990), 208. For further evidence that the essentialism / constructivism debate is taken to comprehend all possible accounts of sexuality, see Edward Stein, ed., *Forms of Desire: Sexual Orientation and the Social Constructionist Controversy* (New York: Routledge, 1992).

and embodiment that is both immoderately antifoundationalist *and* anti-rhetoricalist.

While Butler's fine-tuning of the poststructuralist rhetorical machine enables her to identify in deconstruction a methodological alternative to the constructivism-essentialism debate, I locate that alternative in psychoanalysis.[8] Yet doesn't the notion that sex is discursively constituted derive, in part, from psychoanalysis—specifically, from what Edelman, acknowledging his book's methodological debts, conventionally refers to as "the linguistically oriented psychoanalysis of Jacques Lacan" (xiv)? Lacan's reconstruction of the unconscious as an effect of language ("the unconscious is the discourse of the Other"), his interpretation of the primary process in terms of metaphor and metonymy, and his description of desire as structured metonymically all support this attribution. Yet this attribution leads to a basic misconception. We may begin clarifying the crucial point that distinguishes Lacanian psychoanalysis from other positions by referring to Lacan's insistence that although desire is "in" language, *desire is not itself linguistic.* This distinction is not merely terminological or a question of emphasis, but is the basis for a specifically psychoanalytic conception of desire, sexuality, and rhetoric whose implications directly oppose those derivable from all the impressive and sophisticated constructions of sexuality churned out by the rhetorical machine.

In their failure to consider what in rhetoric or discourse exceeds language—the in-language-more-than-language, to rephrase Lacan's formulation of desire (*Four* 263)—rhetoricalist theories of sexuality effectively evacuate the category of desire from their accounts. Without desire there can be neither rhetoric nor sexuality; without desire, advertising would not exist. To say that explicitly queer-identified theories, such as Butler's and Edelman's, evacuate desire from their accounts could be understood as saying nothing more than that such accounts eschew *heterosexual* desire, concerning themselves instead with queer

---

8. Butler writes:

 Paradoxically, the inquiry into the kinds of erasures and exclusions by which the construction of the subject operates is no longer constructivism, but neither is it essentialism. For there is an "outside" to what is constructed by discourse, but this is not an absolute "outside," an ontological thereness that exceeds or counters the boundaries of discourse; as a constitutive "outside," it is that which can only be thought—when it can—in relation to that discourse, at and as its most tenuous borders. The debate between constructivism and essentialism thus misses the point of deconstruction altogether. (*Bodies,* 8)

desire. Correlative to such a glib interpretation would be the conviction that a psychoanalytic conception of desire is partially or wholly hetero-sexist, so definitively has psychoanalysis "been shaped by homophobic and heterosexist assumptions and histories," as Eve Kosofsky Sedgwick puts it.[9] While the larger argument of *Beyond Sexuality* attempts to dispel this popular misconception, the present chapter contends more point-edly that the rhetoricalist model dispenses with the psychoanalytic framework that enables nonheterosexist *desire*—as opposed to non-heterosexual practices—to be thought at all.

The irony of Butler's and Edelman's elisions of desire lies not only in their attempts to think sexuality without desire, but particularly in their use of psychoanalysis to do so. Both Butler and Edelman are "gay Lacanians"—or so I've been informed on various occasions through the network of "rumors and gossip" allegedly favored by queers.[10] The problem with this common misapprehension is that too many people working in queer studies—and in other fields—remain content to take their understanding of psychoanalysis from accounts such as Butler's and Edelman's. Yet in my view these accounts neglect what is most useful in psychoanalysis for queer intellectual work. To clear up certain misunderstandings about Lacan, it is necessary to recapitulate his devel-opment of a psychoanalytic rhetoric.

Psychorhetoric

Both psychoanalysis and classical rhetoric are concerned with speech's effects on the body, the capacity of speech to produce affect and desire. Lacan exploited this affinity by developing the implications of Freud's account of "dream-work" in rhetorical terms. In his "Rome Discourse"

179

9. Eve Kosofsky Sedgwick, *Tendencies* (Durham: Duke University Press, 1993), 73.

10. Margaret Morrison, "Laughing with Queers in My Eyes: Proposing 'Queer Rhetoric(s)' and Introducing a Queer Issue," *Pre/Text* 13, nos. 3–4 (1992): 22. It was as a response to the special double issue of *Pre/Text* on queer rhetoric that this chapter began. Perhaps it is also worth noting here that the index to *Bodies That Matter* contains more entries under *Lacan* than under any other name. Butler's ambivalence vis-à-vis Lacanian concepts and terminology is signaled by her insistent efforts to qualify her psychoanalytic commitments—for example, by placing the term *unconscious* in scare quotes (22). However, this ambivalence is only compounded when such qualifi-cations are framed in a Lacanian idiom: "The return to psychoanalysis, then, is guided by the question of how certain regulatory norms form a 'sexed' subject in terms that establish the indistinguishability of psychic and bodily formation" (22). This "return to psychoanalysis," unlike Lacan's "return to Freud," explicitly claims fundamental "resignifications" of the theory to which it returns, assuming that, for example, it's safer to speak of "The Lesbian Phallus" than "The Lacanian Phallus."

(1953), Lacan summarized his initial construction of dream "rhetoric" thus:

> Ellipsis and pleonasm, hyperbaton or syllepsis, regression, repeti-
> tion, apposition—these are the syntactical displacements; metaphor,
> catachresis, autonomasis, allegory, metonymy, and synecdoche—
> these are the semantic condensations in which Freud teaches us to
> read the intentions—ostentatious or demonstrative, dissimulating or
> persuasive, retaliatory or seductive—out of which the subject modu-
> lates his oneiric discourse. (*E* 58)

In light of his subsequent revisions of this rhetoric of dreams, it is notable that in 1953 Lacan aligned both metaphor and metonymy with condensation. After Jakobson's famous paper on metaphor and metonymy,
in 1956, these alignments changed significantly.[11] However, Lacan's
revisions of his earlier theory of dream rhetoric are complicated by
the fact that, strongly influenced by Jakobson though he was, not only
did Jakobson's account diverge significantly from the classical divisions
of rhetoric, but Lacan's use of Jakobson subtly and inexplicitly revises
Jakobson's own revisionary model too.[12]

Four years after Jakobson's paper on metaphor and metonymy,
Lacan characterized the rhetoric of the unconscious in this way:

> In this formula [of the linguistic unconscious] . . . the crucial
> term is the signifier, brought back to life from the ancient art of
> rhetoric by modern linguistics, in a doctrine whose various stages

11. Roman Jakobson, "Two Types of Language and Two Types of Aphasic Disturbance," in *Language in Literature,* ed. Krystyna Pomorska and Stephen Rudy (Cambridge: Harvard University Press, 1987), 95–114.

12. In negotiating the complexities of these borrowings, divisions, and debts, I have been aided greatly by Russell Grigg's linguistic analysis of metaphor and metonymy, which makes a series of useful distinctions. See Russell Grigg, "Metaphor and Metonymy," *Newsletter of the Freudian Field* 3 (1989): 58–79 (a revised version of Grigg's essay appeared under the same title in *Pre/Text: A Journal of Rhetorical Theory* 15 [1994]: 27–45). Differentiating between metonymy and three different structures of metaphor (substitution, extension, and apposition), Grigg shows that metonymy and substitution metaphors are produced through substitution, but extension and appositive metaphors are not. "Metonymy is structurally similar to the substitution metaphor, since both have a latent and a manifest term" (71), whereas appositive metaphors (such as "silence is golden") or extension metaphors (such as "the mouth of a river") do not require a latent term in order to function. Making this distinction shows that "while Jakobson's analysis can be applied to metonymy . . . it is unable to account for any form of metaphor" (65). Grigg proceeds to demonstrate that Lacan adopts Jakob-son's account of metonymy (in which a *specific* semantic relation between latent and manifest signifiers holds), but that when Lacan speaks of metaphor he is referring to "substitution metaphors where these relations are absent" (66). My discussion restates Grigg's distinctions in slightly different terms.

cannot be traced here, but of which the names of Ferdinand de Saussure and Roman Jakobson will stand for the dawn and its present-day culmination, not forgetting that the pilot science of structuralism in the West has its roots in Russia, where formalism first flourished. 'Geneva 1910' and 'Petrograd 1920' suffice to explain why Freud lacked this particular tool. But this defect of history makes all the more instructive the fact that the mechanisms described by Freud as those of 'the primary process', in which the unconscious assumes its rule, *correspond exactly* to the functions that this [structuralist] school believes determines the most radical aspects of the effects of language, namely metaphor and metonymy—in other words, the signifier's effects of substitution and combination on the respectively synchronic and diachronic dimensions in which they appear in discourse. (*E* 297– 98; emphasis added)

This remarkably succinct passage establishes a set of alignments that requires clarification and qualification. Lacan's optimistic conviction concerning exact correspondences between rhetorical tropes and unconscious mechanisms is misplaced, for in the domain of rhetoric precise demarcations and unequivocal equations are impossible to maintain, as "Arts of Rhetoric" consistently lament.[13] Perhaps this is another way of

---

13. Conceiving Lacanian theory in periodized terms enables us to view as a form of shorthand the apparent reduction to metaphor and metonymy of the various rhetorical schemes and tropes Lacan described in 1953, rather than as a "lethal generalized restriction" of rhetoric, as Borch-Jacobsen puts it in his critique of psychorhetoric: "Psychoanalytic 'rhetoric,' as it has been understood and practiced for nearly thirty years, is in reality *restricted* rhetoric, rhetoric restricted to the figures of speaking well (or, in this case, the impossibility of speaking well), and also, therefore, to a language amputated from its effective, pragmatic, or persuasive dimension" (Mikkel Borch-Jacobsen, "Analytic Speech: From Restricted to General Rhetoric," in *The Ends of Rhetoric,* ed. Bender and Wellbery, 129–30; original emphasis). Arguing that the Lacanian understanding of rhetoric is restricted by its confining attention to metaphor and metonymy (rather than attending to language's astonishing powers of persuasion), Borch-Jacobsen discusses general (nonrestricted) rhetoric in terms of the persuasive use of language in propaganda and advertising since Freud. In his attempt to reintroduce the dimension of affect to psychorhetoric, Borch-Jacobsen focuses primarily on the functioning of propaganda in group psychology, arguing that "the singular 'logic' of the unconscious is, undoubtedly, the mimo-patho-logic of hypnotic suggestion" (132). However, our reintroducing to Borch-Jacobsen's model the missing question of advertising's persuasive power reveals his model's limits, for it is far more plausible that Madison Avenue exploits desire rather than hypnotic suggestion. Borch-Jacobsen's conception of the unconscious in terms of "the mimo-patho-logic of hypnotic suggestion" reduces the unconscious to an imaginary formation, while simultaneously reducing psychoanalysis to hypnosis. As I explain later in this chapter, Lacanian psychoanalysis theorizes persuasion through the crucial concept of object *a,* which is linked to both affect and desire. Therefore Borch-Jacobsen's avoidance of this concept, which thence restricts his own characterization of unconscious rhetoric (as restricted), displaces the restriction to Lacan's theory of rhetoric that in fact belongs to Borch-Jacobsen's own theory.

saying that there is no way to talk about rhetoric that is not itself rhetorical, no metalanguage extricable from rhetorical discourse. In Lacan's terms, there is no Other of the Other.[14] Given that the appeal to exact correspondences—itself a form of hyperbole—may be read as a sign of this impossibility, we must examine how Lacan theorizes analytic rhetoric in a way that enables psychoanalysis to be assimilated to the rhetoricalist position.

By aligning the mechanisms of the primary process—condensation and displacement—with the rhetorical tropes of metaphor and metonymy, Lacan characterizes the unconscious as rhetorically structured. This alignment depends upon Jakobson's account of metaphor and metonymy as principles of substitution and combination operative on the synchronic and diachronic axes of language respectively. These axes are also described as paradigmatic and syntagmatic, so that the metaphoric substitutions according to which unconscious condensation operates can be understood in literary terms as figuration, while the metonymic combinations according to which unconscious displacement operates can be understood in literary terms as syntax. These necessarily approximate alignments may be summarized thus:

condensation—metaphor—synchronic axis—substitution—paradigm—figure

displacement—metonymy—diachronic axis—combination—syntagm—syntax.

14. The consonance between this Lacanian formulation and the rhetoricalist commitment to the impossibility of metalanguage requires qualification. The rhetoricalist position is stated cogently by Derrida: "Concept is a metaphor, foundation is a metaphor, theory is a metaphor; and there is no meta-metaphor for them" (Jacques Derrida, "White Mythology: Metaphor in the Text of Philosophy," trans. F. C. T. Moore, *New Literary History* 6 [1974]: 23). The antifoundationalist foundation of meta-metaphoricity's impossibility (no Other of the Other) does not entitle metaphor to encompass the entire field of discourse. *Metaphor fails, and its failures are not only metaphoric.* This distinction is highlighted in Butler's "argument" over the Lacanian concept of the real when she asserts that "[t]o claim that the real resists symbolization is still to symbolize the real as a kind of resistance" (*Bodies That Matter*, 207). This assertion bespeaks a sophistic refusal to distinguish between symbolization, discourse, and conceptualization. The notion that a concept is reducible to its discursive conceptualization is a form of the linguistic idealism that Butler ostensibly rejects (*Bodies That Matter*, 8). To say that signification fails, that it is impossible to say everything, is not thereby to eradicate that failure or impossibility. Yet Butler persists with this faulty logic: "The former claim (the real resists symbolization) can only be true if the latter claim ('the real resists symbolization' is a symbolization) is true, but if the second claim is true, the first is necessarily false. To presume the real in the mode of resistance is still to predicate it in some way and to grant the real its reality apart from any avowed linguistic capacity to do precisely that" (*Bodies That Matter*, 207). Butler confuses true and false here. The validity of the "former claim (the real resists symbolization)" is independent

Perhaps these divisions and alignments are unjustifiably schematic; nevertheless this model's great benefit for both psychoanalytic and literary interpretation lies in how—by aligning figuration with condensation, on the one hand, and syntax with displacement, on the other—this version of psychoanalytic formalism reveals an unconscious place in discourse no matter how self-consciously rhetoric is deployed. In other words, one can use this model to interpret written and spoken utterance psychoanalytically without recourse to either the vulgar Freudianism of "thematic" readings or the marginally more sophisticated approach of "symptomatic" readings.[15] For example, while neither symbol hunting nor psychobiography seems at all adequate for the interpretation of discursive practices such as poetry, nevertheless reading poems through the perspective of psychoanalytic formalism encourages one to connect distinctive syntactic patterns and structures of figuration with unconscious processes in a nonpathologizing way.

Furthermore, conceiving unconscious processes linguistically immediately deindividualizes the unconscious: once the unconscious is understood in terms of the discourse of the Other, then the unconscious necessarily exceeds the individual and becomes more readily thinkable as social and cultural (if not "collective" in the Jungian sense). Of course, it's just a hasty step from this conception to the notion that the subject is *constructed* by social discourses and practices. I've tried to suggest why we should think long and hard before taking that easy step. Although irreducible to social constructionism, psychoanalytic formalism is not

---

of the validity of "the latter claim ('the real resists symbolization' is a symbolization)," and since Butler fails to consider the possibility that the first, rather than the second, claim is true, her argument neglects the distinction that would recognize that not every statement (and not every conceptualization) represents a symbolization of the real.

15. The "symptomatic" approach of hunting for parapraxes (as opposed to the "thematic" approach of hunting for symbols) is epistemologically problematic when dealing with highly revised and carefully edited written texts, rather than with unscripted spoken utterance. Nevertheless, critics such as Jane Gallop have had a good measure of success with the symptomatic approach, an ingenious method that seems appropriate when a published text—such as Butler's reading of Žižek—is peppered with terminological slips and conceptual slippages that could be seen as crying out for interpretation. And more recently, in "What Ails Feminist Criticism?" *Critical Inquiry* 24 (1998): 878–902, Susan Gubar interprets a repeated grammatical error in Butler's prose: subject-verb disagreement. Gubar not only identifies an impressive series of instances in which Butler uses the singular verb form when referring to plural grammatical subjects, but she also treats these errors as *meaningful*, as indicating more than mere sloppiness or faulty grammar on Butler's part. Thus Gubar argues that "the most vigilantly antitotalizing theorist of poststructuralism relies on stubborn patterns of totalization (two [grammatical subjects] treated as one)" (898). In discerning meaning— and, indeed, some degree of motivation—behind these grammatical lapses, Gubar's approach is implicitly psychoanalytic, notwithstanding her essay's nonpsychoanalytic argument.

by that token narrowly formalist, for by revealing the degree to which formal properties of discourse are determined by extratextual, historically specific constraints, this psychoanalytic model lays the groundwork for a more nuanced account of what connects a text to the world beyond itself. In maintaining that textual forms are extratextually determined, this account does not suggest that history or culture completely determines texts, or that such determinations operate in a one-to-one fashion. Although psychic determination tends toward overdetermination, these multiple networks of determination and displacement effectively render overdetermination always incomplete, and thus no single sociohistorical, cultural, or subjective determinant can occupy the position of primary cause. The concept of overdetermination does not entail a psychically determinist model, for that would return psychoanalysis to foundationalism. Indeed, by connecting a text's formal or rhetorical features to ostensibly nonformal, historical determinations, psychoanalytic formalism is exonerated from the stereotypical charge leveled at psychoanalytic methods—that they are ahistorical and universalizing.

Yet the psychoanalytic model I'm describing remains troublingly schematic. This can be confirmed by noting that the alignment of metaphor with the substitution axis, on the one hand, and the alignment of metonymy with the combination axis, on the other, ignores "the fact that not all metaphors are substitutions (there are also appositive and extension metaphors) while all metonyms are substitutions," as Grigg indicates.[16] Thus, despite the classical understanding of metaphor as substitutive—the etymology of *meta-phor,* a transfer of burden, suggests this—metaphor intuitively seems to belong on the combination axis (the substitution metaphor "combines" a tenor and vehicle), while metonymy, as *necessarily* substitutive, seems to belong on the substitution axis, rather than vice versa, as Lacan, following Jakobson, aligns them. Furthermore, understanding metonymy in terms of displacement would seem more readily to align metonymy, rather than metaphor, with the substitution axis, since metaphor's alignment with condensation presupposes prior substitutions or displacements that combine various chains of association to form condensation, as Freud suggests in *The Interpretation of Dreams* (*SE* 5:339 ff.).

Although the passage from "Subversion of the Subject" quoted above

16. Grigg, "Metaphor and Metonymy," 64–65.

appears oblivious to the costs of schematism, Lacan anticipated this problem in his seminar *The Psychoses* (1955–56) by showing how the metonymic principle of substitutability is metaphor's condition of possibility. Acknowledging that "[w]hen one reads the rhetoricians, one realizes that they never get to an entirely satisfactory definition of metaphor, or of metonymy," Lacan notes the outcome of this difficulty: "This results in, for example, the formula that metonymy is an impoverished metaphor. One might say that the thing is to be taken in exactly the opposite sense—metonymy exists from the beginning and makes metaphor possible" (*SIII* 227).[17] This excursus on rhetoric in the seminar on psychoses is not tangential but central, a point of some significance given that psychosis represents the most serious—that is, ostensibly the least rhetorical—form of psychical disturbance. In other words, if the most extreme instance of mental illness is to be understood in rhetorical terms, then there seems precious little that would escape this psychoanalytic rhetoricalization of psychic life. Indeed, with respect to rhetorical operations Lacan insists: "This is the heart of Freud's thought. His work begins with the dream, its mechanisms of condensation and displacement, of figuration—these are all of the order of metonymic articulation, and it's on this foundation that metaphor is able to intervene" (*SIII* 228).

Given Lacan's painstaking discussion, in the seminar, of the distinctions between metaphor and metonymy and the implications each has for the other, what are we to make of his subsequent failure in "Subversion of the Subject" to perfectly formalize psychorhetoric? Besides signifying the impossibility of metalanguage, this failure of formalization may be viewed psychoanalytically as a sign of the real: if the real is defined as that which resists symbolization, then symbolization's failures are legible as "signs" of the real. This leads me to suggest that beyond psychoanalytic formalism lies desire—a desire that is structured metonymically but is not itself wholly linguistic. In his *Four Fundamental Concepts,* Lacan explains in highly figurative language how desire is a product of lapses in symbolization:

17. Grigg makes the same point, arguing that one crucial difference between metaphor and metonymy lies in the fact that "there is an established semantic link between latent and manifest terms in metonymy," whereas "metaphors do not just operate by means of a semantic relation between a manifest and a latent signifier, but make use of any means the language has at its disposal" (71–72). Thus although this restriction makes metonymy look like "an impoverished metaphor," Grigg's distinctions enable him to show that nevertheless "the substitution metaphor depends upon the metonymic support the latent term derives from the manifest terms" (73).

185

In this interval intersecting the signifiers, which forms part of the very structure of the signifier, is the locus of what, in other registers of my exposition, I have called metonymy. It is there that what we call desire crawls, slips, escapes, like the ferret. The desire of the Other is apprehended by the subject in that which does not work, in the lacks of the discourse of the Other, and all the child's *whys* reveal not so much an avidity for the reason of things, as a testing of the adult, a *Why are you telling me this?* ever-resuscitated from its base, which is the enigma of the adult's desire. (*Four* 214)[18]

Suggesting that desire originates from negative instances and is therefore not a product of positive linguistic or rhetorical constructions, Lacan's colorful imagery for the mobility of desire provides a useful antidote to the misconception, reiterated in *Bodies That Matter,* that the Lacanian conception of desire is, in its structuralist fixity, intransigently heterosexist. If Butler's project in *Bodies That Matter* is, as she says, "to challenge the structural stasis of the heterosexualizing norm within the psychoanalytic account" (22), then one has only to conjure Lacan's ferret to see how misplaced the charge of "structural stasis" is.[19]

In the spirit of psychorhetoric, both Butler's and Edelman's accounts make much of Lacan's reversing the conventional relation between metaphor and metonymy—his reversing, that is, the place of metonymy for that of metaphor as "foundational" rather than secondary and impoverished. Butler and Edelman exploit this reversal in the process of their rethinking the conventional relation between heterosexuality (as foundational and original) and homosexuality (as secondary and imitative). Since Butler's and Edelman's arguments share a number of misconceptions that nevertheless develop in different directions, it

18. It would be instructive to compare Lacan's notion of the constitutive "enigma of the adult's desire"—an enigma produced by a failure of signification, a gap in the discourse of the Other—with Laplanche's notion of the "enigmatic signifier" and its role in "implanting" sexuality and thence desire. See Jean Laplanche, "The Theory of Seduction and the Problem of the Other," trans. Luke Thurston, *International Journal of Psychoanalysis* 78 (1997): 653–66.

19. In the context of this value-laden opposition between fixity and mobility, I should emphasize that my argument here is consonant with Joan Copjec's crucial point that "[s]ex does not budge, and it is not heterosexist to say so" (*Read My Desire,* 211), because the heterosexist conception of sex depends upon an imaginary complementarity, whereas the psychoanalytic conception of sex as real implies the impossibility of complementarity, the failure of sexual *relation.* It is because sex is real, unsymbolizable, that "sex does not budge." Both Butler and Edelman miss this psychoanalytic point by making sex performative and graphemic—that is, by situating sex at symbolic and imaginary levels of construction, rather than at the level of the real.

makes sense to consider their arguments in turn. In what follows, I want to suggest that by assimilating the category of sexuality to imaginary and symbolic formations, Butler's and Edelman's accounts paradoxically produce queer bodies bearing egos but devoid of subjective desire. That is, their accounts describe subjects of the signifier, not subjects of desire.[20] While the subject of desire is produced through language's impact on bodily materiality—that is, the way language "penetrates to the deepest levels of human experience," in Bender and Wellbery's terms—the subject of desire differs significantly from the subject of imaginary and symbolic identifications. The subject of desire emerges not when an identification (with the father, the mother, or a signifier) is made, but when it fails to be made. In Lacanian terms, we could say that the rhetoricalist account of subjectivity confuses alienation (into the signifier, A) and separation (from an object, a). Failing to distinguish others from Others, Butler's and Edelman's accounts offer us undersubjectivized bodies, bodies so completely rhetoricalized that paradoxically they are devoid of desire.[21] Such suave bodies are queer indeed, though not in any way liberated or liberating.

187

Suave Bodies

I'd like to begin by characterizing Edelman's titular neologism, *homographesis,* since the terms of his substantial, complex, and sophisticated argument require unpacking. Taking seriously Foucault's canonical account of the late-nineteenth-century invention of homosexuality as a discrete ontological identity, Edelman develops the implications of Foucault's description of this new sexual "species" whose sexuality was "written immodestly on his face and body because it was a secret that always gave itself away."[22] Linking Foucault's characterization of homosexuality as something *written* on the body to the ancient tradition of treating homosexuality as "the crime not fit to be *named,*" Edelman persuasively delineates "the historical relationship that has produced gay

---

20. For more on this distinction, see Parveen Adams, *The Emptiness of the Image: Psychoanalysis and Sexual Differences* (London: Routledge, 1996), 55.

21. For more on the implications for queer theory and politics of this distinction between others and Others, see Tim Dean, "Two Kinds of Other and Their Consequences," *Critical Inquiry* 23 (1997): 910–20.

22. Foucault, *The History of Sexuality,* 1:43.

sexuality within a discourse that associates it with figures of nomination or inscription" (4). Associated with writing (graphesis), homosexuality thus figures in Edelman's rhetoricalist account as a "dangerous supplement," undermining all heterosexuality's claims for originality, priority, and naturalness in the way that, for Derrida, writing as supplement undermines similar claims made on behalf of speech.

However, Edelman's rhetoricalization of sexuality is more complex still, since *homographesis* bears the double valence of, on the one hand, indicating the regulatory regime that demands homosexuality be legible (hence necessarily inscribed, textualized) as a discrete identity separate from heterosexuality in the first place; while, on the other hand, *homographesis* suggests the deconstructive possibility inherent in any textualized form for revealing the artificial, secondary, and derivative status of the "natural." Edelman summarizes thus: "Like writing, then, homographesis would name a double operation: one serving the ideological purposes of a conservative social order intent on codifying identities in its labor of disciplinary inscription, and the other resistant to that categorization, intent on *de*-scribing the identities that order has so oppressively inscribed (10). In this way homographesis reveals how heterosexuality is founded not in nature but in the repression of homosexuality, the latter of which then claims a certain priority—not as natural, but as the primary differential in sexuality's constitution. By virtue of its scriptive, rhetorical nature, homosexuality's deconstruction of heterosexuality enables Edelman to claim that gay sexuality "functions in the modern West as the very agency of sexual meaningfulness, the construct without which sexual meaning, and therefore, in a larger sense, meaning itself, becomes virtually unthinkable" (xv). Treating "meaning itself" as an extension of "sexual meaning," Edelman's position in fact directly opposes Lacan's, since Lacan spoke of sexuality in terms of the failure of meaning. To be more precise, we should say that Lacan considered meaning as a substitute for sexuality: "Everything implied by the analytic engagement with human behaviour indicates not that meaning reflects the sexual but that it makes up for it."[23]

This crucial difference notwithstanding, Edelman frames the reversal of priority between hetero- and homosexuality in terms of Lacan's

23. Jacques Lacan, Le séminaire, livre 21, "Les non-dupes errent," 1973–1974, unpublished manuscript, 9. Cited in Jacqueline Rose, *Sexuality in the Field of Vision* (London: Verso, 1986), 71.

reversal of priority between metaphor and metonymy. That is, Edelman rewrites the Foucaultian narrative of homosexuality's invention "as a transformation in the rhetorical or tropological framework through which the concept of 'sexuality' itself is produced":

> a transformation from a reading of the subject's relation to sexuality as contingent or metonymic to a reading in which sexuality is reinterpreted as essential or metaphoric. When homosexuality is no longer understood as a discrete set of acts but as an "indiscreet anatomy," we are in the presence of a powerful tropological imperative that needs to produce a visible emblem or metaphor for the "singular nature" that now defines or identifies a specifically homosexual type of person. That legible marking or emblem, however, must be recognized as a figure for the now metaphorical conceptualization of sexuality itself—a figure for the privileged relationship to identity with which the sexual henceforth will be charged. In keeping, therefore, with the ethnographic imperative of nineteenth-century social science, "the homosexual" could emerge into cultural view through the attribution of essential meaning—which is to say, the attribution of metaphorical significance—to various contingencies of anatomy that were, to the trained observer, as indiscreet in revealing the "truth" of a person's "sexual identity" as dreams or somatic symptoms would be in revealing the "truth" of the unconscious to the emergent field of psychoanalysis. (8)

Like Foucault, Edelman implies—without ever directly stating—that "the emergent field of psychoanalysis" formed part of "the ethnographic imperative of nineteenth-century social science" that enabled—indeed required—the shadowy figure of "the homosexual" to "emerge into cultural view." Edelman reads the historically coincident emergence of homosexuality and psychoanalysis metaphorically rather than metonymically, in that he figures their coincident emergence as essential and therefore causally related, rather than as contingent.

What is at stake in Edelman's rhetoric that encourages us to read homosexuality metonymically but psychoanalysis metaphorically? By suggesting how the cultural project of making homosexuality visible operates through a tropological imperative to produce vital signs, Edelman argues that "sexuality" as sexual orientation is produced when desire as metonymic is misrecognized as metaphoric—in other words,

189

when the contingent is mistaken as essential. In figuring the relation between psychoanalysis and homosexuality as metaphoric, is Edelman performing a misrecognition in the very gesture of unmasking one? Explicitly alluding at this point in his argument to Lacan's conception of desire as metonymically structured (and, indeed, Lacan's reversal of the conventional relation between metaphor and metonymy), Edelman misrecognizes the cultural force of psychoanalysis, for *it is psychoanalysis that discloses the cultural misrecognition whereby sexual identities and orientations are solidified and hierarchized.* Freud's insistence that sexuality undermines identity rather than consolidating it entails a metonymic reading of sexuality at the very moment such metonymies were being culturally misrecognized as metaphoric. Freud's position in his *Three Essays on the Theory of Sexuality* was, as we know, "most decidedly opposed to any attempt at separating off homosexuals from the rest of mankind as a group of a special character" (*SE* 7:145 n.). Thus far from reading sexual signs metaphorically, Freud emphasized such signs' metonymic significance, since he was convinced "that all human beings are capable of making a homosexual object-choice and have in fact made one in their unconscious" (*SE* 7:145 n.).

In pointing to Edelman's misrecognition of psychoanalysis at the very moment he identifies a cultural misrecognition of sexuality, I am not suggesting that psychoanalysis ever could be completely free from social and cultural biases. But I am suggesting that the tropological and ethnographic imperatives Edelman describes should be viewed as less consistent and totalizing than he would have us believe. Edelman's account does have the benefit of delineating a far more elaborate, more explicit way of conceiving resistance to these cultural imperatives than Foucault's notoriously undertheorized notion of resistance. But where Edelman locates resistance in the deconstructive force of writing or language itself, I would locate that resistance more specifically—perhaps more historically—in psychoanalysis. My objection to situating the possibility of disrupting cultural norms at the level of deconstructive "graphesis," in Edelman's case, or "resignification," in Butler's case, is that despite their best efforts they fail to conceive sexuality in anything but binary, overwhelmingly Manichaean terms. Permit me to explain why their conceiving sexuality in this way paradoxically entails evacuating desire from the theoretical picture.

Both Butler and Edelman write about lesbian and gay egos; they

190

treat subjectivity and sexuality as if these dimensions of psychic life were a function of one's self-image rather than, as psychoanalysis insists, a function of the unconscious. Yet neither Butler nor Edelman is up front about this; they imply that Lacan theorizes subjectivity and sexuality as effects of the imaginary order, the realm of ego formation. Hence, for example, in "The Lesbian Phallus" Butler suggests:

> [E]very effort to inhabit fully an identification with the *imago* . . . fails because the sexuality temporarily harnessed and bounded by that ego . . . cannot be fully or decisively constrained by it. What is left outside the mirror frame, as it were, is precisely the unconscious that comes to call into question the representational status of what is shown *in* the mirror. In this sense, the ego is produced through *exclusion,* as any boundary is, and what is excluded is nevertheless negatively and vitally constitutive of what 'appears' bounded within the mirror. (262 n. 23; original emphases)

While it is true that the ego is constituted through exclusion, by means of a perceptual gestalt, it is not the case that this drawing of boundaries produces sexuality or the unconscious. Human sexuality cannot be construed as in any way a result of the mirror stage. However, by relying on Jane Gallop's interpretation of Lacan, Edelman likewise reads sexual identity formation in terms of the mirror stage:

> [T]he symbolic (hetero)sexual order established by the reading of sexual differentiation through the polarizing narrative of the castration complex imposes a (not necessarily necessary) fiction of sexual identity. That fiction reenacts the contradictory temporality of the Lacanian mirror stage, a temporality in which totalized identity is posited by a decree that phobically disavows the definitional incoherence of the bits and pieces imagined as having preceded the constitution of the subject, precisely because the subject anxiously anticipates the possibility of succumbing to such an incoherence once again. The sexual identity so structured is endlessly paranoid in its need to assert the inevitability and security of its narcissistic totalization, and thus the subject actively refuses—indeed, aggressively attempts to efface—whatever would ironize its claim to an identity *intrinsic to and coextensive with the fact of its existence.* (225–26; original emphasis)

It is precisely because the ego produced through this mechanism of identification "is endlessly paranoid" and aggressive that these persistent mischaracterizations of sexuality in imaginary terms are so self-defeating. For by focusing solely on the ego, Butler's and Edelman's accounts not only misrepresent the subjective level at which sexuality is formed and operates, they also seem unable to escape the impasse of paranoid, highly defensive binarity typical of the imaginary structure within whose terms they theorize sexuality. And despite all their loudly proclaimed awareness of constructedness and contingency, lesbian and gay egos—by virtue of being egos—are no less paranoid or aggressive than heterosexual people's egos.

Against Rhetoricality

From a Lacanian viewpoint, all binary relations are imaginary in the sense that they are structured by relations of identification and opposition, one-to-one relations. And all imaginary relations are essentially binaristic. From this it follows that to theorize sexuality in imaginary terms—in terms, that is, of the ego or the self—is to conceptualize sexuality binarily, even if, like Butler and Edelman, one intends otherwise. No amount of subtle theorizing will get you outside a binary system if your model of subjectivity remains focused on the self. All you get from an imaginary relation is an ego and lots of trouble. By "trouble" I mean imaginary aggressivity—imaginary not in the sense of unreal, but in the sense of the extremely violent policing of inside/outside borders by which the ego maintains itself. This is not the kind of subversive trouble Butler intends in *Gender Trouble.* Yet as I suggested in chapter 2, in my discussion of *Gender Trouble,* theorizing gender and sexuality in imaginary terms leaves aspects of subjectivity other than the ego calmly untroubled.

The production of what Butler, following Derrida, calls a "constitutive outside" offers a useful way to think about ego formation, including the formation of collective egos. But in psychoanalytic terms, the *subject* is not formed through the production of a constitutive outside; neither is this exterior equivalent to the category of the unconscious, as Butler seems to think (22). Furthermore, this "constitutive outside" is quite distinct from what Lacan means by the real: "The non-ego is not to be confused with what surrounds it, the vastness of the real" (*Four* 245).

To conceptualize subjectivity in terms of exclusion and the regulation of inside / outside or human / abject borders is simply to think subjectivity imaginarily, to remain caught in binary categories. Thus although Butler at one point notes the Lacanian distinction between subject and ego (261 n. 22), subjectivity—in *Bodies That Matter,* as in *Homographesis*-constantly falls back into the ego.

Neither subjectivity nor sexuality is an effect of imaginary relations. Although some of Lacan's vocabulary when describing the specular construction of the ego—the "lure of the mirror" and suchlike—sounds as if it might have something to do with sexuality, we should be clear that for Lacan sexuality and desire are not produced through binary structures. Since lesbian and gay theorists often remain ambivalent about psychoanalytic methodologies because the binary pairings male / female, masculine / feminine, activity / passivity make psychoanalysis look suspiciously like conceptual support for compulsory heterosexuality, I would like to emphasize that Lacan theorizes sexuality in terms not of gender but of *jouissance.* As I elaborate more fully in the next chapter, this underappreciated dimension of Lacanian theory makes psychoanalysis the ally of theorists—such as Butler, Edelman, and Eve Sedgwick—struggling to think sexuality outside the terms of gender.[24]

For the sake of distinctions that usually evaporate even when people bother to make them, let me summarize Lacan by characterizing the ego as an effect of the imaginary order, the subject as an effect of the symbolic order, and sexuality as an effect of the real order. This leaves us with at least two questions. First, of what is the desiring subject an effect? Second, how are we to understand relations among imaginary, symbolic, and real orders—that is, among the ego, the unconscious, and sexuality? This brings me to the crucial concept of object *a.* Without

24. In *Epistemology of the Closet* (Berkeley and Los Angeles: University of California Press, 1990), Sedgwick makes axiomatic for antihomophobic theory "the imperative of constructing an account of sexuality irreducible to gender" (34); and, in an interview, Sedgwick specifies the following preference: "I like the notion of there being institutional places to think about the likelihood that for some people the most important thing about sexuality is not the gender of sexual object choice" (Sarah Chinn, Mario DiGangi, and Patrick Horrigan, "A Talk with Eve Kosofsky Sedgwick," *Pre / Text* 13, nos. 3–4 [1992]: 86). Butler seems to be approaching a similar commitment to thinking sexuality outside the terms of gender when, in "The Lesbian Phallus," she remarks, "it is unclear to me that lesbians can be said to be 'of' the same sex or that homosexuality in general ought to be construed as love of the same" (*Bodies That Matter,* 65–66). And in the final chapter of *Homographesis,* Edelman similarly criticizes the way "sexual orientation in Western culture is persistently posited through its often contradictory assimilation to the discursive categories associated with differences historically and culturally elaborated to distinguish between the sexes" (197).

a concept of the object, it is practically impossible to maintain a distinction between subject and ego, as *Bodies That Matter* repeatedly shows.

"It is necessary to find the subject as a lost object," Lacan gnomically remarks, adding that "this lost object is the support of the subject and in many cases is a more abject thing than you may care to consider" ("Of Structure" 189). For all their psychoanalytically derived preoccupation with the construction of homosexuality as a zone of abjection, Butler and Edelman never consider the meaning of the abject object. As "the support of the subject," this object counterintuitively (ungrammatically?) appears to precede the subject, to found the subject. Indeed, his notion of object *a* represents the principal foundation that Lacan posits for subjectivity. Yet the apparent foundationalism of object *a* betokens a radically contingent foundation, since as Ellie Ragland points out, "[w]e humans are grounded in objects that are not themselves grounded."[25]

The contingent foundation provided by object *a* is that of desire, an unstable foundation indeed. Lacan refers to the object *a* as "cause of desire." By virtue of its being the cause rather than the aim of desire, object *a* conceptually precedes gender or any particular kind of sexual activity. The place and corporeal form of the object, as it is conceived by Lacan, cannot be deduced from any gender configuration or sexual practice. This status of the object helps explain why it is so easily overlooked in theoretical accounts of desire, but also why the concept of object *a* holds such potential for queer critiques of sexuality. If desire is originally independent of gender, how can Lacanian theory legitimately be accused of promoting a heterosexist model of desire? The heterosexist assumption that desire heads toward the opposite sex is challenged by Lacan's contention that desire heads toward nothing in particular except satisfaction. The object-cause of desire takes so many gender-neutral forms—the gaze, the voice, the phoneme, the lips, "the rim of the anus," and "the slit formed by the eyelids" (*E* 314–15)— that it seems to offer the conceptual basis for a radically nonheterosexist account of sexuality and desire. While it is fairly clear how body parts such as the lips, the nether lips, and "the rim of the anus," may function as object-causes of desire thanks to their direct involvement in sexual activity, it is much less obvious how the gaze, the voice, and the phoneme function as causes of desire.

25. Ellie Ragland, "Rhetoric and Unconscious Desire: The Battle for the Postmodern Episteme," *Studies in Psychoanalytic Theory* 1 (1992): 20.

There is a subtle yet crucial distinction to be made here between thinking of objects *a* as causing desire by virtue of their association with parts of the body, on one hand, and grasping that they cause desire by virtue of their standing in for loss, on the other. For a psychoanalytically informed, gay-positive account of sexuality, it would be plausible to develop Lacan's allusion to "the rim of the anus" in his description of objects *a*. By treating the anus as a legitimate occasion of desire—on a par with more clearly sanctioned sexual body parts—Lacanian theory contributes toward a nonpathologizing understanding of gay sexual practices centered on anal and spintrian eroticism, such as buttfucking, rimming, and fisting. Furthermore, Lacan's characterization of the gaze and voice as objects *a* evokes gay practices of cruising and—in the wake of AIDS and the social imperative to devise safer sexual practices—video sex, phone sex, and virtual sex.[26]

These activities dramatize the psychoanalytic insight that many sexual pleasures do not necessarily involve the genitals. By distinguishing sexual desire and *jouissance* from the irresistible pull of genitalia, Lacan denaturalizes and potentially deheterosexualizes desire. But more than this, Lacan's account of multiple object-causes of desire offers a far less literalist theory of sexuality; in so doing, his account opens a space for us to imagine different configurations of bodies and pleasures. This psychoanalytic understanding of sexuality suggests that the most intense pleasures need not involve genital contact at all: there is no privileged sexual activity or erotic narrative to which we should all aspire, no viable sexual norm for everybody, because desire's origins are multiple

26. In his ambitious reading of Otto Preminger's 1944 Hollywood movie *Laura*, Edelman argues that "the gaze comes to carry the very force of gay sexuality itself" (*Homographesis,* 200). Edelman's argument in his book's final chapter may be summarized thus: "This association of the male homosexual with the aggressive deployment of vision, on the one hand (i.e., in his '"habit" of gazing at . . . male partners'), and with his passive susceptibility to visualization or perceptual recognition on the other (i.e., as the object of the cultural enterprise that seeks to render the gay body legible) makes the cinema a particularly important institution within which to consider the function and effect of gay inscription or homographesis" (200). The problem with his account of the function of this gay gaze in cinema—as with my assimilation of the desirous cruising gaze to the Lacanian concept of the gaze as object *a*—lies in the failure to distinguish between vision and gaze. Without this distinction, we lose the conceptual force of Lacan's account of the gaze as cause of desire. My point is not that this much-misunderstood Lacanian concept cannot be used to theorize scopic dimensions of sexuality, but that the relation between vision and gaze, between cruising and desire, is much more richly complex than gay studies accounts usually allow. Lacan's account of the gaze as object *a* is given in his *Four Fundamental Concepts* (67–119). A useful gloss on the distinctions involved in Lacan's account and their pertinence for theorizing perverse desire may be found in Julia Saville, " 'The Lady of Shalott': A Lacanian Romance," *Word and Image* 8 (1992): 71–87.

and its ambition no more specific than satisfaction. In Lacan's account, this lack of specificity represents not so much a cover for universal sexual norms as the multiplication of possibilities for desire's outcomes.

Gaze, voice, and phoneme connect our bodies to society and culture in a way that suggests the conceptual potential of object *a* for theorizing sexuality as culturally inflected, mediated, even "technologized," without reductively describing sexuality as culturally constructed. Indeed, the concept of object *a* can help us appreciate the way advertising incites desire, as Lacan suggests:

> The features that appear in our time so strikingly in the form of what are more or less correctly called the *mass media* . . . [are] illuminated by the reference to those two objects . . . namely, the voice— partly planeterized, even stratospherized, by our machinery—and the gaze, whose ever-encroaching character is no less suggestive, for, by so many spectacles, so many phantasies, it is not so much our vision that is solicited, as our gaze that is aroused. (*Four* 274; original italics)

This passage suggests the sensitivity of Lacan's account of desire to technological shifts in the organization of social space; in other words, this passage implies that a psychoanalytic understanding of desire need not remain indifferent to historical change. Furthermore, Lacan expands the potential of his account of desire by characterizing object *a* dynamically: "in some cases it is something done" ("Of Structure" 189). If the object that causes desire can take the form of a verb as well as a noun, then we begin to appreciate its multivalent explanatory possibilities.

Lacan's provisional list of the forms object *a* may take centers on the common feature of what he describes somewhat enigmatically as "the mark of a cut." This "cut" refers to bodily borders, wherever inside meets outside. If we can understand how object *a* results from a cut that produces simultaneously subject and object, then it becomes clearer how object *a* can be "something done." This object appears as the effect of some action on my body, rather than preexisting in object form. If, as Butler suggests, matter is always materialized, then we might say that objects *a* are always objected or objectivized. Lacan explains: "The *a*, the object, falls. That fall is primal. The diversity of forms taken by that object of the fall ought to be related to the manner in which the desire of the Other is apprehended by the subject" ("Names" 85). The object's fall is "primal," because in falling the object founds the subject and its desire. But what causes the object to fall? In providing an answer to this question, we shall discover how object *a* links imaginary, symbolic, and real registers. We shall also discover—in Lacan's conception of the body in imaginary, symbolic, and real terms—an alternative to the unidimensional "suave body" of rhetoricalist theory.

Broadly speaking, when language hits the body its impact produces not merely the subject of the signifier but also the subject of desire. The symbolic order has a ripple-like effect on human subjects. Think of the symbolic order as a net settling over the corporeal form, penetrating the body, as Bender and Wellbery say, and slicing the body into erotogenic zones by drawing bodily *jouissance* into pools at its corporeal borders. This process does not happen in a uniform way because there is no single symbolic order that we all inhabit. We move through different, interwoven discourse networks that affect people's bodies unevenly; nevertheless, it should be borne in mind that this process of creating desire begins very early in life, well before anatomical maturation, and usually within familial discourse networks.

Language is the agent of the cut that produces subject and object through the same action. The result of language's impact on the body, object *a* can be thought of as the leftover of *jouissance,* what Lacan calls the *plus-de-jouir.* Without language, desire would not exist. But this does not make desire linguistic. Although object *a* is not prediscursive in the sense that it does not precede language, it also is not a discursive effect in quite the way that rhetoricalism understands the subject and his or her sexuality as discursive effects. Object *a* links the body to language and therefore is crucial for conceptualizing rhetoric, which has a demonstrable effect on bodies. Lacan describes corporeality, subjectivity, and sexuality not simply as discursive or rhetorical effects; rather he provides a way to theorize language's impact on the body in three dimensions—imaginary, symbolic, and real.

Consider the terms in which Lacan formulated the relation between body, language, and desire by defining desire as "neither the appetite for satisfaction, nor the demand for love, but the difference that results from the subtraction of the first from the second, the phenomenon of their splitting *(Spaltung)*" (*E* 287). Distinguishing desire from biological or physical needs, Lacan conceived desire as the excess resulting from the articulation of need in symbolic form. Thus where bodies may be said to have needs such as biological sustenance and physical protection, subjects have desires—principally, overcoming the loss constitutive of subjectivity as such—hence the requirement to "find the subject as a lost object." It is because desire remains distinct from need that sexuality is cultural rather than biological. Yet the widespread insistence on various constituencies' subjective "needs" effectively eclipses desire. Hence the incoherence betrayed in Edelman's account of sexuality by his reference to "the pressure of more immediate psychic needs" (229). No psyche "needs" anything. The confusion indicated by this oxymoronic formulation of "psychic needs" can hardly be excused as merely terminological or rhetorical because, according to Edelman's own account, terminology and rhetoric should be understood as constitutive. This rhetoric of "needs"—which is prevalent in, though not specific to, queer cultural critique—effectively misrecognizes desire in just the way that heterosexist cultural assumptions denigrate and trivialize homosexual desire.

To appreciate the paradox whereby queer cultural critique sometimes unwittingly participates in the conceptual logic of mainstream heterosexist consumer culture, we may extend the argument of this chapter's opening section and suggest that where, from Barthes's semiological perspective, myth transforms history into nature, advertising transforms desire into need—not literally, but rhetorically. The rhetorical effect of this transformation depends on understanding that while desire is impossible to satisfy, need is not. Thus to speak in terms of consumer "needs"—for example, the "communication needs" telephone companies promise to satisfy—is to convert the unsatisfiable into something that ostensibly *can* be satisfied (that is, need) and so promote capitalist consumption while simultaneously perpetuating desire. The demystification of advertising—which so often takes the form of exposing the fallacy that such-and-such completely trivial product could have any significant effect, could change one's life—thus misses how advertising capitalizes on our willingness to confuse need and desire. Since the relatively simple satisfaction of need produces significant effects (a drink of water can save, and therefore immeasurably change, one's life), advertising's notion that desires are needs effectively persuades us that desires can be satisfied, thereby encouraging consumption.

The paradox of the distinction between need and desire is that what can be satisfied (need) sounds so much more legitimate than desire, whose satisfaction remains forever out of reach in a Lacanian framework. Given this distinction, our attention to desire can seem like a luxury, a triviality we should think about only once the more urgent political work of attending to "needs" is accomplished. This hierarchy of political priorities is always implicit in materialist critiques of psychoanalysis.[27] Yet needs concern the biological organism and therefore have little to do with sexuality, which concerns the subject of desire. The issue, then, is how to theorize sexuality in terms of the body without resorting to either a rhetoric of needs—which would return theory to biological foundationalism and hence heterosexism—or a rhetoric of "the body" as pregiven and immutable.

The Body: Imaginary, Symbolic, Real

Butler begins her account of morphogenesis by mimicking a question with which she was reproached in the wake of her theory of gender performativity: " 'What about the materiality of the body, *Judy?*' " (ix). *Bodies That Matter* suggests how "the materiality of the body" can be theorized according to the model of performativity proposed in *Gender Trouble*. My problem with Butler's model differs from those critiques of performativity that charge Butler with failing to take account of "the body." Instead, I am skeptical about the way performativity theorizes the body unidimensionally. This problem becomes clearer when we consider the distinction between the body (which needs) and the subject (which desires). Butler allows no distinction between the body and subjectivity; subjectivity thus collapses back into the ego (American style) and desire is effectively reduced to need (capitalist style).

Arguing for "[t]he indissolubility of the psychic and the corporeal," Butler develops an account of the production of "a 'sexed' subject in terms that establish the indistinguishability of psychic and bodily formation" (66; 22). This account makes all subjectivity imaginary and mistakenly locates sexuality at the level of the ego. Exploiting Freud's axiom, in *The Ego and the Id*, that "the ego is first and foremost a bodily ego" (*SE* 19:26), Butler's analysis provides a nuanced description of nonnormative egos without, however, contributing much to a theory of queer

---

27. For an example of this kind of ordering of political priorities, see Donald Morton, "Birth of the Cyberqueer," *PMLA* 110 (1995): 369–81.

desire. Hence her characterization of "the lesbian phallus" as "transferable" and "plastic property" (62) eloquently describes the play of identifications through which lesbian egos exchange dildos; but this elaboration of a lesbian imaginary fails to register the way egos *occlude*—rather than manifest—desire. Butler's conclusion to her celebrated meditation on "The Lesbian Phallus" makes explicit this emphasis on egos, without considering its psychoanalytic or political implications: "to speak of the lesbian phallus as a possible site of desire . . . is simply to promote an alternative *imaginary* to a hegemonic imaginary" (91; original emphasis). Arguing for the consubstantiality of body and ego—the way bodies do not *precede* egos as models but are themselves embodied, materialized through what Freud calls "the projection of a surface" (*SE* 19:26)— Butler misses the crucial psychoanalytic insight that *desire is predicated on the incommensurability of body and subject.*

We are now in a position to extend our account of language's effect on the body. Although both Butler and Edelman are correct in insisting that we have no unmediated access to our bodies, the forms this mediation takes are more complex than rhetoricalist models allow. The category of "the body" so often invoked in recent theory requires specifying in terms of real, symbolic, and imaginary, as much as in terms of gender, race, and class. If in the realm of the imaginary the body produces— and is indeed produced through—the ego, how should we understand the symbolic order in this production of a visualizable bodily self?

Like Butler, Edelman views the symbolic as essentially an *extension* of the imaginary. Referring to the "policing" effects of what Butler calls "regulatory norms," Edelman argues that "this policing bespeaks the extent to which the symbolic order is mobilized to defend an imaginary self-image against those forces that are seen as threatening to unmask it as always *only* imaginary" (229; original emphasis). Treating the symbolic as a support of the imaginary effectively imaginarizes the symbolic and reduces to the level of the ego the subjectivity of "the gay male body" that Edelman constantly invokes. And, of course, the irony of Edelman's reducing subjectivity to corporeality lies in his insistence that homographesis as "a normalizing practice of cultural discrimination" involves "the process whereby the homosexual subject is represented as being, even more than as inhabiting, a body that always demands to be read, a body on which his 'sexuality' is always already inscribed" (10). To insist on reading the "homosexual subject" in terms of "the gay male body," rather than in terms of that subject's constitutive *dis*embodiment, is thus to perpetuate unwittingly the "normalizing practice of cultural discrimination" at which Edelman levels his critique.

If "the gay male body" is to be credited with a desire beyond that of maintaining his ego—that is, beyond narcissism—this desire will be the result of his disembodiment through language, his subjectivization.[28] The symbolic order's action on dumb corporeal density produces a desubstantialized, symbolic body—the subject ($\mathcal{S}$)—and, as I suggested above, an equally desubstantialized remainder of bodily *jouissance*—the object *(a)*. This process of disembodiment that produces the subject and its causes of desire effectively splits (i) body and subject; (ii) subject and object, thereby constituting desire and the impossibility of its satisfaction; (iii) subject against itself as a consequence of the multiple object-causes of desire that support or contingently ground the subject.[29]

This disembodied, split subject is central to the psychoanalytic theory of sexuality; and it is by conceiving of desire in terms of multiple, partial, not necessarily gendered, not necessarily genital objects that one most fully extricates a model of desire from heterosexist assumptions. By contrast, the unidimensional suave body of the rhetoricalist account—however gussied up in outlandishly queer or sophisticated finery—is simply a product of culturally constrained symbolic and imaginary systems. This "subject's" desire is simply the product of meaning, of a signifying chain; whereas the psychoanalytic subject's desire is a product of that chain's disruption. Regarding this rhetoricalist conception of the subject, Lacan observed that "this subject, who thinks he can accede to himself by designating himself in the statement, is no more than such an [abject] object" *(E* 315).

201

28. The cultural association of homosexuality with narcissism—which stems from the assumption that both homosexuality and narcissism involve love of the same—requires interrogation rather than the endorsement this part of my argument seems to confer. Edelman provides an acute critique of the use of *narcissism* as a term of censure in AIDS activist rhetoric, arguing thus: "It is all the more painful, therefore, when the rhetoric of 'activists,' in its resistance to the dominant discourse, redeploys the ideology of that discourse in order, narcissistically, to reinforce an 'activist' identity by stigmatizing as narcissistic the community, already so-stigmatized, from which they emerged" (*Homographesis*, 108). In "Homo-Narcissism; or Heterosexuality," in *Engendering Men: The Question of Male Feminist Criticism*, ed. Joseph A. Boone and Michael Cadden (New York: Routledge, 1990), 190–206, Michael Warner also provides a strong critique of this association between homosexuality and narcissism. I develop this critique in "Homosexuality and the Problem of Otherness," in *Homosexuality and Psychoanalysis*, ed. Tim Dean and Christopher Lane (Chicago: University of Chicago Press, forthcoming).

29. In *Read My Desire*, chap. 6, Joan Copjec argues for the political purchase of understanding the subject psychoanalytically as disembodied, nonconcrete, universal.

This idea that in language the subject's subjectivity becomes nothing more than "such an object" suggests the difference between a psychoanalytic account (which grounds the subject in the object) and a rhetorical-ist account (which more straightforwardly grounds the subject in language).[30] Lacan's idea suggests also the complex dynamism of a structure in which the language that impacts and dices corporeal density, reducing the subject to an abject object, comes as much from inside the body as outside it. It is for this reason that the phoneme is included in Lacan's catalog of objects *a*. As the smallest linguistic unit capable of signifying difference between otherwise identical words, the phoneme is distinct from Lacan's notion of the signifier, since to make the signifier an object *a* would be to reduce psychoanalysis to rhetoricalism by treating desire as purely linguistic. Our alienation in language is so intense because it is so intimate—that is, because speech operates at the body's borders. Speech comes out of our very mouths, connecting our insides to our outsides. Hence Lacan's reference to "[r]espiratory erogeneity" (*E* 315), the potential for breath itself—not to mention particular words carried on the breath—to produce desire. And thus despite the elaborate protocols surrounding what can be said and to whom, freedom of speech is defended in this culture that seeks to eliminate all other sounds and substances emitted by the body's orifices or at its borders.

Bodies That Mutter

Treating everything except speech that comes out of the body as execrable, North American culture would rather not heed the vital signs emanating from bodies, for to recognize bodies that mutter would require attending to desire, which capitalism prefers to misrecognize as need. Bodies that mutter, that speak almost inaudibly, unintelligibly, are heeded in our culture by psychoanalysis, which first took hysterical symptoms seriously as a form of communication. By producing signs that are not immediately legible even as something requiring reading, bodies that mutter obliquely indicate desire in the form of a failure in the Other's discourse. (Here we might recall Lacan's remarking that "[t]he desire of the Other is apprehended by the subject in that which

---

30. Butler makes this point very clearly in a discussion recorded at a 1991 symposium, "The Identity in Question": "My position is that subjects are constituted in language, but that language is also the site of their destabilization" (*October* 61 [1992]: 113).

does not work, in the lacks of the discourse of the Other.") Bodies that mutter testify to something lacking. Unlike consumer culture, psychoanalysis provides a space in which desire is taken seriously rather than exploited. Whereas rhetoricalism pays attention merely to egos—bodies that matter through imaginary morphogenesis—psychoanalysis pays attention to bodies that mutter, recognizing in the ego a dangerously aggressive façade ("the projection of a surface") that obscures the subject of desire and his or her suffering. Thus we might say that while the ego matters, the body mutters.

Is "bodies that mutter" merely a figure of speech, a play on words? The difference between muttering and speaking concerns the distinction involved in a notion of desire as something *in* language but not itself linguistic. While speech comprises signs and signifiers, muttering comprises the symptom, which represents a literally unspeakable desire. It is a rhetoricalist error to assimilate hysterical symptoms to a model of language or discourse that contains no place for object-causes of desire; if symptoms were simply signs or signifiers, they would be spoken or written. It is because the speaking subject is a disembodied subject that the body mutters. Thus Edelman's unquestioned assumption—that sexuality is written, inscribed, or otherwise textualized on the body—is mistaken in its assigning meaning and legibility, rather than ineliminable opacity, to corporeal marks. Bodies that mutter are bodies whose desire, enmeshed in the symbolic order, is struggling to be heard. The symptom signifies that that desire has not been heard, has not found its signifier. This lack of a signifier is a serious matter, for bodies that mutter are in pain; their muttering is an index of that pain. Yet their muttering also perpetuates that pain. This paradox is what Lacan means by *jouissance,* which Jacques-Alain Miller glosses as "that secret satisfaction which . . . is at the heart of the symptom and attaches the subject to his sickness."[31] By *muttering* I mean a form of signification that condenses and carries with it *jouissance* in a way that ordinary language cannot, since *jouissance* and language conventionally are conceived as antithetical.

Bodies that mutter reveal a relation among language, the body, *jouissance,* and object *a* that illuminates rhetoric—and thence mass culture—as a discourse of persuasion. Desire in language, propelled by

203

---

31. Jean-Paul Morel, "Interview with Jacques-Alain Miller," trans. Dennis Porter, *Newsletter of the Freudian Field* 1, no. 1 (1987): 8.

objects *a,* perturbs language into rhetoric.[32] We might modify the rhetoricalist notion that all language is performative, productive of effects,
by saying that language becomes rhetorical only when it produces affects—that is, when it is imbued with desire. This distinction between
language and rhetoric derives from that elaborated earlier between the
rhetoricalist grounding of subjectivity in language and the psychoanalytic
grounding of subjectivity in objects *a.* Lacan emphasized this distinction
by differentiating signification from discourse: signification comprises a
chain of signifiers, but discourse is made up of both signifiers and objects
a.[33] As Lacan's discourse structures show, there are different ways of
working within language, different ways of speaking, of relating to the
Other, of desiring. As I elaborate in the next chapter, the plurality of
objects *a* suggests great potential for this psychoanalytic theory of desire
to conceive of sexuality outside the terms of normative heterosexuality.
If the plurality of objects *a* finds distorted expression in the range of
rhetorical figures that spoil the fantasy of representational transparency,
then appreciating this link between rhetoric and desire should spoil rhetoricalism's subtler fantasy of "the absolute randomness of language,
prior to any figuration or meaning."[34]

The rhetoricalist model treats some version of this "absolute randomness of language" as the highly contingent foundation of discursive
effects (rhetoric) and subjective affects (guilt, in de Man's example).
By contrast, the psychoanalytic model treats the loss that forms objects
a and hence the subject as foundational. This loss is initiated by language;
and language in the form of rhetoric or discourse—that is, language
infused with desire—tries to overcome this loss. In the face of this
foundational loss, language, "resignification," and deconstruction remain
ultimately inadequate. Thus although psychoanalysis works with nothing
but language, psychoanalytic therapeutics are not directed toward overcoming loss. Instead, psychoanalysis is directed toward admitting desire,
finding ways to inhabit desire.

32. See Ellie Ragland, "Rhetoric and Unconscious Desire," 16.

33. Lacan introduces his discourse structures (that of the master, the university, the hysteric,
and the analyst) in seminar 17, *L'envers de la psychanalyse,* and develops them in seminar 20, *Encore.*
For a demonstration of these discursive structures' potential for rhetorizing aesthetic and gender
relations, see Parveen Adams, *The Emptiness of the Image: Psychoanalysis and Sexual Differences* (London:
Routledge, 1996), chap. 6.

34. Paul de Man, *Allegories of Reading: Figural Language in Rousseau, Nietzsche, Rilke, and Proust*
(New Haven: Yale University Press, 1979), 299.

One best inhabits desire, irrespective of sexual orientation, by acknowledging that the Other is also lacking. That is, the Other (Ø), as well as the subject (𝖲), is "barred." To recognize what Joan Copjec calls "the *unvermögender* Other," the Other who doesn't have what it takes, is to recognize that loss is constitutive of subjectivity rather than the consequence of an oppressive regulatory regime that has arranged the world to one's disadvantage.[35] Recognizing this distinction should not delegitimate the impact of social inequities. Instead, articulating psychoanalysis with politics depends upon differentiating between losses and deficits that represent unequal distribution of social resources, including visibility and dignity, on the one hand, and losses and deficits that are constitutive, that indicate an ineliminable zone of subjective abjection (object *a*), on the other. Despite its ostensibly antifoundationalist commitment to "contingent foundations," rhetoricalism often smacks of conspiracy theory in its unwillingness to countenance the contingency of the real, that which disrupts meaning and, as a by-product of that disruption, leaves objects *a* in its wake. As the desiring subject's contingent foundation, object *a* is, as Lacan suggests, "a more abject thing than you may care to consider." Subjective desire is impossible without abjection. The mistake of the rhetoricalist account is to substantialize that abjection and thus to claim that it can be resignified.

Psychotologic: Arguing with the Real

Butler's commitment to theorizing subjectivity in terms of imaginary formations explains her view of identities and of foundations as being based on exclusions. Since every foundation and identity depends on its "constitutive outside," all foundations are necessarily contingent and therefore subject to critique and—at least in theory—resignification. Grasping the Lacanian principle that symbolic and real orders are mutually exclusive yet also mutually dependent, Butler views the real as open to interrogation. Hence the important chapter in *Bodies That Matter* titled "Arguing with the Real." In fact, this chapter stages an argument with Slavoj Žižek and with what Butler takes to be his account of the real. I want to engage the Butler-Žižek debate here because it frames in more overtly political terms the question of what limits the rhetoricalization

35. Copjec, *Read My Desire*, chap. 6.

of sexuality. My critique of rhetoricalism is, in the end, a political critique, because I see a certain version of psychoanalysis as offering a more radical and workable sexual politics than anything Butler's model promises.

To state my disagreement with Butler in its strongest terms, let me just say that in her rhetoricalizing of psychosis, in "Arguing with the Real," Butler's argument and the politics it implies are psychotic. I hope I will not be misunderstood as suggesting that Judith Butler herself is psychotic; I'm concerned instead with the logic of her argument and its implications for sexual politics. Butler's project to "resignify" the symbolic order by means of psychosis is not political but psychotic. Her turn to psychosis for a politics of sexuality indicates the impasse of Butler's antinormativism and marks the dead-end limits of her thoroughgoing suspicion of all norms.[36]

Butler claims that "[t]he rallying force of politics is its implicit promise of the possibility of a livable and speakable psychosis. Politics holds out the promise of the manageability of unspeakable loss" (209). I have suggested why the "unspeakable loss" immaterialized in object *a* cannot be overcome, and that without this constitutive loss, desire simply would not exist. The "promise of the manageability of unspeakable loss" perpetuates the common fantasy of a world without desire, perhaps even a world without psychoanalysis. To suggest that politics enables "a livable and speakable psychosis," or to advocate "a politically enabling deployment of psychotic speech" (280), nullifies both psychosis and politics by refusing to distinguish between them.

If the category of psychosis represents nothing more than an ideological construction that excludes certain social groups—principally women and queers—by making them the abject real that shores up compulsory heterosexuality, one then must ask exactly what ails clinically diagnosed psychotic patients beyond the interpellation of a normatively deployed diagnosis. A discursive idealism blinds this rhetoricalist position to the seriousness of its argument's implications: by declining

36. I refer here to Amanda Anderson's Habermasian critique of Butler, in "Debatable Performances: Restaging Contentious Feminisms," *Social Text* 54, vol. 16, no. 1 (1998): 1–24. Anderson argues that Butler fails to distinguish between evaluative norms and normalizing norms, thereby foreclosing political possibilities for evaluative norms in feminist and queer praxis. Butler's turn to psychosis as a political model illustrates Anderson's argument and throws into dramatic relief just how politically efficacious is Butler's unexamined jettisoning of evaluative norms.

to acknowledge any legitimate psychosis beyond its disciplinary mobilization (no original apart from its normative citation), Butler's argument euphemizes psychotic suffering as the consequence merely of hegemonic misnaming. If psychosis represents nothing more than a diagnostic category produced and enforced by heterosexism's regulatory regime, mental illness would be curable through *political* resignifications, according to Butler's model. This logic returns us to the 1960s antipsychiatry of David Cooper and R. D. Laing, which implied that even the most serious forms of psychic suffering are amenable to political redemption, since society and its regulatory norms alone are responsible for driving people mad. What leads Butler to this point of maintaining that there is a political purchase to psychotic speech?

Psychotic utterances, crazy though they may sound, are formulated according to a distinct logic, what we may call psychotologic, which is traceable through the use of psychorhetoric. As I suggested above, Lacan shifted the psychoanalytic understanding and treatment of psychosis by conceptualizing this most serious form of psychic suffering in rhetorical terms—that is, in terms of linguistic disorder. Conceiving of psychosis as a specific structural relation between symbolic and real orders, Lacan questioned the psychoanalytic orthodoxy that maintained psychosis was untreatable via the talking cure. In challenging this orthodoxy, Lacan also discredited the conventional fear that engaging the psychotic's symbolic economy through the discursive link of a psychoanalytic encounter necessarily would make the analyst psychotic too. In other words, he spoke to the fear that entering the psychotic's world via the talking cure would send the doctor mad.

There are various ways of engaging psychotologic—some analytic, some crazy, and some neither analytic nor crazy but simply failing to engage. Psychotologic often produces arguments of startling rigor, as Freud discovered with President Schreber, whose impressive erudition confirms, among other things, that Lacan's definition of psychosis as a foreclosure of part of the symbolic order should not imply an equation between psychosis and silence or gobbledygook. Far from being beyond or outside discourse, psychotologic regularly elaborates an intricate and brilliant—if bizarre—discourse of its own. As psychoanalyst Micheline Enriquez comments, psychotic discourse "very often presents this double aspect of being at once a mad delusional discourse outside reason, and at the same time a passionate and often pertinent denunciation of disorders and evils 'glaring within reality.' "[37] I want here to disentangle the steps that lead Butler to promote a form of discursive psychosis as a viable political option.

The first step to note in her argument with the real is Butler's synecdochic sleight of hand that makes Slavoj Žižek stand for Jacques Lacan and psychoanalysis in general. Žižek is one of the most important contemporary psychoanalytic theorists; his work has repoliticized psychoanalysis and shown Lacan's enormous potential for cultural studies. But Žižek's work increases, not diminishes, our responsibility to read Lacan. Working with and against a number of psychoanalytically oriented theorists—Žižek, Laclau and Mouffe, Michael Walsh—Butler's argument relies on secondary sources rather than on Lacan's own texts. Symptomatic of this problem is the fact that, in a long, dense chapter ostensibly devoted to a Lacanian concept, Butler quotes Lacan barely more than once. She constructs an elaborate argument based on only a shred of direct evidence. Her reliance on secondary sources gives the lie to Butler's claim that her argument with the real represents "an effort to underscore the limitations of psychoanalysis when its founding prohibitions and their heterosexualizing injunctions are taken to be invariant" (189). While the Lacanian real undoubtedly raises the question of limits and limitations, Butler's argument underscores nothing so much as the limitations of a certain fantasy about Žižek as theorist of the political.

Should we interpret Butler's refusal to engage Lacan directly as simply a failure of rigor in a critic consistently noted for rigorousness? Since Butler's chapter is full of parapraxes involving persistent misquotation and mischaracterization of Žižek, her reliance on secondary sources perhaps should be read as a sign of something more than intellectual laziness.[38] If, as Butler suggests for Žižek, the Lacanian real is embodied

37. Micheline Enriquez, "Paranoiac Fantasies: Sexual Difference, Homosexuality, Law of the Father," trans. Yifat Hachamovitch and Beátrice Loeffel, in *Psychosis and Sexual Identity: Toward a Post-analytic View of the Schreber Case,* ed. David B. Allison, Prado de Oliveira, Mark S. Roberts, and Allen S. Weiss (Albany: SUNY Press, 1988), 119.

38. Trivial in themselves, the cumulative effect of these parapraxes is serious, suggesting a systemic problem rather than merely superficial or local accidents. For more on Butler's parapraxes, see n. 15 above. In *The Sublime Object,* Žižek describes the symptom as "a stain which cannot be included in the circuit of discourse" (75); in *Bodies That Matter* this description is glossed and misquoted as "the feminine as a 'stain,' 'outside the circuit of discourse' (75)" (Butler, 196). Žižek characterizes Foucault (admittedly somewhat oddly) as one "fascinated by marginal lifestyles con-

by queerness and the feminine, then this characterization might prompt the question of what functions as the real in Butler's psychic economy. I have little interest in defending Žižek. However, in my reading of "Arguing with the Real" I would like to avoid as much as possible psychologizing Butler in the way that her reading of Žižek psychologizes him. I am interested more in the logic of Butler's argument—a logic that, contra rhetoricalism, I take to be irreducible to the rhetoric in which it is formulated. To reduce logic to rhetoric, or to suggest that no logic exists apart from that of rhetoric, is an imaginary fallacy that bespeaks a refusal to recognize the nonrhetorical logic of the real. Hence my disinclination, in this chapter, to discuss the relation between sexuality and rhetoric in terms of either "a rhetoric of sexuality" or "a sexuality of rhetoric," since both these approaches collapse sexuality into rhetoric in a way that forecloses desire.

Given this qualification, a rhetorical analysis of Butler's argument might begin by investigating her strategic use of erotema, the form of rhetorical questioning that implies an answer and so produces an assertion by indirect means. Butler's arguments proceed by posing series of questions whose answers subsequently are assumed as if they were the product of logical argumentation rather than the product of insistent erotema. For example:

209

---

structing their particular mode of subjectivity" (2), which Butler quotes as ". . . constructing their *own* mode of subjectivity" (206; emphasis added). In the passage from *Sublime Object* (99) that Butler provides in indented quotation (208), two extra commas are introduced into the quotation. Let me provide one final quotation of Butler quoting Žižek's *Sublime Object* and indicate her lapses in brackets:

> In Žižek's words, "what is overlooked, at least in the standard version of anti-descriptivism, is that this guaranteeing the identity of an object in all counterfactual situations— through a change of all its descriptive features [Butler omitted a second dash here] is *the retroactive effect of naming itself*: it is the name itself, the signifier, which supports the identity of the object" ([Butler omitted "94–"] 95) . . . Žižek writes, "That 'surplus' in the object which stays the same in all possible worlds is 'something in it more than itself', that is to say the Lacanian *petit objet a* [Žižek had the correct phrase, *"objet petit a"*]: we search in vain for it in positive reality because it has no positive consistency— because it is just an objectification of a void, [Butler omitted "of"] a discontinuity opened in reality by the emergence of the signifier" (95) (*Bodies That Matter*, 216–17).

Needless to say, Butler makes no attempt to assimilate the literally unspeakable *objet petit a* to her argument. In a footnote Butler cites Žižek's book *For They Know Not What They Do*, providing a bibliographical reference omitting the book's subtitle *(Enjoyment as a Political Factor)* and alluding to Žižek's book *Looking Awry: An Introduction to Jacques Lacan through Popular Culture* as published by MIT Press in Boston (rather than Cambridge) (*Bodies That Matter*, 279 n. 14). Together with the more serious misunderstandings of the *spirit* of the Lacanian argument, these examples—each apparently trivial—indicate a constitutive inability to get right anything connected with Žižek's argument or the *letter* of his text.

How might those ostensibly constitutive exclusions be rendered less permanent, more dynamic? How might the excluded return, not as psychosis or the figure of the psychotic within politics, but as that which has been rendered mute, foreclosed from the domain of political signification? How and where is social content attributed to the site of the "real," and then positioned as the unspeakable? Is there not a difference between a theory that asserts that, in principle, every discourse operates through exclusion and a theory that attributes to that "outside" specific social and sexual positions? To the extent that a specific use of psychoanalysis works to foreclose certain social and sexual positions from the domain of intelligibility—and for all time—psychoanalysis appears to work in the service of the normativizing law that it interrogates. How might such socially saturated domains of exclusion be recast from their status as "constitutive" to beings who might be said to matter? (189)

The theory that attributes to the real specific social and sexual positions is Butler's own, since Lacan characterizes the real as asubstantial, unsexed and ungendered. Constructing a Slovenian straw man, Butler proceeds to misrecognize this rhetorical construction and claim that "[t]he production of the unsymbolizable, the unspeakable, the illegible is also always a strategy of social abjection" (190). From this mistaken assumption, produced through erotema, Butler proceeds to deconstruct this "strategy of social abjection" in the name of "beings who might be said to matter."

Butler's characterization of the real as involving "a strategy of social abjection" makes the real far more intransigent and uncompromising than Lacan conceives it. By describing the real in structural rather than substantive terms, Lacan theorizes the real as a variable limit to the speakable and the thinkable. This distinction is politically significant because it implies that although a homophobic culture may figure gay sex, for example, as unspeakable, that figuration is culturally and historically produced rather than necessary or inevitable. The difference between rhetoricalism and psychoanalysis is that although both emphasize the constitutive, determining, and transformative power of language, psychoanalysis recognizes also the constitutive inability of language to say everything. Hence politicizing the real entails distinguishing limits that are amenable to change (limitable limits) from real limits (illimitable limits), limits that won't budge. To substantialize limits—for example,

in the form of acceptable sexual practices—makes those limits ideological, the product of regulatory norms. But to generalize from this and
assume that all limits are ideological, rather than real and therefore
unavoidable, leads to the psychotic conviction that words never fail and
that certain kinds of satisfaction can be achieved without limit.

Hallucinating a straw man in which it urges conviction through
the rhetorical trope of erotema, Butler's argument also rehearses a series of cultural clichés—a collection of moribund metaphors or straw
figures—concerning psychoanalysis. These clichés about psychoanalysis take the following forms: that psychoanalysis is a theory of the self
(confusion of subject and ego); that psychoanalysis is universalizing and
ahistorical (confusion about the relation between history and the real);
that the psychoanalytic category of the real designates reality or real
things (confusion of substance and structure); that Lacan misogynisti-
cally declared women don't exist (confusion of *La femme* and women);
that Freud discovered child abuse, then invented the seduction theory
as a cover-up (confusion of fantasy and reality). Although Butler resists
trotting out Jeffrey Masson's line on seduction, this last cultural cliché
derives from the criticism, which she repeats, that psychoanalysis is
"ahistorical and universalistic" (190). The common academic charge that
psychoanalysis is ahistorical is connected to Masson's more specific
charges against Freud by the assumption that if psychoanalysis were sufficiently attentive to historical realities, especially realities involving
power disequilibriums, then it would not have to euphemize abuses of
power (incest) in terms of universal fantasy (seduction).

Butler rehearses this caricature of psychoanalysis as universalizing and
ahistorical by misquoting and then interpreting the following sentence
from Žižek: "All the different attempts [efforts (Butler, 201)] to attach
this phenomenon to a concrete image ('Holocaust,' 'Gulag' . . .), to reduce
it to a product of a concrete social order (Fascism, Stalinism . . .)—what
are they if not so many attempts to elude the fact that we are dealing here
with the 'real' of our civilization which returns as the same traumatic
kernel in all social systems?"[39] Butler glosses Žižek's sentence thus:

> The effect of this citation is to claim that each of these social
> formations: the family, concentration camps, the Gulag, instantiate

39. Slavoj Žižek, *The Sublime Object of Ideology* (New York: Verso, 1989), 50.

the same trauma, and that what is historically textured about each of these sites of trauma is itself indifferent to and ontologically distinct from the lost and hidden referent that is their traumatic status. They are by virtue of this "same traumatic kernel" equivalent to one another as traumas, and what is historical and what is traumatic are made absolutely distinct; indeed, the historical becomes what is most indifferent to the question of trauma. (202)

I think Žižek is arguing not that traumas are historically or ontologically equivalent, but that the Lacanian concept of trauma enables a different kind of historical understanding. Trauma offers a different perspective on historicity by showing—as Fredric Jameson glosses this Lacanian position—"that history is *not* a text, not a narrative, master or otherwise, but that, as an absent cause, it is inaccessible to us except in textual form, and that our approach to it and to the Real itself necessarily passes through its prior textualization."[40] Far from making "what is historical and what is traumatic . . . absolutely distinct," Žižek suggests that history and trauma can be conceptualized only in relation to each other.

Butler's invoking "the lost and hidden referent" in the passage above points to another common point of confusion—confusing fantasy and reality, or, to put it slightly differently, confusing psychic reality with referentiality. Butler's argument with the real depends upon her substantializing the real as reference—that is, her attributing a content to that zone of psychic negativity that Lacan calls the real. Butler does this by persistently referring to "Žižek's use of the Lacanian 'real' to establish the permanent recalcitrance of the referent to symbolization" (208).[41] Her confusing the real with referentiality connects to Butler's confusing subject and ego, for she initially characterizes the Lacanian position thus: "Following Lacan, Žižek argues that the 'subject' is produced in language through an act of foreclosure *(Verwerfung)*" (189–90). Conceptually, this is complete nonsense. Unsupported by any citation or even allusion to a particular psychoanalytic text, Butler's claim misrecognizes as a theory of subject formation Lacan's explanation of psychosis as following from foreclosure of the Names-of-the-Father, a process I de-

---

40. Fredric Jameson, *The Political Unconscious: Narrative as a Socially Symbolic Act* (Ithaca: Cornell University Press, 1981), 35; original emphasis.

41. This mischaracterization of the real as referentiality is repeated throughout Butler's chapter (207, 208, 209, 215, and 217).

scribed in chapter 3. In effect, Butler is saying that subject formation is a psychotic process. Whether or not she actually believes that, it is hardly fair to characterize Lacan or Žižek as having made such a claim. Lacan argues instead that the subject, as subject of the unconscious, is produced through repression *(Verdrängung)*.

Taken together, these common points of confusion—between real and referent, between subject and ego—enable Butler to conclude that performativity can overcome the real: "Insofar as performatives are their own *referent,* they appear both to signify and to refer and hence to overcome the divide between referent and signification that is produced and sustained at the level of foreclosure" (209; original emphasis). Even more strangely, Butler then proposes performativity as that which might overcome referentiality, as if the fact that words refer to things in the world were in itself a kind of conspiracy: "If referentiality is itself the effect of a policing of the linguistic constraints on proper usage, then the possibility of referentiality is contested by the catachrestic use of speech that insists on using proper names improperly" (217–18).[42] Confusing the real with referentiality, and foreclosure with repression, Butler furthermore conflates *La femme* with women, arguing that women are effectively policed into the real by Lacan and thus excluded from political intelligibility: "if women are positioned as that which cannot exist, as that which is barred from existence by the law of the father, then there is a conflation of women with that foreclosed existence, that lost referent, that is surely as pernicious as any form of ontological essentialism" (218–19). A pernicious conflation indeed, one that derives from Butler's psychotologic itself, since it is not "the law of the father" that bars existence, just as foreclosure does not produce a "lost referent."[43]

213

42. As an antifoundational foundation, catachresis may be seen as the paradoxically stabilized as trope of queerness for rhetoricalist accounts, in that Edelman also treats catachresis as centrally significant for his theory of nonnormative sexuality. By interpreting catachresis as the sign of a fault line in the sexual ideology that esteems heterosexuality as natural and original while repressing homosexuality as artificial and derivative, Edelman argues that

> catachresis, though traditionally construed as aberrant or abusive, as the very trope of "mis-naming," is actually the fundamental principle of language and thus of naming itself. I want to propose that the negotiation between what gets constructed as aberrant and what gets constructed as "natural" in this reading of catachresis and the positing of "face," is implicated in, and bears crucially upon, the logic through which homosexuality takes cognitive shape in the modern West. *(Homographesis,* 232)

43. Although it is not possible to rehearse here Lacan's argument concerning ~~The~~ Woman, we might recall his remark that "Woman does not exist. There are women, but Woman is a dream of men." See Lacan, "Geneva Lecture on the Symptom," trans. Russell Grigg, *Analysis* 1 (1989): 17.

This quite astonishing sequence of conflations, confusions, mischaracterizations, and misquotations leads Butler to characterize Žižek's *The Sublime Object of Ideology* as "a text that defends the trauma of the real, defends the threat of psychosis that the real delivers . . . over and against a different kind of threat . . . that [Žižek's] text proliferates . . . by investing it in a variety of social positions" identified with women, feminism, homosexuality, sadomasochism, and poststructuralism (206). Allegedly aligned with the real by Žižek or Lacan, these "social positions" are constructed psychoanalytically as psychotic, according to Butler. Hence political contestation of women's and queers' social abjection should begin with "a politically enabling deployment of psychotic speech" (280).

In 1975, Lacan publicly corrected a misconception generated by the title of his 1932 doctoral thesis, "De la psychose paranoïaque dans ses rapports avec la personnalité," maintaining that there is no *relation* between paranoid psychosis and the personality (or ego) because they are effectively the same thing.[44] Since Butler's logic stems from a theory of subjectivity grounded in the ego, perhaps we could extend Lacan's point by saying that there is no "politically enabling deployment of psychotic speech," because in the rhetoricalist model all politics—by virtue of its imaginarization—is virtually psychotic. My argument against rhetoricalism dispenses not with all politics, but with the paranoid style of queer politics. One alternative to the paranoid style is a politics in which desire really matters, and in the next chapter I lay out a different political approach based on queer desire.

44. Jacques Lacan, "Le sinthôme," *Ornicar?* 7 (1976): 7.

LACAN MEETS
QUEER THEORY

Chapter 6

This chapter envisions a dialogue between Lacan and queer theory, a sort of roundtable in which various contemporary theorists of sexuality would directly engage Lacan—and he them. But, of course, Lacan died well before queer theory emerged as such; and, as Thomas Yingling observed, queer theorists prepared to grapple with Freud nonetheless have remained relatively shy of tackling the corpus of speculative work bequeathed by Lacan.[1] Furthermore, I discovered to my disappointment at an International Conference on Sexuation (in New York City, April 1997, where I first presented a preliminary version of this chapter) that for their part Lacanian analysts proved far less willing to engage queer theory than I, perhaps naively, had anticipated. Yet spurred on by my conviction that psychoanalysis *is* a queer theory, I've persisted with this imaginary encounter, a dialogue between—to invoke Yeats—self and antiself.

In *Encore*, his seminar devoted most directly to the topic of sexuality, Lacan speaks often of homosexuality, but with the crucial qualification that as far as love is concerned, gender is irrelevant: *"quand on aime, il ne s'agit pas de sexe"* (*SXX* 27). What should we make of this idea that the gender of object-choice remains ultimately inconsequential in

---

1. Thomas E. Yingling, "Homosexuality and the Uncanny: What's Fishy in Lacan," in *The Gay '90s: Disciplinary and Interdisciplinary Formations in Queer Studies,* ed. Thomas Foster, Carol Siegel, and Ellen E. Berry (New York: New York University Press, 1997), 191.

love? Is Lacan merely voicing liberal tolerance, anticipating by a matter of months his transatlantic counterparts' elimination of homosexuality from the *Diagnostic and Statistical Manual of Mental Disorders,* in 1973?[2] Or, more interestingly, could we view Lacan as foreshadowing by a couple of decades the radical move in queer theory to think sexuality outside the terms of gender?[3] Although I consider liberal tolerance far less passé than do most queer theorists, I want to make the case for Lacan as more radical than liberal on the question of homosexuality. I'll make this case by explaining how Lacan's account of sexuality reveals desire as determined not by the gender of object-choice, but by the object *a (l'objet petit a),* which remains largely independent of gender. By detaching desire from gender, Lacan helps to free desire from normative heterosexuality—that is, from the pervasive assumption that *all* desire, even same-sex attraction, is effectively heterosexual by virtue of its flowing between masculine and feminine subject-positions, regardless of the participants' actual anatomy in any given sexual encounter.

I intend to show how Lacan makes good on certain radical moments in Freud, such as the latter's counterheterosexist observation that "the sexual instinct is in the first instance independent of its object; nor is its origin likely to be due to its object's attractions" (*SE* 7:148). Through his concept of object *a,* Lacan alters what Freud means when he speaks of sexual objects, and I intend to use Lacan *with* queer theory to mount a critique of the Freudian notion of sexual object-choice as such. It is

2. For a detailed account of the American Psychiatric Association's decision to remove homosexuality from its official list of mental disorders, see Ronald Bayer, *Homosexuality and American Psychiatry: The Politics of Diagnosis,* 2d ed. (Princeton: Princeton University Press, 1987). For an account of the institutional battles over homosexuality since 1973, see Richard A. Isay, *Becoming Gay: The Journey to Self-Acceptance* (New York: Pantheon, 1996), esp. chap. 7, which suggests that removing homosexuality from *DSM* has not eliminated institutional biases or many psychiatrists' homophobia. Homophobia does not require homosexuality or homosexuals in order to flourish, it just needs signs of queerness.

3. This move to think sexuality outside the terms of gender may be traced to Gayle Rubin's pioneering work, particularly her "Thinking Sex: Notes for a Radical Theory of the Politics of Sexuality," in *Pleasure and Danger: Exploring Female Sexuality,* ed. Carole S. Vance (London: Routledge & Kegan Paul, 1984), 267–319, which argues that feminist theory remains insufficient for conceptualizing sexuality. For an illuminating meditation on Rubin's work, see her interview with Judith Butler: Rubin, "Sexual Traffic," *Differences* 6, nos. 2–3 (1994): 62–99. The move to think sexuality outside the terms of gender remains controversial; for example, Biddy Martin, "Sexualities without Genders and Other Queer Utopias," *Diacritics* 24, nos. 2–3 (1994): 104–21, discusses "the potential obfuscation of misogyny by antinormative stances" (119); and Elizabeth Weed, "The More Things Change," *Differences* 6, nos. 2–3 (1994): 249–73, whose argument is closer to my own, suggests how queer theory's displacing attention from sexual difference also involves neglecting psychoanalytic ways of thinking.

not so much a question of my isolating those moments in psychoanalytic texts that lend support to a progressive sexual politics, nor even of illuminating the fault lines of these texts in order to reinvigorate them, as psychoanalytic readers from Laplanche to Bersani, Davidson, and de Lauretis have done so brilliantly.[4] Instead, I am concerned to demonstrate how Lacan pursues the logic of Freudian insights about sex to a new destination—and how we may push this logic yet further for contemporary sexual politics. Thus I shall argue that this radical Freudian tradition discredits the otherwise amazingly durable nineteenth-century notion that homosexual desire expresses "a feminine soul trapped in a masculine body," or vice versa. In so doing, it also discredits the idea that psychoanalysis is a modern technology designed to regulate and normalize sexuality, as some queer theorists, following Foucault, continue to claim.[5] On the contrary, Lacanian psychoanalysis provides a uniquely valuable source of resistance to just such normalization. In what follows, I'll elaborate on Lacan's antinormative potential and try to account for queer theory's failure to exploit that potential.

217

4. See the following classic readings of Freud's *Three Essays:* Jean Laplanche, *Life and Death in Psychoanalysis,* trans. Jeffrey Mehlman (Baltimore: Johns Hopkins University Press, 1976), chaps. 1, 2; Leo Bersani, *The Freudian Body: Psychoanalysis and Art* (New York: Columbia University Press, 1986), chap. 2; Arnold I. Davidson, "How to Do the History of Psychoanalysis: A Reading of Freud's *Three Essays on the Theory of Sexuality,*" in *The Trial(s) of Psychoanalysis,* ed. Françoise Meltzer (Chicago: University of Chicago Press, 1988), 39–64; and Teresa de Lauretis, *The Practice of Love: Lesbian Sexuality and Perverse Desire* (Bloomington: Indiana University Press, 1994), chap. 1.

5. Although Foucault maintained an especially vexed relation to psychoanalysis, this misguided notion derives less from his work than from its Anglo-American reception; as with Freud, Foucault's transatlantic dissemination deformed his thought in a way that has consequences for the reception of other Continental thinkers, including Lacan. Perhaps the best account of the complexities of Foucault's relation to psychoanalysis is Jacques Derrida's " 'To Do Justice to Freud': The History of Madness in the Age of Psychoanalysis," trans. Pascale-Anne Brault and Michael Naas, *Critical Inquiry* 20 (1994): 227–66. Although in this text Derrida focuses primarily on Foucault's *Madness and Civilization* and only secondarily on *The History of Sexuality,* much of his analysis can be extended to Foucault's treatment of Freud on the topic of homosexuality. Noting the resonance of Foucault's complete silence concerning Lacan (255 n. 19), Derrida argues that "Foucault's project belongs too much to 'the age of psychoanalysis' in its possibility for [Foucault], when claiming to thematize psychoanalysis, to do anything other than let psychoanalysis continue to speak obliquely of itself" (263). The tensions that Derrida identifies in *Madness and Civilization* should encourage us—by which I mean Lacanians *and* Foucaultians—to read Foucault more carefully, to do justice to Foucault in the way that he insisted on the imperative to "do justice to Freud" (*Madness and Civilization: A History of Insanity in the Age of Reason* [New York: Random House, 1965], 198). The kind of careful reading I have in mind is exemplified by John Murchek, "Foucault and Psychoanalysis: 'Quite Near' " (unpublished manuscript), which pursues a fascinating reading of the first volume of *The History of Sexuality* to argue convincingly that Foucault's concept of power can be understood as a version of Freud's concept of libido; that the scenic account of that power can be read in terms of the psychoanalytic theory of fantasy; and that Foucault's spirals of pleasure and power redescribe the concept of transference.

Nature/Nurture—Neither

> *To encounter desire is first of all to forget the difference in*
> *the sexes.*
>
> —Guy Hocquenghem, *Homosexual Desire*

Much of the impasse between Lacan and queer theory stems from problems of translation, difficulties that are as much cultural and ideological as linguistic. To begin with there is the problem of Freud's American reception, which, in seeking to make Viennese speculation about sex palatable in the United States, drastically normalized revolutionary psychoanalytic ideas about sexuality. This is by now a fairly well known story, told in broad historical terms by Russell Jacoby and elaborated with respect to male homosexuality most notably by Kenneth Lewes and Henry Abelove.[6] In his pioneering study of the American domestication of psychoanalysis, historian Abelove argues that Freud's position on homosexuality was far more progressive than those held by his transatlantic followers, both sympathetic and hostile, later in the century: "Freud was perfectly consistent on the subject of homosexuality," Abelove claims; "[w]hat he told the American mother in his letter of 1935, that it was neither advantage, crime, illness, nor disgrace, he had long believed and acted on."[7] However, once Freudianism migrated to the United States, American analysts promoted a fantasy of eradicating homosexuality altogether, willfully disregarding Freud's conclusion, in his *Three Essays on the Theory of Sexuality,* that "all human beings are capable of making a homosexual object-choice and have in fact made one in their unconscious" (*SE* 7:145). Considering this emphasis on the unconscious, we can begin to grasp how the efforts of institutionalized psychoanalysis to "cure" homosexuality remain coeval with American psychoanalytic attempts to cure the *unconscious* out of existence. Seen from

---

6. Russell Jacoby, *Social Amnesia: A Critique of Conformist Psychology from Adler to Laing* (Boston: Beacon, 1975), and Jacoby, *The Repression of Psychoanalysis: Otto Fenichel and the Political Freudians* (Chicago: University of Chicago Press, 1986); Kenneth Lewes, *The Psychoanalytic Theory of Male Homosexuality* (New York: Simon and Schuster, 1988); Henry Abelove, "Freud, Male Homosexuality, and the Americans," in *The Lesbian and Gay Studies Reader,* ed. Henry Abelove, Michèle Aina Barale, and David M. Halperin (New York: Routledge, 1993), 381–93. On the most recent chapter of U.S. anti-Freudianism, see Paul Robinson, *Freud and His Critics* (Berkeley and Los Angeles: University of California Press, 1993).

7. Abelove, "Freud, Male Homosexuality, and the Americans," 384.

this vantage point, Lacan's critique of American ego psychology is readily appropriable for queer theory's critique of institutionalized homophobia.

Freud's view that, at least in the unconscious, *we're all a little queer* conforms to what Eve Kosofsky Sedgwick calls the "universalizing" conception of homosexuality—as distinguished from the "minoritizing" conception, which views same-sex object-choice as characterizing a specific group of people, a sexual minority whose identity is thence defined in contradistinction to that of the majority.[8] "Psychoanalytic research is most decidedly opposed to any attempt at separating off homosexuals from the rest of mankind as a group of a special character," insists Freud, explicitly countering the minoritizing conception of sexual inversion propagated in his own time by figures such as Karl Heinrich Ulrichs, Richard von Krafft-Ebing, and Magnus Hirschfeld (*SE* 7:145). Although the idea of a sexual minority enables a form of political campaigning that culminates in civil rights activism, Abelove's account makes clear how a minoritizing view also serves the American mental health establishment's homophobic purposes by confining homosexuality to a single demographic. And so while I'm persuaded more by the universalizing than by the minoritizing conception of homosexuality, in the end Freud's contention that we've all made a homosexual object-choice (whether we know it or not) doesn't go far enough, because his notion of object-choice remains trapped within the terms of gender. The very possibility of describing object-choice as homosexual or heterosexual takes for granted that the object chosen is gendered and that—no matter how partial or fragmented the object may be—it's somehow identifiable as masculine or feminine. In contrast, Lacan's concept of object *a* radically revises the Freudian notion of object-choice by leaving gender behind, in a move whose far-reaching implications I wish to delineate.

We may approach the ungendered or degendered conception of object-choice by considering a less appreciated dimension of Freud's American reception, one involving the distinction between a psychoanalytic, largely European understanding of sexual difference and a sociological, largely North American understanding of gender. This distinc-

8. Eve Kosofsky Sedgwick, *Epistemology of the Closet* (Berkeley and Los Angeles: University of California Press, 1990), 40–41.

tion is raised by Lacan's comment, quoted above, that *"quand on aime, il ne s'agit pas de sexe."*[9] Although the French word *sexe* roughly conforms to what we mean by gender, this translation elides the specifically psychoanalytic dimension of sex; and so one is forced to confront the conceptual limits of the terms—*sex, gender, sexuality*—available for this discussion.

Conventionally we distinguish sex from gender according to the coordinates of certain well-rehearsed debates—essentialism versus constructionism, or the longer-standing controversy known as nature versus nurture. The force of gender as a concept lies in how it denaturalizes sexual difference, making sex a question of social and historical construction rather than of biological essence. And sexuality, or sexual orientation, tends to be discussed within the framework of these same debates.[10] Indeed, the term *sexuality* is regularly understood to involve questions not only of desire but also of identity, so that the issue of one's sexuality tends to be taken as referring not only to the putative gender of one's object-choice but also to one's *own* gender identity, one's masculinity or femininity. However, we can begin to appreciate the danger of keeping sexuality so closely tied to gender by considering how the diagnosis of "gender identity disorder," in *DSM,* readily takes over the pathologizing role formerly assigned to "homosexuality."[11]

220

9. In an English translation of *Encore* published after I wrote this chapter, Bruce Fink renders the passage in question thus: "Last year I played on a slip of the pen I made in a letter addressed to a woman—*tu ne sauras jamais combien je t'ai aimé* ("you will never know how much I loved you")—*é* instead of *ée*. Since then, someone mentioned to me that that could mean that I am a homosexual. But what I articulated quite precisely last year is that when one loves, it has nothing to do with sex." In this instance, translating *sexe* as *sex* is potentially misleading and so Fink adds this note: "The past participle, *aimé*, is supposed to agree in gender with the sex of the person designated in the phrase by the direct object, *te* (here *t'*); if the person is male, the participle remains *aimé*, if female, an *e* should be added to the end: *aimée*." See Jacques Lacan, *On Feminine Sexuality, The Limits of Love and Knowledge: The Seminar of Jacques Lacan,* Book 20: *Encore, 1972–1973,* ed. Jacques-Alain Miller, trans. Bruce Fink (New York: Norton, 1998), 25.

10. See, for example, the classic contributions collected in Edward Stein, ed., *Forms of Desire: Sexual Orientation and the Social Constructionist Controversy* (New York: Routledge, 1992); and, more recently, Paul R. Abramson and Steven D. Pinkerton, eds., *Sexual Nature, Sexual Culture* (Chicago: University of Chicago Press, 1995). The canonical account of "the construction of homosexuality" is given by David Greenberg in his book of that title (Chicago: University of Chicago Press, 1988), and of heterosexuality in Jonathan Ned Katz, *The Invention of Heterosexuality* (New York: Dutton, 1995).

11. A group of therapists within the American Psychological Association is campaigning to have the category of gender identity disorder removed from the next edition of *DSM,* based on the conviction that this diagnosis, which is used particularly for children, represents a screen for mental health workers' homophobia. See *In the Family: The Magazine for Gays, Lesbians, Bisexuals, and Their Relations,* October 1997, 3.

To free a theory of sexuality from the ideological constraints imposed by gender categories also permits us to divorce sexuality from the straitjacket of identity. Another way of putting this would be to say that psychoanalysis enables us to think sexuality apart from the ego. And, as I've suggested, this way of thinking becomes possible only through some concept equivalent to that of the unconscious: it remains a basic psychoanalytic postulate that while there is always sex, there can be no sexuality without the unconscious. Thus for Lacan sexuality is explicable in terms of neither nature *nor* nurture, since the unconscious cannot be considered biological—it isn't part of my body and yet it isn't exactly culturally constructed either. Instead, the unconscious may be grasped as an index of how both biology and culture *fail* to determine subjectivity and sexual desire. Thinking of the unconscious as neither biological nor cultural allows us to distinguish (among other things) a properly psychoanalytic from a merely psychological notion of the unconscious.

In making such distinctions, I consider it important to specify how Lacan's account of sexuality remains unassimilable to the nature / nurture debate, especially since arguments between essentialists and social constructionists have become increasingly polarized in recent years. Yet I want to emphasize that psychoanalysis does not offer some compromise between these polarities; rather, Lacan furnishes the conceptual means for developing a genuine alternative to them. At the essentialist pole of this debate neuroanatomists and geneticists, such as Simon LeVay and Dean Hamer, search for the biological *cause* of homosexuality in hypothalamic structure or chromosomes.[12] At the social constructionist

12. Simon LeVay, *The Sexual Brain* (Cambridge: MIT Press, 1993); Dean Hamer and Peter Copeland, *The Science of Desire: The Search for the Gay Gene and the Biology of Behavior* (New York: Simon and Schuster, 1994). With respect to the search for the gay gene, Guy Hocquenghem's comment almost one quarter-century earlier still holds good: "The chromosome theory [of homosexuality] appears to be less a biological 'discovery' than an ideological regression" (Guy Hocquenghem, *Homosexual Desire* [1972], trans. Daniella Dangoor [Durham: Duke University Press, 1993], 76). More recently, in *Queer Science: The Use and Abuse of Research into Homosexuality* (Cambridge: MIT Press, 1996), LeVay has examined the history and consequences of scientific explanations of sexual orientation, including psychoanalytic ones. As with the overwhelming majority of lesbian and gay people, LeVay favors the conclusion that homosexuality is innate rather than acquired, essential rather than constructed. This conviction about sexual orientation's innateness can be deemed progressive insofar as it discourages a commitment to reorientation therapy, and, furthermore, it discredits the assumption, so common among conservatives, that homosexuals suffer from a febrile will or poor moral fiber. In other words, the essentialist view of sexual orientation ostensibly makes homosexuality easier to accept—for both queers and straights. On the other hand, scientific evidence of sexual orientation's organic innateness also can support a virulently homophobic politics, insofar

pole philosophers, such as Judith Butler, meticulously deconstruct the sex-gender distinction in order to argue that the ostensibly pregiven, immutable category in this conceptual couple—that is, biological sex— is just as much a result of historically contingent processes of materialization as is gender.[13] As I argued in the previous chapter, the deconstructionist position takes constructionism one step further by arguing that bodies aren't simply the raw material that social processes use to construct gender and sexuality, but rather that corporeal matter itself must be *materialized* through social processes of embodiment. And for this reason the deconstructionist account of sexuality sometimes advertises itself as a critique of and alternative to—rather than simply a refinement of—social constructionism.

222

But from my point of view the various sides in this debate miss the point of a psychoanalytic critique of sex, gender, and sexuality, since the purpose of such a critique is not (like deconstruction) to devise ever subtler ways of revealing that what seemed natural is in fact cultural or a positive effect of the symbolic order. Thus although Butler uses Lacan to support her argument, in the end psychoanalysis authorizes the constructionist (or deconstructionist) account of sexuality no more than it authorizes the essentialist one. Hence Freud's insistence that "[t]he nature of inversion is explained neither by the hypothesis that it is innate nor by the alternative hypothesis that it is acquired" (*SE* 7: 140). And so while it's possible to identify passages in Freud that appear to support either side of the nature/nurture debate, I prefer to draw out a psychoanalytic logic that remains fundamentally irreducible to this debate's terms, even in their most recent, most advanced form. By describing sexuality in terms of unconscious desire, I wish to separate sexual orientation from questions of identity and of gender roles, practices, and performances, since it is by conceiving sexuality outside the terms of gender *and* identity that we can most thoroughly deheterosexualize desire.

---

as genetic engineering and eugenics permit the fantasy of a world in which there would be no homosexuals whatsoever. From this we can see that what attracts both progressives and reactionaries—whether they're experts or laypersons—to scientific evidence concerning the biological innateness of sexual desire is its reassurance that sexuality confers *identity*. This kind of scientific evidence also calms any sense of subjective division, any nagging personal sense that I too could have unconscious conflict about sexual orientation.

13. Judith Butler, *Bodies That Matter: On the Discursive Limits of "Sex"* (New York: Routledge, 1993).

The Queer Critique of Normativity

> Because the logic of the sexual order is so deeply embedded by
> now in an indescribably wide range of social institutions, and is
> embedded in the most standard accounts of the world, queer
> struggles aim not just at toleration or equal status but at chal-
> lenging those institutions and accounts.
>
> —Michael Warner, introduction to *Fear of a Queer Planet:*
> *Queer Politics and Social Theory*

Having reached this point, we should now acknowledge that the problems entailed in confining sexuality to the terms of identity also ignited
queer theory, which emerged as an intellectual and political movement
only during the 1990s, in the wake of feminism, gay liberation, and the
AIDS epidemic.[14] Although queer theory's newness and heterodoxical
configurations make hazardous any attempt at definition, we may nevertheless characterize these new epistemological and ideological configurations in order to distinguish their most salient features.[15] Queer
theory views with postmodern skepticism the minoritizing conception
of sexuality that undergirds gay liberation and women's liberation
(and hence academically institutionalized gay studies and women's
studies too). Building on the civil rights movements of the 1960s, feminism and gay liberation based their claims for political participation
and radical equality, whether assimilationist or separatist, on the foundation of *identity*—female, gay, lesbian, and, more recently, bisexual,
transsexual, transgendered identities. By contrast, queer theory and politics begin from a critique of identity and of identity politics, inspired
primarily by Foucault's analysis of the disciplinary purposes that sexual
identities so easily serve. As Butler encapsulates this Foucaultian critique: "[I]dentity categories tend to be instruments of regulatory regimes, whether as the normalizing categories of oppressive structures
or as the rallying points for a liberatory contestation of that very oppres-

223

14. On the emergence of queer theory and some ramifications of the term itself, see Teresa
de Lauretis, "Queer Theory: Lesbian and Gay Sexualities—An Introduction," *Differences* 3, no. 2
(1991): iii–xviii. Because the word *queer* is intended to be gender neutral, I hesitate to offer the
customary caveat that I'm focusing here primarily on *either* gay men's *or* lesbians' sexuality. Yet in
thus hesitating to specify nonnormative sexualities along gender lines, I want also to emphasize that
queer women's and queer men's concerns aren't identical, symmetrical, or analogous—and therefore psychoanalysis should take greater care not to treat them as if they were.

15. On queer theory's resistance to definition, see Lauren Berlant and Michael Warner, "What
Does Queer Theory Teach Us about *X*?" *PMLA* 110 (1995): 343–49.

sion."[16] Or as Foucault himself put it, ventriloquizing Deleuze and Guattari, "Do not demand of politics that it restore the 'rights' of the individual, as philosophy has defined them. The individual is the product of power."[17] We can see immediately how this blunt admonition flies in the face of Enlightenment postulates of individual liberty and autonomous agency, upon which U.S. society and politics are based. Before discussing the political consequences of this reconceptualization, I'd like to consider further its methodological implications.

Queer theory's Foucaultian suspicion of identity *tout court* leads in two competing directions. On one hand, it has inspired a cautious return to psychoanalytic epistemologies among some queer theorists, given how Freud's theory of the unconscious introduces a constitutive subjective division that undermines the possibility of any seamless identity, sexual or otherwise. Even critics with a more thoroughgoing mistrust of psychoanalysis as a heterosexist and homophobic institution have been led, practically despite themselves, to invent conceptual categories tantamount to that of the unconscious.[18]

Yet, on the other hand, queer theory's critique of identity as a regulatory norm has also led diametrically away from psychoanalytic epistemologies, encouraged in large part by Foucault's displacement of attention from identities to practices. Thus although historicism shares with psychoanalysis the view that identities are essentially illusory, historicism resorts to the empiricist solution of investigating discrete social and cultural practices, whereas psychoanalysis focuses on what, though not exactly illusory, nevertheless resists empirical verification, namely, fantasy. Foucault makes this distinction explicit in a 1982 interview:

> I don't try to write an archaeology of sexual fantasies. I try to make an archaeology of discourse about sexuality, which is really the relationship between what we do, what we are obliged to do, what we are allowed to do, what we are forbidden to do in the field of sexuality, and what we are allowed, forbidden, or obliged to say

16. Judith Butler, "Imitation and Gender Insubordination," *Inside / Out: Lesbian Theories, Gay Theories,* ed. Diana Fuss (New York: Routledge, 1991), 13–14.

17. Michel Foucault, preface to Gilles Deleuze and Félix Guattari, *Anti-Oedipus: Capitalism and Schizophrenia* (1972), trans. Robert Hurley, Mark Seem, and Helen R. Lane (Minneapolis: University of Minnesota Press, 1983), xiv.

18. I discuss the limits of these queer reinventions of psychoanalysis in "On the Eve of a Queer Future," *Raritan* 15 (1995): 116–34.

about our sexual behavior. That's the point. It's not a problem of fantasy; it's a problem of verbalization.[19]

I'll return to this problematic distinction between fantasy and verbalization at the end of this chapter; but even without Foucault it is easy to see how the concrete reality of sexual practices appears to carry greater political weight than the comparative ephemerality of sexual fantasies, which often seem luxurious and trivial in the face of material oppression. Yet I shall argue that such a hierarchy of political seriousness may itself betoken heterosexist logic: fantasy remains so phenomenologically and conceptually inextricable from perversion that the characteristic relegation of fantasy to zones of secondariness, irrationality, passivity, and immaturity should give us pause. Furthermore, the strong vein of utopianism in queer theory suggests the importance of fantasy to its simultaneously political and sexual agendas—"almost everything that can be called queer theory has been radically anticipatory, trying to bring a world into being," note two of queer theory's most prominent spokespersons.[20]

But before we can specify what's so queer about fantasy, we must grasp more precisely what queerness implies. Far more than a handy moniker covering the rainbow coalition of nonnormative sexualities (lesbian, gay, bisexual, transsexual, and so on), "queer" extends the politics of sexuality beyond sex and sexual minorities' civil rights by insisting that "queer" is opposed not simply to "straight," but more broadly to "normal." Defining itself against the normal, queerness exceeds sexuality, sexual practices, sexual identities; indeed, this is how people whose sexual partners are primarily, even exclusively, of the opposite sex get to count as queer. Queer theory depends on identificatory alliances rather than on identities as such; and queer politics thus involves creating alliances between sexual minorities and other social groups whose marginalization or disenfranchisement isn't necessarily a direct consequence of nonnormative sexuality. Hence the centrality accorded ostensibly nonsexual categories—such as race, ethnicity, and nationality—in queer theory, which isn't so much about being inclusive

225

19. Michel Foucault, "An Interview with Stephen Riggins," *The Essential Works of Michel Foucault, 1954–1984,* vol. 1, *Ethics: Subjectivity and Truth,* ed. Paul Rabinow, trans. Robert Hurley et al. (New York: New Press, 1997), 125–26.

20. Berlant and Warner, "What Does Queer Theory Teach Us?" 344.

(under the aegis of an ever-expanding liberal tolerance) as it is about connecting one dimension of social exclusion with others. And in light of this commitment to discerning alliances, I have often wondered why queer theorists have not forged more of an alliance with Lacanian psychoanalysts, given the thoroughgoing antinormative bias in Lacan's work. Yet though Lacan reads to me like a queer theorist *avant la lettre,* the institutional history of psychoanalysis, particularly in the United States, has forestalled any such alliance. As I've already suggested, a good part of this book's intent lies in forging one—with the understanding that such an alliance might require both parties to renounce some of their most cherished shibboleths.

If *queer* represents more than merely a broader or hipper term for gayness and more than a new form of avant-gardism, then queer theory's principal challenge must be to confront the consequences of defining oneself and one's politics against norms as such.[21] The implications of such a stance are radical indeed, particularly in a society whose ideology of individualism guarantees maximum liberty to pursue one's own version of happiness—on condition only that he or she conform. In view of this ideological double bind, Michael Warner correctly identifies queer theory's paradoxically antisocial utopianism:

> Organizing a movement around queerness also allows [queer theory] to draw on dissatisfaction with the regime of the normal in general. Following Hannah Arendt, we might even say that queer politics opposes society itself . . . The social realm, in short, is a cultural form, interwoven with the political form of the administrative state and with the normalizing methodologies of modern social knowledge. Can we not hear in the resonances of queer protest an objection to

226

21. This represents an enormous project, one that bears on the longstanding dispute between Foucault and Jürgen Habermas concerning the function of social norms and normativity. In her stringent critique of Butler's intervention in the feminist version of this debate, Amanda Anderson elaborates a helpful distinction between evaluative norms and normalizing norms. Evaluative norms, associated with the Habermasian position, provide necessary criteria for evaluating the rightness or wrongness of an action or practice. By contrast, normalizing norms, associated with the Foucaultian position, involve mechanisms of social reproduction and identity formation internal to hegemonic social structures (Anderson, "Debatable Performances: Restaging Contentious Feminisms," *Social Text* 54, vol. 16, no. 1 [1998]: 9). This distinction tends to get lost in queer theory's antinormativity, but might prove useful for assessing the role of psychoanalysis as a normalizing discourse or practice, since the reduction of all normativity to normalization—that is, viewing all evaluative criteria as fundamentally insidious—obscures and therefore naturalizes the operation of evaluative norms within queer theory and queer practices themselves.

the normalization of behavior in this broad sense, and thus to the cultural phenomenon of societalization? If queers, incessantly told to alter their "behavior," can be understood as protesting not just the normal behavior of the social but the *idea* of normal behavior, they will bring skepticism to the methodologies founded on that idea.[22]

The capaciousness and force of queerness stem not simply from its opposing sexual norms—or what, almost two decades ago, Adrienne Rich diagnosed as "compulsory heterosexuality"[23]—but from its resistance to the very idea of the normal as such. Thus by contrast with most gay journalism about sexual politics, queer theory, in its avowed opposition to "society itself," assumes that those who've been socially excluded don't *want* to "fit in" or conform as social beings.[24] It is sometimes hard to decide whether this assumption betrays an elitist disregard for the self-perceptions and desires of nonheterosexuals outside the university (particularly working-class queers), or whether it signals a greater ideological awareness enabled by academic freedom and, indeed, promotes a laudatory shouldering of the political responsibilities that accompany institutional privilege.

Queer theory assumes not only that queers' early sense of alienation effectively renders social conformity impossible, but also that queer opposition to social norms represents far more than an expression of aggressivity or "acting out" under the guise of political activism. Furthermore, queer theory stakes its utopian claims on the conviction that opposing "society itself" doesn't necessarily incur the loneliness of psychosis, foreclosed from all social ties, but that, on the contrary, queer political resistance provides access to alternate forms of community and other social ties—perhaps even other *forms* of social tie, different ways of knotting the subject to society and community.[25] Indeed, more than

227

22. Michael Warner, introduction to *Fear of a Queer Planet: Queer Politics and Social Theory*, ed. Warner (Minneapolis: University of Minnesota Press, 1993), xxvii.

23. Adrienne Rich, "Compulsory Heterosexuality and Lesbian Existence," in *Desire: The Politics of Sexuality*, ed. Ann Snitow, Christine Stansell, and Sharon Thompson (London: Virago, 1984), 212–41.

24. For recent arguments on behalf of the desirability of lesbian and gay assimilation into the social mainstream, see Bruce Bawer, *A Place at the Table: The Gay Individual in American Society* (New York: Poseidon, 1993); and Andrew Sullivan, *Virtually Normal: An Argument about Homosexuality* (New York: Knopf, 1995).

25. For a powerful account of community formation based not on identity but instead on nonbelonging, see Giorgio Agamben, *The Coming Community*, trans. Michael Hardt (Minneapolis: University of Minnesota Press, 1993).

a decade before queer theory came along, Foucault was already speculating about the radically different kinds of social tie that homosexuals might establish. Distinguishing between homophobic intolerance of gay sex and horror at the possibility of gay sociality, he explained, in a well-publicized interview, that "[i]t is the prospect that gays will create as yet unforeseen kinds of relationships that many people cannot tolerate."[26]

Lacan's Critique of Normativity

> Strengthening the categories of affective normativity produces disturbing results.
>
> —Jacques Lacan, *The Seminar of Jacques Lacan, Book VII: The Ethics of Psychoanalysis*[27]

228

Rather than directly adjudicating either queer theory's claims or the philosophical presuppositions on which they're based, I want to explore them further by considering how Lacan's account of sexuality harmonizes with queer theory's. In view of its revisionary interventions in social theory, queer politics could be regarded as quintessentially American, as the latest chapter in a long history of native self-invention, utopianism, and experimental communitarianism that characterizes U.S. social politics. Yet on the other hand, queer theory's antinormative, anti-identitarian, and antiliberal commitments make it appear every bit as "un-American" as some of its detractors charge. From this perspective, it is significant that Lacan also directs his critique of norms—including what he pointedly calls "the delusional 'normality' of the genital relation" (*E* 245)—against the American ideology of individualism, particularly as it finds expression in the normalizing ethos of "adaptation

---

26. Michel Foucault, "Sexual Choice, Sexual Act," in *The Essential Works of Michel Foucault,* 153. In what I take to be the most important work of queer theory to date, Leo Bersani provides a useful gloss on Foucault's comment: "The intolerance of gayness, far from being the displaced expression of the anxieties that nourish misogyny, would be nothing more—by which of course Foucault meant nothing less—than a political anxiety about the subversive, revolutionary social rearrangements that gays may be trying out. Indeed, in this scenario there may be no fantasies—in the psychoanalytic sense—on either side, and if there are, they are insignificant in understanding the threat of gayness." (*Homos* [Cambridge: Harvard University Press, 1995], 78).

27. Immediately before this, when speaking explicitly of psychoanalytic ethics, Lacan denounces as particularly normalizing those brands of psychoanalysis that aspire to scientific status: "a form of analysis that boasts of its highly scientific distinctiveness gives rise to normative notions that I characterize by evoking the curse Saint Matthew utters on those who make the bundles heavier when they are to be carried by others" (*SVII* 133).

to reality" that ego psychology promulgates as the goal of psychoanalytic therapy.

Lacan views the conception of therapy in terms of adaptation as a problem not simply because the reality to which one should adapt turns out to be "heteronormative" (in Warner's terms), but more fundamentally because *reality itself is imaginary*. Since we are accustomed to thinking of reality and the imaginary as antithetical, Lacan's paradoxical alignment of the two warrants careful examination. (And even before grasping the full significance of this equation, we can begin to appreciate that what Lacan means by "the real" must be very far from "reality," if reality is imaginary.) It is when one conceives reality in terms of adaptation that it is given over to the imaginary, in that "reality" thus comes to represent a set of norms or ideal forms to which we're supposed to aspire and on the basis of which our egos must be modeled and remodeled. Hence Lacan's objection to the normalizing function of psychology: "Psychology transmits ideals"—to which he adds, "[i]deals are society's slaves" ("Position" 262).

Lacan maintains that so long as psychoanalysts focus exclusively on the ego or individual, they will remain trapped within an essentially prescriptive discourse of norms and normativity. Since the ego comes into being through projective idealization—by means of misrecognitions of images of the other—the ego is nothing but a precipitate of idealized models. Whatever their content, these models are susceptible to idealization insofar as their form appears totalized, bounded, and complete; these imaginary models provide the subject points of coherence with which to identify within a seamless picture of the world. By means of these imaginary identifications the subject finds a place in reality—and so experiences a measure of jubilation, irrespective of how culturally prized or disprized that place may be.[28] Thus "reality" constitutes the sum of these models and norms, the imaginary ideals to which we're supposed to conform not merely in our behavior but in our very existence and perceptions. From this we might say that insofar as reality is imaginary, it is also utopic, a pure projection. Queer theory's counterutopianism makes more sense in this light. And Lacan himself points out that the American ideology of adaptation mystifies reproductive het-

229

28. See Kaja Silverman, *The Threshold of the Visible World* (New York: Routledge, 1996), for an original psychoanalytic argument on behalf of new political uses of the aesthetic that would enable different modes of idealization—specifically, less violent or exclusionary ways of seeing.

erosexuality as the norm: "Goodness only knows how obscure such a pretension as the achievement of genital objecthood (l'objectalité genitale) remains, along with what is so imprudently linked to it, namely, adjustment to reality" (SVII 293).

However, Lacan's response to normativity is not to produce alternative imaginaries, but to elaborate an alternative of a different order—that of the real, a conceptual category intended to designate everything that resists adaptation. As he remarks with characteristic irreverence when alluding to normative accounts of psychosexual development, "what has this absurd hymn to the harmony of the genital got to do with the real?" (E 245).[29] Insofar as the real represents that concept through which Lacan challenges heteronormativity, queer theorist Judith Butler is somewhat mistaken in her claim that the Lacanian real secures heteronormativity.[30] Of course, it could be objected that Lacan's aligning reality with the imaginary over and against the real simply perpetuates a long metaphysical tradition that associates the world of experience and perceptions (so-called reality) with vain appearances, in contradistinction to an ultimate world of essences beyond appearances. Yet as Lacan conceives it, the real isn't simply opposed to reality or the imaginary domain of appearances, since both the imaginary and the real operate only in relation to Lacan's third order, the symbolic (the relation among these three orders—imaginary, symbolic, and real—should be characterized in terms neither of binary opposition nor of dialectic). Furthermore, rather than following the metaphysical tradition, Lacan does not align the order of the real with the world of immutable essences in contrast to an imaginary world of appearances and ephemerality; instead, he situates negativity and mutability on the side of the real rather than on that of appearances. Thus as I shall explain, although the real has no positive content, it has more to do with sex and death than does the imaginary or the symbolic.

29. In his critique of psychoanalytic ethics, Lacan develops this position, sounding very much like a queer theorist:

[Y]ou know that I have often taken aim at the approximate and vague character, so tainted with an optimistic moralism, which marks the original articulations taking the form of the genitalization of desire. That is the ideal of genital love—a love that is supposed to be itself alone the model of a satisfying object relation: doctor-love, I would say if I wanted to emphasize in a comical way the tone of this ideology; love as hygiene, I would say, to suggest what analytical ambition seems to be limited to here. (SVII 8)

30. Judith Butler, "Arguing with the Real," in Bodies That Matter, 187–222. See chapter 5 above.

This understanding of the real accounts for my objection to critically analyzing sex and sexuality in terms of the imaginary and symbolic—that is, in terms of the images and discourses that construct sex, sexuality, and desirability in our culture. Hugely powerful though these images and discourses are, sexuality pertains more to the real than to the imaginary or the symbolic.[31] Put another way, sexuality is comprehended better according to the specific modes of these cultural images' and discourses' failure. I'm suggesting that we should think about sexuality in terms of the limits, rather than the power, of these images and discourses—not simply their limits in representing some objective truth of sexuality but, more precisely, their limits in determining human sexuality. Nevertheless, I'm aware that in the face of the constant media barrage of sexualized imagery, this claim may appear particularly counterintuitive. Since the specificity of a Lacanian perspective on sexuality rests on this claim, permit me to elaborate further.

Much of the difficulty—but also the usefulness—of Lacan's concept of the real lies in its de-essentializing, despecifying abstractness. In this regard, the real resonates with the notion of *queer* underlying queer theory. And as a consequence, the Lacanian real, like queerness, is always relational, oppositional in the subversive sense, rather than substantive (there can be no queer without a norm, and vice versa). From this observation we may take another step and note how the Lacanian real functions similarly to the Freudian unconscious in its constantly undermining social and sexual identities. To grasp what Lacan means by this slippery category, whose quotidian connotations remain so hard to dispel, it helps to bear in mind that the real denotes that concept through which, especially in his later work, Lacan implicitly develops certain aspects of Freud's theory of the unconscious. In so doing, Lacan helps to distinguish a psychoanalytic from a more psychological notion of the unconscious as denoting interiority, depth, or the repository of drives and complexes. If we think of the real in light of the *psychoanalytic* unconscious, we will see more clearly how the real is connected with—indeed, remains inseparable from—sexuality.

The paradox of human sexuality, according to Freud, consists in

31. The most compelling demonstration of this distinction—that sex is of the order of the real rather than of the imaginary or symbolic—may be found in Joan Copjec, "Sex and the Euthanasia of Reason," in *Read My Desire: Lacan against the Historicists* (Cambridge: MIT Press, 1994), 201–36, which uses Kant's antinomies of reason to make this argument about sex and the real.

its diphasic emergence: its initial efflorescence in childhood, prior to maturation of the sexual organs, is succeeded by a period of latency before sexuality reemerges alongside, yet forever out of synch with, organic changes in the body. Freud's claims on behalf of infantile sexuality entail recognizing that sex comes before one is ready for it—either physically or psychically. In the case of children it seems relatively clear what being physically unprepared for sex means; psychically it means that the human infant encounters sexual impulses—its own as well as other people's—as alien, unmasterable, unassimilable to its fledgling ego, and hence ultimately traumatic. As a consequence of this capacity to disorganize the ego or coherent self, sexuality becomes part of the unconscious; and it is owing to this subjectively traumatic origin that Lacan aligns sex with the order of the real. The real—like trauma— is what resists assimilation to any imaginary or symbolic universe. Another way of putting this would be to say that the premature emergence of sexuality in humans—its original noncoincidence with biology— splits sexuality off from reality and reassigns it to the domain of fantasy. In so doing, human sexuality is constituted as irremediably perverse.[32]

The Problem of Perversion

Psychoanalysis inherits the category of perversion from nineteenth-century sexology and transforms it almost beyond recognition. Though Freud followed his predecessors in bracketing homosexuality (along with fetishism, sadism, and masochism) under the rubric of perversion, Lacan rarely aligns homosexuality with perversion. In fact, Lacan says little about homosexuality when discussing perversion; instead, he

---

32. In thus characterizing the diphasic emergence of sexuality, I am summarizing Freud's *Three Essays on the Theory of Sexuality* and drawing on Laplanche's reading of Freud, in *Life and Death in Psychoanalysis,* and his subsequent development of ideas concerning generalized seduction and the enigmatic signifier, in *New Foundations for Psychoanalysis,* trans. David Macey (Oxford: Basil Blackwell, 1989). Whereas Lacan describes the traumatically premature emergence of sexuality in terms of the unsymbolizable real, Laplanche describes the same phenomenon in terms of the enigmatic signifier—an account he presents especially cogently in "The Theory of Seduction and the Problem of the Other," trans. Luke Thurston, *International Journal of Psychoanalysis* 78, no. 4 (1997): 653–66. Although space prevents me from providing even a brief consideration of the relation between Laplanchean and Lacanian theory here, I would like to note the continuing importance of Laplanche's work for Anglophone theorists of nonnormative sexuality, such as Leo Bersani, Jonathan Dollimore, John Fletcher, Teresa de Lauretis, and Mandy Merck. A thorough account of Laplanche's debt to Lacan might provide the key for understanding why these theorists find Laplanche so much more useful than they find Lacan.

seems to prefer fetishism as his example of a perverse manifestation, and he takes Sade—who hardly qualifies as homosexual—as his exemplary pervert.[33] Lacan makes same-sex desire independent of perversion by conceptualizing the latter in terms of an unconscious structure of desire, rather than in terms of its phenomenological manifestations or overt symptomatology. Thus for Lacan perversion is distinguished less from heteronormativity than from neurosis, on one hand, and psychosis, on the other. In this Lacan follows Freud, for whom neuroses are the negative of perversions (SE 7:165). Yet in reconceiving perversion in terms of structure, Lacan departs from Freud—a divergence that, in my view, doesn't necessarily represent an advance, since Lacan's "structures of desire" often have the effect of reinstituting a subjective identity, albeit at the level of the unconscious. In other words, I remain skeptical about how the Lacanian tendency to speak of "the pervert," "the hysteric," and "the psychotic" unwittingly reinscribes a typology of desire and, ultimately, categories of personhood that Freud's account of perversion ostensibly outmoded.[34] Given this skepticism, I am particularly keen to see how theorizing perversion in light of queer theory might ameliorate this problem.[35]

233

Having registered that cautionary note, let me now explain how Freud's theory concerning the irremediably perverse constitution of sexuality is fully consistent with contemporary claims on behalf of sexuality as irremediably queer, resistant to normalization. To take a salient

33. In his contribution to an early psychoanalytic—and profoundly normalizing—symposium on perversion, Lacan offers perhaps the least homophobic account of perversion by avoiding the topic of homosexuality altogether; see Jacques Lacan and Wladimir Granoff, "Fetishism: The Symbolic, the Imaginary, and the Real," in Perversions: Psychodynamics and Therapy, ed. Sandor Lorand (New York: Random House, 1956), 265–76. For Lacan's account of Sadian perversion, see "Kant."

34. See, for example, Jean Clavreul, "The Perverse Couple," in Returning to Freud: Clinical Psychoanalysis in the School of Lacan, ed. and trans. Stuart Schneiderman (New Haven: Yale University Press, 1980), 215–33. Clavreul, who was chair of Lacan's department of psychoanalysis at the University of Paris VIII (Vincennes), writes of perversion and homosexuality as if they were virtually synonymous, thus nullifying his own initial distinction between symptom and structure. He also asserts "[t]he danger that the pervert is always bordering on—I must repeat it here—is psychosis" (225), which gives the lie to any tenable structural distinction between perversion and psychosis—and thus compromises Lacan's invalidation of "borderline" diagnoses. Clavreul's paper combines wonderful insights with the most blatant homophobia, recirculating stereotypes of gay men that one must credit to the period in which Clavreul concocted this mixture—the mid-1960s.

35. The foregoing paragraph registers a provisional critique that is developed in Judith Feher Gurewich, "The Philanthropy of Perversion: Another Kind of Violence," in Jacques Lacan and the Cultural Unconscious: Psychoanalytical Critique for the Twenty-First Century, ed. Jean-Michel Rabaté (forthcoming), and in my "The Pervert Does Not Exist," unpublished manuscript.

example, Sedgwick, attempting to define queerness, writes: "That's one of the things that 'queer' can refer to: the open mesh of possibilities, gaps, overlaps, dissonances and resonances, lapses and excesses of meaning when the constituent elements of anyone's gender, of anyone's sexuality aren't made (or *can't be* made) to signify monolithically." From this Sedgwick concludes that "[s]exuality in this sense, perhaps, can *only* mean queer sexuality."[36] Without acknowledging or apparently even realizing it, Sedgwick is directly echoing Freud's contention that we're all potentially queer and that, paradoxically, perversion *is* the norm. As he concludes the first of his *Three Essays:*

> By demonstrating the part played by perverse impulses in the formation of symptoms in the psychoneuroses, we have quite remarkably increased the number of people who might be regarded as perverts. It is not only that neurotics in themselves constitute a very numerous class, but it must also be considered that an unbroken chain bridges the gap between the neuroses in all their manifestations and normality . . . Thus the extraordinarily wide dissemination of the perversions forces us to suppose that the disposition to perversions is itself of no great rarity but must form a part of what passes as the normal constitution. (*SE* 7:171)

And then, struggling to adjudicate a version of the nature / nurture debate that prevailed in his own time, Freud immediately adds, "It is, as we have seen, debatable whether the perversions go back to innate determinants or arise . . . owing to chance experiences. The conclusion now presents itself to us that there is indeed something innate lying behind the perversions but that it is something innate in *everyone*."

This is what Jonathan Dollimore calls Freud's "deconstructive assault on normality," his universalizing description of perversion not as distinct from or opposed to the norm, but as internal to it.[37] In Freud's

---

36. Eve Kosofsky Sedgwick, *Tendencies* (Durham: Duke University Press, 1993), 8 and 20, respectively; original emphases.

37. Jonathan Dollimore, *Sexual Dissidence: Augustine to Wilde, Freud to Foucault* (Oxford: Clarendon, 1991), 182. Dollimore's most recent work significantly develops this earlier book's discussion of perversion; see *Death, Desire, and Loss in Western Culture* (Harmondsworth: Penguin, 1998), esp. 138–40. There is an important distinction to be made between this sense of generalized perversion—what Jacques-Alain Miller calls "perversion for everyone" ("On Perversion," in *Reading Seminars I and II: Lacan's Return to Freud,* ed. Richard Feldstein, Bruce Fink, and Maire Jaanus [Albany: SUNY Press, 1996], 314)—and the more restricted clinical structure of perversion. Yet as I argue in "The Pervert Does Not Exist," this distinction itself entails a host of conceptual and ideological problems.

theory of sexuality, perversion doesn't represent a detour or falling away from the norm, as it does in the prepsychoanalytic, theological conception of perversion. Instead, for Freud the reverse is true: perversion is primary, rather than a secondary deviation. In the form of polymorphous infantile sexuality, perversion *precedes* the norm, and therefore normal sexuality—that is, reproductive genital heterosexuality—represents a deviation or falling away from perversion. To specify this relation more precisely, perhaps we could say that within the Freudian dialectic of sexuality, the norm *sublates* perversion, ostensibly superseding but never actually eliminating it. There is thus a sense in which, by focusing sexuality on the genitals and on a single prescribed act, normal sex represents "paradise lost" in the psychoanalytic cosmology. This is in direct contrast to the theological understanding of this matter, which equates perversion with original sin. In *Three Essays,* reproductive heterosexuality paradoxically designates both an ideal goal to be striven for and, simultaneously, the loss of an ideal state—that of polymorphous perversity.

Hence Freud's ambivalence toward the process of normalization, his vacillation between speaking on its behalf and speaking sotto voce against it. When he speaks on behalf of perversion Freud enters contradiction, bumping up against inherited categories of pathology.[38] As a doctor he is supposed to treat the sick and cure the pathological; but after situating perversion *internal to* normality, Freud necessarily confronts a fundamental uncertainty about how to determine pathology in the bewildering world of sexual variation. Freud negotiates this uncertainty, which his own theory generates, by identifying pathology with

---

38. Noticing—and no doubt identifying with—Freud's discourse *on behalf of* perversion, Foucault concedes that the psychoanalytic theory of perversion fundamentally altered the category's inherited meanings:

And the strange position of [psychoanalysis] at the end of the nineteenth century would be hard to comprehend if one did not see the rupture it brought about in the great system of degenerescence: it resumed the project of a medical technology appropriate for dealing with the sexual instinct; but it sought to free it from its ties with heredity, and hence from eugenics and the various racisms. It is very well to look back from our vantage point and remark upon the normalizing impulse in Freud; one can go on to denounce the role played for many years by the psychoanalytic institution; but the fact remains that in the great family of technologies of sex, which goes so far back into the history of the Christian West, of all those institutions that set out in the nineteenth century to medicalize sex, it was the one that, up to the decade of the forties, rigorously opposed the political and institutional effects of the perversion-heredity-degenerescence system. (*History of Sexuality,* 1:118.)

exclusiveness, or what he calls fixation. Thus he defines the pathology of perversion formally rather than substantively: "the pathological character in a perversion is found to lie not in the *content* of the new sexual aim but in its relation to the normal"; hence it is only so long as "a perversion has the characteristics of exclusiveness and fixation [that] we shall usually be justified in regarding it as a pathological symptom" (*SE* 7:161). According to Freud, in any isolated instance a perverse manifestation tells you nothing about the subject manifesting it; only when accompanied by "exclusiveness and fixation" can perversion be considered pathological.

Despite the progressive implications of Freud's relativizing perversion, there remains something oddly tautological about his claim that it's not the perversion but its fixation that's pathological; indeed, his critique of sexual exclusiveness can be turned against exclusive *hetero*sexuality, as Freud himself recognized: "from the point of view of psychoanalysis the exclusive sexual interest felt by men for women is also a problem that needs elucidating and is not a self-evident fact based upon an attraction that is ultimately of a chemical nature" (*SE* 7:146 n.). But of course, the pathologization of exclusiveness and fixation has historically been used by the psychoanalytic establishment not to interrogate "the exclusive sexual interest felt by men for women," but to inveigh against any sexual interest felt by men for other men. And as Michael Ferguson has pointed out in a painstaking critique of American psychoanalysts' use of the term "fixation" to pathologize homosexuality, it is when "fixation" is linked to a notion of adaptation that it becomes so destructively normalizing.[39]

236

39. Michael Ferguson, "Fixation and Regression in the Psychoanalytic Theory of Homosexuality: A Critical Evaluation," in *Gay Ethics: Controversies in Outing, Civil Rights, and Sexual Science,* ed. Timothy F. Murphy (New York: Haworth, 1994), 309–27. In *The Language of Psychoanalysis,* trans. Donald Nicholson-Smith (New York: Norton, 1973), 162–65, Jean Laplanche and Jean-Bertrand Pontalis provide a number of useful distinctions concerning fixation. Lacan also points to this notion of fixation in order to suggest a critique of the normalizing impulse in Freud's writing on sexuality:

> In *Three Essays on the Theory of Sexuality,* Freud uses two correlative terms concerning the effects of the individual libidinal adventure: *Fixierarbeit* is the fixation that is for us the register of explanation of that which is, in fact, inexplicable . . . We are caught up in an adventure that has taken a certain direction, a certain contingency, certain stages. Freud didn't finish at a stroke the trail he blazed for us. And it may be that, on account of Freud's detours, we are attached to a certain moment in the development of his thought, without fully realizing its contingent character, like that of every effect of our human history . . . [L]et us remember that psychoanalysis might seem at first to be of an ethical order. It might seem to be the search for a natural ethics—and, my goodness, a certain siren song might well promote a misunderstanding of that kind. And indeed,

Rather than simply dismissing the notion of fixation as ineluctably homophobic, I think we may develop it a little more cogently by recognizing how *the process of normalization itself is what's pathological,* since normalization "fixes" desire and generates the exclusiveness of sexual orientation as its symptom. From this perspective, exclusive homosexuality and exclusive heterosexuality are equally problematic, in that both constrain the mobility of desire, orienting it in increasingly limited ways—first toward persons, then toward persons of the opposite sex, then toward specific sexual acts with persons of the opposite sex, and often toward specific acts with a specific person of the opposite sex. Thus normalization is less a question of inculcating heterosexuality than of coordinating desire with the ego, freezing fragmented and mercurial unconscious effects into the total form of an identity. In the terms that Lacan develops from Jakobson (as discussed in the preceding chapter), normalization involves wrenching the metonymy of desire into the metaphor (or substitutive identity) of the ego.

237

This process of normalization is pathogenic rather than healthy insofar as its totalizing impulse remains fundamentally inimical to the contingency and ambiguity that characterize desire. And the fragility of this normalizing process partly explains the hostility and imaginary aggressivity that emerge in response to whatever or whoever derails its trajectory—for example, queers or those who remain sexually ambiguous.[40] Thus my point here is twofold: first, that normalization itself, by orient-

through a whole side of its action and its doctrine, psychoanalysis effectively presents itself as such, as tending to simplify some difficulty that is external in origin, that is of the order of a misrecognition or indeed of a misunderstanding, as tending to restore a normative balance with the world—something that the maturation of the instincts would naturally lead to. One sometimes sees such a gospel preached in the form of the genital relation that I have more than once referred to here with a great deal of reservation and even with a pronounced skepticism. (*SVII* 88)

It is in light of these sentences that Jacques-Alain Miller's comments regarding lesbians and fixation should be read and severely qualified: "This perversion, this turning to the father *[père-version]*, is nowhere more patent or explicit than in the case of female homosexuals who constantly attest to an intense love for the father, legitimating the use of the Freudian term 'fixation'—the paternal fixation of the female homosexual" ("On Perversion," 308).

Finally, with respect to the Freudian term translated as "fixation," I note that Laplanche and Pontalis give the German word *Fixierung* (162); the original text of seminar 7 gives *Fixierbarkeit* (Jacques Lacan, *Le séminaire, livre VII, L'éthique de la psychanalyse,* ed. Jacques-Alain Miller [Paris: Seuil, 1986], 106); and Dennis Porter's translation gives *Fixierarbeit* (as quoted above).

40. Here I must add that the fragility of normalization also accounts for the hostility many gay people express toward bisexuality—even though bisexuality conceives sexuality in terms of gender rather than beyond gender. On the normalizing implications of "biphobia," see Marjorie Garber's useful *Vice Versa: Bisexuality and the Eroticism of Everyday Life* (New York: Simon and Schuster, 1995).

ing desire toward a stable sexual identity, is potentially pathological irrespective of whether the identity in question is heterosexual, homosexual, or otherwise; and second, more specifically, that homosexuality nevertheless remains a specter haunting this process, signaling the possibility of normalization's failure, its *dis*orientation.

Although homosexuality has functioned since the end of the nineteenth century as a synecdoche for perversion—that is, as perversion's most visible representative—this doesn't warrant our characterizing homosexuality as unequivocally antinormative or subversive. Quite the contrary: as an orientation or identity, homosexuality is normalizing though not socially normative—a distinction that often gets lost in contemporary arguments over its political implications. But, on the other hand, as a sign of desire's perverse *resistance* to orientation or identity (its unconscious, perpetual mobility), homosexuality may remind us of how desire itself remains potentially antinormative, incompletely assimilable to the ego, and hence inimical to the model of the person, fundamentally impersonal.

This subtle distinction—between what in homosexuality is normalizing and what is antinormative—must be maintained if queer theory is to elude the impasses of identity politics that it was originally designed to outwit. In order to be as clear as possible about my dual claims here concerning homosexuality, I'd like to invoke French philosopher Guy Hocquenghem, whose queer manifesto, *Homosexual Desire,* anticipates much of the present argument. Hocquenghem opens his book with a polemic that resonates strikingly with Freud's critique of sexual exclusivity:

> "Homosexual desire"—the expression is meaningless. There is no subdivision of desire into homosexuality and heterosexuality. Properly speaking, desire is no more homosexual than heterosexual. Desire emerges in a multiple form, whose components are only divisible *a posteriori,* according to how we manipulate it. Just like heterosexual desire, homosexual desire is an arbitrarily frozen frame in an unbroken and polyvocal flux. The exclusively homosexual characterisation of desire in its present form is a fallacy of the imaginary; but homosexuality has a specially manifest imagery, and it is possible to undertake a deconstruction of such images. If the homosexual image contains a complex knot of dread and desire, if the homosexual phan-

tasy is more obscene than any other and at the same time more exciting, if it is impossible to appear anywhere as a self-confessed homosexual without upsetting families, causing children to be dragged out
of the way and arousing mixed feelings of horror and desire, then
the reason must be that for us twentieth-century westerners there is
a close connection between desire and homosexuality. Homosexuality
expresses something—some aspect of desire—which appears nowhere else, and that something is not merely the accomplishment of
the sexual act with a person of the same sex.[41]

What homosexuality expresses—indirectly and in popular form—is desire's disquieting disregard for gender and for persons. Or perhaps we
could point the distinction more precisely by saying that this is what
homosexuality *represents*: homosexuality has been historically, not essentially or expressively, associated with what psychoanalysis views as a
transhistorical characteristic of desire. Since transhistorical claims tend
to be regarded as little short of heresy, let me reiterate that what psychoanalysis considers essential to desire is precisely that it obtains no
essential object: *desire's objects remain essentially contingent.*

239

But when homosexuality becomes the basis for an identity, this contingent relation between desire and its objects vanishes. Hocquenghem
frames the conundrum like this: "Homosexual desire is perverse in the
Freudian sense, i.e. it is simply an-Oedipal, as long as it expresses the
disorganisation of the component drives. It becomes neurotically perverse in the ordinary sense when it relates to a face, when it enters the
sphere of the ego and the imaginary."[42] Distinguishing between two
versions of homosexuality and two kinds of perversion (as well as between their respective ideological effects), Hocqenghem raises a question that, even one quarter-century later, queer theory has barely begun
to address, much less to answer. This question concerns how we may
conceive of desire as *not* relating "to a face": how can we depersonify
or impersonalize desire so as to retain its originary perverse force without simply plunging into sexual anarchy? How can we inhibit the pro-
sopopoeia—the face-making trope—that accompanies libidinal investments while still honoring the other's alterity? I think we may profitably
engage these questions by considering Hocquenghem's psychoanalytic

41. Hocquenghem, *Homosexual Desire*, 49–50.
42. Ibid., 149.

antecedents and developing the subterranean Freudian logic that guides his argument; in so doing, we'll push both Lacanian psychoanalysis and queer theory onto new ground.

The Impersonality of Desire

> Relations between human beings are really established before one gets to the domain of consciousness. It is desire which achieves the primitive structuration of the human world, desire as unconscious.
>
> —Jacques Lacan, *The Seminar of Jacques Lacan, Book II: The Ego in Freud's Theory and in the Technique of Psychoanalysis*

Hocquenghem speaks not of "depersonifying" or "impersonalizing" desire but, more austerely, of its *dehumanization:* "The sexualisation of the world heralded by the gay movement pushes capitalist decoding to the limit and corresponds to the dissolution of the human; from this point of view, the gay movement undertakes the necessary dehumanisation."[43] This promulgation of dehumanization sits very uncomfortably with post-Enlightenment liberal politics, which takes as a point of departure the dignity of the human individual. Civil rights is one logical outcome of this political stance, as is the post-'68 gay movement that Hocquenghem invokes; therefore, his advocating dehumanization by means of sexuality might be viewed as pushing gay radicalism into contradiction with its liberal origins. After all, it's not hard to see how discussing gay sex in terms of dehumanization could inflame rather than mitigate homophobia. Yet the reference to "dehumanization" carries more precise resonances—in general, to the tradition of French antihumanism; more specifically, to the work of Deleuze and Guattari; and ultimately, I'll suggest, to the French psychoanalytic tradition of Lacan. Though Hocquenghem follows Deleuze and Guattari to the letter, referring to "capitalist decoding" and suchlike, he follows Lacan in spirit, explicitly developing an account of queer sexuality that remains only implicit in Lacan.

43. Hocquenghem, *Homosexual Desire,* 145. See the French original: "La sexualisation du monde qu'annoncent les mouvements homosexuels correspond à la mise à la limite du décodage capitaliste, à la dissolution de l'humain; de ce point de vue les mouvements homosexuels disent et font brutalement la déhumanisation nécessaire" (*Le désir homosexuel* [Paris: Éditions Universitaires, 1972]).

To boil down a complex philosophical tradition to its most elementary coordinates, let us recall that French antihumanism—for which
the German names Freud, Marx, and Nietzsche can stand just as well
as those of Bataille, Lacan, and Foucault—announces the "death of man"
as a fully autonomous, self-governing agent who is master of his world
because master of himself. Antihumanism extinguishes this conception
of the human in favor of one in which language and various social systems precondition or discipline human agency. Rather than manipulat-
ing signs and wielding power, man is reconceived as the conduit for
and product of nonhuman forces greater than himself. Thus we might
say that man is unmanned in antihumanist philosophy, finding himself
no longer master of his world since no longer master of himself. The
principal name psychoanalysis gives to this loss of mastery or decentering of the human is *the unconscious.* From this it follows that we may
nuance the potentially misleading terms "antihumanism" and "dehumanization" by substituting for them *de-ego-ization,* since it is less the death
of humanity or of Man per se that is at stake than the obsolescence of
a particular conception and ideology of the self. Hocquenghem makes
this clear when he concludes—in a formulation anticipating Bersani's—
that "[h]omosexual desire is neither on the side of death nor on the side
of life; it is the killer of civilised egos."[44]

Deleuze and Guattari's contribution to this antihumanist project
remains somewhat ambiguous—an ambiguity that requires interpreting
if we are to correctly gauge their influence on *Homosexual Desire.* Calling
their critique of the ideology of the self "schizoanalysis" rather than
psychoanalysis, Deleuze and Guattari substitute for the potentially misleading term "antihumanism" the more pointed "anti-Oedipus," thereby
intending to discredit at once the ideology of the sovereign self and the
Freudian metanarrative they claim bolsters that individualist ideology.
In fact, like most readers of Freud, Deleuze and Guattari find in psychoanalysis a duality, whose halves they cast in highly evaluative terms—
the "good" and the "bad" Freud, the liberatory and the repressive dimensions of psychoanalysis. They thus advance their polemic against the
"bad" Freud in the service of a "good" Freud that they incorporate and,
somewhat disingenuously, claim as their own.

44. Ibid., 150. See also Leo Bersani, "Is the Rectum a Grave?" in *AIDS: Cultural Analysis / Cultural
Activism,* ed. Douglas Crimp (Cambridge: MIT Press, 1988), 197–222; and Bersani's *Homos.*

In the Manichaean universe of *Anti-Oedipus,* desire is the hero and Oedipus the villain: "The great discovery of psychoanalysis was that of the production of desire, of the productions of the unconscious. But once Oedipus entered the picture, this discovery was soon buried beneath a new brand of idealism: a classical theater was substituted for the unconscious as a factory."[45] Extolling the promiscuous productivity of the primary process, Deleuze and Guattari object to what they see as the repressive structuring of this process by way of the oedipal triangle, which seems to privatize desire, constraining it within nuclear family dynamics. Like Hocquenghem, they view the anthropomorphization of desire—thinking of desire in terms of persons—as hermeneutically erroneous and ideologically repressive, since, as they point out, "[t]he unconscious is totally unaware of persons as such. Partial objects are not representations of parental figures or of the basic patterns of family relations; they are parts of desiring-machines, having to do with a process and with relations of production that are both irreducible and prior to anything that may be made to conform to the Oedipal figure."[46] Thus, like Hocquenghem, Deleuze and Guattari aim to depersonify desire. And apart from the vocabulary of desiring-machines, their contentions in this matter seem to me wholly compatible with Lacan's theory of desire as unconscious and originating in the object *a,* which is itself "both irreducible and prior to anything that may be made to conform to the Oedipal figure."

However, the problem with Deleuze and Guattari's account appears as soon as they propose liberating desire—conceptually and in reality. Not only do they wish to unleash primary process productivity directly onto the world, without any mediation or regulation whatsoever, but in their utopianist valorization of schizophrenia they render social and psychic processes both transparent and naively beneficent: "We maintain that the social field is immediately invested by desire, that it is the historically determined product of desire, and that libido has no need of any mediation or sublimation, any psychic operation, any transformation, in order to invade and invest the productive forces and the relations of production. *There is only desire and the social, and nothing else.*"[47]

45. Deleuze and Guattari, *Anti-Oedipus,* 24.

46. Ibid., 46.

47. Ibid., 29; original emphasis.

It is claims such as these that prompted the leading historian of French psychoanalysis to characterize *Anti-Oedipus* as a work "whose principal theses are astonishing in their simple-mindedness";[48] such claims also have discouraged many other psychoanalytically oriented intellectuals, including me, from seriously engaging this work. Yet as Elisabeth Roudinesco recognized and, more recently, Jerry Aline Flieger elaborated, the significance of *Anti-Oedipus* lies less in its simpleminded polemic than in how that polemic effectively resuscitates the vitality of what it attacks. Following Flieger, we may read Deleuze and Guattari against themselves, emphasizing not their direct critique of Freudo-Lacanian theory, but rather their indirect revivification of its most radical insights at a time when those insights were ossifying into orthodoxy.[49]

The Repressive Hypothesis Redux

Deleuze and Guattari make their critique of Lacan's theory of desire explicit with the declaration that "[t]he three errors concerning desire

48. Elisabeth Roudinesco, *Jacques Lacan and Co.: A History of Psychoanalysis in France, 1925–1985,* trans. Jeffrey Mehlman (Chicago: University of Chicago Press, 1990), 495. Nevertheless, Roudinesco approaches *Anti-Oedipus* in the right spirit:

> If one restricts oneself to its theses, *Anti-Oedipe* is a work filled with crude formulations, errors, and gross oversights. But the book should not be reduced to its explicit content. For to do so would be to err on the subject of the book as much as a reader of *A la recherche du temps perdu* who would want to transform the Proustian saga into a story of maternal kisses and rosewater. *Anti-Oedipe* is a great book, not through the ideas it conveys but through the form it bestows on them, through its style and tone: in brief, through that febrile syntax in which—with breath held and like a Rimbaldian drunken boat—the forgotten furor of a language of rupture and unreason comes to be couched. Published at a time when the impasse of the structuralist movement was becoming clear, *Anti-Oedipe* anarchically drew to itself all the hopes of an aborted revolution. At the same time, and because it effected a specifically French synthesis of all the ideals of liberation (from Freudo-Marxism to terrorism, and from the quest for a lost paradise to the cult of drugs), it took psychoanalytic conformism as its principal target, noisily designating the degeneration of Lacanianism into a dogma. (496)

49. See Jerry Aline Flieger, "Overdetermined Oedipus: Mommy, Daddy, and Me as Desiring-Machine," *South Atlantic Quarterly* 96 (1997): 599–620, which brilliantly uses Deleuze and Guattari's own theses to show how their work is far more oedipalist than their critique suggests, and that therefore their attack on psychoanalysis should be understood as a mode of disavowal. Flieger argues that far from discrediting *Anti-Oedipus,* this negative modus operandi illuminates psychoanalytic theory in ways that should be of great interest to those who have hitherto dismissed Deleuze and Guattari from serious theoretical consideration. Here it is perhaps worth recalling that the first volume of their magnum opus appeared in 1972, coincident with Hocquenghem's *Homosexual Desire* and Lacan's seminar *Encore,* which, I'm suggesting, separates a theory of sexuality from the terms of both gender and personhood. And in view of the tendency to read *Anti-Oedipus* as an unequivocal denunciation of the Freudo-Lacanian tradition, it is also worth noting that Félix Guattari, who was gay, had been trained by Lacan and remained both a member of his École Freudienne

are called lack, law, and signifier."[50] With respect to Lacan's doctrine of the signifier, we have observed already how Deleuze and Guattari's desire *for* desire permits no room for mediation, allowing no symbolic intervention between desire and the social other than that of repression, which they view as an unnecessary evil: "representation is always a social and psychic repression of desiring-production."[51] Thus whereas Lacan conceptualizes the imaginary and the symbolic as heterogeneous modes of mediating the real, Deleuze and Guattari substitute for these modes of mediation their idea of the machine, which, defined "as a system of interruptions or breaks *(coupures)*" and operating in tripartite mode, serves in displaced form many of the mediating functions performed by the Lacanian symbolic.[52]

Nevertheless, Deleuze and Guattari resist the idea of a symbolic order, since it is through this concept that Lacan rethinks the Oedipus complex. In order to distance their notion of mechanistic interruption from that of symbolic mediation, Deleuze and Guattari insist that "[t]he desiring-machine is not a metaphor."[53] Thus although some critics find their critique of representation fruitful for analyzing cultural production, Deleuze and Guattari's rejection of representation as inherently repressive pushes them toward accepting the repressive hypothesis and

---

de Paris (EFP) and a practicing analyst even after the publication of *Anti-Oedipus.* Hocquenghem too, while composing *Homosexual Desire,* was teaching philosophy at Vincennes, practically next door to Lacan's department of psychoanalysis, and therefore effectively he was working in a Lacanian milieu.

50. Deleuze and Guattari, *Anti-Oedipus,* 111. Having enumerated these three fallacies, they continue:

It is one and the same error, an idealism that forms a pious conception of the unconscious. And it is futile to interpret these notions in terms of a combinative apparatus *(une combinatoire)* that makes of lack an empty position and no longer a deprivation, that turns the law into a rule of the game and no longer a commandment, and the signifier into a distributor and no longer a meaning, for these notions cannot be prevented from dragging their theological cortege behind—insufficiency of being, guilt, signification. Structural interpretation challenges all beliefs, rises above all images, and from the realm of the mother and the father retains only functions, defines *the prohibition and the transgression* as structural operations. But what water will cleanse these concepts of their background, their previous existences—religiosity? Scientific knowledge as nonbelief is truly the last refuge of belief, and as Nietzsche put it, there never was but one psychology, that of the priest. (111; original emphasis)

51. Ibid., 184.

52. Ibid., 36–41. Explaining that "every machine has a sort of code built into it," Deleuze and Guattari acknowledge that "[w]e owe to Jacques Lacan the discovery of this fertile domain of a code of the unconscious" (38).

53. Ibid., 41.

endorsing liberationist psychoanalytic theories, such as those of Wilhelm Reich and Herbert Marcuse, which seem so naively implausible in the wake of Foucault's critique of the repressive hypothesis.[54]

But doesn't this outmoded idea that desire resists norms comport with my claims on behalf of both queer theory and Lacan? I've pointed out that Lacan's category of the real designates that which resists adaptation and remains definitively recalcitrant; and by way of Freud's account of the diphasic emergence of human sexuality, I've suggested that, though the real has no predetermined content, Lacan associates it with the traumatic, unassimilable dimension of sex. I've also suggested that queer theory has something to gain from the psychoanalytic alignment of sex with the unconscious, since this makes sexuality refractive, maladaptive, and therefore always to some extent perverse. In this respect, queer theory is right to claim that perverse sexuality is inherently subversive. And when Warner asks rhetorically, "Can we not hear in the resonances of queer protest an objection to the normalization of behavior in this broad sense, and thus to the cultural phenomenon of societalization?" we now can hear resonances with Deleuze and Guattari's valorization of the schizophrenic, who has indeed effectively resisted "societalization" and stands outside all social norms. But given this conception of the oppositional relation between desire and social norms, we must confront the objection that my theses articulating queer theory with Lacan simply restate the repressive hypothesis.

First, however, Freud's situating perversion as internal, rather than opposed, to the normal requires us to rethink the relation between desire and norms. From a psychoanalytic perspective, the queer is not opposed to the normal, but fissures it from within. Thinking of the relation between normal and queer in this way can be sustained only if we retain a distinction between homosexuality as an orientation or identity, on the one hand, and queerness or perversion on the other. Perversion is always relational, an internal division akin to that of the

245

54. See Foucault's *History of Sexuality,* vol. 1. Flieger makes a similar point, noting that "Deleuze and Guattari adopt the repression hypothesis wholesale" ("Overdetermined Oedipus," 602). This is how their version of it goes: "From the moment desire is welded again to the law—we needn't point out what is known since time began: that there is no desire without law—the eternal operation of eternal repression recommences, the operation that closes around the unconscious the circle of prohibition and transgression, white mass and black mass; but the sign of desire is never a sign of the law, it is a sign of strength *(puissance)" (Anti-Oedipus,* 111). For an example of theoretical cultural criticism based on their critique of representation, see Steven Shaviro, *The Cinematic Body* (Minneapolis: University of Minnesota Press, 1993).

unconscious, rather than being substantive or an external oppositional force. As soon as perversion or queerness becomes ontologized as an identity—whether in the form of "the queer body" invoked by some queer theorists or the figure of "the pervert" invoked by some Lacanians—perversion loses its disruptive potential.[55] And so the definite article that apotropaically unifies perversion into an identity—*the* pervert—should always be barred. If one takes seriously the idea of a subject split by the unconscious, then no structure of desire provides the basis for an identity. The pervert does not exist, except as an ideological construction, an imaginary misrecognition that, in the form of queer identities, lesbians and gays appear almost as ready to make as do psychoanalysts.

We escape the framework of the repressive hypothesis when our understanding of desire treats perversion or queerness as relational rather than substantive, a move that Deleuze and Guattari seem unable to make insofar as their account contains too few conceptual elements to formulate relations in this way. By committing themselves to the axiom that "[t]here is only desire and the social, and nothing else," Deleuze and Guattari foreclose categories of mediation that remain necessary if we are to theorize the relation between desire and the social in terms more nuanced than those of repression or liberation. Beyond even an idea of the symbolic order, their model requires some account of the specific mediating function performed by fantasy. But, like Foucault, they eschew a theory of fantasy in favor of concepts denoting that which seems more concrete, literal, and *real* in a positivist sense.

Not only does fantasy fulfill a crucial mediating function, thereby permitting us to complicate the relation between desire and the social, but it does so by keeping perversion alive and in play. Thus, in my view, queer theory cannot afford to accept Foucault's—or Deleuze and Guattari's—dismissal of fantasy as a ruse of idealism. For me the significance of Lacan's inverting his formula for fantasy ($\$ \lozenge a$) to make

55. Simon Watney gets at this problem when, in a somewhat different context, he argues that the very notion of a "homosexual body" only exposes the more or less desperate ambition to confine mobile desire in the semblance of a stable object, calibrated by its sexual aim, regarded as a "wrong choice." The "homosexual body" would thus evidence a fictive collectivity of perverse sexual performances, denied any psychic reality and pushed out beyond the furthest margins of the social. This, after all, is what the category of "the homosexual" (which we *cannot* continue to employ) was invented to do in the first place. ("The Spectacle of AIDS," in *AIDS: Cultural Analysis/ Cultural Activism,* ed. Crimp, 79)

the formula for perversion ($a \diamondsuit \mathcal{S}$) lies in its maintaining fantasy as always potentially perverse, while also guaranteeing perversion a mobility that defers its solidification into an identity (*the* pervert).[56] Hence the full significance of the $\diamondsuit$ sign (*poinçon*—stamp, punch, or lozenge) that links $\mathcal{S}$ and a, and which Lacan says "is created to allow a hundred and one different readings, a multiplicity that is admissible as long as the spoken remains caught in its algebra" (*E* 313). This $\diamondsuit$ sign indicates a set of possible relations between the subject of the unconscious and its object, a veritable repertoire of relationality. To appreciate how this works, we need to clarify the ambiguous status of the object *(a)*, which, designating neither a person nor a thing, occupies a distinctly multivalent position in Lacan's theory of sexuality.

The Ideology of Lack

Deleuze and Guattari approach a radical conception of the object by repudiating the notion of lack, perhaps the most significant aspect of their critique of psychoanalysis. "Desire does not lack anything," they maintain,[57] whereas Lacan insists just the opposite, namely, that "[d]esire is a relation of being to lack" (*SII* 223). Antithetical though these claims appear, the direction in which they're subsequently elaborated brings Deleuze and Guattari surprisingly close to the Lacanian position: "Desire does not lack anything; it does not lack its object. It is, rather, the *subject* that is missing in desire, or desire that lacks a fixed subject; there is no fixed subject unless there is repression." Here Deleuze and Guattari displace lack from the object to the subject, who thus is decentered by desire. See how similar this originary decentering of the subject by desire sounds to Lacan's version of the matter:

> Desire is a relation of being to lack. This lack is the lack of being properly speaking. It isn't the lack of this or that, but lack of being whereby the being exists . . . The libido, but now no longer as used theoretically as a quantitative quantity, is the name of what animates the deep-seated conflict at the heart of human action. (*SII* 223)

---

56. In *The Plague of Fantasies* (New York: Verso, 1997), Slavoj Žižek says something similar: "fantasy as such is, in its very notion, close to perversion" (14). However, Žižek construes the relation between fantasy and perversion somewhat differently than I'm doing here.

57. Deleuze and Guattari, *Anti-Oedipus*, 26.

For Lacan, as for Deleuze and Guattari, the decentering effect of desire is so fundamental that desire cannot be conceived as following from the loss of any particular object. On the contrary, in this conception of desire what is lost is the fixed, self-identical subject.

Despite the possibility of this dialectical movement, which enables us to discern a deeper compatibility beyond apparent incompatibility, the question of conceptualizing desire in terms of lack remains a stubborn problem, not only for Deleuze and Guattari (and Hocquenghem too), but also more generally for feminism and queer theory. Though the idea that one desires what he or she lacks may be traced back to Plato's *Symposium,* its development in psychoanalysis is especially objectionable to feminists and queer theorists, in part because psychoanalysis tends to explain lack (and hence desire) in terms of castration.[58] Furthermore, institutionalized psychoanalysis exhibits such a poor record of pathologizing homosexuality as lacking, deficient, and developmentally retarded that it is hardly surprising queer theorists consider the very notion of lack to be ideologically suspect. Since the idea of lack has ultimately theological origins (in which it conveys Man's insufficiency in relation to God), we can appreciate queer theorists' skepticism concerning a concept with the potential to resurrect ancient prejudices about same-sex desire as not simply a sin but one of the most abominable. As Dollimore puts it in his very illuminating new work on this subject, "[d]esire implies lack, hence imperfection. To be eternal and hence non-mutable is also to be free of desire."[59]

The crucial issues here concern which master-term—"lack," "loss," "castration," "death," "sexual difference," and so on—we employ to theorize desire; whether that master-term carries positive or negative connotations; and how those connotations imply invidious distinctions or otherwise embed normative ideologies of gender and sexuality. Although, as Dollimore suggests, it is hard to conceive desire in other than negative terms, the alternative view, which queer theory has found

58. Plato has Aristophanes assert that "one desires what one lacks" (*The Symposium,* trans. W. Hamilton [Harmondsworth: Penguin, 1951], 76).

59. Dollimore, *Death, Desire, and Loss in Western Culture,* 81. Dollimore's excellent book provides an extremely thorough and wide-ranging perspective on its topic; its interest for this reader lies in how Dollimore develops a profoundly psychoanalytic logic without psychoanalytic terminology and while maintaining significant critical distance from both Freud and Lacan. For a more narrowly focused approach to the same topic, see Richard Boothby, *Death and Desire: Psychoanalytic Theory in Lacan's Return to Freud* (New York: Routledge, 1991).

248

more congenial, involves situating desire in relation to *excess* rather than lack. In the paradigm that Deleuze and Guattari develop from the Spinozist tradition that runs through Nietzsche to Bataille, desire is a matter of production rather than of reproduction, consumption, or exchange; and desiring production operates within a calculus of abundance rather than scarcity, multiplicity rather than singularity. Hence their early definition: "Desire is the set of *passive syntheses* that engineer partial objects, flows, and bodies, and that function as units of production."[60] And it is on this basis that, as we have seen, Hocquenghem maintains that "[d]esire emerges in a multiple form, whose components are only divisible *a posteriori*, according to how we manipulate it."

It is by mapping desire in relation to excess rather than lack (or abundance rather than scarcity) that we reach an understanding of desire as multiple—an understanding that makes desire essentially pluralistic, with all the inclusive implications of pluralism. Conceiving desire in terms of multiplicity enables us to avoid the problem of castration as an explanatory framework, since castration seems to imply a single, univocal model of desire, one that threatens to return us to the binary categories of complementarity and homogeneity so inhospitable to non-normative sexualities. It is for reasons approximating these that even queer theorists who remain unpersuaded by Deleuze and Guattari nonetheless reject the concepts of castration and lack central to Lacan's theory of desire—or at least the version of Lacan with which we're most familiar.[61]

But, in fact, it isn't hard to demonstrate how Lacan's account of desire depends on a notion of excess that also gives rise to an understanding of desire as multiple and thus in some sense pluralistic. From the very beginning of his return to Freud, Lacan theorizes the unconscious in terms of excess—an excess of meaning:

> The discovery of the unconscious, such as it appears at the moment of its historical emergence, with its own dimension, is that the full significance of meaning far surpasses the signs manipulated by the

249

60. Deleuze and Guattari, *Anti-Oedipus*, 26, original emphasis.

61. See, for example, Bersani, *Homos*, 133: "A theory of homo-ness in desire . . . will lead us to question the Proustian equation of desire with lack"; also 149–51. See also Elizabeth Grosz, *Space, Time, and Perversion: Essays on the Politics of Bodies* (New York: Routledge, 1995), esp. 175–80. And D. A. Miller, "Anal *Rope*," in *Inside / Out*, ed. Fuss, 137: "homosexuality would be characterized not by a problematics of castration, but on the contrary by an exemption from one."

individual. Man is always cultivating a great many more signs than he thinks. That's what the Freudian discovery is about—a new attitude to man. That's what man after Freud is. (*SII* 122)

The new perspective on humanity inaugurated by the discovery or invention of the unconscious involves a sense of loss, but this loss is a consequence of excess—that is, a loss of mastery that stems from an excess of signification. Thus the paradox whereby excess is not so much the alternative to lack as its precondition entails a more specific problem, namely, that the boon of linguistic subjectivity comes at the cost of subjective unity. This excess of meaning called the unconscious generates desire as a multiplicity of possible connections, metonymic links between signifiers that engender subjectivity. Another way of putting this is to point out how linguistic duplicity—the very possibility that language can deceive—produces the perpetual illusion of a secret located beyond language, and it is this enigma that elicits desire. Hence, for Lacan, the subject and desire come into being at the same moment; and he names this constitutive division that founds the subject "object *a*," a term intended to designate the remainder or *excess* that keeps self-identity forever out of reach, thus maintaining desire.

Lacan commonly refers to object *a* as "cause of desire" in order to emphasize that this object is what brings desire into existence. Although the concept of object *a* emerges in his work fairly early, it does not come into its own until the 1960s, the period conventionally designated "late Lacan," which still remains comparatively unfamiliar in cultural studies, feminist theory, and queer theory. As I have been arguing throughout this book, the logic of this concept, object *a,* demotes or relativizes that of the phallus: whereas the phallus implies a univocal model of desire (insofar as all desiring positions are mapped in relation to a singular term), object *a* implies multiple, heterogeneous possibilities for desire, especially since object *a* bears no discernible relation to gender. Indeed, Deleuze and Guattari acknowledge this crucial distinction within Lacan's account of desire:

> Lacan's admirable theory of desire appears to us to have two poles: one related to "the object small *a*" as a desiring-machine, which defines desire in terms of a real production, thus going beyond both any idea of need and any idea of fantasy; and the other related to

the "great Other" as a signifier, which reintroduces a certain notion of lack.[62]

However, Deleuze and Guattari decline to acknowledge that this "notion of lack" introduced by the excess of signification is nothing other than object *a!* And it is hardly the case that the concept of object *a* invalidates "any idea of fantasy," since Lacan's formula for fantasy ($ \$ \diamond a $) describes precisely the subject's multiple relations to object *a*, which itself takes multiple forms.

Object *a* takes multiple forms as a consequence of the drive's partiality; it represents the concept through which Lacan develops Karl Abraham's notion of the partial object, as well as Winnicott's notion of the transitional object. However, by object *a* Lacan designates something different than what object-relations theorists mean by *the object*, as this critical remark suggests: "any theorisation of analysis organised around the object relation amounts in the end to advocating the recomposition of the subject's imaginary world according to the norm of the analyst's ego" (*SII* 254)—a criticism implying not only that psychoanalysis shouldn't concern itself primarily with the patient's object-relations (for example, by attempting to modify the patient's sexual orientation), but also that this antinormative conception of analysis depends on a different conception of the object.

In Lacan's theory the object results from an excess of signification that Freud calls the unconscious; more specifically, it is the effect of this excess on the human body that brings desire into being. In his *Three Essays,* Freud describes this phenomenon in terms of polymorphous perversity, emphasizing the infant's capacity for autoerotic pleasure in any number of bodily openings, surfaces, and activities. As is well known, Freud designates these multiple corporeal apertures and surfaces *erogenous zones,* and this inspires Lacan's account of object *a:*

> The very delimitation of the "erogenous zone" that the drive isolates from the metabolism of the function (the act of devouring concerns other organs than the mouth—ask one of Pavlov's dogs) is the result of a cut *(coupure)* expressed in the anatomical mark *(trait)* of a margin or border—lips, "the enclosure of the teeth," the rim of the

251

---

62. Deleuze and Guattari, *Anti-Oedipus,* 27 n.

anus, the tip of the penis, the vagina, the slit formed by the eyelids, even the horn-shaped aperture of the ear . . . Observe that this mark of the cut is no less obviously present in the object described by analytic theory: the mamilla, faeces, the phallus (imaginary object), the urinary flow. (An unthinkable list, if one adds, as I do, the phoneme, the gaze, the voice—the nothing.) (*E* 314–15)

Erogenous zones—which are always multiple, never singular—come into being as soon as sexuality is separated from organic functions, that is, in the reflexive moment of autoeroticism. Lacan describes this process as "the result of a cut" that occurs at any number of bodily borders. Not only is "this mark of the cut" (which creates objects *a*) multiplied throughout the body, but it is *my own body* on which the symbolic order makes these incisions. Thus for Lacan, as for Freud, sexual desire originates in autoeroticism.

In arguing thus, I find myself parting company with Lacanian analyst Bruce Fink, who claims that

> [a]ccording to Freud, a young boy's masturbatory behavior generally involves fantasies about the boy's mother, which implies that it is already alloerotic—in other words, that it involves another person. I would even go so far as to claim that, beyond an extremely tender age, *there is no such thing as autoeroticism.* Even an infant's masturbatory touching already includes its parents, insofar as they first stimulated certain zones, showed interest in them, paid attention to them, lavished care on them, and so on. The connection to other people— which is evident in the adult's fantasies that invariably accompany "autoerotic behavior"—is so fundamental that there seems to be no *eroticism*, as such, without it. All eroticism is alloeroticism.[63]

This strikes me as a surprisingly commonsensical—that is to say, un-Lacanian—way of thinking about eroticism. While I agree with Fink that there can be no desire (and therefore no eroticism) without the Other, I remain convinced by the Freudian logic that views human sexuality as emerging in the reflexive turning away from functional activities—feeding and suchlike—that involve other people, and the turning around upon itself of the drive, in the direction of fantasy. It is this

63. Bruce Fink, *A Clinical Introduction to Lacanian Psychoanalysis: Theory and Technique* (Cambridge: Harvard University Press, 1997), 269 n. 21, original emphases.

double movement that Freud designates as autoeroticism. The specific-ity of Freud's theory, as he develops it in his *Three Essays,* lies in the idea that sexuality originates in this movement that *breaks* the connection to other people rather than establishing connection.[64]

The significance of this logic for our purposes lies in the implication that desire emerges independently of heterosexuality or homosexuality; and hence the gendering involved in "object-choice" must be a secondary process performed on objects that precede gender—as Lacan's example of "the horn-shaped aperture of the ear" clearly demonstrates. This sec-ondary process, which organizes and thus totalizes objects *a* into a gen-dered object-choice, shows how personification functions as a strategy of normalization. We might even say that the psychoanalytic notion of object-choice is itself a heterosexist invention, one that runs counter to psychoanalysis's own logic of unconscious desire. If within Freudian metapsychology the notion of object-choice could be understood as a sort of conceptual compromise formation, then Lacan's reconception of the object dismantles that compromise and undoes along with it the normalizing implications of gendered object-choice.

Sexuality versus Genitality

Perhaps in homage to Augustine's belief that immaculate conception occurred *per auris,* Lacan's example of "the horn-shaped aperture of the ear" points to the double dimension—tactile and auditory—through which the ear becomes an erogenous zone. This example thus indicates especially cogently the function of fantasy in dispersing erotogenicity throughout the body. The ear can become eroticized not merely because its epidermis is sensitive to tactile stimulation, but because sound elicits our desire too. Thus although the ear is unequivocally distinct from the genital organs—and, unlike the mouth, it rarely if ever approaches di-rect contact with them—it remains no less erotogenic for all that.

This disposition to erotogenicity may be read in two ways. On the one hand, it suggests that by means of fantasy "any other part of the body can acquire the same susceptibility to stimulation as is possessed by the genitals and can become an erotogenic zone"; in such instances, declares Freud, the parts of the body thus affected "behave exactly like

253

---

64. Here again my reading of Freud is inflected by Laplanche's *Life and Death in Psychoanalysis.*

genitals" (*SE* 7:183–84). There is something surreal in this idea that nongenital parts of the body can behave *exactly* like genital organs—as in those pornographic cartoons by Bill Schmeling, a gay artist known as "The Hun," in which the men's nipples are so distended that they become miniature penises. This way of reading the disposition to erotogenicity takes genitalia as the model for which other organs may become hallucinatory analogues.

However, by the third edition of his *Three Essays on the Theory of Sexuality,* Freud's account of this phenomenon has shifted subtly, and he notes that "[a]fter further reflection and after taking other observations into account, I have been led to ascribe the quality of erotogenicity to all parts of the body and to all the internal organs" (*SE* 7:184 n. 1). Part of what has shifted is Freud's distinction between genitality and sexuality; by 1915 the genitals have forfeited their priority as the model for other erogenous zones. From being roughly synonymous in 1905, *genitality* becomes merely a subset of *sexuality* by 1915, so that although the genital is almost always sexual, what Freud means by "sexual" remains fundamentally irreducible to genitality. For example, in an emendation to the third edition of his *Three Essays,* Freud substitutes the word "genital" for "sexual," thereby registering a sharper distinction between the two (*SE* 7:192). And in thus decisively distinguishing sexuality from genitality, Freud also separates sexuality from gender. This irreducibility of sexuality to genitality is one way of describing the mobility of desire, a mobility that makes sexuality all the more difficult to localize. It is insofar as it remains unlocalizable that Lacan explains sexuality in terms of the real. This is worth considering because without localization any disciplinary project is doomed to failure—a fact that should make this psychoanalytic account of sexuality attractive to antinormative politics.

Furthermore, Freud's deprivileging of genitality, which follows from his emphasis on the polymorphous perversity of human sexuality, is clearly useful for queer theory's effort to think about desire outside the terms of heterosexuality. We find a similar deprivileging of genitality in Lacan, who comments that "[t]hese erogenous zones that, until one has achieved a fuller elucidation of Freud's thought, one can consider to be generic, and that are limited to a number of special points, to points that are openings, to a limited number of mouths at the body's surface, are the points where Eros will have to find his source" (*SVII* 93). Describing erogenous zones as "generic"—that is, as multiple members of a single class—Lacan specifies their genre through the figure of the mouth. Rather than figuring the mouth as a displaced or secondary analogue for more primary orifices or organs—as, for example, Freud does with Dora—Lacan reverses this priority, thereby eliminating any potential gender bias with his implication that genital orifices represent displaced or secondary analogues for the mouth.

This surreal image of multiple mouths at the body's surface is highly resonant.[65] Lacan takes the mouth as his model for erogenous zones owing to the mouth's multivalence as a site of entry and exit: it is not

65. Lacan may draw this image from *Julius Caesar,* in which Caesar's multiple wounds are graphically figured by Mark Antony as mouths eliciting desire:

> Over thy wounds now do I prophesy—
> Which like dumb mouths do ope their ruby lips
> To beg the voice and utterance of my tongue—
> A curse shall light upon the limbs of men . . .   (3.1.262–65)

255

> Let but the commons hear this testament—
> Which, pardon me, I do not mean to read—
> And they would go and kiss dead Caesar's wounds
> And dip their napkins in his sacred blood . . .   (3.2.132–35)

> Show you sweet Caesar's wounds, poor poor dumb mouths,
> And bid them speak for me. But were I Brutus,
> And Brutus Antony, there were an Antony
> Would ruffle up your spirits, and put a tongue
> In every wound of Caesar that should move
> The stones of Rome to rise and mutiny.   (3.2.220–25)

Though he does not mention *Julius Caesar,* Shakespeare scholar Joel Fineman elaborated this connection in "Shakespeare's Ear" (an essay left incomplete at his death, in 1989, and published in Fineman, *The Subjectivity Effect in Western Literary Tradition: Essays toward the Release of Shakespeare's Will* [Cambridge: MIT Press, 1991], 222–31). In this essay Fineman develops his thesis that "the Lacanian subject in particular, and the psychoanalytic subject in general, were epiphenomenal consequences of the Renaissance invention of the literary subject" (225) by way of a discussion of the famous Rainbow Portrait of Queen Elizabeth I (attributed to Isaac Oliver and dated circa 1600), one of whose most notable features is the design of individual eyes, mouths, and ears that cover the queen's dress. Unlike other designs on the queen's garments these eyes, mouths, and ears do not appear embroidered; they represent allegorical signs rather than realistic ornamentation. Whereas the multiple mouths on Shakespeare's Caesar's body and those on Lacan's psychoanalytic body are figured as sexualized openings in the corporeal integument, the multiple mouths in the Renaissance portrait are on Elizabeth's clothing rather than directly on her skin—and are therefore in some sense detachable, part of the sublime body of the monarchical function, rather than part of her. And although Fineman does not connect this figuration with Lacan's description of erogenous zones, nevertheless he remarks that "what is genuinely mysterious and surprising about the Rainbow Portrait, especially if we assume this large picture was originally displayed at court, is the way the painting places an exceptionally pornographic ear over Queen Elizabeth's genitals, in the crease formed where the two folds of her dress fold over on each other, at the wrinkled conclusion of the arc projected by the dildo-like rainbow clasped so imperially by the Virgin Queen" (228). This detail from the painting provides the image that adorns the jacket of Fineman's book; and when read in light of Lacan's description of erogenous zones it supports Fineman's argument better than he was able to say.

only food that traverses this border (and not only other parts of the body), but also less tangible objects—words, breath, voice. Thus, in the first instance, the mouth is a model for erogenous zones because it's the most obvious corporeal point at which inside meets outside (and, of course, life itself depends on the continuousness of this meeting and exchange). But in the second instance, the mouth is Lacan's model for erogenous zones because it's an organ of speech; and desire involves language as well as the body. Or, to be more precise, desire involves symbolic—as well as material and corporeal—phenomena. Thus although food mainly goes into the mouth and words mainly come out of it, in fact nothing that crosses this border is restricted to unidirectional movement. By following the same trajectory, intangible objects are liable to become confused with tangible ones, to be fantasized as nourishing, poisonous, or otherwise physically stimulating to the body in the way that tangible objects are. This explains why words become libidinally invested and vocalization itself can be eroticized.[66]

But if the mouth remains the most obvious corporeal zone where inside meets outside—where, that is, something within the body is relinquished to the world outside—it is certainly not the only one. Lacan suggests that from a psychoanalytic viewpoint the body is covered in mouths. And though he refers to "a *limited number* of mouths," his catalogue of bodily borders characterized by a "mark of the cut" points to their multiplicity. What if we were to extend this metaphor of mouths to include all those bodily openings where inside meets outside? If, following Lacan's figure, we may think of the anus as a mouth, why not even smaller holes in the body? Why not think of the pores in our skin—which also breathe, absorb, and excrete—as mouths?

Deleuze and Guattari suggest this interpretive possibility in their sequel to *Anti-Oedipus,* in a discussion of the Wolf Man, where they characterize Freud as asserting, in effect, that "it would never occur to a neurotic to grasp the skin erotically as a multiplicity of pores, little spots, little scars or black holes"; but "[t]he psychotic can."[67] Deleuze

256

---

66. See Renata Salecl and Slavoj Žižek, eds., *Gaze and Voice as Love Objects* (Durham: Duke University Press, 1996).

67. Gilles Deleuze and Félix Guattari, "One or Several Wolves," *A Thousand Plateaus: Capitalism and Schizophrenia,* trans. Brian Massumi (Minneapolis: University of Minnesota Press, 1987), 27. Thanks to Shannon McRae for drawing my attention to this passage.

and Guattari's criticisms notwithstanding, Freud does in fact come very close to conceptualizing integument in this way when he moves from thinking of the genitals as his model for erogenous zones to thinking about skin as the model: "We have already discovered in examining the erotogenic zones that these regions of the skin merely show a special intensification of a kind of susceptibility to stimulus which is possessed in a certain degree by the whole cutaneous surface" (*SE* 7:201). Here Freud is struggling to maintain a primarily physiological account of erotogenicity. Yet his inclusion of "all the internal organs" in the repertoire of potential erogenous zones suggests that it is less a susceptibility to physical stimulus that is the key to erotogenicity than it is a susceptibility to fantasmatic investment.

On this question, Deleuze and Guattari's critique of Freud for constantly subordinating multiplicity to unity carries some merit, in that Freud pursues his insight concerning libidinal investments of the skin in terms not of the proliferating possibilities of multiple holes and surface zones, but of the total form of the ego as a libidinal object: "The ego is first and foremost a bodily ego; it is not merely a surface entity, but is itself the projection of a surface" (*SE* 19:26). In thus functioning as the surface by means of which the ego is projected, the skin loses its permeability, its porosity, and thence its potential for multiplicity. This is Freud's *imaginary* account of the skin.[68] By contrast, Lacan's account of fantasy shows how the surface of the body is subject to *symbolic* operations too. It is language's effect on the body that gives rise to fantasy and, in the process, decomposes imaginary unities into fragments *(a),* thereby multiplying desire's possibilities. The possibilities for desire proliferate only when one detotalizes the bodily form on which the ego depends. Thus like the politics this book advocates, fantasy involves a strategy of de-ego-ization or impersonalization that needn't entail chaos or schizophrenic fragmentation, since it follows a certain logic.

257

---

68. This account has been developed most notably by Didier Anzieu in *The Skin Ego: A Psychoanalytic Approach to the Self,* trans. Chris Turner (New Haven: Yale University Press, 1989). In Anzieu's model, unlike Freud's, integument retains the crucial attribute of permeability, a distinction that enables Anzieu to draw suggestive comparisons between the skin and the mouth: "the third function [of the Skin Ego]—which the skin shares with the mouth and which it performs at least as often—is as a site and a primary means of communicating with others, of establishing signifying relations" (40).

The Queer Logic of Fantasy

Tell me where is fancy bred?
Or in the heart, or in the head?
How begot, how nourishèd?

—William Shakespeare, *The Merchant of Venice*[69]

In speaking of a *logic* of fantasy, I am alluding to one of Lacan's unpublished seminars and, more specifically, to the paradox whereby fantasy isn't opposed to the rational and the logical, as it was customarily denigrated as being, but can be shown to have an order and rationality all its own.[70] Long before Freud made it into a psychoanalytic concept, fantasy played a central role in aesthetic theory, in which it was often (though not always) treated as interchangeable with the category of imagination. I mention this elementary fact of intellectual history because Freud inherited from nineteenth-century German idealism a distinction between fantasy and imagination that pertains to my argument here. This distinction concerns the superior synthesizing power that Kant (and Coleridge after him) attributes to the imagination *(die Einbildungskraft)* in contrast to fantasy *(die Phantasie)*. Describing imagination as "an active faculty of synthesis," in his *Critique of Pure Reason,* Kant extends this account of imagination's power in *Critique of Judgment,* arguing that aesthetic imagination is unfettered by "the laws of association" that govern cognition, since imagination follows a higher law or logic of its own.[71]

The two main points I wish to extract from the myriad scholastic

259

69. Shakespeare, *The Merchant of Venice,* 3.2.63–65. "Fancy" abbreviates "fantasy."

70. Jacques Lacan, "Le séminaire," bk. 14, "La logique du fantasme, 1966–1967" (unpublished manuscript).

71. My lines from Kant are cited by A. S. P. Wodehouse, "Imagination," in *Princeton Encyclopedia of Poetry and Poetics,* ed. Alex Preminger, Frank J. Warnke, and O. B. Hardison Jr. (Princeton: Princeton University Press, 1974), 370–77, esp. 374; see also Leo Hughes, "Fancy," in *Princeton Encyclopedia,* 270–72. In Anglophone aesthetics the canonical topos for these distinctions is *Biographia Literaria,* chap. 13, in which Coleridge elevates imagination above fantasy and then subdivides imagination into primary and secondary forms:

> The primary IMAGINATION I hold to be the living Power and prime Agent of all human Perception, and as a repetition in the finite mind of the eternal act of creation in the infinite I AM. The secondary I consider as an echo of the former, co-existing with conscious will, yet still as identical with the primary in the *kind* of its agency, and differing only in *degree,* and in the *mode* of its operation. It dissolves, diffuses, dissipates, in order to re-create; or where this process is rendered impossible, yet still at all events it struggles to idealize and to unify. (*Collected Works of Samuel Taylor Coleridge,* ed. James Engell and Walter Jackson Bate [London: Routledge & Kegan Paul, 1983], 7:304)

discriminations involved in nineteenth-century aesthetic theory are these: first, that the basis on which philosophers, poets, and aestheticians subordinated fantasy to imagination (or vice versa) concerned a capacity for synthesis that Lacan describes in terms of the imaginary order; second, that no matter which faculty ended up privileged in these debates, it invariably was characterized as adhering to a logic or laws distinct from those of positivist science. These two points enable us to appreciate the full significance of Freud's reformulating the logic of fantasy in terms of the unconscious and his describing laws of substitution, association, and combination that he identified with the primary process. Indeed, these laws are both higher *and* lower than those of ordinary rationality, since the incessant productions of the primary process can seem akin to the faculty of divine creation that aestheticians associated with the primary imagination; whereas, on the other hand, some unconscious effects, such as repetition compulsion and uncanniness, appear positively demonic.

259

Let me make clear that Freud's theory of fantasy intervenes in long-standing philosophical debates not simply to redescribe the imagination in different terms, but, more substantially, to elaborate a new category or level of determination. Hence, to the distinction between artistic imagination and daydreaming on one hand, and the distinction between diurnal reveries and nocturnal dreams on the other, Freud adds the dimension of unconscious fantasy, which is not so much opposed to everyday reality (in the mode of illusion) as it is meant to designate a new mode of reality—what he calls *psychical reality*. Given my contention that Lacan's category of the real may be read as a rewriting of some aspects of the Freudian unconscious, we can see how psychical reality may be aligned with the Lacanian real (as Slavoj Žižek often has noted). And given the heteronomous relation between the imaginary and the real, we can begin to grasp how the psychoanalytic understanding of fantasy radically distinguishes it from the imagination. Thus if the imagination may be coordinated with the Lacanian imaginary as a synthesizing power, then fantasy must be coordinated with the Lacanian real as a disintegrating force, one that ultimately resists all efforts at assimilation and domestication.

However, this unruliness of fantasy is complicated by Freud's insight that psychical reality *mediates* our access to mundane reality, and therefore fantasy can never be separated completely from more material concerns. As Victor Burgin puts it, "[p]sychoanalysis deconstructs the positivist dichotomy in which fantasy is seen as an inconsequential addendum to 'reality.' It reveals the supposedly marginal operations of fantasy to be constitutive of our identity, and to be at the centre of all our perceptions, beliefs and actions."[72] In supplying this mediation, fantasy offers itself as an indispensable concept for discussing subjectivity and sociality together, without reducing one to the other. And owing to the psychoanalytic insistence on distinguishing the subject of fantasy ($) from the individual who may be characterized as having the fantasy, this concept justifies our speaking of social fantasy or national fantasy, since fantasy, no matter how private it may seem, is not a strictly individual phenomenon. Indeed, Deleuze and Guattari make exactly this point: "fantasy is never individual: it is *group fantasy*—as institutional analysis has successfully demonstrated."[73] My epistemological point here is that the idea of "social fantasy" isn't merely a metaphor or a result of viewing the collective analogically, as if it were an individual. Rather, the concept of fantasy describes how a dimension of sociality—the Other—inhabits the innermost, ostensibly private zone of the subject.[74]

Not only is the unruliness of fantasy complicated by its crucial mediating function, but it also must be qualified by fantasy's logic—an issue that returns us to the question of fantasy's relation to verbalization (which was raised earlier by Foucault), as well as to that of fantasy's connection with perversion. Freud's key text on the logic of fantasy is " 'A Child Is Being Beaten,' " his 1919 study of beating fantasies, which he subtitles "A Contribution to the Study of the Origin of Sexual Perversions." As our consideration of perversion might have encouraged us to expect, Freud's labeling these beating fantasies "perverse" remains equivocal, since he readily concedes that they're so common as to qualify statistically as normal. Examining these fantasies, Freud observes something peculiar about them, namely, that the person having the fan-

72. Victor Burgin, "Fantasy," in *Feminism and Psychoanalysis: A Critical Dictionary,* ed. Elizabeth Wright (Oxford: Basil Blackwell, 1992), 87.

73. Deleuze and Guattari, *Anti-Oedipus,* 30; original emphasis.

74. For exemplary critical studies that exploit these implications of the psychoanalytic concept of fantasy, see Lauren Berlant, *The Anatomy of National Fantasy: Hawthorne, Utopia, and Everyday Life* (Chicago: University of Chicago Press, 1991); Renata Salecl, *The Spoils of Freedom: Psychoanalysis and Feminism after the Fall of Socialism* (London: Routledge, 1994); Eric L. Santner, *My Own Private Germany: Daniel Paul Schreber's Secret History of Modernity* (Princeton: Princeton University Press, 1996); and the work of Jacqueline Rose and Slavoj Žižek.

tasy is not immediately identifiable as either the child being beaten in the fantasy or the one doing the beating, and, moreover, that "there is no constant relation between the sex of the child producing the phantasy and that of the child being beaten" (*SE* 17:185).

In the course of investigating these enigmas, Freud isolates three phases of the fantasy, each with its own distinct locution. The initial phase, which the subject is able to remember (though with some effort), runs: *My father is beating the child (whom I hate)*. However, the locution in which the fantasy is usually expressed goes: *A child is being beaten (I am watching)*. Between these two phases Freud infers an intermediate one, which remains permanently inaccessible to the subject's consciousness and runs: *I am being beaten by my father*. This intermediate phase permits Freud to argue with respect to the version in which the fantasy is usually expressed—*A child is being beaten (I am watching)*—that "only the *form* of this phantasy is sadistic; the satisfaction which is derived from it is masochistic" (*SE* 17:191). Although in the fantasy as it is consciously expressed, the subject occupies merely the role of spectator, unconsciously he or she is in the position of the one being beaten. This shift from sadism to masochism is accomplished grammatically by the transformation from an active to a passive construction: in order for the subject of the fantasy to remain disguised in it this fantasy must be expressed using the indefinite article and the passive voice—"A child is being beaten."

Freud's attention to the determining role of these grammatical transformations enables us to grasp that fantasy is not antithetical to verbalization, as Foucault claimed; on the contrary, the logic of fantasy *is* that of verbalization—that of the structure and effects of language. In their classic 1964 paper on fantasy, Laplanche and Pontalis reach a similar conclusion: "In fantasy the subject does not pursue the object or its sign: he appears caught up himself in the sequence of images . . . [T]he subject, although always present in the fantasy, may be so in a desubjectivized form, that is to say, in the very *syntax* of the sequence in question."[75] From this reference to desubjectivization we may deduce that fantasy *impersonalizes* the subject, decomposing his or her ego in the *mise-en-scène* of desire. Thus it is owing to the subject's mercurial

261

75. Jean Laplanche and Jean-Bertrand Pontalis, "Fantasy and the Origins of Sexuality," in *Formations of Fantasy,* ed. Victor Burgin, James Donald, and Cora Kaplan (London: Methuen, 1986), 26, emphasis added.

positioning in a sequence of mutating terms that fantasy permits identifications across a number of socially regulated boundaries—between active and passive, masculine and feminine, gay and straight, black and white, perhaps even the boundary between the living and the dead. In so doing, fantasy undermines the distinctions such categories are intended to uphold, thereby disqualifying these social categories from providing the grounds for anything but *imaginary* identities.[76]

This notion of identification *across* is central to queer theory, since the word "queer" derives etymologically from the Indo-European root *-twerkw,* meaning "athwart" or "across."[77] Although fantasy's potential for subjective mobility carries a broad range of political implications, it has tended to be construed in distinctly utopian terms, in part because fantasmatic identification furnishes an important raison d'être for sympathies and allegiances that otherwise might remain unaccountable on the basis of material interests. Hence utopian fantasy remains indispensable for queer theory's identificatory alliances and its effort to connect queerness with categories of social exclusion that aren't obviously grounded in sexuality. Indeed, it may be in queer theory and politics that the otherwise exhausted tradition of left utopianism finds its greatest vitality.

Furthermore, this celebrated potential for subjective mobility stems from fantasy's exploitation of component or partial drives—those that lend the child its polymorphous perversity—and therefore, according to Freud, this kind of unconscious fantasy must "be regarded as a primary trait of perversion" (*SE* 17:181).[78] Lacan indicates the indissoluble link between fantasy and perversion not only by writing his formulas for these concepts as mirror images of each other ($\mathcal{S} \lozenge a / a \lozenge \mathcal{S}$),

76. This idea has generated some very insightful work in cultural studies, one particularly fascinating example of which is Constance Penley's study of Kirk/Spock "slash" fandom, a subcultural phenomenon in which the two male leads from *Star Trek* are figured as gay lovers—often pornographically—in fantasy scenarios produced by and for a community of predominantly heterosexual women. See Penley, "Feminism, Psychoanalysis, and the Study of Popular Culture," in *Cultural Studies,* ed. Lawrence Grossberg, Cary Nelson, and Paula A. Treichler (New York: Routledge, 1992), 479–500.

77. See Sedgwick, *Tendencies,* xii; also Judith Butler and Biddy Martin, "Cross-Identifications," introduction to a special queer issue of *Diacritics* (24, nos. 2–3 [1994]: 3).

78. Hence also Lacan's point that "[a] drive, insofar as it represents sexuality in the unconscious, is never anything but a partial drive. That is the essential failing [*carence*], namely the absence [*carence*] of anything that could represent in the subject the mode of what is male or female in his being" ("Position" 276). This is another way of saying that sexual difference belongs to the order of the real more than to the imaginary or symbolic.

but also by requiring the ◇ sign to figure the multiple transformations and hence subjective mobility that fantasy entails.[79] This inseparability of fantasy and perversion suggests that queer theory's tendency
to follow Foucault in dismissing the claims of fantasy in favor of vari-
ations in sexual practice is thoroughly misguided. Indeed, the rationale
for characterizing fantasy's logic as queer stems from the terms of Lacan's formula ($ ◇ a), which insists that in fantasy the subject relates not
to another subject, but to an "object" generated by the symbolic
order's impact on one's own body. This psychoanalytic account of fantasy reveals heterosexuality as utterly secondary to a more primary
structure of relationality that remains stunningly oblivious to both persons and gender.

Yet fantasy's potential for subjective mobility is not unlimited.
Laplanche and Pontalis's emphasis on the syntax of the fantasy sequence—which accords with Freud's on the grammatical transformations that fantasy entails—suggests that subjective mobility in fantasy
is constrained by the logic and laws of language. It is to this constraint
that Lacan is referring when he inverts Coleridge's hierarchy, in *Biographia Literaria,* and asserts polemically that "any temptation to reduce
[phantasy] to the imagination . . . is a permanent misconception, a
misconception from which the Kleinian school, which has certainly carried things very far in this field, is not free, largely because it has been
incapable of even so much as suspecting the existence of the category of
the signifier" (*E* 272). This distinction between fantasy and imagination
clarifies how fantasy involves the imaginary order (the domain of images) only when the latter has been captured and fragmented by the
nets of language: "once it is defined as an image set to work in the
signifying structure, the notion of unconscious phantasy no longer presents any difficulty" (*E* 272).[80] Thus what should be kept in mind, partic-

79. With respect to these Lacanian formulas, Judith Feher Gurewich writes: "In the unconscious, desire aims at the place where the *jouissance* of an object can plug the lack in the Other,
repeating therefore at the level of the repressed the logic of the perverse scenario" ("The Philanthropy
of Perversion: Another Kind of Violence"). This vital point depends on how we interpret the ◇
sign, which Lacan used to designate a whole range of possible relations. In one discussion of fantasy
he noted that "[t]he sign ◇ registers the relations envelopment — development — conjunction —
disjunction" (*E* 280). A useful gloss on the history of Lacan's formula for fantasy, particularly the
significance of the ◇ sign, is provided by James B. Swenson Jr. in his annotations to "Kant with
Sade," 85.

80. This sentence makes clear that Lacan's text coincides almost verbatim with Laplanche and
Pontalis's later formulations concerning fantasy, as quoted above.

ularly in view of the tendency in cultural studies to discuss formations of fantasy in purely imaginary terms, is that fantasy involves all three orders—imaginary, symbolic, and real—together.

Nevertheless, the final term in Lacan's formula for fantasy, object *a,* does not belong unequivocally to any one of these three orders. In order to reach my concluding thesis, I'd like to look a little harder at the material object Lacan takes as his prototype for object *a*—the turd. Looking unblinkingly at a psychoanalytic theory of excrement offers the benefit of enabling us to gauge just how incidental to Lacan's account of fantasy, sexuality, and desire is the phallus. Perhaps surprisingly, such an examination will also permit us to say something more concerning the place of love in psychoanalytic theory, a topic that was raised by my chapter's opening quotation from *Encore*—*"quand on aime, il ne s'agit pas de sexe"*—but deferred until now.

The Triumph of Love

> *Every love is an exercise in depersonalization.*
> —Gilles Deleuze and Félix Guattari,
> *A Thousand Plateaus*

In a formulation rebarbative even by his standards, Lacan locates his paradigm of object *a* in scat. Speaking of what happens to the human organism in the process of subjectification—when, that is, language impacts the body—he explains:

> It is important to grasp how the organism is taken up in the dialectic of the subject. The organ of what is incorporeal in the sexuated *[sexué]* being is that part of the organism the subject places when his separation occurs . . . In this way, the object he naturally loses, excrement, and the props he finds in the Other's desire—the Other's gaze or voice—come to this place. ("Position" 276)

Here Lacan's model for subjective loss is not the phallus but feces, an ungendered object. In the face of *this* object-cause of desire, the controversy over the concept of the phallus pales into insignificance, since whether or not we're all—men as well as women—missing the phallus, certainly we've all lost objects from the anus. And this distinction remains universally true—irrespective of gender, race, class, nation, culture, or history—in that although we never may be completely certain that nobody has the phallus, we can be sure everybody has an anus. Castration isn't Lacan's only rubric for loss. Or, to put it slightly differently, *phallus* isn't his only term for describing what's lost in symbolic castration. Indeed, as Žižek points out, object *a* is in the first instance the anal object.[81] The explanatory virtue of turds over the phallus lies not only in the fact that everybody loses them, but also in the fact that their loss is repeated: it's because loss from this part of the body is multiplied over and over that feces so aptly figure objects *a*. Now this formulation confronts us with the disturbing implication that in fantasy ($ \cancel{S} \diamondsuit a$) we find the subject relating to its shit. Though in one sense this is true, we also must bear in mind that the Lacanian object isn't, in fact, a material object; instead it designates an absence or loss for which material objects function as both the prototype and the imaginary fulfillment.

When Lacan refers to gaze and voice as "the props [the subject] finds in the Other's desire," he implies that anality cannot be considered a presymbolic "stage," because the Other is already present—a point that Freud clarifies by emphasizing the child's use of bowel movements to communicate with its caretakers. In his discussion of anal eroticism, Freud elaborates on this notion of shit as signifier by comparing the anal zone to the mouth, which "is well suited by its position to act as a medium through which sexuality may attach itself to other somatic functions" (*SE* 7:185). If Freud considers mouth and anus as analogous or in some sense interchangeable, then Lacan's image for the erogenous zones could be reformulated yet more surreally to suggest that the body exhibits a number of assholes at its surface.

Furthermore, in some highly evocative sentences added to the third

265

81. Slavoj Žižek, *The Metastases of Enjoyment: Six Essays on Woman and Causality* (New York: Verso, 1994), 179. Writing very illuminatingly of the object *a*, Žižek continues:

> In Lacanian theory, one usually conceives of the anal object as a signifying element: what effectively matters is the role of shit in the intersubjective economy—does it function as proof to the Other of the child's self-control and discipline, of his complying with the Other's demand, as a gift to the Other . . . ? However, prior to this symbolic status of a gift, and so on, the excrement is *objet a* in the precise sense of the non-symbolizable surplus that remains after the body is symbolized, inscribed into the symbolic network: the problem of the anal stage resides precisely in how we are to dispose of this leftover. For that reason, Lacan's thesis that animal became human the moment it confronted the problem of what to do with its excrement is to be taken literally and seriously: in order for this unpleasant surplus to pose a problem, the body must already have been caught up in the symbolic network. (179)

edition of his *Three Essays,* Freud makes clear exactly why feces as object *a* take explanatory priority over the phallus:

> The contents of the bowels, which act as a stimulating mass upon a sexually sensitive portion of mucous membrane, behave like forerunners of another organ, which is destined to come into action after the phase of childhood. But they have other important meanings for the infant. They are clearly treated as a part of the infant's own body and represent his first "gift": by producing them he can express his active compliance with his environment and, by withholding them, his disobedience . . . The retention of the faecal mass . . . is thus carried out intentionally by the child to begin with, in order to serve, as it were, as a masturbatory stimulus upon the anal zone or to be employed in his relation to the people looking after him. (*SE* 7:186–87)

To transpose Freudian into Lacanian terms, we can say that by using feces as both a sexual stimulus and a means of communication the child's relation to shit involves *l'objet petit a* and *le grand Autre*—that is, anality entails both "big" and "little" others, the different modes of alterity that constitute the subject and his or her desire. But let us be more explicit about what Freud is saying here. His initial claim is that feces, by sexually stimulating the anus, act like "another organ"—presumably the penis. From this we may deduce that the phallus is less a figure for the penis than, more fundamentally, a figure for the turd. Lacanians have been remarkably reticent about this ineluctable implication, perhaps because a theory of sexuality organized around feces appears even more questionable than one centered on the phallus. Nevertheless, it is to this point that the logic of Lacan's concept of object *a* has brought us.

Perhaps it takes a gay man to observe that the phallus is simply a turd in disguise; though Freud points out that Lou Andreas-Salomé inferred this connection in her paper on anal sexuality, where she argues that "the history of the first prohibition which a child comes across—the prohibition against getting pleasure from anal activity and its products—has a decisive effect on his whole development" (*SE* 7:187 n.).[82] In this perspective, symbolic prohibition begins with anal sexuality and a form of pleasure easily confused with genital pleasure, since as Freud

82. Freud is referring to Lou Andreas-Salomé, "'Anal' und 'Sexual,'" *Imago* 4 (1916): 249 ff.

remarks elsewhere, "The excremental is all too intimately and insepara-
bly bound up with the sexual; the position of the genitals—*inter urinas
et faeces*—remains the decisive and unchangeable factor" (*SE* 11:189).
Having alluded to Augustine (who remarked that we are born between
urine and feces), Freud immediately proceeds to quote Napoleon:
"Anatomy is destiny." However, we should note that Freud isn't referring to sexual difference, as is usually supposed when this aphorism is
hauled out as an objection to psychoanalysis, but rather to the inseparability of genital and anal that follows, in part, from their anatomical
proximity.

Let me make clear that I'm claiming not that sexual difference is
inconsequential to this account of sexuality, just that it is secondary.
Desire emerges before sexual difference, through the anal object, and
therefore there can be no a priori gendering of the object-cause of desire. Hence Hocquenghem's much misunderstood assertion that "to
encounter desire is first of all to forget the difference in the sexes"
and his correlative insistence on focusing on anal erotics. In my view
Hocquenghem's *Homosexual Desire* is not so much a critique of Lacanian
psychoanalysis (as many readers seem to think) as it is an elaboration
of Lacan's most radical ideas in the wake of May '68 and Stonewall '69.

Yet this reassessment of Hocquenghem raises the question of why
it hasn't been easier to articulate queer politics with psychoanalysis since
1972. Besides the institutional histories, the prejudice and exclusions,
I can't help thinking that this failure of articulation may be explained in
part by reference to the fact that excrement remains an extraordinarily
difficult topic for sustained discourse: the anal object tests the limits of
sexual tolerance far more stringently than mere homosexuality or other
manifestations of queerness. Indeed, homosexuality's being branded
"the love that dare not speak its name" must have been a consequence
primarily of its association with anality. Even Freud, whose broad-
mindedness still retains the capacity to astonish, deems perversion most
unequivocally pathological when it involves sexual contact with shit:

> [I]n some of these perversions the quality of the new sexual aim
> is of a kind to demand special examination. Certain of them are
> so far removed from the normal in their content that we cannot
> avoid pronouncing them "pathological." This is especially so where
> (as, for instance, in cases of licking excrement or of intercourse with

dead bodies) the sexual instinct goes to astonishing lengths in successfully overriding the resistances of shame, disgust, horror or pain. (*SE* 7:161)

In the face of this scenario worthy of Sade, Freud makes a quite remarkable observation: "It is impossible to deny that in their case a piece of mental work has been performed which, in spite of its horrifying result, is the equivalent of an idealization of the instinct. The omnipotence of love is perhaps never more strongly proved than in such of its aberrations as these" (*SE* 7:161). According to Freud the triumph of love consists in fucking corpses and eating shit. Or, to put it another way, the triumph of love entails a kind of "mental work" that—by overriding shame, disgust, horror, or pain—could be identified as specifically queer, because this work consists in struggling against the affect-laden social norms regulating sexuality. Queer politics involves not only the negative effort to resist norms, but also the positive work of intense, almost superhuman loving.

By pointing to one extreme outcome of the discontinuity between sexual instinct and sexual object, Freud reminds us that originally the object of desire is not another person, much less a member of the opposite sex, but something rather more abject. Thinking of sexual object-choice in terms of persons entails a kind of sublimation, an idealizing consolidation of the object, rather than the idealization of the instinct manifested in Freud's examples of necrophilia and coprophagy. When we grasp the idea that erotic desire for another person itself depends on some sort of sublimation—rather than sublimation standing as the alternative to interpersonal desire, as is commonly supposed—then we can begin to appreciate just how strange, how distant from the normalizing perspective on love and sex, psychoanalytic theory really is. In its most fundamental formulations psychoanalysis is a queer theory.

THE INELUCTABILITY
OF SUBLIMATION

Conclusion

The primary status of jouissance *is not sexual.*
—Jacques-Alain Miller, "The Drive Is Speech"

This book has attempted to bring out the strangeness of a psychoanalytic perspective on sex by arguing against psychological understandings of sexuality. I have argued that this bizarre conception of sex should be regarded as a queer theory in its own right. And while insisting on the specificity of psychoanalysis in contradistinction to psychology, I have tried to articulate Lacan's account of sexuality with Foucault's in a new way. Certainly sexuality has a history, and one that isn't over. Here I want to put some pressure on the idea of an *ongoing* history of sexuality, in order to imagine possible futures that don't simply repeat our current deployment of sex. In so doing, however, the imperative to specify more concretely what the next chapter in our ongoing history of sex might look like comes into conflict with my reluctance to speak programmatically about erotic, subjective, and political options. The project of imagining what lies beyond sexuality is necessarily speculative and cannot be reduced to an individual enterprise.

Imagining a future history of sex requires more than a commitment to the standard Foucaultian position that sexuality is a historical rather than a natural phenomenon. This is true as far as it goes; the problem is that it doesn't go far enough. Sexuality is only partly historical; its other dimension has to do not with nature but with the unconscious and with what Lacan calls the traumatic real—unfamiliar aspects of existence that are no more biological than they are historically produced. If the unconscious were purely a historical construct, it would be manipulable in a way that it clearly is not. Historical explanations of sexuality remain too tied to commonsensical psychological notions of personhood and gender to account for the radical impersonality of desire. Paradoxically, it's the very recognizability of these explanations that limits their heuristic value.[1]

Because sexuality forms part of everybody's experience, there is a persistent tendency to understand it intuitively. Any reader of these pages may say, "I have at least a sense—if not a fully fledged theory— of sexuality because it's something that's happened to me, something in which I've personally participated." But while sexuality is part of everybody's experience, it is also part and parcel of the unconscious, and therefore there's a fundamental aspect of sexuality that remains definitively inaccessible to experience, regardless of one's erotic adventurousness. *Beyond Sexuality* has emphasized the importance for cultural meaning-making enterprises of this dimension of sexuality that we never experience. My focus on object *a*—the object of unconscious fantasy— has tried to show how social and cultural phenomena that might not appear to be sexual are in fact permeated by psychical processes and unconscious desire.

By emphasizing the unconscious dimension of sexuality, psychoanalysis dramatically enlarges the scope of the sexual, inferring that ostensibly nonsexual realms of experience actually derive from erotic impulses. Psychoanalysis troubles the border between the sexual and the nonsexual almost to the point of unintelligibility. Freud does not extend sexuality merely from the genital regions throughout the entire body ("any part of the skin and any sense-organ—probably, indeed, *any* organ— can function as an erotogenic zone" [*SE* 7:233; original emphasis]). Far more radically, Freud is inclined to sexualize all human experience, even going so far as to claim that "[i]t may well be that nothing of considerable importance can occur in the organism without contributing

1. See, for example, David M. Halperin, *One Hundred Years of Homosexuality: And Other Essays on Greek Love* (New York: Routledge, 1990); and Thomas Laqueur, *Making Sex: Body and Gender from the Greeks to Freud* (Cambridge: Harvard University Press, 1990).

some component to the excitation of the sexual instinct" (*SE* 7:205). Intellectual work, muscular activity, the mechanical stimulation of railway travel, and even emotional reactions of fear and fright—all these and more Freud views as contributing to erotic excitation. Far from taking us beyond sexuality, psychoanalysis would appear to imprison us within sexuality more thoroughly than—and with a maniacal insistence unrivaled by—other modes of thinking. And, indeed, this has been one of the principal objections to psychoanalysis from the very beginning— an objection that, in its turn, queer theory now faces for finding sexuality everywhere.[2]

The troubling way in which a psychoanalytic conception of the unconscious seems to authorize our interpreting almost anything as "sexual" raises a number of important questions that I'd like to address briefly here. Doing so will help clarify what I mean by my book's title. To begin with, if everything is ultimately "sexual" or somehow traceable to erotic impulses, then the explanatory force of sexuality as a concept is diluted and the adjective *sexual* becomes virtually meaningless. For psychoanalysis sexuality starts to seem like a determinist concept; hence a dangerously totalizing universalism and loss of specificity—historical and otherwise—rears its hydra head. Given such apparent epistemological coarseness, there is considerable warrant for objecting to any project that reads all signs as, at some level, sexual signs. To this extent, complaints about the pansexualizing perspective of both queer theory and psychoanalysis would be justified.

On the other hand, however, a certain innovative potential lies in projects—whether they be psychoanalytic or queer—that defamiliarize what we mean by sex and sexuality. Freud's expansion of the sexual beyond the genital is redescribed by Lacan in terms of *jouissance,* a form of enjoyment so intense as to be barely distinguishable from suffering and pain. One of the most striking features about *jouissance* as a concept is that its primary status is not sexual, according to Jacques-Alain Miller. Anglophone commentators tend to miss this feature by constantly reminding us that *jouissance* derives from the French word for orgasm. But when the term *sexual* starts to lose or alter its meaning—which it does even as soon as it is uncoupled from genitality—all sorts of possi-

271

---

2. For this kind of objection to queer theory, see Lee Siegel, "The Gay Science: Queer Theory, Literature, and the Sexualization of Everything," *New Republic,* November 9, 1998, 30–42.

bilities emerge for shifting our habits of mind away from both normative heterosexuality and any politics that would require sexuality to be securely wedded to the sovereign self. This helps explain what I intend by the phrase "beyond sexuality": a conceptual move beyond not only genitality and heterosexuality as paradigm and norm, but also beyond identity politics. Queer politics is "beyond sexuality" in this sense, because it concerns itself with dimensions of exclusion that are seen as connected to sexuality, though they are not themselves sexual.

But I have something else in mind, too, by this book's title. Disarticulating sexuality from identity, from the self, and from personhood by conceiving it nonpsychologically, this book's aim also has been to develop Foucault's critique of sexuality as the truth of our being. Speaking of the modern deployment of sex, Foucault concludes the first volume of his *History of Sexuality* thus:

> [W]e have arrived at the point where we expect our intelligibility to come from what was for many centuries thought of as madness; the plenitude of our body from what was long considered its stigma and likened to a wound; our identity from what was perceived as an obscure and nameless urge. Hence the importance we ascribe to it, the reverential fear with which we surround it, the care we take to know it. Hence the fact that over the centuries [sex] has become more important than our soul, more important almost than our life.[3]

Psychologizing sex has centered and privileged it, making sexuality utterly crucial to our lives and identities, even if in negative modes of self-understanding. Certainly there is no easy or immediate way for getting beyond what Foucault viewed as a rather absurd condition of living. But once sexuality is grasped impersonally—that is, in terms of the unconscious rather than the self—then we may find ourselves inhabiting a different deployment of sexuality, one in which sex might no longer seem "worth dying for," as Foucault put it. Here I am inferring, in contradistinction to Foucault, that psychoanalysis may not only be less responsible for our reigning deployment of sexuality than is often charged, but also that a certain version of psychoanalysis may contain within itself the conceptual means for taking us beyond sexuality.

3. Michel Foucault, *The History of Sexuality*, vol. 1, *An Introduction*, trans. Robert Hurley (New York: Random House, 1978), 156.

Foucault recognized that psychoanalysis was central, not peripheral, to our deployment of sexuality, and that its function of prioritizing sex within the self was far from unambiguous:

> The history of the deployment of sexuality, as it has evolved since the classical age, can serve as an archaeology of psychoanalysis. We have seen in fact that psychoanalysis plays several roles at once in this deployment: it is a mechanism for attaching sexuality to the system of alliance; it assumes an adversary position with respect to the theory of degenerescence; it functions as a differentiating factor in the general technology of sex.[4]

Psychoanalysis both contributes to *and resists* the modern understanding of sex. Tracing one abortive outcome of its resistance, Foucault gets only as far as Wilhelm Reich's libertarianism. However, Lacan's de-psychologizing of sex could take much further the inchoate psycho-analytic resistance to our current deployment of sexuality, though of course Lacan himself didn't go far enough in this direction.

This is unsurprising, insofar as the notion that sex might become less important—not only theoretically, but also in our day-to-day self-understanding—immediately reveals the intransigent difficulty of any such enterprise, for it is far easier to stop having sex than it is to stop thinking about it in certain habitual ways. Strange though it may sound, often greater pleasure derives from contemplating erotic activity than from actually doing it. Relinquishing certain habits of mind about the sexual proves more taxing than renouncing genital stimulation itself. Having said this, I also must acknowledge that these propositions about sex generate considerable anxiety, if not bafflement, especially among gay men. Let me reiterate that I'm suggesting not that anybody modify his or her sexual practices, only that we transform our mental activity about sex. Since this is an enormous project, I'd like to sketch it out here a little more explicitly—not in order to recast "beyond sexuality" in more familiar terms (its promise lies precisely in its unfamiliarity), but to clarify just what's at stake. Having insisted that a crucial dimension of sexuality is unconscious and that the unconscious resists manipulation, I'm not about to suggest that we can somehow transform our unconscious fantasies about sex or otherwise educate the unconscious.

4. Ibid., 130.

The unconscious is, by definition, immune to consciousness raising. Yet we might get beyond sex as the truth of our being by thinking harder about sexuality in nongenital terms and grasping how fantasies about sex may be about something else entirely.

This book has argued for an impersonalist conception of sexuality, suggesting that desire and fantasy involve an object—Lacan's *objet petit a*—that is not a person and is prior to gender. The advantage of this notion of the object lies in its revealing the origin of desire as nonheterosexual. Lacan's theory of desire gives the lie to compulsory heterosexuality. It follows that if desire is, in the first instance, impersonal, then our primary relations aren't with other persons. The human infant relates to its mother not as a person but as an object. We start to see that, harsh though it may sound to say so, other people provide merely contingent supports for psychical relations that are at bottom impersonal. This being the case, the impersonalist conception of sexuality gives rise to different ideas about relationality. It might be possible to develop some of our most intense and satisfying relations within realms of experience other than the interpersonal or intersubjective. One of the things I find *epistemologically* appealing about the kinds of gay sex that typically receive so much censure is that anonymous sex dramatizes a fundamental impersonality that no amount of love or humanizing intimacy can eradicate. While arguments extolling the democratic utopianism of queer public sex totally mystify what actually goes on in sex clubs and outdoor venues where men gather for sex, nevertheless the sexual activity in these places has the virtue of emphasizing connections with body parts rather than with persons. Gay public sex is often thoroughly impersonal in a way that throws into relief how relationality involves other persons only contingently. Men having sex through a gloryhole reveal that sexual relationality is as much about the Other and the object *a* as it is about interpersonal connection. Sometimes the gay man relates to his partner not as a person but as an object—and there is something to praise as well as lament in this form of relating.[5]

5. In "Cruising in the Homosexual Arena" (*Being a Character: Psychoanalysis and Self Experience* [New York: Hill and Wang, 1994], 144–64), psychoanalyst Christopher Bollas interprets this impersonal dimension of gay sexuality rather differently. Without referring to AIDS, Bollas pathologizes impersonal relationality—which he characterizes in terms of " 'it-to-it' encounters" (149)—because it entails "an erasure of self" that he cannot see as anything but negative and harmful. From my

This view of sexuality raises the question of how desire gets attached to persons at all. At the end of the previous chapter I suggested that intersubjective desire itself entails a kind of sublimation, in that taking as one's sexual object another person requires idealizing object *a* into a totalized form. Though Freud subsequently distinguished sublimation from idealization, his first published reference to sublimation, in 1905, points the concept in exactly the direction I'm pursuing here:

> The progressive concealment of the body which goes along with civilization keeps sexual curiosity awake. This curiosity seeks to complete the sexual object by revealing its hidden parts. It can, however, be diverted ("sublimated") in the direction of art, if its interest can be shifted away from the genitals on to the shape of the body as a whole. (*SE* 7:156)

This remarkable passage suggests that the question of how desire gets attached to persons and the question of how one understands sublimation are versions of the same question. For Freud any diversion of interest away from genitalia initiates a sublimating movement "in the direction of art." One immediate consequence of this strange claim is that Freudian speculation, in its insistence on expanding the sexual so far beyond the genital as to render the latter often incidental, must be considered a sublimating theory quite as much as a theory of sublimation. Perhaps this explains why psychoanalysis has always experienced such difficulties generating anything approaching a coherent account of sublimation, and why there nonetheless exists such a large body of psychoanalytic literature on the subject. Yet the difficulty with sublimation lies also in establishing how and when the sexual tips into the nonsexual, and where the boundary between the two may be said to lie. Expanding the reach of the sexual—as do queer theory and psychoanalysis—leads ineluctably to the problematic of sublimation, and hence, I'm suggesting, to that of aesthetics.

Freud's general contention that sublimation represents the transformation of erotic into cultural aims becomes especially ambiguous when one grasps "culture" in its broader, anthropological sense, since we are always participating in cultural practices, institutions, and networks of

point of view, however, it is just this self-erasure that holds such positive potential for conceiving relationality beyond the normative coordinates set by "His Majesty, the Ego."

meaning. From a certain perspective, it would seem that human beings rarely cease sublimating. Lacan makes just this point in a discussion of Freud's "Instincts and Their Vicissitudes," commenting upon sublimation as one of the drives' vicissitudes:

> [I]n this article, Freud tells us repeatedly that sublimation is also satisfaction of the drive, whereas it is *zielgehemmt*, inhibited as to its aim—it does not attain it. Sublimation is nonetheless satisfaction of the drive, without repression.
>
> In other words—for the moment, I am not fucking, I am talking to you. Well! I can have exactly the same satisfaction as if I were fucking. That's what it means. Indeed, it raises the question of whether in fact I am not fucking at this moment. (*Four* 165–66).[6]

Sublimation entails no detour via the unconscious and, according to this account, produces "exactly the same satisfaction" as explicitly sexual activity. Indeed, if we take *satisfaction of the drive without repression* as our definition of sublimation—as Freudian metapsychology urges us to do—then we're led to the counterintuitive conclusion that heterosexual copulation itself constitutes a kind of sublimation.

Although from this point of view we are all always sublimating to one degree or another, for Freud sublimation nevertheless bears an intimate connection with homosexuality, because sublimation takes up "what are known as the *perverse* elements of sexual excitation" (*SE* 9:189; original emphasis). In his study of Leonardo da Vinci, Freud hints at a model of sublimation in which it is not a question of something culturally prized, such as aesthetic creation, substituting for something culturally disprized, such as homosexuality; rather, it is a question of normative psychosexual development requiring the eradication of homosexual *and* aesthetic tendencies, since both evidence a failure to subordinate polymorphous perversity to the cultural dictates of reproductive genitality. Thus sublimation may be understood as not the repressively redemptive desexualization of sexuality, but its much more interesting and progressive degenitalization.[7]

6. While Lacan devotes seminar 7, *The Ethics of Psychoanalysis*, to his most sustained discussion of sublimation, this passage from a later seminar (seminar 11) seems to me quite as profound as anything he says on the topic in that earlier seminar.

7. See Sigmund Freud, *Leonardo da Vinci and a Memory of His Childhood* (1910), in *SE* 11:57–137. Here I'm summarizing an argument about sublimation developed at greater length in my "Paring His Fingernails: Homosexuality and Joyce's Impersonalist Aesthetic," in *Quare Joyce*, ed. Jo-

When Freud claims that diverting attention away from genitalia initiates a sublimation "in the direction of art," he implies that our relations to art, just as much as interpersonal relations, may count as in some sense sexual. In a way that his own writing on art never fully grasped, Freud's conception of sublimation suggests that we can have intensely pleasurable experiences and intimate relationships with verbal and visual forms even when these forms aren't ostensibly erotic at all. Such relationships should not be considered secondary to or necessarily less intense than interpersonal sexual relationships, because they draw on the same libidinal sources and fantasies. An impersonalist perspective on sexuality reveals intersubjective relations as simply one subset of a far broader matrix of relationality, in which aesthetic investments might be viewed less hierarchically. In other words, aesthetic experiences should be considered no better or worse—no higher or lower—than sexual ones. For me the fascination of Leo Bersani and Ulysse Dutoit's recent explorations of new kinds of relationality through their meditation on artworks lies in the implication that human connections with visual and verbal artifacts represent a primary rather than secondary form of relationality. Bersani and Dutoit's redefinition of relationality entails seeing how we relate to other persons only by way of our mediating relationships with nonhuman forms.[8]

This understanding of relationality raises the possibility that some people "love literature" *in exactly the same way* as others love sex. Indeed, some gay men love art and aesthetic forms in just the way that others love screwing. What in his latest novel gay writer Andrew Holleran contemplates as "the beauty of men" involves aesthetic considerations just as much as erotic ones.[9] Gay men's appreciation of beauty extends from architecture, art, and music, through interior decor and gardens, to the physical appearance of other men. The high estimation of male beauty that is so common among certain men should be understood as a subset of a more general aesthetic commitment to beauty, rather than as a specifically sexual preference, since connoisseurs of male beauty

---

seph Valente (Ann Arbor: University of Michigan Press, 1998), 241–72. This understanding of sublimation derives largely from Jean Laplanche, *Problématiques III: La Sublimation* (Paris: PUF, 1980). Part of Laplanche's seminar on sublimation is available in English as Jean Laplanche, "To Situate Sublimation," trans. Richard Miller, *October* 28 (1984): 7–26.

8. See Leo Bersani and Ulysse Dutoit, *Arts of Impoverishment: Beckett, Rothko, Resnais* (Cambridge: Harvard University Press, 1993); and *Caravaggio's Secrets* (Cambridge: MIT Press, 1998).

9. Andrew Holleran, *The Beauty of Men: A Novel* (New York: William Morrow, 1996).

tend to focus more on the entire bodily form than on the genitals alone.[10] Not only would it be narrow-minded to treat aesthetic passion as either superior or inferior to sexual passion, but there exist ample historical grounds for claiming that homosexual investments in art precede our current definition of gayness in primarily erotic terms. From a psychoanalytic perspective, the leather queen's admiration of bodies at the gym is just as much a sublimation as the opera queen's passion for arias. In particularly intense moments operatic arias can induce an ecstatic self-loss—or syncope—similar to that which may be experienced in the raunchiest sex.[11]

It is not only that sublimation draws on the same libidinal components as does perverse sexuality, but also that aesthetic experience can have an effect on human subjects similar to that of sex. One can be ravished by art, especially music, as well as by other people's bodies. This is what Miller is getting at with his contention that "[t]he primary status of *jouissance* is not sexual." For historical reasons we aim at *jouissance* through sex, but this is a result of the deployment of sexuality, rather than an invariable necessity. Indeed, an impersonalist theory of sexuality shows that interpersonal relations offer only one arena for engaging the truth of our being. Writing this conclusion exactly thirty years after Stonewall, the New York City barroom insurrection that sparked our modern gay rights movement, I find myself wondering whether sufficient time has passed for us to invent new relational ways of being gay, instead of merely rehearsing nostalgic references to this historical touchstone. I'm arguing for a more expansive sense of gayness in the spirit of—though differently from—*queerness* as an especially capacious and looser understanding of the connection between sexuality and selfhood. Of course, any shift from a primarily sexual conception of homosexuality threatens a loss of specificity that critics today find politically dubious. Yet in its emphasis on thinking sexuality outside— or apart from—genitality, this book has been arguing all along for a positive, politically progressive deracination of sexual specificity. A particular psychoanalytic notion of sublimation represents the point at

278

10. Lesbian relations to the aesthetic are another question entirely and not within my purview here. A historical consideration of this issue might begin with Kathy Alexis Psomiades, *Beauty's Body: Femininity and Representation in British Aestheticism* (Stanford: Stanford University Press, 1997).

11. See Catherine Clément, *Syncope: The Philosophy of Rapture,* trans. Sally O'Driscoll and Deirdre M. Mahoney (Minneapolis: University of Minnesota Press, 1994).

which, by way of Freud's expanding eroticism beyond genitalia, that loss of specificity reaches epistemological crisis.

The suggestion that we cultivate aesthetic as well as erotic practices for approaching *jouissance* need not be mistaken for an elitist proposition, since it isn't necessary to be initiated into high culture to have one's relational activity intensively engaged by visual and verbal phenomena. The ravishing effects of *jouissance* are as likely to be experienced in the mosh pit as they are in the opera hall. And when we bear in mind that it is often a collective aesthetic experience that induces this self-loss, we start to see that aesthetics is no less political—only differently so—than more familiar kinds of group activity. Far from a poor substitute for sex, art may represent a more inventive mode of approaching *jouissance*. Having cultivated explicitly erotic impersonalist modes of relating, gay men might now develop alternative ways of being open to forms of otherness that exceed the comparatively familiar otherness of other persons. Beyond sexuality lie the myriad possibilities of aesthetics.

279

References

Abelove, Henry. "Freud, Male Homosexuality, and the Americans." In *The Lesbian and Gay Studies Reader*. Ed. Henry Abelove, Michèle Aina Barale, and David M. Halperin, 381–93. New York: Routledge, 1993.

Abramson, Paul R., and Steven D. Pinkerton, eds. *Sexual Nature, Sexual Culture*. Chicago: University of Chicago Press, 1995.

Adams, Parveen. *The Emptiness of the Image: Psychoanalysis and Sexual Differences*. London: Routledge, 1996.

Agamben, Giorgio. *The Coming Community*. Trans. Michael Hardt. Minneapolis: University of Minnesota Press, 1993.

Allison, David B., Prado de Oliveira, Mark S. Roberts, and Allen S. Weiss, eds. *Psychosis and Sexual Identity: Toward a Post-analytic View of the Schreber Case*. Albany: SUNY Press, 1988.

Althusser, Louis. *Lenin and Philosophy and Other Essays*. Trans. Ben Brewster. New York: Monthly Review, 1971.

———. *Writings on Psychoanalysis: Freud and Lacan*. Ed. Olivier Corpet and François Matheron. Trans. Jeffrey Mehlman. New York: Columbia University Press, 1996.

Anderson, Amanda. "Debatable Performances: Restaging Contentious Feminisms." *Social Text* 54, vol. 16, no. 1 (1998): 1–24.

Anderson, Benedict. *Imagined Communities: Reflections on the Origin and Spread of Nationalism*. New York: Verso, 1983.

Andreas-Salomé, Lou. " 'Anal' und 'Sexual.' " *Imago* 4 (1916): 249–60.

Anzieu, Didier. *The Skin Ego: A Psychoanalytic Approach to the Self*. Trans. Chris Turner. New Haven: Yale University Press, 1989.

Apter, Emily. "Fantom Images: Hervé Guibert and the Writing of 'Sida' in France." In *Writing AIDS: Gay Literature, Language, and Analysis*. Ed. Timothy F. Murphy and Suzanne Poirier, 83–97. New York: Columbia University Press, 1993.

Barthes, Roland. *Mythologies*. Trans. Annette Lavers. New York: Hill and Wang, 1972.

REFERENCES

————. *The Pleasure of the Text*. Trans. Richard Miller. New York: Hill and Wang, 1975.

Barzilai, Shuli. "Reading Lacan, or Harlaquanage: An Essay Review." *American Imago* 52 (1995): 81–106.

Bawer, Bruce. *A Place at the Table: The Gay Individual in American Society*. New York: Poseidon, 1993.

Bayer, Ronald. *Homosexuality and American Psychiatry: The Politics of Diagnosis*. 2d ed. Princeton: Princeton University Press, 1987.

Beachy, Stephen. "20+, HIV+." *New York Times Magazine*, April 17, 1994, 52–53.

Bender, John, and David E. Wellbery, eds. *The Ends of Rhetoric: History, Theory, Practice*. Stanford: Stanford University Press, 1990.

————. "Rhetoricality: On the Modernist Return of Rhetoric." In Bender and Wellbery, *Ends of Rhetoric*, 1–30.

Benjamin, Harry. *The Transsexual Phenomenon*. New York: Julian Press, 1966.

————. "Transvestism and Transsexualism." *American Journal of Psychotherapy* 8 (1954): 219–30.

Benjamin, Jessica. *Like Subjects, Love Objects: Essays on Recognition and Sexual Difference*. New Haven: Yale University Press, 1995.

Benveniste, Emile. *Problems in General Linguistics*. Trans. Mary Elizabeth Meek. Coral Gables: University of Miami Press, 1971.

Berlant, Lauren. *The Anatomy of National Fantasy: Hawthorne, Utopia, and Everyday Life*. Chicago: University of Chicago Press, 1991.

Berlant, Lauren, and Michael Warner. "Sex in Public." *Critical Inquiry* 24 (1998): 547–66.

————. "What Does Queer Theory Teach Us about *X*?" *PMLA* 110 (1995): 343–49.

Bersani, Leo. *The Culture of Redemption*. Cambridge: Harvard University Press, 1990.

————. *The Freudian Body: Psychoanalysis and Art*. New York: Columbia University Press, 1986.

————. *Homos*. Cambridge: Harvard University Press, 1995.

————. "Is the Rectum a Grave?" In Crimp, *AIDS*, 197–222.

Bersani, Leo, and Ulysse Dutoit. *Arts of Impoverishment: Beckett, Rothko, Resnais*. Cambridge: Harvard University Press, 1993.

————. *Caravaggio's Secrets*. Cambridge: MIT Press, 1998.

Bérubé, Allan. "Prophesy, 1984." *Harvard Gay and Lesbian Review* 5, no. 2 (1998): 10.

Billings, Dwight B., and Thomas Urban. "The Socio-medical Construction of Transsexualism: An Interpretation and Critique." *Social Problems* 29 (1982): 266–82.

Bollas, Christopher. "Cruising in the Homosexual Arena." In *Being a Character: Psychoanalysis and Self Experience*, 144–64. New York: Hill and Wang, 1994.

Boothby, Richard. *Death and Desire: Psychoanalytic Theory in Lacan's Return to Freud*. New York: Routledge, 1991.

Borch-Jacobsen, Mikkel. "Analytic Speech: From Restricted to General Rhetoric." In Bender and Wellbery, *Ends of Rhetoric*, 127–39.

————. *The Emotional Tie: Psychoanalysis, Mimesis, Affect*. Trans. Douglas Brick. Stanford: Stanford University Press, 1993.

————. *The Freudian Subject*. Trans. Catherine Porter. Stanford: Stanford University Press, 1988.

————. *Lacan: The Absolute Master*. Trans. Douglas Brick. Stanford: Stanford University Press, 1991.

————. *Remembering Anna O: A Century of Mystification*. Trans. Kirby Olson. New York: Routledge, 1996.

Bordowitz, Gregg. "Picture a Coalition." In Crimp, *AIDS,* 183–96.

Bornstein, Kate. *Gender Outlaw: On Men, Women, and the Rest of Us.* New York: Routledge, 1994.

Bronski, Michael. *The Pleasure Principle: Sex, Backlash, and the Struggle for Gay Freedom.* New York: St. Martin's Press, 1998.

———. "Behind the Sex Panic! Debate." *Harvard Gay and Lesbian Review* 5, no. 2 (1998): 29–32.

Brown, Rebecca. *The Gifts of the Body.* New York: HarperCollins, 1994.

Buhle, Mari Jo. *Feminism and Its Discontents: A Century of Struggle with Psychoanalysis.* Cambridge: Harvard University Press, 1998.

Burgin, Victor. "Fantasy." In *Feminism and Psychoanalysis: A Critical Dictionary.* Ed. Elizabeth Wright, 84–88. Oxford: Basil Blackwell, 1992.

———. "Geometry and Abjection." In *Abjection, Melancholia and Love: The Work of Julia Kristeva.* Ed. John Fletcher and Andrew Benjamin, 104–23. New York: Routledge, 1990.

Butler, Judith. *Bodies That Matter: On the Discursive Limits of "Sex."* New York: Routledge, 1993.

———. "Contingent Foundations: Feminism and the Question of 'Postmodernism.'" In *Feminists Theorize the Political.* Ed. Judith Butler and Joan W. Scott, 3–21. New York: Routledge, 1992.

———. "Critical Exchanges: The Symbolic and Questions of Gender." In *Questioning Foundations: Truth / Subjectivity / Culture.* Ed. Hugh J. Silverman, 134–49. New York: Routledge, 1993.

———. *Excitable Speech: A Politics of the Performative.* New York: Routledge, 1997.

———. *Gender Trouble: Feminism and the Subversion of Identity.* New York: Routledge, 1990.

———. "Imitation and Gender Insubordination." In Fuss, *Inside / Out,* 13–31.

———. "Lana's 'Imitation': Melodramatic Repetition and the Gender Performative." *Genders* 9 (1990): 1–18.

Butler, Judith, and Biddy Martin. "Cross-Identifications." *Diacritics* 24, nos. 2–3 (1994): 3.

Callen, Michael. *Surviving AIDS.* New York: HarperCollins, 1990.

Champagne, John. *The Ethics of Marginality: A New Approach to Gay Studies.* Minneapolis: University of Minnesota Press, 1995.

Chinn, Sarah, Mario DiGangi, and Patrick Horrigan. "A Talk with Eve Kosofsky Sedgwick." *Pre / Text* 13, nos. 3–4 (1992): 79–95.

Clavreul, Jean. "The Perverse Couple." In Schneiderman, *Returning to Freud,* 215–33.

Clément, Catherine. *Syncope: The Philosophy of Rapture.* Trans. Sally O'Driscoll and Deirdre M. Mahoney. Minneapolis: University of Minnesota Press, 1994.

Clendinen, Dudley. "When Negative Meets Positive." *Gentlemen's Quarterly,* October 1994. 236–39, 265.

Coleridge, Samuel Taylor. *Biographia Literaria.* Vol. 7 of *Collected Works of Samuel Taylor Coleridge.* Ed. James Engell and Walter Jackson Bate. London: Routledge and Kegan Paul, 1983.

Copjec, Joan. *Read My Desire: Lacan against the Historicists.* Cambridge: MIT Press, 1994.

Corbett, Edward P. J. *Classical Rhetoric for the Modern Student* [1965]. 3d ed. rev. Oxford: Oxford University Press, 1990.

Crain, Caleb. "Pleasure Principles: Queer Theorists and Gay Journalists Wrestle over the Politics of Sex." *Lingua Franca,* October 1997, 26–37.

Crimp, Douglas. "AIDS: Cultural Analysis / Cultural Activism." In Crimp, *AIDS,* 3–16.

———, ed. *AIDS: Cultural Analysis / Cultural Activism.* Cambridge: MIT Press, 1988.

———. "How to Have Promiscuity in an Epidemic." In Crimp, *AIDS,* 237–70.

283

REFERENCES

————. "Mourning and Militancy." *October* 51 (1989): 3–18.

Crimp, Douglas, and Adam Rolston, eds. *AIDS Demo Graphics*. Seattle: Bay Press, 1990.

Cullen, Deborah, ed. *Bataille's Eye and ICI Field Notes 4*. New York: Studley Press, 1997.

Davidson, Arnold I. "Closing Up the Corpses: Diseases of Sexuality and the Emergence of the Psychiatric Style of Reasoning." In *Homosexuality and Psychoanalysis*. Ed. Tim Dean and Christopher Lane. Chicago: University of Chicago Press, forthcoming.

————. "How to Do the History of Psychoanalysis: A Reading of Freud's *Three Essays on the Theory of Sexuality*." In *The Trial(s) of Psychoanalysis*. Ed. Françoise Meltzer, 39–64. Chicago: University of Chicago Press, 1988.

Daum, Meghan. "Safe-Sex Lies." *New York Times Magazine*, January 21, 1996, 32–33.

Dean, Tim. "Homosexuality and the Problem of Otherness." In *Homosexuality and Psychoanalysis*. Ed. Tim Dean and Christopher Lane. Chicago: University of Chicago Press, forthcoming.

————. "On the Eve of a Queer Future." *Raritan* 15, no. 1 (1995): 116–34.

————. "Paring His Fingernails: Homosexuality and Joyce's Impersonalist Aesthetic." In *Quare Joyce*. Ed. Joseph Valente, 241–72. Ann Arbor: University of Michigan Press, 1998.

————. "The Pervert Does Not Exist." Unpublished manuscript.

————. "Sex and Syncope." *Raritan* 15, no. 3 (1996): 64–86.

————. "Two Kinds of Other and Their Consequences." *Critical Inquiry* 23 (1997): 910–20.

————. "Wanting Paul de Man: A Critique of the 'Logic' of New Historicism in American Studies." *Texas Studies in Literature and Language* 35 (1993): 251–77.

De Lauretis, Teresa. *The Practice of Love: Lesbian Sexuality and Perverse Desire*. Bloomington: Indiana University Press, 1994.

————. "Queer Theory: Lesbian and Gay Sexualities—An Introduction." *Differences* 3, no. 2 (1991): iii–xviii.

Deleuze, Gilles, and Félix Guattari. *Anti-Oedipus: Capitalism and Schizophrenia*. Trans. Robert Hurley, Mark Seem, and Helen R. Lane. Minneapolis: University of Minnesota Press, 1983.

————. *A Thousand Plateaus: Capitalism and Schizophrenia*. Trans. Brian Massumi. Minneapolis: University of Minnesota Press, 1987.

De Man, Paul. *Allegories of Reading: Figural Language in Rousseau, Nietzsche, Rilke, and Proust*. New Haven: Yale University Press, 1979.

Derrida, Jacques. *Of Grammatology*. Trans. Gayatri Chakravorty Spivak. Baltimore: Johns Hopkins University Press, 1976.

————. *Positions*. Trans. Alan Bass. Chicago: University of Chicago Press, 1981.

————. " 'To Do Justice to Freud': The History of Madness in the Age of Psychoanalysis." Trans. Pascale-Anne Brault and Michael Naas. *Critical Inquiry* 20 (1994): 227–66.

————. "White Mythology: Metaphor in the Text of Philosophy." Trans. F. C. T. Moore. *New Literary History* 6 (1974): 5–74.

Diaz, Rafael M. *Latino Gay Men and HIV: Culture, Sexuality, and Risk Behavior*. New York: Routledge, 1997.

Dollimore, Jonathan. *Death, Desire, and Loss in Western Culture*. Harmondsworth: Penguin, 1998.

————. *Sexual Dissidence: Augustine to Wilde, Freud to Foucault*. Oxford: Clarendon, 1991.

Domenici, Thomas, and Ronnie C. Lesser, eds. *Disorienting Sexuality: Psychoanalytic Reappraisals of Sexual Identities*. New York: Routledge, 1995.

Duberman, Martin. "Epidemic Arguments." *Nation*, May 5, 1997, 27–29.

Düttmann, Alexander García. *At Odds with AIDS: Thinking and Talking about a Virus.* Trans. Peter Gilgen and Conrad Scott-Curtis. Stanford: Stanford University Press, 1996.

Dyess, Cynthia, and Tim Dean. "Gender: The Impossibility of Meaning." *Psychoanalytic Dialogues.* Forthcoming.

Edelman, Lee. *Homographesis: Essays in Gay Literary and Cultural Theory.* New York: Routledge, 1994.

Eigo, Jim. "Sexual Ecology: An Activist Critique." http://www.geocities.com/~sexpanicnyc/revo.htm.

Elliot, Patricia, and Katrina Roen. "Transgenderism and the Question of Embodiment: Promising Queer Politics?" *GLQ* 4 (1998): 231–61.

Enriquez, Micheline. "Paranoiac Fantasies: Sexual Difference, Homosexuality, Law of the Father." Trans. Yifat Hachamovitch and Beátrice Loeffel. In *Psychosis and Sexual Identity: Toward a Post-analytic View of the Schreber Case.* Ed. David B. Allison, Prado de Oliveira, Mark S. Roberts, and Allen S. Weiss, 102–29. Albany: SUNY Press, 1988.

Epstein, Julia, and Kristina Straub, eds. *Body Guards: The Cultural Politics of Gender Ambiguity.* New York: Routledge, 1991.

Feinberg, Leslie. *Transgender Warriors: Making History from Joan of Arc to RuPaul.* Boston: Beacon, 1996.

Feldstein, Richard, Bruce Fink, and Maire Jaanus, eds. *Reading Seminar XI: Lacan's Four Fundamental Concepts of Psychoanalysis.* Albany: SUNY Press, 1995.

Ferguson, Michael. "Fixation and Regression in the Psychoanalytic Theory of Homosexuality: A Critical Evaluation." In *Gay Ethics: Controversies in Outing, Civil Rights, and Sexual Science.* Ed. Timothy F. Murphy, 309–27. New York: Haworth, 1994.

Fineman, Joel. *The Subjectivity Effect in Western Literary Tradition: Essays toward the Release of Shakespeare's Will.* Cambridge: MIT Press, 1991.

Fink, Bruce. *A Clinical Introduction to Lacanian Psychoanalysis: Theory and Technique.* Cambridge: Harvard University Press, 1997.

Fish, Stanley. "Rhetoric." In *Critical Terms for Literary Study.* Ed. Frank Lentricchia and Thomas McLaughlin, 203–22. Chicago: University of Chicago Press, 1990.

Fitzpatrick, Michael, and Don Milligan. *The Truth about the AIDS Panic.* London: Junius, 1987.

Fletcher, John. "Freud and His Uses: Psychoanalysis and Gay Theory." In Shepherd and Wallis, *Coming On Strong,* 90–118.

Fletcher, John, and Martin Stanton, eds. *Jean Laplanche: Seduction, Translation, Drives.* Trans. Martin Stanton. London: ICA, 1992.

Flieger, Jerry Aline. "Overdetermined Oedipus: Mommy, Daddy, and Me as Desiring Machines." *South Atlantic Quarterly* 96 (1997): 599–620.

Forrester, John. *Dispatches from the Freud Wars: Psychoanalysis and Its Passions.* Cambridge: Harvard University Press, 1997.

———. *Truth Games: Lies, Money, and Psychoanalysis.* Cambridge: Harvard University Press, 1997.

Foucault, Michel. *The Essential Works of Michel Foucault, 1954–1984.* Vol. 1. *Ethics: Subjectivity and Truth.* Ed. Paul Rabinow. Trans. Robert Hurley, et al. New York: New Press, 1997.

———. *The History of Sexuality.* Volume 1: *An Introduction.* Trans. Robert Hurley. New York: Random House, 1978.

———. "An Interview with Stephen Riggins." In *The Essential Works,* 121–33.

———. *Madness and Civilization: A History of Insanity in the Age of Reason.* Trans. Richard Howard. New York: Random House, 1965.

REFERENCES

————. Preface to Deleuze and Guattari, *Anti-Oedipus*, xi–xiv.

————. "Sexual Choice, Sexual Act." In *The Essential Works*, 141–56.

Freud, Sigmund. *Beyond the Pleasure Principle* (1920). In *Standard Edition*, 18:1–64.

————. " 'A Child Is Being Beaten': A Contribution to the Study of the Origin of Sexual Perversions" (1919). In *Standard Edition*, 17:175–204.

————. *Civilization and Its Discontents* (1930). In *Standard Edition*, 21:57–145.

————. " 'Civilized' Sexual Morality and Modern Nervous Illness" (1908). In *Standard Edition*, 9:177–204.

————. *The Ego and the Id* (1923). In *Standard Edition*, 19:3–66.

————. "Instincts and Their Vicissitudes" (1915). *Standard Edition*, 14:109–40.

————. *The Interpretation of Dreams*. Vols. 4 and 5 of *Standard Edition*.

————. *Leonardo da Vinci and a Memory of His Childhood* (1910). *Standard Edition*, 11:57–137.

————. "Mourning and Melancholia" ([1915] 1917). In *Standard Edition*, 14:237–58.

————. *On the History of the Psychoanalytic Movement* (1914). In *Standard Edition*, 14:1–66.

————. "On the Universal Tendency to Debasement in the Sphere of Love" (1912). In *Standard Edition*, 11:177–90.

————. "Recommendations to Physicians Practising Psychoanalysis" (1912). In *Standard Edition*, 12:109–20.

————. "Some Character-Types Met with in Psychoanalytic Work" (1916). In *Standard Edition*, 14:309–33.

————. *Standard Edition of the Complete Psychological Works of Sigmund Freud*. Ed. and trans. James Strachey. London: Hogarth, 1953–74.

————. "Thoughts for the Times on War and Death" (1915). In *Standard Edition*, 14:273–300.

————. *Three Essays on the Theory of Sexuality* (1905). In *Standard Edition*, 7:123–243.

————. "The Unconscious" (1915). In *Standard Edition*, 14:159–204.

————. "Zeitgemässes über Krieg und Tod." *Gesammelte Werke*, 10:324–55. London: Imago, 1946.

Fumento, Michael. *The Myth of Heterosexual AIDS*. New York: Basic Books, 1990.

Fuss, Diana, ed. *Inside / Out: Lesbian Theories, Gay Theories*. New York: Routledge, 1991.

Gallagher, John. "Slipping Up." *Advocate*, July 8, 1997, 33–34.

Gallop, Jane. *The Daughter's Seduction: Feminism and Psychoanalysis*. Ithaca: Cornell University Press, 1982.

————. *Reading Lacan*. Ithaca: Cornell University Press, 1985.

————. *Thinking through the Body*. New York: Columbia University Press, 1988.

Garber, Marjorie. *Vested Interests: Cross-Dressing and Cultural Anxiety*. New York: Routledge, 1992.

————. *Vice Versa: Bisexuality and the Eroticism of Everyday Life*. New York: Simon and Schuster, 1995.

Garrett, Laurie. *The Coming Plague: Newly Emerging Diseases in a World out of Balance*. New York: Penguin, 1995.

Gever, Martha. "Pictures of Sickness: Stuart Marshall's *Bright Eyes*." In Crimp, *AIDS*, 109–26.

Goudsmit, Jaap. *Viral Sex: The Nature of AIDS*. New York: Oxford University Press, 1997.

Granon-Lafont, Jeanne. *La topologie ordinaire de Jacques Lacan*. Paris: Point Hors Ligne, 1985.

Green, Jesse. "Flirting with Suicide." *New York Times Magazine*, September 15, 1996, 39–45, 54–55, 84–85.

Greenberg, David. *The Construction of Homosexuality*. Chicago: University of Chicago Press, 1988.

Grigg, Russell. "Metaphor and Metonymy." *Newsletter of the Freudian Field* 3, nos. 1 and 2 (1989): 58–79.

Grosz, Elizabeth. *Volatile Bodies: Toward a Corporeal Feminism.* Bloomington: Indiana University Press, 1994.

———. *Space, Time, and Perversion: Essays on the Politics of Bodies.* New York: Routledge, 1995.

Gubar, Susan. "What Ails Feminist Criticism?" *Critical Inquiry* 24 (1998): 878–902.

Guibert, Hervé. *To the Friend Who Did Not Save My Life.* Trans. Linda Coverdale. New York: High Risk, 1994.

Gurewich, Judith Feher. "The Philanthropy of Perversion: Another Kind of Violence." In *Jacques Lacan and the Cultural Unconscious: Psychoanalytical Critique for the Twenty-First Century.* Ed. Jean-Michel Rabaté. Forthcoming.

Halperin, David M. *One Hundred Years of Homosexuality: And Other Essays on Greek Love.* New York: Routledge, 1990.

———. *Saint Foucault: Towards a Gay Hagiography.* New York: Oxford University Press, 1995.

Hamer, Dean, and Peter Copeland. *The Science of Desire: The Search for the Gay Gene and the Biology of Behavior.* New York: Simon and Schuster, 1994.

Harper, Phillip Brian. "Gay Male Identities, Personal Privacy, and Relations of Public Exchange: Notes on Directions for Queer Critique." *Social Text,* 52/53, vol. 15, no. 3/4 (1997): 5–29.

———. " 'The Subversive Edge': *Paris Is Burning,* Social Critique, and the Limits of Subjective Agency." *Diacritics* 24, nos. 2–3 (1994): 90–103.

Harris, Daniel. "AIDS and Theory." *Lingua Franca,* June 1991, 1, 16–19.

Harris, Thomas. *The Silence of the Lambs.* New York: St. Martin's Press, 1988.

Hausman, Bernice L. *Changing Sex: Transsexualism, Technology, and the Idea of Gender.* Durham: Duke University Press, 1995.

Haver, William. *The Body of This Death: Historicity and Sociality in the Time of AIDS.* Stanford: Stanford University Press, 1996.

Heitz, David. "Men Behaving Badly." *Advocate,* July 8, 1997, 26–29.

Hocquenghem, Guy. *Homosexual Desire.* Trans. Daniella Dangoor. Durham: Duke University Press, 1993. Originally published as *Le désir homosexuel* (Paris: Éditions Universitaires, 1972).

Holleran, Andrew. *The Beauty of Men: A Novel.* New York: William Morrow, 1996.

hooks, bell. *Black Looks: Race and Representation.* Boston: South End Press, 1992.

Hyppolite, Jean. "A Spoken Commentary on Freud's *Verneinung.*" In Lacan, *The Seminar,* bk. 1, 289–97.

The Identity in Question. Special issue of *October* 61 (1992).

L'inconscient homosexuel. Special issue of *La cause freudienne* 37 (1997).

Irigaray, Luce. *Je, Tu, Nous: Toward a Culture of Difference.* Trans. Alison Martin. New York: Routledge, 1993.

Isay, Richard A. *Becoming Gay: The Journey to Self-Acceptance.* New York: Pantheon, 1996.

Jacoby, Russell. *The Repression of Psychoanalysis: Otto Fenichel and the Political Freudians.* Chicago: University of Chicago Press, 1986.

———. *Social Amnesia: A Critique of Conformist Psychology from Adler to Laing.* Boston: Beacon, 1975.

Jakobson, Roman. "Two Types of Language and Two Types of Aphasic Disturbance." In *Language in Literature.* Ed. Krystyna Pomorska and Stephen Rudy, 95–114. Cambridge: Harvard University Press, 1987.

Jameson, Fredric. *The Political Unconscious: Narrative as a Socially Symbolic Act.* Ithaca: Cornell University Press, 1981.

Kant, Immanuel. *Critique of Practical Reason.* Ed. and trans. Lewis Beck White. New York: Macmillan, 1993.

Katz, Jonathan Ned. *The Invention of Heterosexuality.* New York: Dutton, 1995.

Kettelhack, Guy. *Dancing around the Volcano: Freeing Our Erotic Lives: Decoding the Enigma of Gay Men and Sex.* New York: Crown, 1996.

King, Edward. *Safety in Numbers: Safer Sex and Gay Men.* New York: Routledge, 1994.

Kramer, Larry. *Faggots.* New York: Random House, 1978.

———. "Ten Years of Plague: 110,530 Deaths . . . and Counting." *Advocate,* July 2, 1991, 62–63.

Lacan, Jacques. "Aggressivity in Psychoanalysis." In *Écrits,* 8–29.

———. "Desire and the Interpretation of Desire in *Hamlet.*" In *Literature and Psychoanalysis, The Question of Reading: Otherwise.* Ed. Shoshana Felman, 11–52. Baltimore: Johns Hopkins University Press, 1982.

———. "The Direction of the Treatment and the Principles of Its Power. In *Écrits,* 226–80.

———. *Écrits: A Selection.* Trans. Alan Sheridan. New York: Norton, 1977.

———. *Feminine Sexuality: Jacques Lacan and the école freudienne.* Ed. Juliet Mitchell and Jacqueline Rose. Trans. Jacqueline Rose. New York: Norton, 1982.

———. *The Four Fundamental Concepts of Psychoanalysis.* Ed. Jacques-Alain Miller. Trans. Alan Sheridan. Harmondsworth: Penguin, 1977.

———. "The Function and Field of Speech and Language in Psychoanalysis." In *Écrits,* 30–113.

———. "Geneva Lecture on the Symptom." Trans. Russell Grigg. *Analysis* 1 (1989): 7–26.

———. "Intervention on Transference." In *Feminine Sexuality,* 61–73.

———. "Introduction to the Names-of-the-Father Seminar." In *Television: A Challenge to the Psychoanalytic Establishment.* Text established by Jacques-Alain Miller. Ed. Joan Copjec. Trans. Denis Hollier, Rosalind Krauss, Annette Michelson, and Jeffrey Mehlman, 81–95. New York: Norton, 1990.

———. "Kant with Sade." Trans. James B. Swenson Jr. *October* 51 (1989): 55–104.

———. *The Language of the Self: The Function of Language in Psychoanalysis.* Trans. Anthony Wilden. Baltimore: Johns Hopkins University Press, 1968.

———. "Of Structure as an Inmixing of an Otherness Prerequisite to Any Subject Whatever." In *The Structuralist Controversy: The Languages of Criticism and the Sciences of Man.* Ed. Richard Macksey and Eugenio Donato, 186–200. Baltimore: Johns Hopkins University Press, 1972.

———. "On a Question Preliminary to any Possible Treatment of Psychosis." In *Écrits,* 179–225.

———. *On Feminine Sexuality, The Limits of Love and Knowledge: The Seminar of Jacques Lacan. Book 20: Encore, 1972–1973.* Ed. Jacques-Alain Miller. Trans. Bruce Fink. New York: Norton, 1998.

———. "Position of the Unconscious." In Feldstein, Fink, and Jaanus, *Reading Seminar XI,* 259–82.

———. *Le séminaire, livre VII, L'éthique de la psychanalyse, 1959–1960.* Ed. Jacques-Alain Miller. Paris: Seuil, 1986. Translated as *The Seminar of Jacques Lacan,* bk. 7, *The Ethics of Psychoanalysis, 1959–1960,* ed. Jacques-Alain Miller, trans. Dennis Porter (New York: Norton, 1992).

————. *Le séminaire, livre VIII: Le transfert, 1960–1961*. Ed. Jacques-Alain Miller. Paris: Seuil, 1991.

————. "Le séminaire." Bk. 14, "La logique du fantasme, 1966–1967." Unpublished manuscript.

————. *Le séminaire, livre XVII: L'envers de la psychanalyse, 1969–1970*. Ed. Jacques-Alain Miller. Paris: Seuil, 1991.

————. *Le séminaire, livre XX: Encore, 1972–1973*. Paris: Seuil, 1975.

————. *The Seminar of Jacques Lacan. Book 1: Freud's Papers on Technique, 1953–1954*. Ed. Jacques-Alain Miller. Trans. John Forrester. Cambridge: Cambridge University Press, 1988.

————. *The Seminar of Jacques Lacan. Book 2: The Ego in Freud's Theory and in the Technique of Psychoanalysis, 1954–1955*. Ed. Jacques-Alain Miller. Trans. Sylvana Tomaselli. Cambridge: Cambridge University Press, 1988.

————. *The Seminar of Jacques Lacan. Book 3: The Psychoses, 1955–1956*. Ed. Jacques-Alain Miller. Trans. Russell Grigg. New York: Norton, 1993.

————. "The Signification of the Phallus." In *Écrits*, 281–91.

————. "Le sinthôme." *Ornicar?* 7 (1976): 3–18.

————. "The Subversion of the Subject and the Dialectic of Desire in the Freudian Unconscious." In *Écrits*, 292–325.

————. *Television: A Challenge to the Psychoanalytic Establishment*. Text established by Jacques-Alain Miller. Ed. Joan Copjec. Trans. Denis Hollier, Rosalind Krauss, Annette Michelson, and Jeffrey Mehlman. New York: Norton, 1990.

Lacan, Jacques, and Wladimir Granoff. "Fetishism: The Symbolic, the Imaginary, and the Real." In *Perversions: Psychodynamics and Therapy*. Ed. Sandor Lorand, 265–76. New York: Random House, 1956.

Laclau, Ernesto, and Chantal Mouffe. *Hegemony and Socialist Strategy: Towards a Radical Democratic Politics*. Trans. Winston Moore and Paul Cammack. London: Verso, 1985.

Lane, Christopher. *The Burdens of Intimacy: Psychoanalysis and Victorian Masculinity*. Chicago: University of Chicago Press, 1999.

Laplanche, Jean. *Life and Death in Psychoanalysis*. Trans. Jeffrey Mehlman. Baltimore: Johns Hopkins University Press, 1976.

————. *New Foundations for Psychoanalysis*. Trans. David Macey. Oxford: Basil Blackwell, 1989.

————. *Problématiques III: La Sublimation*. Paris: PUF, 1980.

————. "To Situate Sublimation." Trans. Richard Miller. *October* 28 (1984): 7–26.

————. "The Theory of Seduction and the Problem of the Other." Trans. Luke Thurston. *International Journal of Psychoanalysis* 78 (1997): 653–66.

Laplanche, Jean, and Jean-Bertrand Pontalis. *The Language of Psychoanalysis*. Trans. Donald Nicholson-Smith. New York: Norton, 1973.

————. "Fantasy and the Origins of Sexuality." In *Formations of Fantasy*. Ed. Victor Burgin, James Donald, and Cora Kaplan, 5–34. London: Methuen, 1986.

Laqueur, Thomas. *Making Sex: Body and Gender from the Greeks to Freud*. Cambridge: Harvard University Press, 1990.

Leavitt, David. *Family Dancing*. New York: Knopf, 1984.

LeVay, Simon. *Queer Science: The Use and Abuse of Research into Homosexuality*. Cambridge: MIT Press, 1996.

————. *The Sexual Brain*. Cambridge: MIT Press, 1993.

Lewes, Kenneth. *The Psychoanalytic Theory of Male Homosexuality*. New York: Simon and Schuster, 1988.

REFERENCES

Listing, Johann. *Introduction à la topologie*. Trans. Claude Léger and Michael Turnheim. Paris: Navarin, 1989.

Livingston, Jennie, dir. *Paris Is Burning*. Off-White Productions.

Macey, David. *Lacan in Contexts*. New York: Verso, 1988.

Martin, Biddy. "Sexualities without Genders and Other Queer Utopias." *Diacritics* 24, nos. 2–3 (1994): 104–21.

Merleau-Ponty, Maurice. *The Visible and the Invisible*. Ed. Claude Lefort. Trans. Alphonso Lingis. Evanston: Northwestern University Press, 1968.

Merlis, Mark. *American Studies*. New York: Houghton Mifflin, 1994.

Metz, Christian. *Psychoanalysis and Cinema: The Imaginary Signifier*. Trans. Celia Britton, Annwyl Williams, Ben Brewster, and Alfred Guzzetti. London: Macmillan, 1982.

Meyerowitz, Joanne. "Sex Change and the Popular Press: Historical Notes on Transsexuality in the United States, 1930–1955." *GLQ* 4 (1998): 159–87.

Michie, Helena. "A Few Words about AIDS." *American Literary History* 2 (1990): 328–38.

Miklitsch, Robert. "'Going through the Fantasy': Screening Slavoj Žižek." *South Atlantic Quarterly* 97 (1998): 475–507.

Miller, D. A. "Anal *Rope*." In Fuss, *Inside/Out*, 119–41.

———. "Sontag's Urbanity." *October* 49 (1989): 91–101.

Miller, Jacques-Alain. "Context and Concepts." In Feldstein, Fink, and Jaanus, *Reading Seminar XI*, 3–15.

———. "The Drive Is Speech." Trans. Kirsten Stolte. *Umbr(a)* 1 (1997): 15–33.

———. "*Extimité*." In *Lacanian Theory of Discourse: Subject, Structure, Society*. Ed. Mark Bracher, Marshall W. Alcorn Jr., Ronald J. Corthell, and Françoise Massardier-Kenney, 74–87. New York: New York University Press, 1994.

———. "Michel Foucault and Psychoanalysis." In *Michel Foucault, Philosopher*. Ed. and trans. Timothy J. Armstrong, 58–64. London: Harvester Wheatsheaf, 1992.

———. "On Perversion." In *Reading Seminars I and II: Lacan's Return to Freud*. Ed. Richard Feldstein, Bruce Fink, and Maire Jaanus, 306–20. Albany: SUNY Press, 1996.

———. "Teachings of the Case Presentation." In Schneiderman, *Returning to Freud*, 42–52.

Millot, Catherine. *Horsexe: Essay on Transsexuality*. Trans. Kenneth Hylton. New York: Autonomedia, 1990.

Morel, Jean-Paul. "Interview with Jacques-Alain Miller." Trans. Dennis Porter. *Newsletter of the Freudian Field* 1, no. 1 (1987): 5–10.

Morris, Martina, and Laura Dean. "Effect of Sexual Behavior Change on Long-Term Human Immunodeficiency Virus Prevalence among Homosexual Men." *American Journal of Epidemiology* 140 (1994): 217–32.

Morrison, Margaret. "Laughing with Queers in My Eyes: Proposing 'Queer Rhetoric(s)' and Introducing a Queer Issue." *Pre/Text* 13, nos. 3–4 (1992): 11–36.

Morton, Donald. "Birth of the Cyberqueer." *PMLA* 110 (1995): 369–81.

Moss, Donald. "*Disorienting Sexuality:* A Commentary." *Gender and Psychoanalysis* 2 (1997): 185–90.

Muller, John P. *Beyond the Psychoanalytic Dyad: Developmental Semiotics in Freud, Peirce, and Lacan*. New York: Routledge, 1995.

Murchek, John. "Foucault and Psychoanalysis: 'Quite Near.'" Unpublished manuscript.

Nelson, James L. "The Silence of the Bioethicists: Ethical and Political Aspects of Managing Gender Dysphoria." *GLQ* 4 (1998): 213–30.

Newton, Esther. *Mother Camp: Female Impersonators in America* (1972). 2d ed. Chicago: University of Chicago Press, 1979.

Nunokawa, Jeff. " 'All the Sad Young Men': AIDS and the Work of Mourning." In Fuss, *Inside / Out,* 311–23.

Odets, Walt. *In the Shadow of the Epidemic: Being HIV-Negative in the Age of AIDS.* Durham: Duke University Press, 1995.

Ogas, Ogi. "Spare Parts." *City Paper* (Baltimore), March 9, 1994, 10–15.

O'Hara, Scott. *Autopornography: A Memoir of Life in the Lust Lane.* New York: Harrington Park, 1997.

———. "Safety First?" *Advocate,* July 8, 1997, 9.

O'Sullivan, Sue, and Pratibha Parmar. *Lesbians Talk (Safer) Sex.* London: Scarlet, 1992.

Oppenheimer, Joshua. " 'Sexual Ecology' = Sexual Apartheid." *Harvard Gay and Lesbian Review* 5, no. 2 (1998): 15–18.

Ozick, Cynthia. *The Shawl.* New York: Vintage, 1990.

Patsalides, André. "*Jouissance* in the Cure." *Anamorphosis: Journal of the San Francisco Society for Lacanian Studies and the Lacanian School of Psychoanalysis* 1 (1997): 3–12.

Patton, Cindy. *Fatal Advice: How Safe-Sex Education Went Wrong.* Durham: Duke University Press, 1996.

———. *Inventing AIDS.* New York: Routledge, 1990.

———. *Sex and Germs: The Politics of AIDS.* Boston: South End Press, 1985.

Pêcheux, Michel. *Language, Semantics, and Ideology: Stating the Obvious.* Trans Harbans Nagpal. London: Macmillan, 1982.

Pendleton, Eva, and Jane Goldschmidt. "Sex Panic!—Make the Connections." *Harvard Gay and Lesbian Review* 5, no. 3 (1998): 30–33.

Penley, Constance. "Feminism, Psychoanalysis, and the Study of Popular Culture." In *Cultural Studies.* Ed. Lawrence Grossberg, Cary Nelson, and Paula A. Treichler, 479–500. New York: Routledge, 1992.

The Phallus. Special issue of *Differences* 4, no. 1 (1992).

Plato. *The Symposium.* Trans. W. Hamilton. Harmondsworth: Penguin, 1951.

Preminger, Alex, Frank J. Warnke, and O. B. Hardison, eds. *The Princeton Encyclopedia of Poetry and Poetics.* Princeton: Princeton University Press, 1974.

Psomiades, Kathy Alexis. *Beauty's Body: Femininity and Representation in British Aestheticism.* Stanford: Stanford University Press, 1997.

Queer Rhetoric. Special double issue of *Pre / Text* 13, nos. 3–4 (1992).

Ragland, Ellie. "The Passion of Ignorance in the Transference." In *Freud and the Passions.* Ed. John O'Neill, 151–65. University Park: Pennsylvania State University Press, 1996.

———. "Rhetoric and Unconscious Desire: The Battle for the Postmodern Episteme." *Studies in Psychoanalytic Theory* 1 (1992): 4–24.

Ragland-Sullivan, Ellie. "The Paternal Metaphor: A Lacanian Theory of Language." *Revue internationale de philosophie* 46 (1992): 49–92.

———. "Seeking the Third Term: Desire, the Phallus, and the Materiality of Language." In *Feminism and Psychoanalysis,* ed. Richard Feldstein and Judith Roof, 40–64. Ithaca: Cornell University Press, 1989.

Raymond, Janice G. *The Transsexual Empire: The Making of the She-Male.* Boston: Beacon, 1979.

Restuccia, Frances. "The Subject of Homosexuality: Butler's Elision." *Clinical Studies* 5, no. 1 (1999): 19–37.

Rich, Adrienne. "Compulsory Heterosexuality and Lesbian Existence." In *Desire: The Politics of*

Sexuality. Ed. Ann Snitow, Christine Stansell, and Sharon Thompson, 212–41. London: Virago, 1984.

Richards, Renée. *Second Serve: The Renée Richards Story.* New York: Stein and Day, 1983.

Rieff, Philip. *The Triumph of the Therapeutic: Uses of Faith after Freud.* New York: Harper and Row, 1966.

Robinson, Paul. *Freud and His Critics.* Berkeley and Los Angeles: University of California Press, 1993.

Rofes, Eric. *Reviving the Tribe: Regenerating Gay Men's Sexuality and Culture in the Ongoing Epidemic.* New York: Harrington Park, 1996.

Rose, Jacqueline. "Introduction II." In Lacan, *Feminine Sexuality,* 27–57.

———. "On the 'Universality' of Madness: Bessie Head's *A Question of Power.*" *Critical Inquiry* 20 (1994): 401–18.

———. *Sexuality in the Field of Vision.* London: Verso, 1986.

———. *Why War? Psychoanalysis, Politics, and the Return to Melanie Klein.* Oxford: Blackwell, 1993.

Rosser, B. R. Simon. *Male Homosexual Behavior and the Effects of AIDS Education: A Study of Behavior and Safer Sex in New Zealand and South Australia.* New York: Praeger, 1991.

Rotello, Gabriel. *Sexual Ecology: AIDS and the Destiny of Gay Men.* New York: Dutton, 1997.

Rothblatt, Martine. *The Apartheid of Sex: A Manifesto on the Freedom of Gender.* New York: Crown, 1995.

Rothenberg, Molly Anne, and Joseph Valente. "Fashionable Theory and Fashion-able Women: Returning Fuss's Homospectatorial Look." In *Identities.* Ed. Kwame Anthony Appiah and Henry Louis Gates, 413–23. Chicago: University of Chicago Press, 1995.

———. "Performative Chic: The Fantasy of a Performative Politics." *College Literature* 24 (1997): 295–304.

Roudinesco, Elisabeth. *Jacques Lacan and Co.: A History of Psychoanalysis in France, 1925–1985.* Trans. Jeffrey Mehlman. Chicago: University of Chicago Press, 1990.

Roustang, François. *Dire Mastery: Discipleship from Freud to Lacan.* Trans. Ned Lukacher. Baltimore: Johns Hopkins University Press, 1982.

———. *The Lacanian Delusion.* Trans. Greg Sims. Oxford: Oxford University Press, 1990.

———. *Psychoanalysis Never Lets Go.* Trans. Ned Lukacher. Baltimore: Johns Hopkins University Press, 1983.

Rubin, Gayle. "Thinking Sex: Notes for a Radical Theory of the Politics of Sexuality." In *Pleasure and Danger: Exploring Female Sexuality.* Ed. Carole S. Vance, 267–319. London: Routledge and Kegan Paul, 1984.

———. "Sexual Traffic: Interview [with Judith Butler]." *Differences* 6, nos. 2–3 (1994): 62–99.

Ruskin, Cindy, Matt Herron, and Deborah Zemke. *The Quilt: Stories from the NAMES Project.* New York: Simon and Schuster, 1988.

Russo, Vito. "A Test of Who We Are as a People." In *Democracy: A Project by Group Material.* Ed. Brian Wallis. Seattle: Bay Press, 1990.

Ryan, Joanna. "Reflections on *Disorienting Sexuality.*" *Gender and Psychoanalysis* 2 (1997): 177–84.

Saalfield, Catherine, and Ray Navarro. "Shocking Pink Praxis: Race and Gender on the ACT UP Frontlines." In Fuss, *Inside / Out,* 341–69.

Sade, Marquis de. *Justine, Philosophy in the Bedroom, and Other Writings.* Trans. Richard Seaver and Austryn Wainhouse. New York: Grove, 1966.

Sadownick, Douglas. *Sex between Men: An Intimate History of the Sex Lives of Gay Men, Postwar to Present.* New York: HarperCollins, 1996.

Safouan, Moustafa. "Contribution to the Psychoanalysis of Transsexualism." In Schneiderman, *Returning to Freud,* 195–212.

———. "Is the Oedipus Complex Universal?" In *The Woman in Question: M/F.* Ed. Parveen Adams and Elizabeth Cowie, 274–82. Cambridge: MIT Press, 1990.

Salecl, Renata. *The Spoils of Freedom: Psychoanalysis and Feminism after the Fall of Socialism.* London: Routledge, 1994.

Salecl, Renata, and Slavoj Žižek, eds. *Gaze and Voice as Love Objects.* Durham: Duke University Press, 1996.

Santner, Eric L. *My Own Private Germany: Daniel Paul Schreber's Secret History of Modernity.* Princeton: Princeton University Press, 1996.

Sartre, Jean-Paul. *Being and Nothingness: An Essay in Phenomenological Ontology.* Trans. Hazel E. Barnes. Secaucus, N.J.: Citadel, 1977.

Savage, Dan. "Life after AIDS." *The Stranger* (Seattle), January 16, 1997, 8–12.

Saville, Julia. " 'The Lady of Shalott': A Lacanian Romance." *Word and Image* 8 (1992): 71–87.

Scarry, Elaine. *The Body in Pain: The Making and Unmaking of the World.* New York: Oxford University Press, 1985.

Schneiderman, Stuart, ed. *Returning to Freud: Clinical Psychoanalysis in the School of Lacan.* Trans. Stuart Schneiderman. New Haven: Yale University Press, 1980.

Schwartz, Adria E. *Sexual Subjects: Lesbians, Gender, and Psychoanalysis.* New York: Routledge, 1997.

Schwartzberg, Steven. *A Crisis of Meaning: How Gay Men Are Making Sense of AIDS.* New York: Oxford University Press, 1996.

Sedgwick, Eve Kosovsky. *Epistemology of the Closet.* Berkeley and Los Angeles: University of California Press, 1990.

———. *Tendencies.* Durham: Duke University Press, 1993.

Shapiro, Judith. "Transsexualism: Reflections on the Persistence of Gender and the Mutability of Sex." In Epstein and Straub, *Body Guards,* 248–79.

Shaviro, Steven. *The Cinematic Body.* Minneapolis: University of Minnesota Press, 1993.

Shepherd, Simon, and Mick Wallis, eds. *Coming On Strong: Gay Politics and Culture.* London: Unwin Hyman, 1989.

Shepherdson, Charles. "The Epoch of the Body: Need and Demand in Kojève and Lacan." In *Perspectives on Embodiment: The Intersections of Nature and Culture.* Ed. Gail Weiss and Honi Fern Haber, 183–211. New York: Routledge, 1999.

———. "The Gift of Love and the Debt of Desire." *Differences* 10, no. 1 (1998): 30–74.

———. "History and the Real: Foucault with Lacan." In *Rhetoric in an Antifoundational World: Language, Culture, and Pedagogy.* Ed. Richard R. Glejzer and Michael F. Bernard-Donals, 292–317. New Haven: Yale University Press, 1998.

———. "The *Role* of Gender and the *Imperative* of Sex." In *Supposing the Subject.* Ed. Joan Copjec, 158–84. New York: Verso, 1994.

Shernoff, Michael, and Steven Ball, moderators. "Sex, Secrets, and Lies" (roundtable). *Out,* April 1997, 104–6, 144–47.

Shilts, Randy. *And the Band Played On: Politics, People, and the AIDS Epidemic.* New York: St. Martin's Press, 1987.

Siegel, Lee. "The Gay Science: Queer Theory, Literature, and the Sexualization of Everything." *New Republic,* November 9, 1998, 30–42.

REFERENCES

Signorile, Michelangelo. *Life Outside: The Signorile Report on Gay Men: Sex, Drugs, Muscles, and the Passages of Life*. New York: HarperCollins, 1997.

———. "Nostalgia Trip." *Harvard Gay and Lesbian Review* 5, no. 2 (1998): 25–28.

———. "Unsafe Like Me." *Out*, October 1994, 22–24, 128.

Silin, Jonathan G. *Sex, Death, and the Education of Children: Our Passion for Ignorance in the Age of AIDS*. New York: Teachers College, 1995.

Silverman, Kaja. *The Threshold of the Visible World*. New York: Routledge, 1996.

Sobo, Elisa Janine. *Choosing Unsafe Sex: AIDS-Risk Denial among Disadvantaged Women*. Philadelphia: University of Pennsylvania Press, 1995.

Sontag, Susan. *AIDS and Its Metaphors*. New York: Farrar, Straus and Giroux, 1989.

Stein, Edward, ed. *Forms of Desire: Sexual Orientation and the Social Constructionist Controversy*. New York: Routledge, 1992.

Stoller, Robert J. *Sex and Gender*. Vol. 1, *The Development of Masculinity and Femininity*. New York: Science House, 1968.

———. *Sex and Gender*. Vol. 2, *The Transsexual Experiment*. New York: Aronson, 1975.

Stone, Sandy. "The *Empire* Strikes Back: A Posttranssexual Manifesto." In Epstein and Straub, *Body Guards*, 280–304.

Sullivan, Andrew. *Virtually Normal: An Argument about Homosexuality*. New York: Knopf, 1995.

———. "When Plagues End: Notes on the Twilight of an Epidemic." *New York Times Magazine*, November 10, 1996, 52–62, 76–77, 84.

Tort, Michel. "The New Testament of Lacan." Unpublished manuscript.

Traits de perversion dans les structures cliniques. Paris: Navarin, 1990.

Treichler, Paula A. "AIDS, Homophobia, and Biomedical Discourse: An Epidemic of Signification." In Crimp, *AIDS*, 31–70.

———. *How to Have Theory in an Epidemic: Cultural Chronicles of AIDS*. Durham: Duke University Press, 1999.

Turkle, Sherry. *Psychoanalytic Politics: Jacques Lacan and Freud's French Revolution*. 2d ed. New York: Guilford, 1992.

Tyler, Carole-Anne. "Boys Will Be Girls: The Politics of Gay Drag." In Fuss, *Inside / Out*, 32–70.

Valenzuela, Tony. "Let's Talk about Sex without Condoms." http://www.geocities.com/~sexpanicnyc.

Vergetis, Dimitris. "Deux axiomatiques des psychoses." *Ornicar?* 44 (1988): 52–64.

Walsh, Michael. "Reading the Real in the Seminar on the Psychoses." In *Criticism and Lacan: Essays and Dialogue on Language, Structure, and the Unconscious*. Ed. Patrick Colm Hogan and Lalita Pandit, 64–83. Athens: University of Georgia Press, 1990.

Warner, Michael, ed. *Fear of a Queer Planet: Queer Politics and Social Theory*. Minneapolis: University of Minnesota Press, 1993.

———. "Homo-Narcissism; or Heterosexuality." In *Engendering Men: The Question of Male Feminist Criticism*. Ed. Joseph A. Boone and Michael Cadden, 190–206. New York: Routledge, 1990.

———. "Media Gays: A New Stone Wall." *Nation*, July 14, 1997, 15–19.

———. "Why Gay Men Are Having Risky Sex." *Village Voice*, January 31, 1995, 32–37.

Watney, Simon. *Policing Desire: Pornography, AIDS, and the Media*. Minneapolis: University of Minnesota Press, 1987.

———. *Practices of Freedom: Selected Writings on HIV / AIDS*. Durham: Duke University Press, 1994.

————. "Psychoanalysis, Sexuality, and AIDS." In Shepherd and Wallis, *Coming On Strong*, 22–38.

————. "The Spectacle of AIDS." In Crimp, *AIDS*, 71–86.

————. "Taking Liberties: An Introduction." In *Taking Liberties: AIDS and Cultural Politics*. Ed. Erica Carter and Simon Watney, 11–57. London: Serpent's Tail, 1989.

Weed, Elizabeth. "The More Things Change." *Differences* 6, nos. 2–3 (1994): 249–73.

White, Edmund. "What Century Is This Anyway?" *Advocate*, June 23, 1998, 58.

Yingling, Thomas E. "Homosexuality and the Uncanny: What's Fishy in Lacan." In *The Gay '90s: Disciplinary and Interdisciplinary Formations in Queer Studies*. Ed. Thomas Foster, Carol Siegel, and Ellen E. Berry, 191–98. New York: New York University Press, 1997.

Žižek, Slavoj. *For They Know Not What They Do: Enjoyment as a Political Factor*. New York: Verso, 1991.

————. "Grimaces of the Real, or When the Phallus Appears," *October* 58 (1991): 45–68.

————. *Looking Awry: An Introduction to Jacques Lacan through Popular Culture*. Cambridge: MIT Press, 1991.

————. *The Metastases of Enjoyment: Six Essays on Woman and Causality*. New York: Verso, 1994.

————. *The Plague of Fantasies*. New York: Verso, 1997.

————. *The Sublime Object of Ideology*. New York: Verso, 1989.

————. "The Undergrowth of Enjoyment: How Popular Culture Can Serve as an Introduction to Lacan." *New Formations* 9 (1989): 7–29.

301